# New York Yankees

## Seasons of Glory

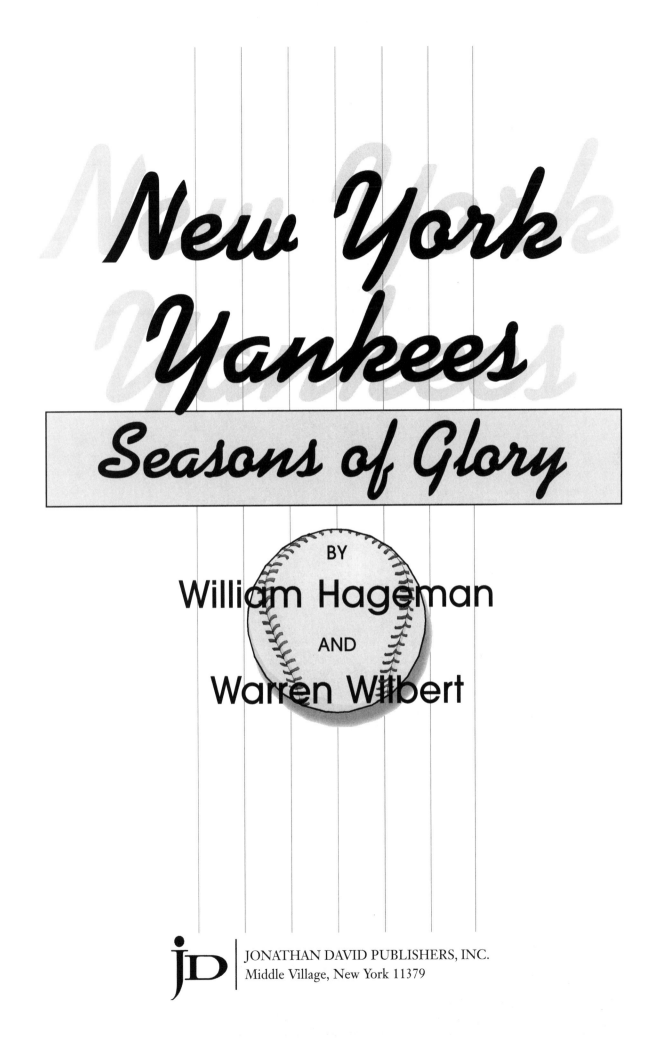

# New York Yankees
## Seasons of Glory

BY

## William Hageman

AND

## Warren Wilbert

JD

JONATHAN DAVID PUBLISHERS, INC.
Middle Village, New York 11379

# NEW YORK YANKEES:
# SEASONS OF GLORY

Jonathan David Publishers, Inc.
68-22 Eliot Avenue
Middle Village, New York 11379


www.jdbooks.com

**Library of Congress Cataloging-in-Publication Data**

Hageman, William.
    New York Yankees : seasons of glory / by William Hageman, Warren Wilbert.
        p.      cm.
    Includes index.
    ISBN 0-8246-0438-5 pb
    1. New York Yankees (Baseball team)—History.    2. New York Yankees (Baseball team)—
Statistics.     3. Baseball—Records—United States. I. Wilbert, Warren N.     II. Title.
    GV875.N4H35  2001
    796.357'64'097471—dc21

99-10732
CIP

*Book design and composition by John Reinhardt Book Design*


**Printed in the United States of America**

In memory of Chuck Leonard.

—William Hageman

To my grandsons Josh, the Captain, and Jeff, the Wizard of Oz:
two of God's more precious gifts.

—Warren Wilbert

# Acknowledgments

This book would not have been possible without the help and support of a lot of people. First and foremost, my coauthor, Warren Wilbert. I can't imagine a better writing partner, and it has been a pleasure working with him.

Others to whom I am indebted: Doran and Elsie McFadden for their hospitality and wonderful stories, Jim and Lora Gooden for the use of the camper, the ever vigilant Margaret Knight for chasing down reference material for the book, Jack Thompson for keeping an eye on things for me, and Estelle Hageman, Ann Schatz, and Dave, Barbara, and Laura Lukas for their interest and encouragement.

Also, thanks to the employees at the Harold Washington Library in Chicago, the Carnegie in Pittsburgh, the Aurora, Illinois, Public Library, and the Milford, Delaware, Public Library, and the Yankees' Media Relations Department. And George and Mary Brace, of course, for access to their tremendous photo collection.

I also wish to remember two wonderful people who, sadly, aren't here to see this finished product: Frances Sarna and Mabel Aston Thornhill. They are deeply missed.

Lastly, thanks to my wife, Dona, for tolerating my preoccupation with this project for the last two years, and to my daughters, Julie, Kelly, and Katie, for letting me use the computer once in a while. You guys are the greatest.

—WILLIAM HAGEMAN

A note of continuing appreciation is in order not only for Pete Palmer's expertise in the field of baseball statistics and analysis, which is considerable, but for his patience and availability. He's been just a helpful e-mail away. I am much obliged.

A special note of thanks is in order for my good wife, Ginny, who was very considerate and made many sacrifices, for my eldest daughter, Karen, who is always on the lookout for those "special baseball books," and for the rest of a long-suffering family who patiently put up with all of Papa's "baseball stuff."

—WARREN WILBERT

# Contents

*Foreword by Dan Schlossberg* ...................... xi

*Introduction by John Sterling* ...................... xiii

*A Welcome From the Authors* ...................... xv

*America's Team* ........................................ xix

## From the Top

1. Babe Ruth 1923 ........................ 1
2. Mickey Mantle 1956 ................ 11
3. Lou Gehrig 1934 ..................... 21
4. Rickey Henderson 1985 .......... 29
5. Snuffy Stirnweiss 1945 .............. 35
6. Jack Chesbro 1904 .................. 41
7. Lefty Gomez 1937 .................... 47
8. Joe DiMaggio 1941 ................ 53
9. Ron Guidry 1978 ..................... 61
10. Carl Mays 1921 ...................... 67
11. Spud Chandler 1943 .............. 75
12. Bobby Murcer 1971 ................ 81
13. Joe Gordon 1942 ................... 87
14. Bill Dickey 1937 ..................... 93
15. Roger Peckinpaugh 1919 ....... 99
16. Don Mattingly 1984 ............... 103
17. Tony Lazzeri 1929 ................... 109
18. Wilcy Moore 1927 .................. 115
19. Red Ruffing 1939 .................... 121
20. Mariano Rivera 1997 ............. 127
21. Goose Gossage 1978 ........... 133
22. Dave Righetti 1986 ................ 139
23. Whitey Ford 1956 ................... 145
24. Roy White 1971 ..................... 151
25. Sparky Lyle 1977 ................... 157

## An Outstanding Supporting Cast

26. Charlie Keller 1942 ................ 165
27. Russ Ford 1910 ...................... 171
28. Luis Arroyo 1961 .................... 177
29. Bob Shawkey 1920 ................ 183
30. Yogi Berra 1956 ..................... 189
31. Reggie Jackson 1980 ........... 195
32. Elston Howard 1961 ............... 203
33. Gil McDougald 1957 ............. 209
34. Phil Rizzuto 1950 .................... 215
35. Paul O'Neill 1994 ................... 221
36. Graig Nettles 1976 ................. 227
37. Andy Pettitte 1997 ................. 233
38. Clete Boyer 1962 ................... 239
39. Dave Winfield 1984 ............... 245
40. Allie Reynolds 1952 ............... 251
41. Mel Stottlemyre 1969 ............ 257
42. Catfish Hunter 1975 ............... 263
43. Del Pratt 1919 ........................ 269
44. Thurman Munson 1973 .......... 273
45. Roger Maris 1960 ................... 281
46. Herb Pennock 1924 ............... 291
47. Willie Randolph 1980 ............ 297
48. Tommy John 1979 .................. 303
49. Wade Boggs 1994 ................. 309
50. Joe Page 1949 ...................... 315

*More Than an Afterthought* ...................... 321

*Total Player Ratings (TPR)* .......................... 327

*About the Authors* ...................................... 329

# Foreword

## by Dan Schlossberg

*Dan Schlossberg, a columnist for* Yankees Magazine, *is author of* The New Baseball Catalog, *a hardcover history of the game.*

From 1920, when Babe Ruth arrived from Boston, through 1998, when they won the most games in American League history, the New York Yankees have been baseball's most successful team. Their record of 35 pennants and 24 World Championships seems as formidable as Mark McGwire's mark of seventy home runs in one season.

The list of Yankee legends is almost endless. Babe Ruth, Lou Gehrig, Joe DiMaggio, Bill Dickey, Phil Rizzuto, Yogi Berra, Mickey Mantle, Roger Maris, Whitey Ford, Elston Howard, Thurman Munson, Don Mattingly, and Reggie Jackson were so sensational that their numbers were retired. Most have since advanced to the Baseball Hall of Fame.

Even before 1998, when the Yankees finished with 114 regular-season victories and another eleven in postseason play, the team's success was built upon the considerable contributions of individual performers. Picking the top fifty is a herculean task, but authors William Hageman and Warren Wilbert present plausible cases not only for their selections but also for the sequence of their rankings.

Without doubt, they will stir up considerable controversy.

Did Roger Maris have a better year in 1960, his first in the Bronx, than he did in 1961, the year he hit sixty-one home runs? Was the 19-6 season of Whitey Ford in 1956 better than his 25-4 campaign of '61?

According to the authors, Babe Ruth's best year was neither 1927, when he hit sixty home runs, nor 1921, considered by most experts the most productive offensive season ever produced by an individual. They chose 1923, when revenues produced by Ruth's robust bat allowed the Yankees to open Yankee Stadium ("The House that Ruth Built").

Other selections are also certain to ignite serious debates:

- Bill Dickey's .362 batting average of 1936 was the best by a catcher until Mike Piazza matched it in 1997, but the Dickey season detailed in the pages that follow is 1937.

- Sparky Lyle had more saves and a better ERA in 1972, but the authors insist he was more valuable to the Yankees in 1977.

- In 1981, his first year with the Yanks, Dave Winfield provided the power to fill the Reggie Jackson void and lead the team back to the World Series, but the authors opt for his .340 campaign of 1984—and batting title battle with teammate Don Mattingly—for this volume.

But there's a method to their madness. It's a science called Sabermetrics, devised by Bill James, a Kansas college professor who is also a well-known author, computer guru, and prominent member of the Society for American Baseball Research. The James formula measures individual performance against league averages for any given year, and also allows comparisons of players and clubs across different eras.

That makes it easier to match modern-day players against Babe Ruth, whose career ended before night games, jet lag, relief pitching, artificial turf, domed ballparks, and television scrutiny made conditions much more difficult.

In Ruth's day, the Yankees played a 154-game schedule of day games in an eight-team league whose champion went directly to the World Series.

The Derek Jeter Yankees of '98 played 162 games, mostly at night, before advancing to a best-of-five Division Series and a best-of-seven League Championship Series before reaching the Fall Classic. The 1949–53 Yankees, winners of five straight World Series, did not have to survive two rounds of preliminary playoffs first.

This is a book not only for Yankee fans but for lovers of baseball history. Who can forget Luis Arroyo, the journeyman reliever who came out of nowhere to save so many Whitey Ford wins in '61? But how many will remember Del Pratt, a solid second baseman whose all-around play helped set the stage for the Yankees' success in The Roaring Twenties?

Even Snuffy Stirnweiss, the hero of the wartime team of 1945, has a chapter in this book. Once the war ended, he went from batting king to utility man, but he still merits a niche in Yankee lore.

*New York Yankees: Seasons of Glory* provides a complete historical perspective, including quotes, boxscores, and baseball and world news headlines of the featured seasons.

One such headline, from 1953, says "Flying saucers spotted everywhere."

Maybe it was actually Yankee fans showering confetti on their heroes. It happened that fall—and so many others.

—DAN SCHLOSSBERG

# Introduction

## by John Sterling

*Since 1976, John Sterling has done play-by-play for the New Jersey Nets, the New York Islanders, and the Atlanta Hawks. Since 1989, he has been the exciting voice of the New York Yankees. His radio show,* Sports Talk, *which he co-anchors with Michael Kaye, currently airs on WABC in New York City.*

As the third-rate emcee would say, here's an act that needs no introduction! Well, no one needs less of an introduction than the New York Yankees, the most famous, accomplished franchise in the history of professional sports.

It's both interesting, and highly ironic, that this excellent book documenting the gloried exploits of the Yankees and their many stars is written by William Hageman and Warren Wilbert, two men who through unfortunate circumstance are Chicago White Sox fans. The Sox last played in a World Series in 1959, and last won the Series in 1917. Of course, maybe it's not ironic; at least Hageman and Wilbert are able to bask in the spotlight of Yankees history—and what a history!

While the 1998 Yankees team was the best, at least statistically, to truly appreciate the greatness of the Bronx Bombers you must go back, way back to 1920. That's when Boston Red Sox owner and Broadway producer Harry Frazee sold a fella named George Herman Ruth to the Yanks and used the case to produce *No, No, Nanette.*

Babe Ruth became the most celebrated sports star in history, and the years haven't diminished that. Mohammed Ali and Michael Jordan may have challenged his greatness, but have never reached his level. Still, the Babe left the Yankees in 1934 and the Bombers have never stopped being the dominant baseball franchise through the decades. Thirty-five pennants, twenty-four championships, plus a division flag in 1980 and two wild-card playoff appearances in the 1990s. Seventy-seven years since the first pennant in 1921, thirty-eight playoffs, or one every two years! That's a rare combination of consistency and brilliance.

So, when you've achieved the continual success of the Yankees, it speaks volumes about the organization and, most important, about the players you'll meet in the ensuing pages. Recalling Casey Stengel's tongue-in-cheek line, "I couldn't have done it without the players," the Yankees have had an endless stream of great athletes leading them to victory. Players, victories, consistency, brilliance. The New York Yankees won no fewer that five pennants in the '20s, '30s, '40s, '50s, and '60s. Three more in the '70s, one in the '80s, and one other division championship. And then in the '90s, two pennants, two World Series victories, two wild-card playoff appearances, one 6½ game first-place mid-August lead erased by the labor management strife of 1994.

To fully understand the New York Yankees and to comprehend the power and glory of the Yankees name, examine closely one period of Yankees history. In an amazing stretch of almost three decades—1936 to 1964, twenty-nine baseball seasons—the Yanks compiled a record that never will be approached. In the then one-winner-take-all in the American and National Leagues, the Bombers won twenty-two pennants in the twenty-nine years, along with sixteen Championships.

It all began in 1936 when the Yankees welcomed a new outfielder from the Pacific Coast League, Joseph Paul DiMaggio. The Yankee Clipper spearheaded a run of four straight pennants and World Series victories from 1936 to 1939. After a year off in 1940, the Yankees won three straight pennants and two Series from 1941 to 1943. After the war, in 1947, the Yankees won another pennant and World Championship. And then, from 1949 through 1953, Casey Stengel's first year as manager, the Yankees won an unprecedented five straight championships.

Dimag retired in 1951, passing the torch to newcomer Mickey Mantle. Four straight pennants and two Series followed in 1955 through 1958. And after finishing third in 1959, the Yankees rebounded with five straight pennants and two more World Championships from 1960 through 1964.

One more timely note. One year when the Yankees lost, 1954, the Yankees finished second but won 103 games. That, of course, was the year Cleveland won 111 games, the all-time American League record until the remarkable 1998 season when the Yankees smashed that Indian mark with 114 victories.

In *New York Yankees: Seasons of Glory*, this fabulous history will be traced through the exploits of the stars who made it all possible.

In choosing the top fifty for this volume, Hageman and Wilbert opted to use the rating system known as Sabermetrics. "The numbers speak for themselves" or "You can't argue with the numbers" are oft-spoken phrases by those backyard baseball commentators who spend endless hours debating statistics and heralding the accomplishments of their favorite Yankee players. The authors' choices will undoubtedly fuel these heated discussions, spark new debates, or perhaps settle longstanding friendly arguments.

*New York Yankees: Seasons of Glory* offers up a veritable baseball galaxy featuring such stars as Babe Ruth, Lou Gehrig, Tony Lazzeri, Joe DiMaggio, Bill Dickey, Phil Rizzuto, Tommy Henrich, Red Ruffing, Yogi Berra, Whitey Ford, Mickey Mantle, Roger Maris, Catfish Hunter, Thurman Munson, Reggie Jackson, Ron Guidry, and Don Mattingly, on up to the 1998 record-setting ballclub that had nothing but stars who hid their egos in a cloak of teamwork that led to 114 regular season wins and an 11-2 record in the playoffs, culminating in a season of 125 wins and fifty losses, a mark that probably will never be surpassed—or will it? As they say, stay tuned to WABC and the Yankees radio network. With the New York Yankees it is always possible.

—JOHN STERLING
*Yankee Stadium*

# A Welcome From the Authors

In the interests of full disclosure, the authors have an admission to make: We are Chicago White Sox fans. We hope you won't hold that against us. In fact, that probably helped us as we researched this book. As Sox fans we were painfully aware Mickey Mantle was good. But it wasn't until we did a game-by-game study of his greatest season, 1956, that we appreciated just *how* good. The same goes for Lou Gehrig. And Whitey Ford. And Thurman Munson. And on and on. By not being Yankee fans, we were able to take a more objective view of the team and its players, giving us a new appreciation of them.

Before we explain how we chose the greatest seasons of the fifty individuals discussed in this book, a little history is necessary. The Yankees were a late arrival in Ban Johnson's American League, appearing on the scene in 1903 as the New York Highlanders. (The Yankee moniker wouldn't come along until 1906.) The early returns were modest—there were second-place finishes in 1904, 1906, and 1910, but most of the time the ball club found itself in the dank recesses of the American League's second division. That all changed, of course, in 1920, when the Yankees brought Babe Ruth to New York and unleashed him not only on the rest of the league, but on an entire nation as well. Baseball and America were never the same.

The great Yankee teams of the 1920s were the foundation on which was built the most illustrious sports franchise in history. The Green Bay Packers? The Boston Celtics? The Montreal Canadiens? Small potatoes compared to the Yankees. Ruth, Gehrig, and DiMaggio; Mantle, Berra, and Ford; Munson, Guidry, and Jackson; Pettitte, Rivera, and Jeter. More than seventy-five years of greatness, and still going strong.

We're not here, though, to sing the praises of the franchise. Our purpose is to present—to celebrate—the greatest seasons of fifty of the Yankees' greatest players. Such a daunting undertaking needs some explanation, especially in terms of how we picked and ranked our top fifty players.

First, using the rating system and criteria described below, we calculated scores that measure the performance of each team member in Yankee history, for every year that a team member played. Then we compiled a list of the scores, from the highest to the lowest. Some of the most outstanding players had multiple seasons in which they scored very high, according to our system. Thus, if you look at Appendix A, which ranks the top fifty performance scores, you will see that certain players, such as Babe Ruth and Mickey Mantle, are listed a number of times. But we felt it would be more interesting to present fifty different high-ranking players, rather than focus on the top fifty scores (which belong to only twenty-seven players). So, starting from the top of the list, we eliminated multiple listings of the same player (keeping only the score from the player's best season as a Yankee). We moved down the list in this way until we had determined fifty players with the highest performance scores. Thus, some of the men we included in this book did not, strictly speaking, achieve a top-50 performance in their careers.

Now comes the tough part—explaining our rating system. How could we rank Ruth's 1923 season ahead of his performance in 1927? Or how was Dave Winfield's 1984 effort better than Roger Maris' in 1960? Indeed, why would we choose Maris' 1960 campaign over his home run record-setting season of 1961? It all comes down to numbers.

Every season of every player who has ever stepped on a baseball diamond can be analyzed and broken down using a sabermetric rating system. ("Sabermetric" is derived from SABR, which stands for the Society for American Baseball Research.) Sabermetricians have developed a series of complex mathematical formulas that not only analyze a player's statistics for a given season, but also take into account other factors that affect player performance, such as the ballparks they play in and the overall strength or weakness of the league, as well as overall team stats. It's all based on the premise that the basic unit of measurement in baseball is the run. Scoring runs and preventing runs—that's the name of the game. When all the numbers are plugged into the formula, the resulting figure can be used as a way to compare, and thus rank, players' performances. (For a much more thorough explanation of the sabermetric formulas, refer to *Total Baseball* [HarperPerennial] by stats gurus John Thorn and Pete Palmer. In the words of that great statesman Casey Stengel, you could look it up.)

Sounds complicated, right? Dry? Maybe a little. But let's walk through a couple of examples. We'll look at outfielder Willie Keeler's 1904 season and pitcher Phil Niekro's 1984 campaign. Neither of these Hall of Famers made our top fifty, as fine as their seasons were, once their numbers were run through the sabermetric formulas.

In 143 games in 1904, Keeler hit .343, with 186 hits, 78 runs, two home runs, 24 extra base hits, 40 RBIs, 21 stolen bases, a .390 on-base percentage, a .409 slugging average, and a .935 fielding average as the Highlanders' right fielder. On the surface a remarkable performance. But let's look deeper, using two sabermetric categories: Batting Runs and Fielding Runs.

Batting Runs/Adjusted (abbreviated as "BR" in this book's stats tables) is a figure that indicates thenumber of runs a player produces beyond the league-average batter

(in sabermetric terms the average player rates a 0.0; Batting Runs can range from -50 to more than 100). The process used to arrive at this figure takes into account a variety of factors, from the number of times a player is hit by a pitch to the number of times he was caught stealing, to the idiosyncracies of the player's home park. Hilltop Park, where Keeler played half his games in 1904, was a singles hitter's paradise—365 feet to the left-field fence, 454 feet to center, and 400 feet to right. It was made to order for a slap hitter like Keeler (160 of his 186 hits were singles) and helps account for his .343 batting average. When Keeler's numbers are plugged into the formula, he gets a Batting Runs/Adjusted figure of 28. That's well above average, but, putting things in perspective, it's well below the numbers posted by players like Ruth, Gehrig, Ted Williams, and Jimmie Foxx, who produced numbers of 70-plus.

Fielding Runs (abbreviated as "FR" in this book's stats tables), similarly, is a figure that indicates the number of runs a player prevents beyond the number of runs a league-average ballplayer in the same position prevents. It's the defensive counterpart to run production. A player's fielding stats are used in this calculation, as well as a formula that takes into account the particular demands of different positions. In Keeler's case, his rating for 1904 was -3. (A rating of -0.5 to 0.5 is about average, so Keeler's lackluster -3 hurt his overall rating.)

Taking the Batting Runs/Adjusted, Fielding Runs, and Base Stealing Runs (another category) and plugging them into yet another formula produces a Total Player Rating, or TPR. That number is the bottom line—how players from any era can be compared. The higher the number, the greater the player's contribution, and the number roughly corresponds with the number of victories a player contributes to his team's total. Keeler's TPR for 1904 was 1.9, roughly two victories. Interestingly, his 1904 teammate Jimmy Williams, who hit just .263, had a higher TPR of 2.7 (accounting for three victories). How could that be? Remember, we're talking about contributions to the team, and everything is based on the scoring and preventing of runs. Williams drove in thirty-four more runs, his fielding average was sixteen points higher, and he accumulated twenty more Fielding Runs. As a point of reference, the highest TPR ever recorded was Ruth's 10.8 in 1923 (hence that season's inclusion in this book, rather than his 1927 season, when he had an 8.9).

Now let's look at Niekro and the separate calculations that go into deriving a Total Pitcher Index (TPI), the pitcher's equivalent of the TPR. In 1984 Niekro was 16-8 with five complete games, one shutout, 136 strikeouts, 76 walks, and a 3.09 ERA, and opposing batters hit .267 against him. The sabermetric categories that go into the TPI include Pitching Runs/Adjusted (abbreviated as "PR" in ourstats lines), Pitcher-As-Hitter Index (PHI), and Pitcher's Defense (DEF). Pitching Runs is a figure that indicates the number of runs saved beyond that of a league-average pitcher (rated at 0.0). In Niekro's case, after all his stats are plugged into one of the formulas, his PR is 22. Adjusted to Yankee Stadium, he has a 17. In comparison, the fifteen highest PR totals begin at around 70, with the highest belonging to the New York Giants' Amos Rusie, who had a monstrous 125.7 in 1894.

The Pitcher-As-Hitter Index is the pitcher's equivalent of the position player's Batting Runs figure; it's an adjusted number that quantifies the pitcher's contribution as a hitter to the team's success. (Niekro, of course, rates a 0 because of the DH.)

Pitcher's Defense assigns a value to the pitcher's contributions as a fifth infielder. This is similar to the position player's Fielding Runs category, with a couple of modifications for strikeouts and a pitcher's style (some pitchers induce a large number of ground balls, for example). Niekro had a PD figure of 2.0.

All the numbers are plugged into a formula to produce the Total Pitcher Index, which is comparable to the Total Player Rating. Again, 0.0 is average; Niekro's figure for 1984 was a 2.0, giving him credit for producing roughly two victories more than what an average American League pitcher produced that season. Good, but not high enough to warrant inclusion here.

Whew!

What all this adds up to is hundreds of Yankee players with TPRs and TPIs that can be compared. That we did, and we've taken the top seasons of the fifty top performers and described them here. From Babe Ruth's phenomenal 1923 effort to Joe Page's 1949 performance, they were all great fun to research and write about. Even for a couple of White Sox fans.

So sit back, relax, relive some of the greatest individual performances in baseball history, and, most of all, enjoy.

# America's Team

The New York Yankees . . . America's team?

With apologies to the once-great Dallas Cowboys, why not?

America loves baseball.

America loves winners.

America loves those who stand tall in times of tragedy.

The New York Yankees fit the bill.

Between 1996 and 2001, they made five postseason appearances in six years, winning four World Series. And after being thrust into the spotlight following the horrors of September 11, 2001, the Yankees provided inspiration to all Americans and brought back at least a modicum of normalcy.

As Chicago White Sox owner Jerry Reinsdorf said when asked what he'd remember most about 2001: "It has to be the sympathy, respect, and love shown to New York and the New York Yankees following the attacks of September 11. . . . The Yankees visited Comiskey Park when play resumed one week [after the attacks]. I was amazed by the emotion of the pregame ceremony that first night back, and the positive response White Sox fans had for the Yankee team and the city of New York. It's not often that the Yankees are cheered in Chicago, but September 11 changed a great many things in this nation."

In the month and a half since, right down to the thrilling—and stunningly disappointing—conclusion of the World Series, New York's team became America's team. Yet even before September 11, the Yankees had reestablished themselves as the preeminent team in baseball, so much so that they were being compared to the greatest clubs of all time.

*Aerial view of the ticker-tape parade hosted by New York following the Yankees' 1998 World Series sweep.*

## Consecutive World Series Champs

| | |
|---|---|
| 1907–1908 Chicago Cubs | **1949–1953 New York Yankees** |
| 1910–1911 Philadelphia Athletics | **1961–1962 New York Yankees** |
| 1915–1916 Boston Red Sox | 1972–1974 Oakland Athletics |
| 1921–1922 New York Giants | 1975–1976 Cincinnati Reds |
| **1927–1928 New York Yankees** | **1977–1978 New York Yankees** |
| 1929–1930 Philadelphia Athletics | 1992–1993 Toronto Blue Jays |
| **1936–1939 New York Yankees** | **1998–2000 New York Yankees** |

The debate began in earnest after a phenomenal 1998 season in which they dominated the game with 114 regular-season victories: How did this team rank when compared to the legendary 1927 Yankees of Babe Ruth, Lou Gehrig, and Tony Lazzeri?

Then, in 1999, when the Yankees went on to capture their third World Championship in four years, the team was likened to others that had strung together consecutive seasons of glory, such as Charley Finley's Oakland A's of the early '70s and Cincinnati's Big Red Machine later in that decade.

But following the Yankees' victory over the New York Mets in the 2000 "Subway Series," the talk entered a whole new level: dynasty.

And why not? Only the Yankees of 1936-1939 and 1949-1953 had won more than three consecutive World Series. And baseball was a very different game in those days, with fewer teams—and thus, stronger competition—and no long, multitiered playoff system.

"Our run of five postseasons, four World Series appearances in five years, is pretty damn good," manager Joe Torre said after his team polished off the Mets in five games. "Our ballclub, for what they've accomplished, should be right up there with any of the clubs that have put something together."

• • •

How good have these guys been in recent years? Their postseason record from 1996-2001 speaks for itself: four World Championships, including three in a row from 1998 to 2000; a 56-22 postseason record from '96 to '01; and a 19-7 World Series mark, including 19 of their last 24 games and 14 in a row at one point. The only glitches came in 1997, when the Yankees were eliminated by Cleveland in the American League Division Series, and in 2001, when they came within three outs of yet another World Series title, only to be beaten by a dramatic, bottom-of-the-ninth Arizona comeback.

"To be the best, they had to beat the best, and that's what they've done," said Yankees general manager Brian Cashman of the Diamondbacks after his team lost to them in the 2001 World Series. "That's why they're world champions. . . . I'll tell you what. We really do realize how difficult it is to be world champions."

"We can put our record, our dedication, our resolve up against any team that's ever played the game of baseball," Torre said after the 2000 World Series. "We may not have the best players, but we certainly have the best team."

• • •

That was never truer than in 1998, a season that set the benchmark for success.

The secret that year was teamwork. There were no MVP seasons, no Ruth or Mantle or DiMaggio. The Yankees didn't even have a player voted to start in the 1998 All-Star Game. All they did was win.

"When people remember us, it won't be a name, but the team itself," Torre said.

*New York fans salute the record-breaking 1998 Yanks as they parade up the "Canyon of Heroes." Derek Jeter raises his fist in victory.*

The Yanks tore through the competition. They won 22 of 24 during a stretch in April and early May and were 37-13 with a 7½-game AL East lead by the end of the month. They won nine in a row to open June and ten straight in July, which ended with New York holding a 76-27 record. When the dust settled, they had won 114 games, an AL record until it was eclipsed by Seattle in 2001, finished 66 games over .500, and outdistanced second-place Boston by 22 games in the AL East.

The story was the same in the playoffs. The Yankees swept Texas in three games, beat Cleveland in six, and defeated the Padres in four in the World Series, finishing the season with a record 125 victories.

Heroes? The 1998 roster was full of them. David Wells threw a perfect game against Minnesota; a fight-marred game against Baltimore was won when Tim Raines, the first batter after order was restored, ripped a two-run homer; David Cone, Tino Martinez, Chad Curtis, Scott Brosius, Darryl Strawberry, and Jorge Posada all had their time in the spotlight.

"We've had an uncanny knack all season," Cone said. "When we need to pitch well, when we win 1-0 or 2-1, we get great pitching performances. And when we need to score runs, it seems like we're able to match up and do that. Is that character? Is that integrity? It's a team that really picks each other up and pulls for each other."

# The Very Best

Here are the winningest teams by percentage, including regular season and postseason records.

| | Regular Season | | | Overall | | |
|---|---|---|---|---|---|---|
| | W | L | Pct. | W | L | Pct. |
| 1906 Chicago Cubs | 116 | 36 | .763 | 118 | 40 | .747 |
| 2001 Seattle Mariners | 116 | 46 | .716 | 120 | 52 | .698 |
| 1927 New York Yankees | 110 | 44 | .714 | 114 | 44 | .722 |
| 1927 New York Yankees | 110 | 44 | .714 | 114 | 44 | .722 |
| 1909 Pittsburgh Pirates | 110 | 42 | .724 | 114 | 45 | .717 |
| 1998 New York Yankees | 114 | 48 | .704 | 125 | 50 | .714 |
| 1907 Chicago Cubs | 107 | 45 | .704 | 111 | 45 | .712 |
| 1954 Cleveland Indians | 111 | 43 | .721 | 111 | 47 | .703 |
| 1939 New York Yankees | 106 | 45 | .702 | 110 | 45 | .702 |

• • •

The 1999 Yankees had a tough act to follow, but they succeeded.

"Our expectations going into the [1999] season were to win the division, try to get back to the playoffs, and win the World Series," outfielder Paul O'Neill said midway through that campaign. "It just seems like everybody else's expectations from Day One were for us to be as good as or better than we were last year. It's a different team and a different year."

That it was. Seldom has a team had to overcome as many problems as the '99 ball club. It began in spring training when Torre was diagnosed with prostate cancer. In his absence, the team went 21-15. Another early-season casualty was outfielder Darryl Strawberry, who was suspended after being arrested on drug and solicitation charges.

There were other off-field distractions as well. Three players—O'Neill, Brosius, and Luis Sojo—lost their fathers in the last two months of the season. The deaths of Joe DiMaggio and Catfish Hunter also contributed to the grim atmosphere.

On the field, second baseman Chuck Knoblauch had defensive difficulties, pitcher Andy Pettitte struggled to reach .500 and was the subject of seemingly constant trade rumors, Roger Clemens, obtained in a spring trade for fan favorite David Wells, was booed at Yankee Stadium, and a number of players suffered nagging injuries.

"Obviously, we were expected to win again," first baseman Martinez said. "But to win as many games as we won [in 1998], nobody expected that. The struggles we had early on, the media kind of got carried away with it. We felt we were just battling through some tough times like a lot of teams do."

The 1999 Yankees clinched their division on September 30—as compared to September 9 during the magical 1998 season—and finished with 98 victories, best in the American League. They swept Texas in the first round of the playoffs, then needed five games to eliminate the Boston Red Sox.

The 1999 World Series against the Atlanta Braves—winners of five National League pennants in the '90s—was supposed to determine which club deserved "Team of the Decade" bragging rights. It took the Yankees an economical four games to settle the issue.

Again, heroes were everywhere—Orlando Hernandez and three relievers teamed up on a two-hitter in Game 1; Cone allowed just one hit over seven innings in Game 2; part-time leftfielder Curtis hit two homers, including the game-winner in the 10th, in Game 3; and in Game 4, Clemens, who went just 14-10 with a 4.60 earned-run average in the regular season, shut down the Braves for $7^2/_3$ innings before turning the game over to the bullpen, which closed out the game.

# The Yankees In Postseason Play

## WORLD SERIES (Won 26, Lost 12)

| | |
|---|---|
| 1921—Lost to New York Giants, 5-3 | 1953—Beat Brooklyn Dodgers, 4-2 |
| 1922—Lost to New York Giants, 4-0 | 1955—Lost to Brooklyn Dodgers, 4-3 |
| 1923—Beat New York Giants, 4-2 | 1956—Beat Brooklyn Dodgers, 4-3 |
| 1926—Lost to St. Louis Cardinals, 4-3 | 1957—Lost to Milwaukee Braves, 4-3 |
| 1927—Beat Pittsburgh Pirates, 4-0 | 1958—Beat Milwaukee Braves, 4-3 |
| 1928—Beat St. Louis Cardinals, 4-0 | 1960—Lost to Pittsburgh Pirates, 4-3 |
| 1932—Beat Chicago Cubs, 4-0 | 1961—Beat Cincinnati Reds, 4-1 |
| 1936—Beat New York Giants, 4-2 | 1962—Beat San Francisco Giants, 4-3 |
| 1937—Beat New York Giants, 4-1 | 1963—Lost to Los Angeles Dodgers, 4-0 |
| 1938—Beat Chicago Cubs, 4-0 | 1964—Lost to St. Louis Cardinals, 4-3 |
| 1939—Beat Cincinnati Reds, 4-0 | 1976—Lost to Cincinnati Reds, 4-0 |
| 1941—Beat Brooklyn Dodgers, 4-1 | 1977—Beat Los Angeles Dodgers, 4-2 |
| 1942—Lost to St. Louis Cardinals, 4-1 | 1978—Beat Los Angeles Dodgers, 4-2 |
| 1943—Beat St. Louis Cardinals, 4-1 | 1981—Lost to Los Angeles Dodgers, 4-2 |
| 1947—Beat Brooklyn Dodgers, 4-3 | 1996—Beat Atlanta Braves, 4-2 |
| 1949—Beat Brooklyn Dodgers, 4-1 | 1998—Beat San Diego Padres, 4-0 |
| 1950—Beat Philadelphia Phillies, 4-0 | 1999—Beat Atlanta Braves, 4-0 |
| 1951—Beat New York Giants, 4-2 | 2000—Beat New York Mets, 4-1 |
| 1952—Beat Brooklyn Dodgers, 4-3 | 2001—Lost to Arizona Diamondbacks, 4-3 |

## LEAGUE CHAMPIONSHIP SERIES (Won 9, Lost 1)

| | |
|---|---|
| 1976—Beat Kansas City Royals, 3-2 | 1996—Beat Baltimore Orioles, 4-1 |
| 1977—Beat Kansas City Royals, 3-2 | 1998—Beat Cleveland Indians, 4-2 |
| 1978—Beat Kansas City Royals, 3-1 | 1999—Beat Boston Red Sox, 4-1 |
| 1980—Lost to Kansas City Royals, 3-0 | 2000—Beat Seattle Mariners, 4-2 |
| 1981—Beat Oakland A's, 3-0 | 2001—Beat Seattle Mariners, 4-1 |

## DIVISIONAL PLAYOFF SERIES (Won 6, Lost 2)

| | |
|---|---|
| 1981— Beat Milwaukee Brewers, 3-2 | 1998—Beat Texas Rangers, 3-0 |
| 1995—Lost to Seattle Mariners, 3-2 | 1999—Beat Texas Rangers, 3-0 |
| 1996—Beat Texas Rangers, 3-1 | 2000—Beat Oakland A's, 3-2 |
| 1997—Lost to Cleveland Indians, 3-2 | 2001—Beat Oakland A's, 3-2 |

"Coming into this series, I would have said, 'No way we'll get swept,'" said Braves third baseman Chipper Jones. "But the Yankees played pretty much a perfect series. When they play a perfect series, they can beat anybody out there."

. . .

The 2000 World Series champs probably best exemplify that notion.

The Yankees had no Most Valuable Player, no batting champion, no Cy Young Award winner. They were a *team*—some stars, of course—but they were also loaded with talented role players who were able to step to the fore when needed.

Exhibit A: Luis Sojo.

A member of the 1996, '98, and '99 champions, the backup infielder was let go before the 2000 season, signed with Pittsburgh, then was reacquired in August after the Pirates put him on waivers. Two-and-a-half months later, it was Sojo—using a bat borrowed from fellow reserve Clay Bellinger—who bounced a single up the middle in Game 5 of the World Series to bring home the two runs that beat the Mets and gave the Yankees their twenty-sixth World Championship.

"This is a *group* of MVPs," shortstop Derek Jeter once said.

"Every game we have a new hero. You could pick a name out of a hat. . . . That's how you win. It's not just one guy."

Whereas the 1998 team just blew everyone away and the 1999 club won in a businesslike manner, the 2000 Yankees had to work hard for everything they got. At the end of June, they were just two games over .500 (38-36), three games out of first, and struggling.

"By mid-June, we realized changes had to be made," said general manager Cashman. He began making moves, trading for David Justice, Denny Neagle, and Glenallen Hill, and picking up Dwight Gooden, José Canseco, and Sojo on waivers.

All six contributed as the Yankees righted the ship. Justice hit 20 homers in pinstripes and was later named MVP of the American League Championship Series; Neagle won seven games; Hill hit 16 homers in only 132 at-bats; Gooden won four games; Canseco hit six homers; and Sojo, his World Series heroics aside, brought a spark to a team that desperately needed it.

Cashman's maneuvers paid off even better than he expected. "I didn't envision everyone stepping up and playing as well as they did," he admitted.

The Yankees pulled out to an 82-58 record and had a nine-game lead in the American League East on September 10. But then they went into a slump and staggered to the finish line, losing 15 of their last 18 games, including their last seven in a row. They won the division by a mere 2½ games and entered the postseason with an 87-74 record, worst of any playoff team.

Once the Yankees made the playoffs, though, they got down to business. They needed the full complement of five games to beat Oakland in the division series, then had to go six games before eliminating Seattle in the ALCS.

It took the Yankees only five games to beat the Mets in the World Series, but that might be deceptive. Three of the Yankees' victories were by one run; the other, in Game 5, was by two. Winning the close ones was just further evidence of the 2000 team's experience and professionalism.

"The Yankees are a different ball club in the postseason," pointed out Seattle Mariners manager (and former Yankee) Lou Piniella. "They have a confidence, a swagger that says, 'We've done this before. We can do it again.'"

⚫ ⚫ ⚫

That attitude—call it swagger, call it businesslike efficiency—was equally evident in 2001, when the Yankees came within one inning of a fourth straight World Championship.

Their season started slowly, and they were in a three-way battle in the AL East with Boston and Toronto through much of May. The Blue Jays soon fell out of contention, leaving the race between the Yankees and Red Sox. The teams were even as late as July 21, but then New York began pulling away, thanks in large part to the utter collapse of the Red Sox.

Nonetheless, the Yankees were sluggish over the last month of the season—a month interrupted by the terrorist attacks on the World Trade Center in New York and the Pentagon in Washington—hitting just .234. Nonetheless, they managed to coast to the AL East title by 13½ games, finishing with 95 wins and 65 losses, only the third-best record in the American League.

The 2001 offense was led by Derek Jeter (.311), Bernie Williams (.307), and Tino Martinez (.280, 34 homers, 113 RBIs). The pitching staff was led by Roger Clemens (20-3), free agent acquisition Mike Mussina (17-11, 3.15 ERA), and Andy Pettitte (15-10).

His flashy record aside, Clemens showed again in 2001 how important he was to the New York club, whose two key pitchers, Pettitte and Hernandez, missed time because of injuries. On his way to an unprecedented sixth Cy Young Award, Clemens won 16 in a row between May 26 and September 19 and was 20-1.

"This year was so special because in a lot of those wins there wasn't a lot of room for

## Cy Young Awards of Roger Clemens

| | | |
|---|---|---|
| 1986 (Boston) | 1991 (Boston) | 1998 (Toronto) |
| 1987 (Boston) | 1997 (Toronto) | 2001 (New York) |

error," Clemens said. "The time when Andy was down, Moose [Mussina] and I had to carry the mail. Joe [Torre] and Mel [Stottlemyre, the Yankees' pitching coach] would tell us in the clubhouse how much the pitching staff had to come through. . . . El Duque [Hernandez] was down, and you know you can't afford a long losing streak."

That was something the Yankees didn't have to worry about with Clemens as the stopper.

There may have been some detractors: Clemens didn't have a complete game all season; he was supported by an average of 6.6 runs per game, second highest among all AL pitchers; and he had the second-highest ERA among AL Cy Young Award winners. But the bottom line was success, and the Yankees won 27 of his 33 starts.

"What I'm most proud of is that I think we only lost six or seven ball games this year that I participated in," Clemens said after becoming, at age thirty-nine, the third oldest Cy Young Award winner. "I love those numbers."

After injuring a hamstring and struggling in the first round of the playoffs, he rebounded to pitch well in the League Championship series and was the Yankees' most consistent pitcher in the World Series. In five postseason appearances, he was 1-1 with a 2.36 ERA and 32 strikeouts in $26^{2}/_{3}$ innings.

For a time, though, it appeared the Yankees might not get a chance to defend their World Series crown. Just as they had for much of the 2001 season, they stumbled at the outset of the playoffs. They lost the first two games in the best-of-five first-round series against Oakland, but then swept the next three to advance. In the ALCS, they eliminated Seattle—winner of a league-record 116 games in the regular season—in five games.

"They play human all summer, and then in the postseason they turn it up a notch,"

Piniella said after his team's season ended.

The 2001 World Series against the Arizona Diamondbacks also started badly for the Yankees, as they lost Games 1 and 2 to Curt Shilling and Randy Johnson, respectively, in Phoenix. But then came three magical games in New York—a city still recovering from the attacks of September 11—that seemed to confirm these Yankees as a team of destiny.

They won Game 3 behind the pitching of Clemens and Mariano Rivera and the sixth inning tie-breaking single of Scott Brosius. Games 4 and 5 will be talked about as long as there are baseball fans. Martinez's two-out, ninth-inning homer tied the game and sent it into extra innings, and Jeter's homer in the 10th won it. As implausible as that was, the Yankees did it again the next night in Game 5, Brosius hittting a two-run, two-out homer in the bottom of the ninth to tie the score, and Alfonso Soriano singling the winning run across in the 12th.

The Diamondbacks took Game 6, then staged a two-run ninth-inning rally of their own in Game 7—improbably, against Rivera, the best reliever in postseason history—to stun the Yankees and end their three-year reign atop baseball.

"In my mind, when you get beat like that, you get beat," O'Neill said. "It's utter disappointment, yes."

*  *  *

Despite their success over the last few years, or perhaps because of it, the Yankees are still the target of criticism. One of the most-repeated knocks is that they're the best team money can buy, implying that George Steinbrenner bought these championships simply by pulling out his checkbook. But other teams have spent nearly as much—the Orioles and Dodgers, for example—without comparable success. If you're going to throw money around, you have to know where to throw it.

But that's only one aspect of the franchise's success. The other is its emphasis on the development of young talent. In the late '80s and early '90s, the Yankees thought nothing of trading away their young minor-league prospects for veteran players. These trades usually didn't pay off. Today, the team grooms its young talent—core players like Jeter, Pettitte, Rivera, and Williams—in the minors, then moves them into the majors, where they achieve star status. Steinbrenner, Cashman, and the rest of the brass bring aboard complementary players through trades and signings.

Of course, no discussion of the World Championship Yankee teams of recent years can leave out Joe Torre. He came to the Bronx in 1996, going to work for a man who had made nineteen managerial changes in his first twenty years as owner.

"Like everyone else, I had read about the fights, or George screaming at somebody," Torre said. "I realized a lot of those things weren't baseball-related other than that they involved the Yankees. So I wanted to keep distractions out of the clubhouse. That was important for me because they had given some players this built-in excuse, a reason they couldn't concentrate."

"He came in, took over, had an evenness about him," said David Cone. "He's a straight shooter. . . . He heads off situations that might arise or have arisen in the past and stops them before any trouble happens."

A solid manager, a hard-driving owner willing to spend money to win, a front office that's able to go after the player it needs to fill a hole, a nucleus of stars surrounded by bit players who take turns rising to the occasion . . . the Yankees have put all those pieces together, building themselves into the most dominant team in baseball. Beyond that, they demonstrated an ability to play a great game following an event of unspeakable horror.

"We felt the NY on our caps represented the rescue workers at ground zero," Torre said a couple of days after the Series ended.

Are they America's team?

The character and spirit of the 2001 Yankees provided much needed inspiration for an entire nation. Without a doubt, the term fits perfectly.

# Champions Among Champions

Between their first World Series appearance, in 1921, and the end of the 2001 season, the Yankees have participated in the prestigious fall classic thirty-eight times. Amazing! But of all those Yankee championship teams, which can be characterized as the best? Everyone has their favorite, of course. And so do we, presented here as our Elite Eight.

*Baseball Dynasties* (W.W. Norton & Co., 2000), by ESPN's Rob Neyer and sportswriter Eddie Epstein, is a persuasively written book that attempts to sort out the very best teams in baseball history on the basis of their seasonal run differential. The basic premise is that the team with the largest differential in runs scored during the season, versus runs scored by its opponents, are ranked as the best.

Run differential may not be the only criterion used in judging baseball's best teams, but it certainly is the most basic. It's where Neyer and Epstein start, and we think they're on to something. So we're going to look at the Yankee champions with run differential in mind and add a stat or two that might be helpful in

rounding out the picture of our Elite Eight.

These eight Yankee championship teams (see chart below) played a total of 37 games, winning 32, an astounding .865 winning percentage. In five of the eight Series, there were four-game sweeps. During the course of those 37 games, they limited their opponents to one run or less 10 times, recording shutouts in four of those 10 victories. That's domination. These World Series triumphs garnish the many Seasons of Glory that Yankee heroes have contributed to the history of the game.

Of the recent Yankee championship teams, the 1998 club comes in at a lofty No. 4 of the Elite Eight. The 1999 team gets our vote as a very efficient winner, but that doesn't put it among the greatest of the Yankee powerhouses. As for the 2000 champions, let's give them our "Gritty Greats" title. They did what they had to do, came up with the big hits and big outs, and won the Subway Series!

Winning. That's the bottom line in any of the Seasons of Glory.

| Year | RS | ORS | RD | WSO | WSR | OWSR | WSRD | WSRD/G | SERA | OSERA |
|------|------|------|------|------|------|------|------|--------|------|-------|
| 1939 | 967 | 556 | 411* | NYG | 20 | 8 | 12 | 3.00 | 1.22 | 4.29 |
| 1927 | 975 | 599 | 376 | PITTS | 23 | 10 | 13 | 3.25 | 2.00 | 5.19 |
| 1936 | 1,065 | 731 | 334 | NYG | 43 | 23 | 20 | 3.33 | 3.33 | 6.79 |
| 1998 | 965 | 656 | 309 | SD | 26 | 13 | 13 | 3.25 | 2.75 | 5.82 |
| 1937 | 979 | 671 | 308 | NYG | 28 | 12 | 16 | 3.20 | 2.45 | 4.81 |
| 1932 | 1,002 | 724 | 278 | CHI | 37 | 19 | 18 | 4.50 | 3.25 | 4.50 |
| 1938 | 966 | 710 | 256 | CINC | 22 | 9 | 13 | 3.25 | 1.75 | 5.03 |
| 1961 | 827 | 612 | 215 | CINC | 27 | 13 | 14 | 2.80 | 1.50 | 4.91 |

RS—runs scored in the season; ORS—opponents' runs scored in the season; RD—run differential;
WSO—World Series opponent; WSR—runs scored in the World Series; OWSR—runs scored by opponent in World Series;
WSRD—World Series run differential; WSRD/G—World Series run differential per game; SERA—World Series earned-run average;
OSERA opponents' World Series earned-run average.

* The 1939 Yankee team is rated No. 1 of all time by Neyer and Epstein.

# From the Top

From Babe Ruth, the Sultan of Swat, on through the colorful reliever Sparky Lyle, the top twenty-five players in Yankee history demonstrated phenomenal skills in their peak seasons. Not only did legends like Ruth, DiMaggio, Guidry, Ruffing, Gehrig, and Mattingly put together extraordinary single seasons, but also lesser known stars like Spud Chandler, Roger Peckinpaugh, Bobby Murcer, Snuffy Stirnweiss, Roy White, and Luis Arroyo contributed more victories to the Yankee cause than the league's average player might have contributed (explained in the Preface).

The top twenty-five players, on average, contributed between five and six more victories in their featured seasons than league-average players in the same season. The top twenty-five averaged 5.5, from Ruth's 10.6 season to Lyle's 4.4. Those five to six victories in many cases made a significant difference in the final standings of the team. In some cases it even meant a pennant.

For example, in 1921 the Yankees won their first pennant, beating out the second-place Indians by 4½ games. That year, pitcher Carl Mays rated a 5.8 Total Pitcher Index, which translates roughly into six victories. Take those six wins away, and the Yankees finish *behind* the Indians.

More recently, Rickey Henderson's 7.4 season in 1985 was a major factor in the Yankees' second-place finish in the AL East. They finished two games behind Toronto. Without Henderson's contribution, the Yankees would have been distant also-rans and 1985 would have been just another year at Yankee Stadium.

So let's take a closer look at the top twenty-five players to see what it was that made their peak seasons so special.

# 1

# Season of Glory

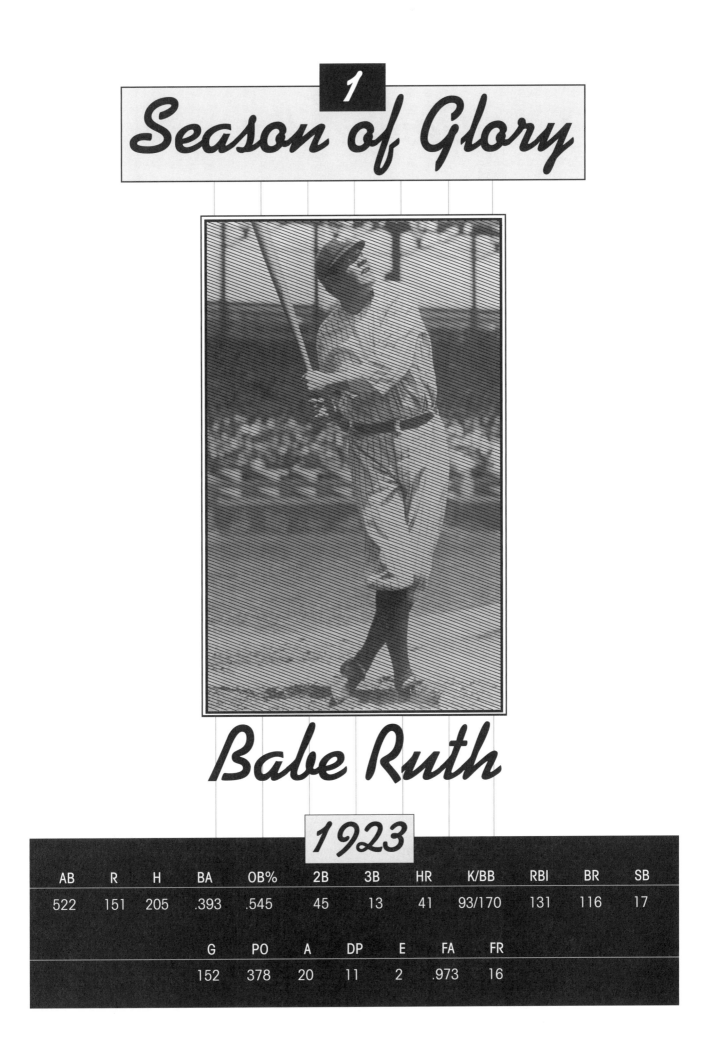

## Babe Ruth

### 1923

| AB | R | H | BA | OB% | 2B | 3B | HR | K/BB | RBI | BR | SB |
|-----|-----|-----|------|------|-----|-----|-----|--------|-----|-----|-----|
| 522 | 151 | 205 | .393 | .545 | 45 | 13 | 41 | 93/170 | 131 | 116 | 17 |

| | | | G | PO | A | DP | E | FA | FR | | |
|--|--|--|-----|-----|-----|-----|-----|------|-----|--|--|
| | | | 152 | 378 | 20 | 11 | 2 | .973 | 16 | | |

# George Herman Ruth

BORN
February 6, 1895
Baltimore, Maryland

DIED
August 16, 1948
New York

HEIGHT
6-2

WEIGHT
215

THREW
left hand

BATTED
left hand

New York Yankees
1920–1934

Hall of Fame
1936

*1923*

*H*e had a big, round face, a beer belly, and skinny legs. He was loud and vulgar. He ate too much, drank to excess, smoked big cigars, and spent many a sleepless night chasing some of life's other pleasures. And America worshipped him. George Herman Ruth, who could hit a baseball like no one before him, was the greatest sports hero the United States had ever known.

Ruth was a man for his times, the unbridled, extravagant, outrageous Roaring Twenties. It was America's golden age of sports—Dempsey, Grange, Tilden, and Jones were at the top of their games. But Ruth was bigger than all of them. With performances like his phenomenal 1923 season he reshaped a game that was already the national pastime.

"He was a parade all by himself," wrote sportswriter Jimmy Cannon, "a burst of dazzle and jingle, Santa Claus drinking his whiskey straight and groaning with a bellyache caused by gluttony. Babe Ruth made the music that his joyous years danced to in a continuous party. What Babe Ruth is comes down, one generation handing it to the next, as a national heirloom."

Ruth's story, which seems too implausible to be true, began in Baltimore, where he was born on February 6, 1895. His father, George, worked in his father's saloon-grocery store. By the time Little George, as the younger George Ruth was called, was six, his father was running a saloon of his own. The boy had little direction in his life—by all accounts he was something of a hellion—and when he was seven his parents shipped him to St. Mary's Industrial School, a training school where delinquents, orphans, and children from broken homes or impoverished families could get the education and discipline they couldn't find elsewhere.

Although George—he quickly outgrew the "Little" tag—was very happy at St. Mary's, he left the school on at least three occasions and returned to live with his parents. But the homecomings never lasted, and he was sent back to the good brothers who ran the school, the last time when he was seventeen.

There was one constant during Ruth's turbulent childhood: baseball. His sister Mamie said that almost from the time he could walk, he had a bat in his hand. St. Mary's, then, with its almost four dozen baseball teams, was the perfect home for George. He became a star on the school's top team, first as a catcher, then as a pitcher, outfielder, and infielder.

George Herman Ruth

# Game of Glory • July 11, 1923

The Babe's bat is too much for the White Sox in a July 11 victory in Chicago. This time he does his damage with four singles, driving in one run and scoring two more.

| NEW YORK | AB | R | H | E | | CHICAGO | AB | R | H | E |
|---|---|---|---|---|---|---|---|---|---|---|
| Hendricks, lf | 4 | 0 | 0 | 0 | | Hooper, rf | 4 | 0 | 1 | 0 |
| Dugan, 3b | 4 | 0 | 0 | 0 | | McClellan, ss | 5 | 0 | 1 | 1 |
| Ruth, cf | 4 | 2 | 4 | 1 | | Mostil, cf | 4 | 1 | 2 | 0 |
| Pipp, 1b | 2 | 0 | 0 | 0 | | Sheely, 1b | 3 | 0 | 0 | 0 |
| Smith, rf | 4 | 0 | 3 | 0 | | Falk, lf | 4 | 0 | 0 | 0 |
| Ward, 2b | 2 | 0 | 0 | 0 | | Kamm, 3b | 4 | 0 | 2 | 0 |
| Scott, ss | 4 | 0 | 1 | 0 | | Hapenny, 2b | 3 | 0 | 1 | 0 |
| Hofmann, c | 2 | 0 | 0 | 0 | | Graham, c | 2 | 0 | 1 | 0 |
| Bengough, c | 2 | 0 | 1 | 0 | | Faber, p | 0 | 0 | 0 | 0 |
| Hoyt, p | 2 | 1 | 0 | 0 | | Thurston, p | 0 | 0 | 0 | 0 |
| Strunk, ph | 1 | 0 | 0 | 0 | | Collins, ph | 1 | 0 | 0 | 0 |
| Elsh, ph | 1 | 0 | 0 | 0 | | | | | | |
| **Totals** | **32** | **3** | **9** | **1** | | | **30** | **1** | **8** | **1** |

| | | | | | | |
|---|---|---|---|---|---|---|
| New York | 0 0 0 | 1 1 0 | 0 1 0 | — 3 |
| Chicago | 0 0 0 | 0 0 0 | 0 1 0 | — 1 |

Double plays—New York 1, Chicago 1. Stolen base—Smith.

| New York | IP | H | BB | K |
|---|---|---|---|---|
| Hoyt | 9 | 8 | 0 | 2 |

| Chicago | IP | H | BB | K |
|---|---|---|---|---|
| Faber | 7 | 6 | 1 | 3 |
| Thurston | 2 | 3 | 0 | 2 |

Hit by pitcher—Sheely (by Hoyt).

Time—1:47.

By the time Ruth was eighteen, word was spreading about the big, gawky, hard-throwing left-hander at St. Mary's. Soon the buzz reached Jack Dunn, owner and manager of the Baltimore Orioles of the International League. He offered Ruth $600 for the 1914 season, and on March 2, 1914, Ruth left St. Mary's for good.

Dunn had landed an incredible talent. The 6-foot-2-inch, 170-pound youngster could not only pitch, but he was a powerful home run hitter—this was still the dead-ball era. What's more, he could run and field.

Soon nicknamed "Babe"—one of the Oriole veterans referred to him as "Dunn's new baby" when he first saw him—Ruth won eight straight games for the Orioles. But that success didn't translate into fan support, and the cash-strapped Dunn decided to sell off his top talent. So in July 1914, just a few months after Ruth left St. Mary's, he was sold to the Boston Red Sox.

Harry Hooper was a member of the Red Sox when Ruth came aboard. In *The Glory of Their Times*, he told author Lawrence S. Ritter about Ruth's first season with Boston:

He was a left-handed pitcher then, and a good one. He had never been anywhere, didn't know anything about manners or how to behave among people—just a big overgrown green pea. You probably remember him with that big belly he got later on. But that wasn't there in 1914. George was six foot two and weighed 198 pounds, all of it muscle. He had a slim waist, huge biceps, no self-discipline, and not much education—not so very much different from a lot of other nineteen-year-old would-be ball players. Except for two things: he could eat more than anyone else, and he could hit a baseball further . . .

You know, I saw it all happen, from beginning to end. But sometimes I still can't believe what I saw: this nineteen-year-old kid, crude, poorly educated . . . gradually transformed into the idol of American youth and the symbol of baseball the world over—a man loved by more people and with an intensity of feeling that perhaps has never been equaled before or since. I saw a man transformed from a human being into something pretty close to a god.

Ruth made his major-league debut on July 11, beating Cleveland 4-3. Ruth spent part of the season in the minors, with Boston's Providence ball club, then came back to the majors to stay in late September. His 1914 record for the Red Sox was 2-1, but he won another 22 games for Baltimore and Providence that year.

Ruth soon became a bonafide star in Boston. In 1915 he had an 18-8 record, a 2.44 ERA, and a team-leading four homers in 42 games for the World Series champion Red Sox. He won 23 games in 1916—Boston won the World Series again that year—and 24 in 1917. He slipped to 13-7 in 1918, but that year the Red Sox started using him in the outfield and at first base to take advantage of his hitting skills. He responded with 11 homers, tops in the majors, as the Red Sox won their third AL pennant in four years. Then he won two games against the Cubs in the World Series, running his Series shutout streak to a record 29²/₃ innings.

Life was good, too, off the field. As Paul

Gallico once wrote, Ruth had "all the food he could eat, beer and whiskey, girls with red or black or yellow hair and soft lips, baseball every day, nice warm places to sleep, silk underwear, fine warm clothing, plenty of pals, money in the pants pocket, more where that came from, name and pictures in the papers, a big shiny automobile to ride around in—wow!"

The 1919 season marked a turning point for baseball and for Ruth. A new era was arriving, with the home run replacing the hit-and-run, station-to-station game that had been the trademark of the dead-ball era of Honus Wagner and Ty Cobb. The long ball was in, and no one was better at it than Ruth.

By this time, Ruth was being used primarily as an outfielder—he appeared in only 17 games as a pitcher in 1919, going 9-5. That season he had 432 at-bats, more than 100 more than in any previous season. He responded with 29 home runs, a single-season record and more than twice as many as anyone else in the majors that year.

The fans loved the home runs. Other players, equating the crowd-pleasing homers with bigger paydays, changed their approach and began swinging for the fences. Owners, too, realized that home runs translated into profits. A livelier ball was introduced, trick pitches like the spitter and emery ball were banned, and umpires were instructed to put new, clean balls in play. All the changes were made for the benefit of the hitter, especially the home run hitters. Baseball was entering a new age, with Ruth leading the way.

"His home runs were to baseball what the forward pass was to football, the knockout punch of Jack Dempsey and Joe Louis to boxing," Tom Meany wrote in *Baseball's Greatest Hitters*. "Baseball owes as much to Ruth as it does to Doubleday, providing Abner actually did invent the game. Regardless of who conceived baseball, it was Ruth who made it a big business."

At twenty-four, Ruth was the game's biggest star, making $9,000 a season and receiving hundreds of letters from fans each week. Everyone, including New York Yankees owners Jacob Ruppert and Tillinghast Huston, knew that Ruth was ready for a bigger stage. And on December 26, 1919, Red Sox owner Harry Frazee, who was in financial trouble, sold Ruth to the Yankees for $125,000, a $300,000 loan, and other considerations.

The deal was announced on January 3, the dawn of the Roaring Twenties. The timing couldn't have been better. The horrors of World War I were fading, and although Prohibition became law less than three weeks after Ruth was sold to the

> "To understand him you had to understand this: he wasn't human. No human could have done the things he did and lived the way he lived and been a ballplayer. Cobb? Could he pitch? Speaker? The rest? I saw them. I was there. There was never anybody close. When you figure the things he did and the way he lived and the way he played, you got to figure he was more than an animal even. There was never anyone like him. He was a god."
>
> —Teammate Joe Dugan

Yankees, America was ready to celebrate. And Babe Ruth was going to be the life of the party.

With more than a dozen daily newspapers and some of the best sportswriters ever in their prime, New York was the perfect place for Ruth and his escapades. And when he hit 54 homers that first season, he owned the town. "To whatever engaged him, he was the mightiest: hitter, pitcher, womanizer, drinker, eater," wrote Donald Honig in *Baseball America*. "He was the greatest player on the greatest team in the greatest stadium in the greatest city. He was power. He was New York. He was baseball." "Life was worth livin' with that guy," former teammate Whitey Witt told Kal Wagenheim, author of *Babe Ruth: His Life and Legend*, published in 1974. "He was our star, our meal ticket.

Some of the guys may have been jealous, but not me! I had enough brains to know that he was makin' money for me!"

Ruth, though, was more than just a larger-than-life character and a meal ticket for his teammates. He turned out to be the savior of his sport. In 1920, when the future of baseball was in question as a result of the 1919 World Series scandal, Ruth went on his home run rampage. He hit 54, individually more than fourteen of the fifteen other teams in the majors, and captivated (and distracted) fans not only in New York, but across the nation.

Ruth remained on the national stage in 1921. His remarkable performance that year included 59 homers, 177 runs scored, 171 RBIs, a .378 batting average, and an .846 slugging percentage. With a supporting cast of people like Carl Mays (27-9), Waite Hoyt (19-13), and Bob Meusel (.318, 135 RBIs), the Yankees won the AL pennant, only to lose to the Giants in eight games in the World Series.

In 1922 the Yankees again won the AL pennant, yet that season was extremely disappointing for both Ruth and the Yankees. Although Ruth became the highest-paid player in baseball when he signed a three-year contract at $52,000 per year before the start of the season, he spent the first month of the campaign on the sidelines, suspended by Commissioner Kenesaw Mountain Landis for participating in a barnstorming tour after the 1921 season. (Players from championship teams were prohibited from barnstorming on the theory that players who hadn't received World Series shares should be allowed to pick up the extra cash.) Thus, Ruth's season began in mid-May, and it was less than a week old when it started to unravel. He went into the stands after a heckler and was later fined $200. More trouble followed: There was a fight with teammate Wally Pipp, a confrontation with umpire Bill Dineen that resulted in a five-game suspension, an operation on an abscess on his calf, and another multiple-game suspension for disagreeing with an umpire. The Yankees ended the year by losing to the Giants in the World Series in four

*Babe Ruth and Ty Cobb*

games, with Ruth hitting just .118 in the Series.

Ruth was held accountable for his unprofessional behavior. During the off-season, at a dinner held in his honor in New York, Ruth was subjected to some biting criticism from the sportswriters and politicians in attendance. The climax of the night was a speech by rising politician and future New York mayor Jimmy Walker. "Babe Ruth is not only a great athlete, but also a fool!" Walker began. Ruth, first stunned, then seemingly angry, listened as Walker accused him of letting down his biggest fans, kids, by the off-field escapades that diminished his game. By the time Walker was finished, Ruth was in tears. He took his turn at the podium and promised to change his ways. "When I think of important turning points in his career," Ruth's daughter Dorothy Ruth Pirone once recalled, "that night belongs at the top. From that moment on, Dad really had something to prove."

True to his word, Ruth retreated to his farm over the winter and slimmed down to 215 pounds. He reported to spring training in shape, eager for the new season. It would turn out to be the finest season of his career.

Ruth had a new stage for his comeback: Yankee Stadium, a $2.5 million showplace (the Yankees had been asked to leave the Polo Grounds, which was owned by the Giants, in 1920). And he christened it in typical fashion in the Yankees' season opener on April 18 against Boston. "Governors, generals, colonels, politicians, and baseball officials gathered solemnly today to dedicate the biggest stadium in baseball," the *Chicago Tribune* reported, "but it was a ballplayer who did the real dedicating. In the third inning, with two teammates on the base lines, Babe Ruth smashed a savage home run into the right-field bleachers, and that was the real baptism of the new Yankee stadium." Ruth's homer was all the Yankees needed as they beat the Red Sox 4-1.

The next day he had two hits and a walk in another victory over Boston, and the following afternoon he went 3-for-5, including a game-winning two-run double in the ninth. The season was three days old, and the reformed Babe was 6-for-10 and had reached base in nine of his first fifteen trips to the plate.

Ruth cooled off over the next ten days, hitting just .240 to close out the month at .343 (12-for-35). April ended with the Yankees in second place, 1½ games behind Cleveland. In May, though, they took control of the AL race, moving into first with a 3-2 victory over the Indians on May 8. By the end of the month, they had a seven-game lead over their closest competition.

With the drama gone from the pennant race, attention soon turned to Ruth and his pursuit of his single-season home run record. In May he had 11 homers and a .341 batting average. The homers seemed to come in bunches—he homered in three consecutive games, May 17–19, against St. Louis, and there were back-to-back shots on May 30 in a double-header sweep of Washington.

Soon, pitchers realized the best way to stay out of trouble was to walk Ruth. On June 11, for example, he doubled in the first inning of a game against Cleveland. The next four times he came up to bat, he was walked intentionally. The following afternoon, with two men on, the Indians elected to pitch to Ruth. He blasted his thirteenth home run—and was walked two more times that afternoon. (Ruth walked 170 times that season, a major-league record.)

Ruth's greatest season continued to unfold in magnificent fashion. He opened July with an 8-for-16 series against Washington (all Yankee victories) that included two homers, three doubles, and a triple, and raised his average to .362. He had a 4-for-4 day against the White Sox on July 11, and the next day he hit his twentieth homer in another victory. He had three hits against Detroit on July 19, raising his average to .381. He ended July at .390 with 24 homers.

Ruth hit a remarkable .500 (40-for-80) in August. He ended the month with a .401 average and 32 homers, and was slightly ahead of Detroit's Harry Heilmann (.396), Ruth's closest competition in the batting race. But Ruth began tailing off in early September, and Heilmann finally passed him on September 20. The two stayed neck-and-neck to the wire. Ruth, who missed three games during the last week because of a bad ankle, closed with a rush, hitting .607 in his last seven games, but still finished second to Heilmann, .403 to .393.

The batting race notwithstanding, Ruth dominated the AL stats in 1923. He was first in homers (41), runs (151), total bases (399), RBIs (131), walks (170), on-base percentage (.545), and slugging average (.764). And he was fourth in hits (205) and third in doubles (45). He reached base an incredible 379 times. In mid-September, baseball writers voted him the American League's Most Valuable Player.

"The difference between the Yanks of last year . . . and the American League champions of this year lies in Ruth's altered plan of life," wrote the esteemed Hugh Fullerton in the October 3 *Chicago Tribune*. "The big boy is sincere and earnest, is hustling, fighting, playing for his team instead of for his individual record—and the result is that his record, save for those ballyhoo home runs, is better than ever and he is the greatest ballplayer of all."

Still, his season wasn't complete. He needed to prove that he could win a World Series. The Yankees' Series opponent in 1923, for the third straight year, was the Giants.

The Giants took Game 1 thanks to Casey Stengel's inside-the-park home run in the ninth inning. Ruth got the Yankees back in the Series in Game 2, hitting two long home runs in consecutive innings—he was the first player to do it—to provide a 4-2 victory. Stengel's seventh-inning homer was the only run scored in Game 3, giving the Giants a 2-1 edge. But the Yankees swept the next three games to win their first World Series.

Ruth hit .368 in the Series, with three homers, two singles, a double, and triple in 19 at-bats. He scored eight runs and drove in three.

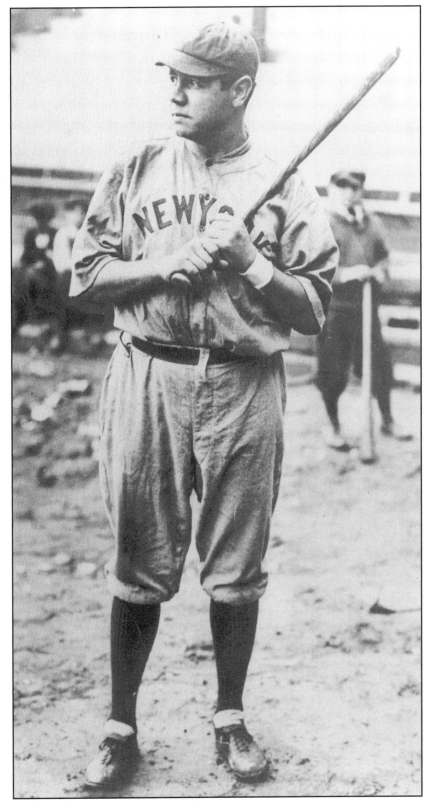

George Herman Ruth

The Babe's redemption was complete.

Ruth, of course, would have other great years for the Yankees. He had 46 homers and a league-leading .378 batting average in

1924; 47 homers with 146 RBIs in 1926; and 60 homers, 164 RBIs and 158 runs for the legendary 1927 ballclub. Any of those seasons would be worthy of inclusion in this book. But Ruth's 1923 season was his best defensively, when he fielded, according to one writer, "with the deft touch of a thief in the black of night." That year he threw out 20 base runners, had 378 putouts, and recorded one of his best career fielding averages (.973), which was tops among regular AL right-fielders. Those defensive contributions were enough to tip the scales in favor of 1923.

During the next eleven years Ruth played for the Yankees, the team won four more pennants and three more World Series crowns. In his twenty-two-year career, he had more than 700 homers, more than 2,000 runs, more than 2,000 RBIs, and more than 2,000 walks. He had a slugging average of .690—still the best ever—and he still holds several single-season records more than seventy years after he set them.

He was the game's greatest drawing card, its most colorful personality, a hero around the world. There's not much more he could have done. Well, maybe. . . .

"If I'd tried for them dinky singles," he once observed, "I could've batted around .600."

And who's to doubt it?

## Baseball News Of 1923

- Yankee first baseman Wally Pipp had a twenty-one-game hitting streak.
- Yankee pitcher Sam Jones no-hit the Athletics on September 4 in Philadelphia.
- Pirate first baseman Charley Grimm began the season with a National League-record twenty-three-game hitting streak.
- Everett Scott of the Yankees played in his 1,138th straight game.
- On September 17 the New York Giants' George Kelly became the first major-leaguer to hit home runs in three consecutive innings.
- The top seven hitters in the NL were all future Hall of Famers: Rogers Hornsby, Zack Wheat, Jim Bottomley, Edd Roush, Frankie Frisch, Pie Traynor, and Ross Youngs.

## Around The World In 1923

- Henry Ford's Model T had its biggest sales year to date.
- The Teapot Dome scandal exploded.
- Edna St. Vincent Millay won the Nobel Prize in poetry.
- President Harding withdrew the last U.S. forces from Germany.
- U.S. Steel's agreement to implement the eight-hour workday was hailed as a milestone for the labor movement.

# 2

# Season of Glory

## Mickey Mantle

## 1956

| AB | R | H | BA | OB% | 2B | 3B | HR | K/BB | RBI | BR | SB |
|---|---|---|---|---|---|---|---|---|---|---|---|
| 533 | 132 | 188 | .353 | .467 | 22 | 5 | 52 | 99/112 | 130 | 89 | 10 |

| | | G | PO | A | DP | E | FA | FR | |
|---|---|---|---|---|---|---|---|---|---|
| | | 150 | 370 | 10 | 3 | 4 | .990 | 8 | |

# Mickey Charles Mantle

**BORN**
October 20, 1931
Spavinaw, Oklahoma

**DIED**
August 13, 1995
Dallas

**HEIGHT**
5-11

**WEIGHT**
198

**THREW**
right hand

**BATTED**
both

New York Yankees
1951–1968

Hall of Fame
1974

**1956**

*M*ickey Charles Mantle came out of Commerce, Oklahoma, a strapping, switch-hitting teenager who could cream a baseball, who could run like few of his peers, and who had an arm like fewer still. From the start, the Mick was destined for greatness. "He was a true baseball hero of that era, the athlete as mythic figure," David Halberstam wrote in his book *October 1964*. ". . . Everything about Mantle seemed to come from a storybook about the classic American athlete; he was the modest country boy with a shock of blond hair that turned the color of corn silk every summer, who became a superstar in the big city." But the path to greatness, to that superstardom, to his becoming the greatest New York Yankee of his era, was not an easy one.

Mantle was born on October 20, 1931, in Spavinaw, Oklahoma. Almost from birth, Mickey was immersed in baseball by his father, Elvin "Mutt" Mantle, a zinc and lead miner who also played semipro ball. (Mutt named his son after Tiger great Mickey Cochrane.)

Mickey was a standout athlete at Commerce High School, and it was there that he almost lost the chance to fulfill his destiny. While playing football as a sophomore, he was kicked in the left shin, an injury that developed into osteomyelitis, a bone disease that results in inflammation of the bone marrow. Doctors considered amputation; Mantle's mother steadfastly refused. Slowly he regained his health, and by his senior year he was again performing heroically at shortstop for the baseball team.

Tom Greenwade, a scout for the Yankees, signed Mantle in June 1949, on the night of Mantle's high school graduation, to a Class D contract. Greenwade, unlike some other major-league scouts, was undeterred by Mantle's history of leg trouble. "The first time I saw Mantle," Greenwade said years later, "I knew how Paul Krichell felt when he first saw Lou Gehrig. He knew that as a scout he'd never have another moment like it. I felt the same way about Mantle."

Mantle spent his first season in professional ball in Independence, Missouri; the next year he moved up to Class C ball, playing for the Joplin, Missouri, team and hitting .383. He was promoted to the Yankees' Triple-A Kansas City farm team and was invited to the Yankees' prespring training camp, which was held in Phoenix before the start of the 1951 season.

Mantle had such a great spring that instead of being sent to Kansas City for seasoning, he was put on the major-league roster. Yankee manager Casey Stengel decided to move Mantle from shortstop to the outfield. There were several reasons: 1951 was going to be Joe DiMaggio's last season, and the fleet Mantle—he could cover a lot of Yankee Stadium turf—was the best prospect in the organization to replace DiMaggio, even if he would have to be switched from the infield. Also, the Yankees had 1950 MVP Phil Rizzuto entrenched at short.

By midsummer, though, he was struggling at the plate and found himself being shipped to Kansas City. The demotion was only temporary; he hit .361 with 11 homers and 50 RBIs in just 40 games and was soon headed back to New York, where he finished out the season, hitting .267 over his two tours of duty.

Mantle blossomed into the player everyone expected him to be the next season, hitting .311 with 23 homers and 87 RBIs and making the American League All-Star team. He followed that with three more outstanding seasons, hitting .295, .300, and .306, and leading the league in runs in 1954 and in triples, homers, on-base percentage, and slugging percentage in 1955.

Clearly, Mickey Mantle was one of the best young players in the game. However, people wanted—no, expected—a lot more. "Mantle has been a terrific ballplayer—one of the greatest of the great Yankees," wrote Dan Daniel, the baseball writer for the *New York World-Telegram and Sun*, in the January 4, 1956, edition of *The Sporting News*. "But the fact remains that, as yet, he has not come up to the spectacular expectations that had been set up for him by Stengel and the experts when he jumped into the Yankee ranks from Class C Joplin in 1951." And Mantle himself knew that he had not yet reached his full potential. "I had a pretty good year in 1955," Mantle said in *My*

*Mickey Mantle*

# Game of Glory · September 18, 1956

With his fiftieth homer of the season, a mighty eleventh-inning blast into the upper deck in left field at Comiskey Park on September 18, Mantle beats Chicago 3-2 and clinches the pennant for the Yankees.

| NEW YORK | AB | R | H | RBI | CHICAGO | AB | R | H | RBI |
|----------|----|----|----|----|---------|----|----|----|----|
| Bauer, rf | 5 | 0 | 1 | 0 | Aparicio, ss | 5 | 0 | 1 | 0 |
| Martin, 2b | 5 | 2 | 1 | 0 | Fox, 2b | 5 | 0 | 0 | 0 |
| Mantle, cf | 5 | 1 | 2 | 2 | Doby, cf | 4 | 1 | 1 | 1 |
| Berra, c | 5 | 0 | 1 | 1 | Minoso, lf | 4 | 0 | 1 | 0 |
| Skowron, 1b | 4 | 0 | 0 | 0 | Dropo, 1b | 4 | 1 | 2 | 1 |
| Collins, 1b | 0 | 0 | 0 | 0 | Delsing, pr | 0 | 0 | 0 | 0 |
| McDougald, ss | 3 | 0 | 0 | 0 | Lollar, c | 4 | 0 | 2 | 0 |
| Howard, lf | 4 | 0 | 0 | 0 | Phillips, rf | 3 | 0 | 0 | 0 |
| Carey, 3b | 4 | 0 | 1 | 0 | Rivera, rf | 2 | 0 | 0 | 0 |
| Ford, p | 4 | 0 | 0 | 0 | Hatfield, 3b | 2 | 0 | 0 | 0 |
| Grim, p | 0 | 0 | 0 | 0 | Esposito, 3b | 0 | 0 | 0 | 0 |
| | | | | | Pierce, p | 4 | 0 | 1 | 0 |
| | | | | | Jackson, ph | 1 | 0 | 0 | 0 |
| Totals | 39 | 3 | 6 | 3 | Totals | 38 | 2 | 8 | 2 |

```
New York    0 0 0    1 0 0    0 0 1    0  1 — 3
Chicago     1 0 0    0 0 0    0 1 0    0  0 — 2
```

Errors—McDougald, Fox. Double—Lollar. Triple—Martin. Home runs—Doby, Dropo, Mantle. Double plays—New York 2, Chicago 1. Left on base—New York 4, Chicago 8.

| New York | IP | H | R | ER | BB | K |
|----------|----|----|----|----|----|----|
| Ford (W, 19-5) | 10 | 8 | 2 | 2 | 5 | 1 |
| Grim | 1 | 0 | 0 | 0 | 0 | 1 |

| Chicago | IP | H | R | ER | BB | K |
|---------|----|----|----|----|----|----|
| Pierce (L, 20-8) | 11 | 6 | 3 | 2 | 1 | 8 |

Time—2:55. Attendance—31,694.

*Favorite Summer 1956*, written in 1991 with Phil Pepe. "But I wasn't satisfied. I hadn't achieved what I knew I could and I was determined to start producing in 1956 the way everyone expected me to."

The Yankee questions in 1956 went beyond Mantle. They had lost a hard-fought seven-game World Series to the Brooklyn Dodgers in 1955 (Mantle appeared in only three games—as a starter in two and as a pinch-hitter in one—because of a leg injury).

Would they be able to go that additional step in 1956? They had the talent, but they'd have to stay healthy, and that was a concern as the 1956 campaign dawned: outfielder Hank Bauer had continued problems with a groin pull; outfielder Irv Noren was recovering from surgery on both knees; shortstop Billy Hunter was coming back from a leg fracture that had sidelined him almost half of the previous season.

Still, they were the defending AL cham-

Yankees, with the best pitching and catching staffs in the league, a team whose strong infield would be strengthened even more by having Billy Martin, back from the service, available for a full season. And this was a team with Mickey Mantle.

This would be the greatest season of Mantle's career, one that would show everyone once and for all just how good he was. It took Mantle only until the second exhibition game of the spring to start producing. His three-run homer gave the Yankees a 4-3 victory over St. Louis. He added another homer the next afternoon to help beat Chicago, and a triple, two singles, and a two-run homer in the ninth a few days later in a 7-5 victory over Detroit. The hitting was there, all right. But so was something else. In 1955 Mantle had led the AL with 97 strikeouts. In the spring of 1956, he didn't strike out until his twelfth exhibition game, a total of 36 at-bats without fanning.

As well as Mantle performed during the exhibition season, there were still concerns about his frequent injuries. He wore out his arm after the team's first three exhibition games and needed a day off. A few days later he pulled a tendon in his right leg and missed several more games. It was starting to sound like the injury-prone Mantle of the past. "That Mantle can hit the ball farther than anybody else I have seen in baseball," Stengel said. "But can he keep from getting hurt? Can he stay in the lineup? Can he cut down on them 97 strikeouts?"

At the Yankees' first regular-season game on April 17, 1956, in Washington, D.C., however, Mantle showed that he meant business. With President Eisenhower, whom Mantle

A young Mickey Mantle.

always considered a good-luck charm, cheering him on, he belted two homers over the center-field fence. It was the first time anyone had done it twice in one game at Griffith Stadium, and it prompted Yankee coach Bill Dickey to compare Mantle to one of his old teammates. "I only saw one ball hit over that fence before," he said, "and that was by the Babe. Mantle's got more power than any hitter I ever saw, including the Babe."

By the end of April, Mantle was hitting .415 (with four homers) and the Yankees were in first place. Even after the Yankee infield went into a horrible slump in early May,

## Triple Crown Winners

| Player | Year | Avg. | HR | RBI |
|---|---|---|---|---|
| Ty Cobb, Detroit | 1909 | .377 | 9 | 115 |
| Rogers Hornsby, St. Louis (NL) | 1922 | .401 | 42 | 152 |
| Rogers Hornsby, St. Louis (NL) | 1925 | .403 | 39 | 143 |
| Chuck Klein, Philadelphia (NL) | 1933 | .368 | 28 | 120 |
| Jimmie Foxx, Philadelphia (AL) | 1933 | .356 | 48 | 163 |
| Lou Gehrig, New York (AL) | 1934 | .363 | 49 | 165 |
| Joe Medwick, St. Louis (NL) | 1937 | .374 | 31 | 154 |
| Ted Williams, Boston (AL) | 1942 | .356 | 36 | 137 |
| Ted Williams, Boston (AL) | 1947 | .343 | 32 | 114 |
| **Mickey Mantle, New York (AL)** | **1956** | **.353** | **52** | **130** |
| Frank Robinson, Baltimore | 1966 | .316 | 49 | 122 |
| Carl Yastrzemski, Boston | 1967 | .326 | 44 | 121 |

the team was able to keep winning behind Mantle (.391, with 11 homers and 25 RBIs, through the first week of May) and Yogi Berra (.340, 28 RBIs).

Mantle was back up to .400 (40-for-100) and had 13 homers by the middle of the month. Many of the home runs were dramatic—he connected from both sides of the

> "He can hit better than anyone else, he can field better than anyone else, he can throw better and he can run better. What else is there?"
>
> —BALTIMORE ORIOLES MANAGER PAUL RICHARDS IN THE AUGUST 29, 1956, EDITION OF *THE SPORTING NEWS*

plate against Chicago on May 18, the second one tying the game in the ninth inning—and some were moon-shots like his monstrous blast out of the ballpark three days later in Kansas City, his sixteenth of the year.

He celebrated Memorial Day in a big way, leading the Yankees to a double-header sweep of the Senators in New York. In the first game, he hit a home run off the facade of the right-field stands, coming within two feet or less of knocking it out of Yankee Stadium. And in the second game, he broke a 3-3 tie with a 400-foot shot off Camilo Pascual. As Yankee teammate Joe Collins put it, "He hits them as though they don't count if they're under 400 feet."

The two homers and two other hits that day raised his average to .425, tops in the majors. And his twenty homers put him eleven games ahead of Ruth's record-setting 60-home run pace of 1927. But the comparisons soon stopped as Mantle suffered through his first extended slump of 1956, going 11-for-40 (.275) over the next ten games. And only one of those hits was a home run.

He got back on track around the middle of June, at least as far as chasing the legend of Ruth was concerned. His twenty-second home run came on June 14 in a victory over Chicago; he homered the next day in a win over Cleveland and the next day in another win over the Indians. On June 18 he hit one out of Briggs Stadium in Detroit, and two days later he hit a pair of 400-footers against the Tigers, giving him 27 home runs and a .380 average.

The month ended with Mantle at .383 and the Yankees holding a two-game lead over the second-place White Sox, who had helped their own cause by sweeping a four-game

*Mickey Mantle with the "Old Professor," manager Casey Stengel.*

series at Comiskey Park from June 22 through June 24.

What looked like a good pennant race suddenly threatened to get even closer when Mantle was hurt July 4 in Boston. He was injured on the last play of the first game of a holiday double-header when he twisted his right knee breaking for Jimmy Piersall's blooper to short right-center in the bottom of the eleventh. Once he got to the ball, he further aggravated the knee with an off-balance futile throw to the plate.

Mantle was sent back to New York, where X-rays showed a strained ligament that sidelined him until July 8, when he returned for four innings in an 8-2 victory over Washington. The next afternoon he had a home run and three strikeouts in the American League's 7-3 All-Star Game loss in Washington.

The Yankees were 52-26 at the All-Star break, led by Mantle (.371, 71 RBIs and 29 homers, one ahead of Ruth's pace) and pitch-ers Johnny Kucks (11-4) and Whitey Ford (10-4). But in the first week of the second half of the season, they showed once and for all who was best.

The second half started with a big series against the second-place Indians in New York. The Yankees won all three games impressively—a pinch grand slam by Bauer won one, Martin's bases-loaded single off Bob Feller in the tenth won another, and the score of the other contest was 10-0—to widen their lead to 9½ games. Chicago came to town next, and the Yankees won both games of that series (a third was rained out), increasing their winning streak to ten games. (They would win one more before Detroit ended it on July 18.) Except for a couple of slumps that caused the Yankees' lead to dwindle to a half-dozen games, the pennant race was all but decided.

Attention was now focused on Mantle and his pursuit of Ruth's record and of that most elusive of baseball feats, the Triple Crown.

*"Joltin'Joe" DiMaggio with the Yankees' young sensation, Mickey Mantle.*

On August 1 he led the AL in the requisite categories: batting average (.368), home runs (34), and runs batted in (89). He also had the most hits (128).

The month was filled with more big hits and heroics: a pair of homers on August 4 against Detroit; his thirty-eighth, surpassing his 1955 total, on August 8 against Washington; an RBI single in the ninth to beat Baltimore 5-4 two days later; two singles and a homer (his forty-first, which put him thirteen games ahead of Ruth's pace) against the Orioles on August 12 (cheering him on as he circled the bases was Ruth's widow, Claire); and the forty-seventh homer on August 31 in Washington with Eisenhower again in the seats, breaking a 4-4 tie and giving the Yankees a 6-4 victory.

Mantle's home run pace, though, slackened. He went one nine-game stretch without hitting one, and by the middle of August, he was only five games ahead of Ruth. By the first week in September, he was only two ahead, and he soon fell victim to Ruth's sensational September, when the Babe hit 17 (Mantle had 13 in August, the month Ruth hit only 9). By September 10 Mantle was four games behind the Bambino and no longer a threat to the record. At least not for another five years.

Mantle was not only a victim of Ruth's scorching September performance, but of the pressure he was putting on himself. He was being too anxious at the plate, lunging at pitches good and bad and taking too big a stride. He hit just .152 (5-for-33), with no homers or RBIs between September 1 and 12. "I wasn't worried about the homers in that spell," he later recalled of the ten-game homerless stretch. "All I wanted to do was hit singles, or even a double now and then. I couldn't even bunt . . . I just wasn't doing anything good."

Stengel and Dickey took him aside before

the Yankees' September 16 game in Cleveland for some hitting instruction. Mantle responded with his forty-ninth homer in a 10-3 victory that clinched a tie for the pennant. On September 18 in Chicago, the Yankees beat the White Sox 3-2 on Mantle's fiftieth home run, in the eleventh off Billy Pierce, to win the twenty-second pennant in their history.

The early September slump had put Mantle's Triple Crown chances in jeopardy. The day the Yankees won the pennant, he led the league in home runs and RBIs but trailed Boston's Ted Williams in the batting race .355 to .350. Mantle regained the lead thanks to a successful series in Boston from September 21 to September 23, when he went 6-for-9. He appeared as only a pinch-hitter in five of the last six games (he had a pulled thigh muscle, and Stengel wanted to make sure he would be ready for the World Series) and was able to maintain his lead in all three offensive categories.

Detroit's Al Kaline and Williams made things interesting in the closing days of the season, however. With two games to go, Kaline was only four RBIs behind Mantle, 128 to 124. In the last game of the season, Mantle got his 130th on an infield grounder; Kaline drove home two in his finale and finished with 128. Williams was within five or six percentage points of Mantle for most of the last week. By the last day of the season, though, Mantle had an eight-point lead, and Williams conceded by not playing the final game of the season.

"That last week or so I was very conscious of it," Mantle later said in recalling those hectic final days of the Triple Crown race. "To tell you the truth, I even dreamed about it at night. . . . The last few days I kept telling myself I had better not get into another fuss like this, because it certainly was nerve-wracking."

At the end of the 1956 season, Mantle was the runaway winner of the AL Most Valuable Player Award (this was the first of three

The "Mick" with Willie Mays.

times he would win the award). He was the Triple Crown winner with 52 homers, 130 RBIs, and a .353 batting average. He also led the AL in runs (132), total bases (376), and slugging percentage (.705), was second in walks (112) and on-base percentage (.467), and fourth in hits (188).

The 1956 World Series—a rematch of the 1955 Series, in which the Yankees had lost to the Dodgers—gave Mantle another opportunity to demonstrate his abilities. His most important contribution was helping pitcher Don Larsen throw the only perfect game in World Series history (in the fifth game of a tied Series). Larsen got help from Mantle offensively (his third homer of the Series had staked him to a 1-0 lead in the fourth) and, perhaps more importantly, defensively.

Mantle made a heroic defensive play in

the Dodger fifth, when Larsen hung a slider to Gil Hodges on a 2-2 pitch, and the Brooklyn first baseman pounced on it, sending a long drive to left-center. What happened next is best described by Larsen himself in his book on that historic day, *The Perfect Yankee* (written with Mark Shaw).

"At the crack of the bat I watched as Mickey Mantle raced to his right and headed toward the deepest part of left-center field. He was motorin' and with his blazing speed, he raced toward Hodges's hit. The ball would surely have been a home run in most any other park, but it looked to me that while the ball wouldn't go over the wall, it would drop near the base of the fence and Hodges would end up with either a double, triple, or perhaps even an inside-the-park home run.

"Back-pedaling from his starting position moving swiftly to his left, the Mick drew a bead on the spiraling ball. Just when it appeared that it would fall to the ground, Mickey stretched full-length toward ground level and snagged the ball into his glove."

The catch preserved the perfect game and was yet another Mantle-provided boost as the Yankees went on to their sixth World Series championship in eight years, a fitting cap to Mantle's finest season.

"I had the best year of my career in 1956," Mantle recalled in his book. "Winning the Triple Crown was the highlight. But perhaps more important, 1956 was the first time I accomplished the things that had been predicted for me, and I finally established myself in the major leagues. And that's why, at least from a personal standpoint, 1956 was my favorite summer."

## Baseball News Of 1956

- Reds' pitchers Johnny Klippstein (seven hitless innings), Hershell Freeman (one), and Joe Black (two) held the Braves hitless for ten innings on May 26. Milwaukee then got four hits off Black in the eleventh to win.

- Stan Musial was named Player of the Decade in a poll of 260 players and sportswriters conducted by *The Sporting News*. Joe DiMaggio was second, Ted Williams third.

- Jim Derrington, age 16, became the youngest pitcher in modern baseball history to start a game when he took the mound for the White Sox against the Athletics on September 30. He allowed nine hits in six innings and took the loss.

- The Dodgers sold Ebbets Field to a real estate developer who agreed to lease it back to them through the 1959 season.

- Phil Rizzuto, a Yankee since 1941, was released.

## Around The World In 1956

- Six marine recruits drowned while on a disciplinary march at Paris Island, South Carolina, on April 8. A platoon sergeant was later convicted of drinking on duty and negligent homicide, had his rank reduced and served three months in prison.

- Frank Lloyd Wright began work on the Guggenheim Museum in New York.

- Artist Jackson Pollock, 44, was killed in an automobile accident on August 11.

- Pulitzer Prizes were awarded to MacKinlay Kantor for *Andersonville*, Talbot F. Hamlin for *Benjamin Henry Latrobe*, Richard Hofstadter for *The Age of Reform*, and Francis Goodrich and Albert Hackett for *The Diary of Anne Frank*.

- Elvis Presley burst upon the music scene. Parents were all shook up.

# 3

# Season of Glory

# Lou Gehrig

## 1934

| AB | R | H | BA | OB% | 2B | 3B | HR | K/BB | RBI | BR | SB |
|----|----|----|------|------|----|----|----|--------|-----|----|----|
| 579 | 128 | 210 | .363 | .465 | 40 | 6 | 49 | 31/109 | 165 | 98 | 9 |

| | | G | PO | A | DP | E | FA | FR | | |
|--|--|-----|-------|----|-----|---|------|----|--|--|
| | | 154 | 1,284 | 80 | 126 | 8 | .994 | 1 | | |

# *Henry Louis Gehrig*

**BORN**
June 19, 1903
New York

**DIED**
June 2, 1941
New York

**HEIGHT**
6-0

**WEIGHT**
200

**THREW**
left hand

**BATTED**
left hand

New York Yankees
1923–1939

Hall of Fame
1939

**1934**

The 1934 season marked a turning point in Yankee history. The greatest Yankee of them all, Babe Ruth, was at the end of the line. At thirty-nine, and in his twenty-first season in the majors, Ruth was no longer the offensive terror of years past. In the field he had become a defensive liability, to put it charitably. It would be his final season as a Yankee.

Other familiar faces were absent—pitcher Herb Pennock and third baseman Joe Sewell had been released—and room had to be made for newcomers Red Rolfe, Don Heffner, Myril Hoag, Jimmy DeShong, Johnny Murphy, and others. Overhauling his infield, manager Joe McCarthy started the season with veteran shortstop Frank Crosetti on the bench, and Tony Lazzeri—one of only four Yankee starters left from the glory days of 1927—moved from second base to third. There would also be a spate of injuries to further complicate McCarthy's rebuilding efforts in 1934.

One of the few things he would be able to count on this season was Lou Gehrig. At this point, Gehrig was a legend. An eleven-year veteran with a career batting average of .342 in 1933, he had broken Everett Scott's record for consecutive games played. With Ruth fading, Gehrig would finally eclipse Babe as the heart of the Yankees (to the general public, at least; he had already become Ruth's superior on the field).

The Gehrig story was—and is today—familiar to every fan. The son of immigrant parents, he was signed by the Yankees out of Columbia University. He got his big break in 1925, when regular first baseman Wally Pipp asked to come out of a game because of a headache. Manager Miller Huggins put the strapping left-handed slugger in the lineup, where he would stay for the next fourteen seasons.

For the first eleven of those fourteen years, though, these were Babe Ruth's Yankees. The biggest star the game has ever known, the boisterous, fun-loving Ruth commanded attention—sometimes to the detriment of his teammates. Gehrig hit behind Ruth in the lineup and for those eleven years had to play second fiddle. "When I get to bat," he once said, "people are still talking about what Ruth has done. If I stood on my head and held the bat in my teeth, none of the fans would pay the slightest attention. But I'm not kicking."

And that was Gehrig's way. Quiet, shy, a man of impeccable character, he was cheered by fans, respected by his peers, and appreciated by management (though that never translated into large salaries). He was satisfied to do his job—and do it extremely well—with little fanfare.

*Gehrig conferring with "Marse Joe" McCarthy, Yankee manager.*

But in 1934 it would be different. The Yankees were becoming Lou Gehrig's team.

The season opened on April 17 at Yankee Stadium, the Yankees dropping a 6-5 decision to Philadelphia when the A's scored twice in the ninth. Gehrig got his greatest season off to a fast start with a pair of hits in the losing cause.

April ended with the Yankees in first place, a half-game ahead of the Detroit Tigers, who were led by pitching sensation Schoolboy Rowe. The teams met for a two-game series in early May, the Yankees winning both games, putting some distance between themselves and Detroit, at least temporarily.

Gehrig contributed substantially to the Yankees' early-season success. On April 29, for example, his RBI single in the ninth beat

Boston 3-2; he had a double and home run with three RBIs the next afternoon to help beat Washington 7-4; on May 6 he almost single-handedly beat St. Louis, homering in the fourth inning, doubling in one run and scoring another in the eighth to tie the score at 5, then singling home the winning run of the Yanks' 6-5 victory in the ninth. On May 10 he went 4-for-4 in a 13-3 rout of Chicago in New York—two homers and two doubles, with seven RBIs—to get his average to .400. And he did it while suffering from a bad cold that caused him to come out of the game in the sixth inning.

Several times during the 1934 season, Gehrig's consecutive game streak was threatened by injuries. In early June Gehrig missed an exhibition game to have a tooth pulled. It

# Game of Glory • June 25, 1934

On June 25 Gehrig hits for the cycle to help rout Chicago and put the Yankees back in first place. In the eighth, he is thrown out at home trying for an inside-the-park home run; it goes into the books as a triple, completing his cycle.

| CHICAGO | AB | R | H | RBI | NEW YORK | AB | R | H | RBI |
|---|---|---|---|---|---|---|---|---|---|
| Uhalt, rf | 4 | 1 | 2 | 0 | Combs, lf | 5 | 1 | 3 | 2 |
| Haas, cf | 4 | 1 | 3 | 0 | Saltzgaver, 3b | 3 | 2 | 1 | 0 |
| Simmons, lf | 4 | 0 | 1 | 1 | Chapman, cf | 5 | 1 | 1 | 0 |
| Bonura, 1b | 4 | 0 | 1 | 1 | Gehrig, 1b | 5 | 3 | 4 | 3 |
| Boken, 2b | 4 | 0 | 1 | 0 | Hoag, rf | 5 | 2 | 3 | 4 |
| Dykes, 3b | 4 | 0 | 1 | 0 | Dickey, c | 5 | 2 | 2 | 0 |
| Chamberlin, ss | 4 | 0 | 0 | 0 | Crosetti, ss | 4 | 2 | 2 | 0 |
| Shea, c | 2 | 0 | 1 | 0 | Heffner, 3b | 4 | 0 | 2 | 3 |
| Fehring, c | 1 | 0 | 0 | 0 | Broaca, p | 5 | 0 | 0 | 0 |
| Earnshaw, p | 1 | 0 | 0 | 0 | | | | | |
| Ruel, ph | 1 | 0 | 0 | 0 | | | | | |
| Gallivan, p | 0 | 0 | 0 | 0 | | | | | |
| Lyons, ph | 1 | 0 | 0 | 0 | | | | | |
| Kinzy, p | 0 | 0 | 0 | 0 | | | | | |
| Swanson, ph | 1 | 0 | 0 | 0 | | | | | |
| Totals | 35 | 2 | 10 | 2 | Totals | 41 | 13 | 18 | 12 |

| | | | | | | |
|---|---|---|---|---|---|---|
| Chicago | 1 0 1 | 0 0 0 | 0 0 0 — 2 | | | |
| New York | 2 1 2 | 0 1 4 | 2 1 * — 13 | | | |

Error—Chamberlin. Doubles—Dickey (2), Gehrig, Heffner, Boken. Triples—Haas, Hoag, Gehrig. Home runs—Gehrig, Hoag, Combs. Stolen bases—Dykes, Crosetti. Double plays—New York 2. Left on base—Chicago 7, New York 8.

| Chicago | IP | H | BB | K |
|---|---|---|---|---|
| Earnshaw (L) | 3 | 6 | 3 | 2 |
| Gallivan | 3 | 8 | 1 | 3 |
| Kinzy | 2 | 4 | 0 | 1 |

| New York | IP | H | BB | K |
|---|---|---|---|---|
| Broaca (W) | 9 | 10 | 1 | 5 |

Time—1:54.

was the first time he'd been out of the lineup—in both regular season and exhibition games—since his streak started on June 1, 1925.

A slightly more serious situation came up two weeks later. During a June 17 double-header at Yankee Stadium, he fouled a ball off his right foot. It fractured his big toe, but the next day, despite obvious pain, he was in the lineup for his 1,404th consecutive game—going 2-for-5, including his seventeenth home run.

A worse injury—and a threat to his well-being, not just his streak—occurred on June 29. During an exhibition in Norfolk, Virginia, he was hit in the head by a pitch from Ray White, a former Columbia student, oddly enough. Gehrig, who had homered his first time up, was unconscious for five minutes. Teammates Bill Dickey and Crosetti accompanied him back to the team's hotel, where he told reporters, "I will be in there tomorrow."

True to his word, the next day in Washington, D.C. after morning X-rays showed he didn't have a skull fracture, he was in the lineup. He smashed consecutive triples his first three times up, but the feat failed to go into the record books because the game was washed out in the fifth inning.

Keeping the streak alive also involved some machinations on the part of McCarthy and Gehrig. In July, for example, Gehrig was suffering from leg and back problems that would have sidelined most players. On July 13 in Detroit, he had to leave a game in the second inning because of the pain. The next day McCarthy made out his lineup card and listed Gehrig as his shortstop, hitting leadoff. After Gehrig batted in the top of the first—he got a hit to raise his average to .365—he came out of the game and was replaced by Rolfe, who "took over" at short for Gehrig when the Yankees took the field in the bottom of the inning. (Gehrig obviously benefited from the short workday; he returned to the lineup on July 15 with a 4-for-4 day.)

But in 1934 Gehrig didn't need much help, as he performed heroically on an almost daily basis: He hit a ninth-inning homer on June 20 to beat Cleveland 3-2; he hit for the cycle—he was one of only two players to do it twice in the 1930s—to help beat Chicago 13-2 on June 25, putting the Yankees back in first place; he had a phenomenal first week of July—15-for-31 with sixteen runs batted in, in seven games—and he had seven hits in a row on August 2 and 3, which raised his average to over .375.

The Yankees and Tigers, meanwhile, were battling it out for the AL pennant. New York's chances suffered a huge blow on July 24, when outfielder Earle Combs crashed into a wall in St. Louis and was nearly killed. Combs, who was hitting .319 when he was hurt, spent two months in the hospital and

> "Gehrig was a strange character. If he had thought he was half as good as he really was, he would have been much greater. Lou never became cocky or puffed up. Saying that seems superfluous. He was REAL. His feats never impressed him."
>
> —Former teammate Earle Combs, quoted in The Sporting News, April 16, 1942

never fully recovered from the fractured skull and other injuries. Dickey, Rolfe, and Ruth were also sidelined by injuries (Ruth was hurt when he was struck by a Gehrig line-drive in batting practice in mid-July). Detroit took over first place for good on August 1 and went on to win the pennant by seven games, paced by Rowe, who won sixteen consecutive games between June 15 and August 25.

A more competitive race, though, developed over the last two months of the season as Gehrig, Detroit's Charlie Gehringer, and Washington's Heine Manush chased the AL batting crown. (Gehrig was already the season's home run leader, and early in the season he had assumed the lead in runs batted in—during one stretch, he drove in runs in ten consecutive games for a total of twenty-two in the streak). Manush was the early batting leader, flirting with .400 into August and leading Gehrig by twenty points and Gehringer by twenty-five on August 8. A week later, though, Manush was down to .380, with Gehringer at .374 and Gehrig at .365. On September 6 Gehrig took over the lead from Gehringer, .363 to .362, when he went 2-for-5 in a victory over Chicago (Manush was at .357). The race was even closer two weeks later, with Gehrig at .357, Manush at .355, and Gehringer at .354.

The batting chase went down to the final days of the season. After a 4-for-6 day

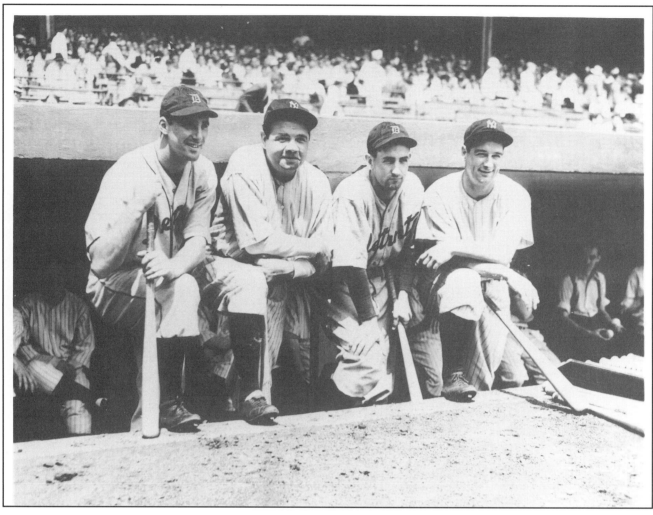

*Greenberg, Ruth, Cochrane, and Gehrig*

on September 26, Gehringer led Gehrig .3593 to .3590. The Yankees didn't play the next day, but Gehrig took over the lead when Gehringer went 0-for-4 to fall to .357. In his final game of the season, Gehrig went 3-for-4, while Gehringer finished up 2-for-7 in a double-header. Gehrig's final batting average was .363, while Gehringer's was .356.

By winning the batting championship, Gehrig became the Triple Crown winner— he was the first Yankee ever to achieve the feat. He finished with 49 home runs (to 44 for runner-up Jimmie Foxx of Philadelphia) and 165 runs batted in (Cleveland's Hal Trosky was a distant second at 142). All of Gehrig's figures were not only best in the AL, but tops in the majors. He also led in on-base percentage (.465), total bases (409), and slugging average (.706). He was second in the AL in hits (210) and walks (109), and third in runs (128). Nineteen thirty-four was truly a spectacular season for Gehrig. (But, inexplicably, it was not good enough for Gehrig to win the Most Valuable Player award, which went to Detroit's Mickey Cochrane, who had a .320 average, with two home runs and 76 RBIs).

With Ruth's departure after the 1934 season, Gehrig had assumed the Yankee leadership. But they would be Gehrig's Yankees only briefly. He had three more strong seasons and then fell ill with the disease that ended his streak and his life in 1941, at the age of thirty-seven.

"What a wonderful fellow that Gehrig was," McCarthy would later say. "Always hustled. Never gave a moment's trouble. Just went out every day and played his game and hit the ball. I'll say he hit the ball . . ."

# "Luckiest Man On The Face Of The Earth"

On July 4, 1939, 61,808 fans turned out at Yankee Stadium to honor the dying Lou Gehrig. After several politicians spoke, Gehrig stepped to the microphones and delivered one of the most memorable speeches in history:

"Fans, for the past two weeks, you have been reading about a bad break I got. Yet today I consider myself the luckiest man on the face of the Earth. I have been in ballparks for seventeen years and I have never received anything but kindness and encouragement from you fans. Look at these grand men. Which of you wouldn't consider it the highlight of his career just to associate with them for even one day? Sure, I'm lucky. Who wouldn't consider it an honor to have known Jacob Ruppert? Also, the builder of baseball's greatest empire, Ed Barrow? To have spent six years with that wonderful little fellow, Miller Huggins? Then to have spent the next nine years with that outstanding leader, that smart student of psychology, the best manager in baseball today, Joe McCarthy? Sure, I'm lucky. When the New York Giants, a team you would give your right arm to beat and vice versa, sends you a gift, that's something. When everybody down to the groundskeepers and those boys in white coats remember you with trophies, that's something. When you have a wonderful mother-in-law who takes sides with you in squabbles against her own daughter, that's something. When you have a father and mother who work all their lives so that you can have an education and build your body, it's a blessing. When you have a wife who has been a tower of strength and shown more courage than you dreamed existed, that's the finest I know. So I close in saying that I might have had a bad break, but I have an awful lot to live for."

# Baseball News Of 1934

- Former Giants manager John McGraw, 60, died of cancer on February 25.
- The Wall made its debut at the Red Sox' home opener in newly remodeled Fenway Park on April 17.
- In his first two starts of the season, the Cubs' Lon Warneke narrowly missed two no-hitters. On April 17 the Reds' Adam Comorosky singled in the ninth, and on April 22 Ripper Collins got the Cardinals' only hit, a fifth-inning double.
- Babe Ruth hit the 700th homer of his career July 13 in Detroit.
- The Yankees obtained Joe DiMaggio from San Francisco of the Pacific Coast League for $25,000 and four players.
- Schoolboy Rowe won sixteen straight games for the Tigers.

# Around The World In 1934

- Public Enemy Number 1 John Dillinger was gunned down by FBI agents outside a Chicago movie house on July 22.
- The Midwest suffered through the worst drought in history.
- Only fifty-eight banks failed in 1934—a huge improvement over the average of 901 that had failed each year since 1921.
- What later became known as nylon was first produced by Dr. Wallace H. Carothers, a Du Pont research scientist.
- Unemployment dropped by more than four million, evidence that the Depression was winding down.
- A new child star was introduced: Shirley Temple.

# 4
# Season of Glory

## Rickey Henderson

### 1985

| AB | R | H | BA | OB% | 2B | 3B | HR | K/BB | RBI | BR | SB |
|-----|-----|-----|------|------|-----|-----|-----|-------|-----|-----|-----|
| 547 | 146 | 172 | .314 | .422 | 28 | 5 | 24 | 65/99 | 72 | 48 | 80 |

| | | G | PO | A | DP | E | FA | FR | |
|---|---|-----|-----|---|---|---|------|-----|---|
| | | 143 | 439 | 7 | 3 | 9 | .980 | 16 | |

# 4 *Rickey Henley Henderson*

BORN
**December 25, 1958**
**Chicago**

HEIGHT
**5–10**

WEIGHT
**195**

THREW
**left hand**

BATTED
**right hand**

**New York Yankees**
**1985–1989**

*I*t was March 1986, and Rickey Henderson was holding court near the batting cage at the Yankees' spring training camp in Ft. Lauderdale. "I was born on Christmas Day in the back of a '56 Chevy," he told reporters while he waited his turn in the cage. "My father was driving to the hospital, but I couldn't wait. I came right out there. I guess I was born to run, and I haven't stopped."

Talented, colorful, outspoken—at times controversial—Rickey Henderson was the best leadoff man in the history of baseball. He could hit for average or for power, and he was blessed with the speed and smarts that made him the greatest base stealer of all time. As he told the reporters that morning, "I try to be a complete player."

Henderson began his athletic career in Oakland, where he excelled not only in baseball (he hit .716 his junior year in high school and .465 his senior year), but in football and basketball as well. He was chosen by his hometown team, the Oakland Athletics, in the June 1976 free-agent draft. In his first season of pro ball, with Oakland's Boise Rookie League team, he made two big adjustments. First, because he was relatively short—he was only 5 feet-10 inches—and because he was so fast, he was moved from first base to the outfield. And second, he developed his trademark batting stance. Years later, *Chicago Tribune* columnist Bernie Lincicome described it thus:

> Henderson stands at the plate like a man on one roller skate. His left leg is straight out, his right leg is bent, his shoulders are tilted at an angle that wouldn't hold snow and his body is folded in on itself like a road map.
>
> The target he offers to pitchers in the American League is about the size of a shoe box. They don't know whether to throw him the ball or give him the name of their chiropractor.

Henderson blossomed that first season, hitting .336 in 140 at-bats and stealing 29 bases in 36 tries. He then climbed through the Oakland minor-league system—moving to Class A (Modesto) in 1977, to Double-A (Jersey City) in '78, and to Triple-A (Ogden) in '79. Early in the 1979 season, he made his major-league debut with the Oakland A's. He performed well that season, batting .274 and stealing 33 bases in eighty-nine games.

In 1980 the A's hired Billy Martin as manager. Martin encouraged his team to play more aggressively—"Billy Ball" the writers called it—

and as a result the A's and Henderson benefited greatly. Oakland, which had won only fifty-four games and finished last in the AL West in 1979, won 83 games and was runner-up to Kansas City in 1980. Henderson also improved dramatically under Martin's leadership; he led the AL in stolen bases for four straight years, stealing 100 in 1980, 56 in '81, 130 in '82 and 108 in '83.

Despite Henderson's impressive performance, however, Oakland management became increasingly dissatisfied with him for a number of reasons, and vice versa. First, after the 1983 season, Henderson and the A's couldn't come to terms on a new contract. The dispute went to arbitration, and Henderson won a $950,000 contract. Second, Henderson was reluctant to follow the orders of new A's manager Steve Boros, who told him to steal fewer bases and concentrate on being a power hitter. "I'd made my living getting on base and running, and I didn't understand," he told a *Sports Illustrated* writer in July 1986. Finally, as the 1984 season wore on, Henderson displayed a lackadaisical attitude that soured A's management even more. So on December 8, 1984, they traded Henderson to the Yankees in a seven-player deal.

The baseball world was shocked, as was Henderson. "I'm glad to be here, but I don't know if I'm a New York-type person or not," he told Thomas Boswell of *The Washington Post.*

Henderson's much-anticipated Yankee debut was delayed for more than two weeks while he recovered from an ankle sprain suffered in spring training. In his first game as a Yankee, a 5-4 loss to Boston on April 23, he was 1-for-6. His luck soon changed, however, when on April 28 the faltering Yankees (6-10) fired manager Yogi Berra and replaced him with Henderson's old pal, Billy Martin. Soon it was just like old times.

Henderson had hit just .120 in his first six games as a Yankee. After Billy Martin came aboard, he hit .419 in his next eleven contests. The Yankees, too, began turning things around. They were in last place at the end

*Rickey Henderson*

of April (6-12), but they managed to win twelve of their next fifteen games, putting them within 2½ games of first place. By the end of May, the Yankees were in fourth place at 24-20, 5½ games behind Toronto. And Henderson, who had raised his average to .293, was just shifting into high gear.

He was a terror in June, hitting .416—with six homers and twenty-two stolen bases—to earn the AL Player of the Month award. Among his highlights that month were a 3-for-4 day on June 10 in a 4-2 victory over the first-place Blue Jays; a 5-for-5 effort on June 17—the first five-hit day of his career—in a 10-0 victory over Baltimore that raised his average to .332 and gave him the AL lead; a 21-for-35 (.600) stretch in nine games between June 17 and June 25 that put him at .360 for the season; and four stolen bases on June 26 in a game against the Orioles.

Henderson had a .357 average by the time of the All-Star Game—one point behind Kansas City's George Brett—11 homers, and

# Game of Glory • May 21, 1985

On May 21 Henderson is practically a one-man team with three hits, three runs, four RBIs, three stolen bases in an 11-1 rout of Seattle.

| NEW YORK | AB | R | H | RBI | | SEATTLE | AB | R | H | RBI |
|---|---|---|---|---|---|---|---|---|---|---|
| RHenderson, cf | 5 | 3 | 3 | 4 | | Perconte, 2b | 3 | 1 | 0 | 0 |
| Mattingly, 1b | 6 | 1 | 2 | 1 | | Bradley, lf | 4 | 0 | 2 | 0 |
| Hassey, 1b | 0 | 0 | 0 | 0 | | DHenderson, cf | 4 | 0 | 0 | 1 |
| Winfield, rf | 6 | 3 | 4 | 1 | | Thomas, dh | 2 | 0 | 0 | 0 |
| Moreno, rf | 0 | 0 | 0 | 0 | | Calderon, dh | 2 | 0 | 0 | 0 |
| Baylor, dh | 4 | 1 | 2 | 1 | | Davis, 1b | 3 | 0 | 1 | 0 |
| Wynegar, c | 4 | 0 | 1 | 1 | | Cowens, rf | 3 | 0 | 0 | 0 |
| Griffey, lf | 5 | 0 | 0 | 1 | | Presley, 3b | 3 | 0 | 0 | 0 |
| Cotto, cf | 0 | 0 | 0 | 0 | | Kearney, c | 3 | 0 | 0 | 0 |
| Randolph, 2b | 4 | 2 | 3 | 1 | | Owen, ss | 3 | 0 | 1 | 0 |
| Berra, 3b | 2 | 0 | 0 | 0 | | | | | | |
| Pagliarulo, 3b | 1 | 0 | 0 | 1 | | | | | | |
| Meacham, ss | 5 | 1 | 0 | 0 | | | | | | |
| **Totals** | **42** | **11** | **15** | **11** | | **Totals** | **30** | **1** | **4** | **1** |

| | | | | | | | | |
|---|---|---|---|---|---|---|---|---|
| New York | 4 0 0 | 0 1 3 | 1 0 2 — 11 | | | | | |
| Seattle | 0 0 0 | 1 0 0 | 0 0 0 — 1 | | | | | |

Errors—Bradley, Berra. Doubles—Winfield, RHenderson.
Triple—RHenderson. Home run—RHenderson.
Double plays—New York 2. Left on base—New York 12, Seattle 3.

| NEW YORK | IP | H | R | ER | BB | K |
|---|---|---|---|---|---|---|
| Guidry (W, 4-3) | 8 | 3 | 1 | 1 | 1 | 6 |
| Cooper | 1 | 1 | 0 | 0 | 0 | 0 |

| SEATTLE | IP | H | R | ER | BB | K |
|---|---|---|---|---|---|---|
| Langston (L, 5-4) | .1 | 4 | 4 | 4 | 1 | 0 |
| Barojas | 5 | 3 | 3 | 3 | 1 | 3 |
| Stanton | 1.1 | 2 | 2 | 2 | 2 | 0 |
| Vandeberg | 1.1 | 2 | 0 | 0 | 2 | 1 |
| Nunez | 1 | 4 | 2 | 2 | 1 | 1 |

Hit by pitch—by Langston (Baylor). Passed ball—Kearney.

*1985*

41 stolen bases. In the first inning of the All-Star Game, on July 16 in Bloomington, Minnesota, he demonstrated his true potential, singling, stealing second and advancing to third base on NL catcher Terry Kennedy's error, and scoring on George Brett's sacrifice fly.

July ended with Brett at .360 and Henderson at .355—and trouble on the horizon for baseball. Players, unable to reach an agreement with owners on a number of issues, were threatening to strike in the first week of August. The strike occurred on August 6 but lasted only until August 7, when owners gave in to the players' demand.

Expecting a long walkout, and against the

advice of several teammates, Henderson had flown home to Oakland when the strike began. After the settlement, he was unable to return in time for a double-header in Cleveland on August 8—the Yankees swept—and was docked three days' pay, an estimated $22,000.

"There is a discipline on this club that Rickey is going to find out about in a hurry," owner George Steinbrenner told reporters. "We're in a pennant race and here he is missing two crucial games. He is being paid enough money that I think he should be here for every game. I have no sympathy for him. Whatever he has to say will fall on deaf ears."

The next day Henderson returned from Oakland, hitting a two-run single in a six-run sixth inning, scoring a second run and stealing his fifty-first base in a 10-6 victory over Boston.

Henderson's average declined during the second half of the season, but he still finished at .314, fourth in the league. He was No. 1 in the AL in runs (146) and stolen bases (a Yankee record of 80), fourth in bases on balls (99) and on-base percentage (.422), and was seventh in slugging percentage (.516). As a result, he finished third in the AL MVP award voting—behind teammate Don Mattingly (who benefited immensely from hitting behind Henderson, driving in 145 runs) and Brett.

The Yankees, too, were unable to move to first place by the end of the 1985 season. Although they came within 1½ games of the lead when they beat Toronto on September 12, they lost the next three games in the series to fall 4½ back. The race for the AL East title came down to a season-ending three-game series in Toronto.

In the opening game, Henderson contributed an RBI single in the fourth inning—his 172nd and last hit of the season—and his 80th stolen base, and the Yankees pushed across a run in the top of the ninth for a 3-2 victory, coming within two games of the lead with two to play. The next day, though,

Toronto beat the Yankees 5-1 to clinch the AL East title.

Henderson played for the Yankees for four more seasons, making the AL All-Star team in 1986, 1987, and 1988. But all was not well. He suffered a hamstring injury midway through the 1987 season that bothered him the rest of the year and limited him to forty-one stolen bases. He hit only six homers with just 50 RBIs in 1988. At times, he seemed to lose interest on the field. And in 1989, with his contract due to expire at the end of the season, Henderson and the Yankees haggled over a new deal. He had clearly worn out his welcome in New York. The Yankees, figuring they

> "Lots of people can run fast but still can't steal. You have to work at it, know the pitchers, be able to psyche yourself. You must believe you're going to be safe."
>
> —RICKEY HENDERSON

would lose him to free agency at season's end, decided to get what they could for him.

On June 20 he was traded back to Oakland for three players. The deal rejuvenated his career. Henderson was hitting .247 when he left the Yankees. He hit .378, had a .487 on-base percentage, scored 41 runs, and stole 23 bases in his first 37 games with the A's, who went on to win the AL West title.

He continued his Hall-of-Fame career in Oakland, where he became baseball's all-time stolen base leader in 1991. Over the next few years he played in Toronto, San Diego and Anaheim. He returned to the A's in 1998. The New York Mets signed Rickey Henderson to a one-year contract for the 1999 season.

"All you have to do," teammate Dave Winfield once said, "is watch Rickey, see what he does at the plate or on the basepaths, to be convinced that here's a guy who matches up with the best of any era."

# Baseball News Of 1985

- The Pittsburgh Pirates made twenty-year-old Barry Bonds their first pick—and the sixth selection overall—in the June free-agent draft.

- The Angels' Rod Carew collected his 3,000th hit, a single off the Twins' Frank Viola on August 4.

- On August 6 major league players went on strike over free agency, arbitration, and salary minimums. The walkout ended after two days and twenty-five canceled games.

- On September 11, exactly fifty-seven years after Ty Cobb played his last game, Cincinnati's Pete Rose got his 4,192nd hit, breaking Cobb's career record.

- On December 14 Roger Maris died at 51.

- Dwight Gooden, at 20, became the youngest Cy Young Award winner ever. He won twenty-four games, struck out 268 batters, and had a 1.53 ERA for the Mets.

# Around The World In 1985

- President Reagan had a cancerous tumor removed from his colon.

- Former Senator Sam Ervin Jr., the folksy North Carolina Democrat who chaired the Senate Watergate investigation, died on April 23, at age 88.

- The wreck of the *Titanic*, which sank in 1912, was found on the floor of the North Atlantic by a joint U.S.-French exploratory team.

- Simultaneous terrorist attacks at airports in Rome and Vienna left eighteen dead and 110 wounded.

- Among 1985's obituaries: Marc Chagall (March 28, age 97), Stepin Fetchit (November 19, age 83), Ruth Gordon (August 28, age 88), Rock Hudson (October 2, age 59), Eugene Ormandy (March 12, age 85), and Orson Welles (October 10, age 70).

# 5
# Season of Glory

## Snuffy Stirnweiss

### 1945

| AB | R | H | BA | OB% | 2B | 3B | HR | K/BB | RBI | BR | SB |
|-----|-----|-----|------|------|-----|-----|-----|-------|-----|-----|-----|
| 632 | 107 | 195 | .309 | .385 | 32 | 22 | 10 | 62/78 | 64 | 34 | 33 |

| G | PO | A | DP | E | FA | FR |
|-----|-----|-----|-----|-----|------|-----|
| 152 | 432 | 492 | 119 | 29 | .970 | 16 |

# George Henry Stirnweiss

**BORN**
October 26, 1918
New York

**DIED**
September 15, 1958
Newark Bay, New Jersey

**HEIGHT**
5-8½

**WEIGHT**
175

**THREW**
right hand

**BATTED**
right hand

New York Yankees
1943–1950

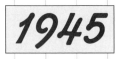

*I*t's unfortunate that when George "Snuffy" Stirnweiss is thought of—if he's thought of at all these days—it's usually as a player who made his mark against inferior competition. Granted, he led the American League in hitting in 1945, when the game's best players were in the service. And, yes, his .309 average was the second lowest ever for an AL batting champion. But Snuffy Stirnweiss—the nickname was the result of a lifelong sinus condition—*was* the best at what he did that year (and parts of several others), the key man for the Yankees that season. And he wasn't just a wartime oddity. "That sawed-off runt playing second base is the only ballplayer who could've gotten a uniform when the Yankees really had a ball club," Babe Ruth once said.

George Henry Stirnweiss was born on October 26, 1918, in New York, the son of a New York police officer. Despite his size—he stood just 5 feet 8 inches and weighed 175 pounds—he excelled in baseball, football, and basketball. Quick and surehanded, he was offered an athletic scholarship to Fordham University but left school after only a month. He enrolled at the University of North Carolina, where he was a star player on the school's baseball team and was All-America in football. After graduation in 1940, he signed a Yankee contract.

Stirnweiss, a second baseman, spent two seasons in the Minors, first making headlines when he stole an International League-record 73 bases for Newark, the Yankees' top farm team, in 1942. His talent attracted interest from other teams, and he was nearly sold to the Brooklyn Dodgers late in the 1942 season. Yankee general manager Ed Barrow—who was feuding with Dodger management—changed his mind, however, perhaps recognizing Stirnweiss's skills or perhaps just to spite Brooklyn. Either way, Barrow was fortunate he didn't make the deal.

Given an $8,000 contract for 1943, Stirnweiss was brought up to the big club, but not as a second baseman. Joe Gordon was coming off a career season, and there was no way a rookie was going to replace him. Stirnweiss was switched to shortstop, with disappointing results. He hit just .219 in 83 games, finally finding himself on the bench. But he had a great seat. Joe McCarthy had Stirnweiss sit next to him in the dugout, and the Yankee manager, who had taken a liking to the scrappy, hustling infielder, imparted his baseball wisdom to the rookie on a daily basis.

Stirnweiss's big break came when Gordon went into the service before the 1944 season (Snuffy was rejected because of gastric ulcers, which had plagued him since college). Gordon's departure gave him the second base job, and he grabbed it by the throat. As the Yankees' leadoff hitter, he led the AL in runs (125), hits (205), triples (16) and stolen bases (55), and finished with a .319 average, fourth in the league. He was second in total bases (296) and led the league's second basemen in fielding. By midseason, McCarthy was calling him "the best second baseman in the game today."

If there were doubters, Stirnweiss's 1945 season should have convinced them. He got off to a solid start and was hitting .333 by the end of April. Despite a ten-game hitting streak, he slipped below .300 in late May. Still, he was making his hits count—a homer leading off the game was all the offense the Yankees needed to beat Boston on May 6; his single sparked a five-run inning in a victory over Cleveland on May 12; and he contributed an RBI triple and scored a run in a three-run eighth in a victory over Chicago on May 25 that moved the Yankees into first place.

Early in the season, Stirnweiss's bat was carrying the Yankees. On May 11 McCarthy dropped him from the leadoff spot to third in the batting order, where he could do more good. But the experiment lasted only a week, as he went just 3-for-18 in the number 3 slot. Back where he felt more comfortable, he hit .405 (15-for-37) over the last week of May to raise his average to .324.

Stirnweiss was about all the Yankees could brag about in 1945. They lost first place to Detroit in early June, and although they stayed close—even moving into a first-place

Snuffy Stirnweiss

tie later in the month—they were never able to gain the upper hand. They were four games back by the start of August but soon faded, dropping as low as sixth place. They wound up fourth, 6½ games behind the pennant-winning Tigers.

Meanwhile, however, there was a far more exciting race taking place between Stirnweiss and Chicago third baseman Tony Cuccinello for the AL batting crown. The thirty-seven-year-old Cuccinello, who was playing his final season, got off to a tremendous start, hitting better than .360 over the first month

# Game of Glory • September 29, 1945

On September 29, which was designated Snuffy Stirnweiss Day at Yankee Stadium in recognition of his performance over the season, the man of the hour has three hits to lead a 5-0 victory over Boston.

| BOSTON | AB | R | H | RBI | NEW YORK | AB | R | H | RBI |
|---|---|---|---|---|---|---|---|---|---|
| Lake, ss | 4 | 0 | 2 | 0 | Stirnweiss, 2b | 5 | 1 | 3 | 1 |
| LaForest, lf | 4 | 0 | 0 | 0 | Metheny, rf | 4 | 0 | 0 | 0 |
| Metkovich, rf | 4 | 0 | 0 | 0 | Stainback, cf | 5 | 0 | 1 | 0 |
| McBride, 1b | 4 | 0 | 3 | 0 | Keller, lf | 4 | 2 | 2 | 1 |
| Bucher, 3b | 4 | 0 | 0 | 0 | Etten, 1b | 4 | 1 | 2 | 2 |
| Newsome, 2b | 3 | 0 | 1 | 0 | Grimes, 3b | 4 | 0 | 2 | 1 |
| Tobin, cf | 2 | 0 | 1 | 0 | Crosseti, ss | 4 | 0 | 0 | 0 |
| Steiner, c | 3 | 0 | 0 | 0 | Robinson, c | 2 | 1 | 1 | 0 |
| V. Johnson, p | 2 | 0 | 0 | 0 | Chandler, p | 4 | 0 | 1 | 0 |
| Hausman, p | 0 | 0 | 0 | 0 | | | | | |
| Totals | 30 | 0 | 7 | 0 | Totals | 36 | 5 | 12 | 5 |

```
Boston      0 0 0   0 0 0   0 0 0 — 0
New York    2 0 0   0 0 1   2 0 * — 5
```

Triple—Keller. Home run—Etten. Stolen bases—Lake, Stirnweiss.
Double plays—New York, 3. Left on base—Boston 5, New York 10.

| BOSTON | IP | H | BB | K |
|---|---|---|---|---|
| Johnson (L) | 6 | 11 | 2 | 3 |
| Hausman | 2 | 1 | 0 | 0 |

| NEW YORK | IP | H | BB | K |
|---|---|---|---|---|
| Chandler (W) | 9 | 7 | 2 | 3 |

Hit by pitcher—by Johnson (Metheny).

Time—1:50. Attendance—10,364.

and grabbing the lead from the outset. Through June, July, and August, Stirnweiss trailed by about 25 points. He was just 16 points back, though in fifth place, at the end of August.

By September 13 Cuccinello had surrendered his lead to Boston's Johnny Lazor. There were only eight players over .300, and several of them, Lazor included, would not finish the season with the requisite number of at-bats to be considered for the batting crown. Stirnweiss was at .297 on September 15, but he had some excellent games over the last two weeks of the month, including a 3-for-8 day in a double-header with St. Louis on September 16, a 4-for-10 in another double-header three days later, and a 4-for-7 series against Washington.

Cuccinello ended his season on September 25, when he went 1-for-3 in a White Sox loss at St. Louis, finishing at .308. The Sox's last three games were rained out, leaving Cuccinello as a spectator as Stirnweiss closed in, in dramatic fashion. On September 29, Stirnweiss had three hits in a 5-0 victory over Boston to raise his average to

.306. On September 30, in the Yankees' season finale, he had three more hits, with his last one, a single in the eighth off Otis Clark, inching him to .309 and giving him the batting crown.

Stirnweiss thus became the first AL hitter to win a batting crown without ever having led until the last day of the season. His .309 average was the second-lowest leading average in AL history (only Elmer Flick at .306 in the dead-ball year of 1905 was lower). But the batting crown and his other numbers— AL bests in hits (195), runs (107), triples (22), slugging (.476), stolen bases (33), putouts by a second baseman (432), and double plays (119)—add up to make his greatest year one of the top five individual Yankee seasons.

In 1946, with the war over and Gordon back in a Yankees uniform, Stirnweiss was moved to third base. His average declined by 58 points, and he would never again hit over .261. By 1949 his legs were giving him trouble and he had become a part-time player. The next year he was traded to the St. Louis Browns, and he finished out his career in Cleveland in 1952.

Snuffy Stirnweiss's story had a tragic fi-

> "You cannot overlook his general hustle and competitive spirit. I've never known a player to take a defeat more to heart, especially after losing a tough one. A manager simply has to go all-out for a player like that."
>
> —Yankee manager Joe McCarthy

nal chapter. After his baseball career was over, he became a banker and a foreign freight agent, and also served as the director of a sandlot baseball program run by the *New York Journal-American*. On September 15, 1958, he caught a commuter train in Red Bank, New Jersey, for the ride into New York, where he had a noon business meeting. In Elizabeth, New Jersey, the train—the engineer was apparently incapacitated—ran several signals and plunged off an open drawbridge into a river. More than three dozen people were killed, Stirnweiss among them. He left a wife and six children.

## Baseball News Of 1945

- Pete Gray, who lost his right arm in an accident as a child, made his major-league debut on April 18 for the St. Louis Browns. He had a single in four at-bats against the Tigers and went on to hit .218 in 77 games for the Browns.

- Detroit's Les Mueller pitched $19\frac{2}{3}$ innings as the Tigers and A's played to a 24-inning 1-1 tie on July 21.

- The Cubs bought pitcher Hank Borowy from the Yankees in July after he cleared waivers. He won 11 games to lead the Cubs to the NL pennant.

- On October 23 the Brooklyn Dodgers signed Jackie Robinson to play for their Montreal farm team.

- The Cubs swept twenty double-headers; they also beat Cincinnati twenty-one times.

- Hank Greenberg returned from the army and hit 13 homers and drove in 60 runs in 78 games to help the Tigers win the AL pennant.

# Around The World In 1945

- World War II ended with VE Day, on May 8, and VJ Day, on August 15.
- President Franklin D. Roosevelt died on April 12 in Hot Springs, Georgia. He was 63.
- The United Nations charter was signed on June 26.
- The first atomic bomb was detonated at 5:30 a.m. on July 16 near Alamogordo, New Mexico.
- U.S. soldiers left their mark—"Kilroy was here"—on walls, sidewalks, and just about any other available surface around the world.
- Humorist Robert Benchley died on November 21 at age 56.
- War correspondent Ernie Pyle was killed on Iwo Jima on April 18; he was 44.
- A B-52 bomber crashed into the seventy-eighth floor of the Empire State Building in New York on July 28, leaving thirteen dead.

# 6
# Season of Glory

## Jack Chesbro

## 1904

| W | L | PCT. | IP | GS | CG | SH | SV | K/BB | OPP. BA | ERA |
|---|---|------|-----|----|----|----|----|------|---------|-----|
| 41 | 12 | .774 | 454.2 | 51 | 48 | 6 | 0 | 239/88 | .208 | 1.82 |

| | | GP | PO | A | DP | E | FA | ER/R | PR | DEF |
|---|---|----|----|----|----|----|-----|------|-----|-----|
| | | 55 | 24 | 166 | 7 | 12 | .942 | 92/128 | 45 | 5 |

# John Dwight Chesbro

**BORN**
June 5, 1874
North Adams, Massachusetts

**DIED**
November 6, 1931
Conway, Massachusetts

**HEIGHT**
5-9

**WEIGHT**
180

**THREW**
right hand

**BATTED**
right hand

New York Highlanders
New York Yankees
1903–1909

Hall of Fame
1946

*1904*

*I*magine looking through a Yankee photo album, where memorable moments in the franchise's storied history are captured in single images—snapshots of history, if you will. There's Lou Gehrig standing at the microphones, delivering his "Luckiest Man on the Face of the Earth" speech. And Carl Mays firing the pitch that killed Cleveland's Ray Chapman. Roger Maris hitting his sixty-first home run. Left-fielder Yogi Berra watching Bill Mazeroski's home run clear the wall at Forbes Field. Then there's the faded, sepia-toned photo of the Jack Chesbro pitch that cost the Highlanders (later the Yankees) the 1904 American League pennant. The wild pitch, on the last day of the season, was a sobering end to a spectacular campaign, arguably the best season of any pitcher this century.

How good was Chesbro in 1904? The numbers tell the story. He won forty-one games, nearly half of New York's ninety-two wins. He was the starting pitcher in fifty-one games and appeared in four more as a relief pitcher. He had forty-eight complete games and worked 454⅔ innings. His ERA was 1.82, and opponents hit just .208 against him.

Chesbro came to New York before the 1903 season, lured from the National League's Pittsburgh Pirates to the upstart American League by AL President Ban Johnson. Johnson wanted to ensure that the league's new New York franchise—the AL's crown jewel—would be competitive on two fronts—against its AL opponents and, for obvious financial reasons, against the National League's Giants. To that end, Johnson chose Clark Griffith, manager and pitcher for the Chicago White Sox, to be the first manager for the New York franchise, dubbed the Highlanders. He also recruited a number of other stars from the NL besides Chesbro, including outfielder Wee Willie Keeler, pitcher Jesse Tannehill, third baseman Wid Conroy, and catcher Jack O'Connor. During their inaugural AL season, the Highlanders finished fourth, a respectable ten games over .500, with Chesbro going 21-15.

By the start of the 1904 season, the Highlanders—and Jack Chesbro—were ready to begin making their way to the top. In the season opener, Chesbro got the better of Boston and Cy Young, helping the team win 8-2. The game marked the start of a season-long battle between the Highlanders and the Pilgrims, a battle that wasn't decided until the last day of the season.

Along the way, Chesbro put on a show never equaled, before or

Jack Chesbro

# Game of Glory • August 23, 1904

Chesbro outduels Chicago ace Doc White on August 23 at Hilltop Park.

| CHICAGO | AB | H | PO | A | E | | NEW YORK | AB | H | PO | A | E |
|---|---|---|---|---|---|---|---|---|---|---|---|---|
| Holmes, cf | 4 | 0 | 3 | 0 | 0 | | Dougherty, lf | 4 | 1 | 2 | 0 | 0 |
| Green, rf | 4 | 1 | 1 | 0 | 0 | | Keeler, rf | 4 | 1 | 0 | 0 | 0 |
| Callahan, lf | 4 | 0 | 0 | 0 | 0 | | Fultz, cf | 3 | 1 | 1 | 0 | 0 |
| Davis, ss | 3 | 0 | 1 | 1 | 0 | | Anderson, 1b | 4 | 1 | 13 | 1 | 0 |
| Isbell, 1b | 3 | 0 | 6 | 2 | 0 | | Elberfield, ss | 4 | 0 | 4 | 4 | 0 |
| Tannehill, 3b | 3 | 1 | 3 | 1 | 0 | | Ganzel, 2b | 3 | 3 | 0 | 5 | 0 |
| Dundon, 2b | 3 | 1 | 2 | 3 | 0 | | Conroy, 3b | 3 | 2 | 0 | 2 | 0 |
| Sullivan, c | 2 | 0 | 6 | 2 | 0 | | Kleinow, c | 2 | 0 | 6 | 1 | 0 |
| White, p | 3 | 1 | 2 | 2 | 1 | | Chesbro, p | 4 | 0 | 1 | 3 | 0 |
| **Totals** | **29** | **4** | **24** | **11** | **1** | | **Totals** | **31** | **9** | **27** | **16** | **0** |

```
Chicago      0 0 0    0 0 0    0 0 0 — 0 4 1
New York     0 0 0    0 0 0    1 0 * — 1 9 0
```

Doubles—Fultz, White. Double plays—Chicago 1, New York 1.
Stolen bases—Ganzel (2).
Strikeouts—Chesbro 6, White 6.
Bases on balls—White 4, Chesbro 0.
Passed ball—Sullivan.

*1904*

since. He had two winning streaks, one fourteen games long, the other nine. In a game in late April against Washington, he gave up a leadoff single then pitched no-hit ball the rest of the way. He had 31 games in which he limited his opponents to two runs or fewer. After a 2-2 start, he was 9-3 at the end of May, 18-3 by July 4, and 35-8 by mid-September.

Chesbro was at his finest as the Highlanders and Pilgrims jostled for first place near the end of the season. From mid-August through late September, he was 12-1, and during the last month of the season, he was 9-2.

A typical performance was his 1-0 victory on August 23 against the visiting White Sox. Chicago ace Doc White, whom Chesbro faced five times that season (3-1-1) fought it out with Chesbro for 6⅓ innings—before

New York pushed a run across that Chesbro made stand up.

Chesbro's forty-first victory, on October 7, put New York back in first place by a half game. His luck ran out the next day, however, when he was hammered by the Pilgrims 13-2 in the first game of a double-header. Boston also took the nightcap, going into a season-ending double-header on October 10 back in New York with a 1½-game lead.

Obviously tired after nearly 450 innings of work—60 more than anyone else in baseball that season—Chesbro still managed a gutsy performance in the first game. The score was 2-2 going into the top of the ninth. Lou Criger led off with a scratch infield single and was sacrificed to second. He took third on an infield out. Chesbro then let slip a spitball that flew over the head of catcher Red Kleinow, letting Criger score the run that de-

# Finishing What They Started

In 1904 major-league pitchers completed more games than in any other year of the twentieth century. The numbers, in comparison with those of today, are staggering. Finishing what you started was simply de rigueur in 1904. The figures below chart this phenomenal development at the height of the dead-ball era. An interesting note: Although Highlander pitchers completed seventy-nine percent of their games, they were still last in the majors. Manager Clark Griffith was already developing the notion of relief specialists and would soon pioneer that idea with his Washington Senators in the 1920s.

| Pitcher/ Team | Complete | Starts | Pct. | IP | Shutouts | ERA |
|---|---|---|---|---|---|---|
| Jack Taylor, St. Louis (NL) | 39 | 39 | 1.000 | 352 | 2 | 2.22 |
| Bill Dineen, Boston (AL) | 37 | 37 | 1.000 | 335.2 | 5 | 2.20 |
| Cy Young, Boston (AL) | 40 | 41 | .976 | 380 | 10 | 1.97 |
| George Mullin, Detroit | 42 | 44 | .955 | 382.1 | 7 | 2.40 |
| Casey Patten, Washington | 37 | 39 | .950 | 357.2 | 2 | 3.07 |
| Jack Chesbro, New York (AL) | 48 | 51 | .949 | 454.2 | 6 | 1.82 |
| Oscar Jones, Brooklyn | 38 | 41 | .927 | 377 | 0 | 2.75 |
| Vic Willis, Boston (NL) | 39 | 43 | .907 | 350 | 2 | 2.85 |
| Joe McGinnity, New York (NL) | 38 | 44 | .864 | 408 | 9 | 1.61 |
| Eddie Plank, Philadelphia (AL) | 37 | 43 | .860 | 357.1 | 7 | 2.17 |

## Team figures

| Team | Games | Complete | Pct. | Shutouts | ERA |
|---|---|---|---|---|---|
| Boston (AL) | 157 | 148 | .943 | 21 | 2.12 |
| St. Louis (NL) | 155 | 146 | .942 | 10 | 3.59 |
| Cleveland | 154 | 141 | .916 | 20 | 2.22 |
| Cincinnati | 157 | 142 | .904 | 10 | 3.01 |
| Chicago (NL) | 156 | 139 | .891 | 18 | 2.30 |
| Boston (NL) | 155 | 136 | .887 | 14 | 3.52 |
| Philadelphia (AL) | 155 | 136 | .887 | 26 | 2.35 |
| Detroit | 162 | 143 | .883 | 15 | 2.77 |
| Brooklyn | 154 | 135 | .877 | 7 | 3.76 |
| Washington | 157 | 137 | .873 | 7 | 3.62 |
| St. Louis (AL) | 156 | 135 | .865 | 13 | 2.83 |
| Chicago (AL) | 156 | 134 | .859 | 26 | 2.30 |
| Pittsburgh | 156 | 133 | .853 | 12 | 2.86 |
| Philadelphia (NL) | 155 | 131 | .845 | 12 | 2.81 |
| New York (NL) | 158 | 127 | .804 | 18 | 2.39 |
| New York (AL) | 155 | 123 | .794 | 15 | 2.57 |

"I still remember the first day he threw (the spitter) in a regular game. We were playing Cleveland. He had a tough first inning. They hit him for three runs. He came back to the bench and said, 'Griff, I haven't got my natural stuff today. I'm going to give 'em the spitter the next inning, if it's all right with you.' I told him to go to it, and you know what? He fanned 14. They didn't get another run, and we won the game 4-3."

—New York manager Clark Griffith

termined the game and the winner of the AL pennant.

For some years after that loss, Chesbro's wife campaigned to get the call on the fateful pitch changed from a wild pitch to a passed ball. But it was not to be. Still, the wild pitch could not dull the luster of Chesbro's greatest season.

He had two more winning seasons in New York, going 19-15 in 1905 and 23-17 in 1906, but went 24-34 over the next 3½ years. He was sold to Boston, of all teams, in 1909, his last year in the majors. Chesbro died in 1931, and fifteen years later became the first Yankee pitcher to be inducted into baseball's Hall of Fame.

## Baseball News Of 1904

- On their way to winning the NL pennant, the Giants won eighteen games in a row.
- The Red Sox' Cy Young threw the American League's first perfect game, on May 5, beating the A's and Rube Waddell in Boston.
- Wee Willie Keller hit two inside-the-park homers in one game—his only homers of the season—to help the Highlanders beat the Browns 9-1.
- The Giants refused to play the AL pennant-winning Red Sox in the World Series.
- Bill Yawkey, heir to a lumber and mining fortune, purchased the Detroit Tigers for $50,000.
- Rube Waddell of the Philadelphia A's fanned 348 batters, 110 more than his closest rival, Jack Chesbro.

## Around The World In 1904

- Work began on the Panama Canal.
- The United States hosted the third modern Olympics in St. Louis, in conjunction with the 1904 World's Fair.
- The first portion of New York's subway system was opened.
- The American Lung Association was founded.
- The *General Slocum*, an excursion steamer, burned and sank in New York's East River, killing 1,030 people.

# 7

# Season of Glory

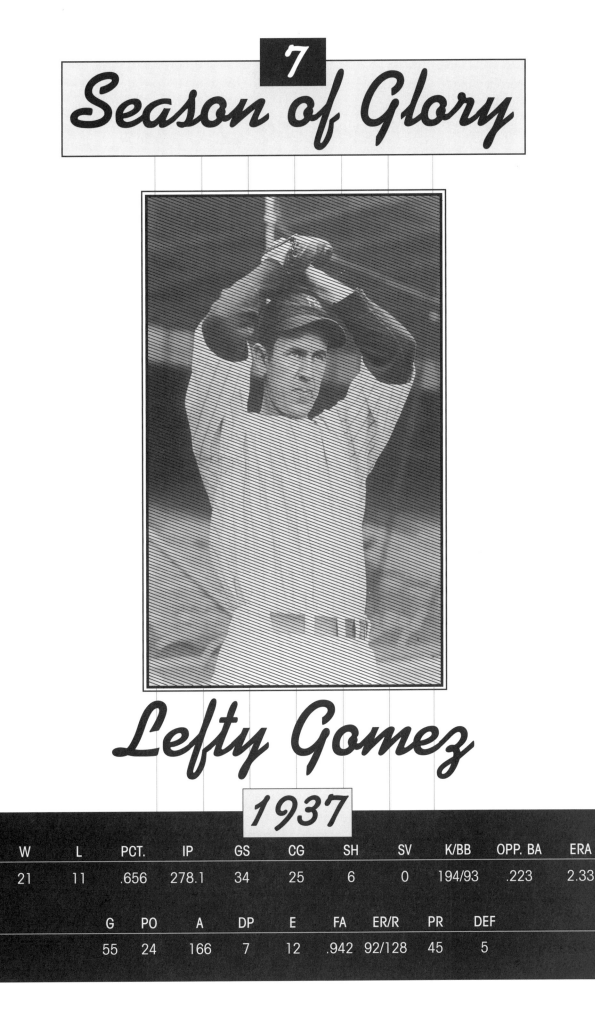

# Lefty Gomez

## 1937

| W | L | PCT. | IP | GS | CG | SH | SV | K/BB | OPP. BA | ERA |
|---|---|------|-----|----|----|----|----|------|---------|-----|
| 21 | 11 | .656 | 278.1 | 34 | 25 | 6 | 0 | 194/93 | .223 | 2.33 |

| | G | PO | A | DP | E | FA | ER/R | PR | DEF |
|---|---|----|---|----|---|----|------|----|----|
| | 55 | 24 | 166 | 7 | 12 | .942 | 92/128 | 45 | 5 |

# Vernon Louis Gomez

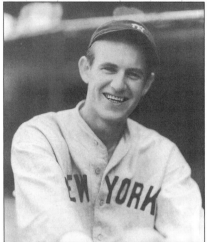

**BORN**
November 26, 1908
Rodeo, California

**DIED**
February 17, 1989
Greenbrae, California

**HEIGHT**
6-2

**WEIGHT**
175

**THREW**
left hand

**BATTED**
left hand

New York Yankees
1930–1942

Hall of Fame
1972

**1937**

When Lefty Gomez was in his prime out on the mound, few hitters could get past him. Even fewer ballplayers could touch him when Gomez was on a roll.

Over thirteen years he won 189 games for the Yankees, four times winning twenty in a season, twice leading the American League in victories, and three times leading the league in strikeouts.

Lefty Gomez was one of the most colorful ballplayers in an era that gave the game characters like Babe Ruth, Hack Wilson, Art "the Great" Shires, and "Jolly Cholly" Grimm. Always ready with a wisecrack, he was a newspaperman's dream.

On slugger Jimmie Foxx: "He's got muscles in his hair."

On the secret of his pitching success: "Clean living and a fast outfield."

On the one time in his career the notoriously bad hitter broke a bat: "I ran over it backing out of the garage."

Clean living and a fast outfield? How about a great fastball and, later in his career when he lost some of his zip, good control, a knuckleball, and an extremely effective curveball? That's what made Gomez the Yankee ace.

Vernon Louis Gomez was born in Rodeo, California, on November 26, 1908. He made a name for himself pitching for the San Francisco Seals (Pacific Coast League) and was purchased by the Yankees on August 17, 1929, for a reported $35,000. He played half of the 1930 season with the Yankees—he was a lackluster 2-5 in fifteen games, mostly in relief—before being sent to St. Paul (American Association). The following spring, he was back in New York to stay.

Gomez went 21-9, 24-7, and 16-10 in his first three full seasons. Then he had a triumphant 1934 season, during which he went 26-5 and led the league in wins, winning percentage (.839), complete games (25), shutouts (6), innings pitched (281), strikeouts (158), and earned-run average (2.33).

As good as that was, Yankee general manager Ed Barrow thought Gomez could be even better, if only the gangly (6 feet 2 inches tall, 175 pounds) left-hander would put on some weight. Barrow told Gomez he could make people forget forty-one-game winner Jack Chesbro. The idea backfired. Instead, "I put on twenty pounds and almost made them forget Gomez," Lefty said, referring to a dismal—for him—1935 season (12-15), when the Yankees finished three games behind Detroit.

Gomez and his teammates righted themselves in 1936, as he went 13-7 and the Yankees ran away with the pennant by 19½ games. New York was favored to win the pennant again in '37, and after less than three weeks of spring training, it was obvious why. Second-year man Joe DiMaggio was hitting .400, the eight position players averaged nearly one RBI each per game against major-league competition, and even Gomez, a career .165 hitter, got into the act, pounding out three hits in one exhibition game.

The defending champions opened their season at home on April 20. But the Washington Senators, led by Al Simmons, who had three hits, knocked off Gomez and the Yankees 3-2 (it was the third straight year that Gomez had lost the opener by one run).

With that tradition out of the way, Gomez embarked on what would be his greatest season. He picked up his first victory on April 28, a five-hitter against the Senators. And six days later, his four-hitter stopped Detroit.

After losing two of his next three decisions—he was 3-3 halfway through May—Gomez won three in a row, then lost two more, then won four of his next five.

Manager Joe McCarthy began juggling his rotation in late June so he could set up Gomez to start in the All-Star Game, scheduled for July 7 in Washington. McCarthy started Gomez out of turn on June 30, and it turned out to be his most impressive performance of the season. He held Philadelphia to one hit—Bob Johnson's leadoff homer in the fifth—and walked just two men, both with two out in the fifth. He retired

*Vernon Louis Gomez, more popularly known as "Lefty" or "El Goofo."*

the A's 1-2-3 in the other eight innings, and only one ball was hit out of the infield after the fifth.

The All-Star Game was always special to Gomez. He was a member of the AL pitching staff for the first seven years of the All-Star Game, and he started in 1933, '34, '35, '37, and '38. His 3-1 record made him the winningest pitcher in All-Star history, and he drove in the first run in All-Star history, in 1933 in Chicago. "Nothing I did in baseball gave me more satisfaction than getting that base hit," he reflected years later. "I hit only .113 that year. I think 300 fans fainted in the stands when that ball fell in."

# Game of Glory • June 30, 1937

On June 30 Gomez holds Philadelphia to one hit—Bob Johnson's leadoff homer in the fifth. He walks just two men, both in the fifth, and he retires the A's 1-2-3 in the other eight innings.

| NEW YORK | AB | R | H | RBI | PHILADELPHIA | AB | R | H | RBI |
|---|---|---|---|---|---|---|---|---|---|
| Heffner, ss | 5 | 0 | 1 | 0 | Finney, 1b | 4 | 0 | 0 | 0 |
| Rolfe, 3b | 5 | 1 | 1 | 0 | Moses, rf | 4 | 0 | 0 | 0 |
| DiMaggio, cf | 4 | 2 | 1 | 1 | Rothrock, cf | 4 | 0 | 0 | 0 |
| Gehrig, 1b | 3 | 2 | 0 | 0 | Johnson, lf | 3 | 1 | 1 | 1 |
| Dickey, c | 4 | 0 | 3 | 2 | Peters, 3b | 3 | 0 | 0 | 0 |
| Selkirk, rf | 4 | 0 | 2 | 2 | Newsome, ss | 3 | 0 | 0 | 0 |
| Powell, lf | 4 | 0 | 0 | 0 | Ambler, 2b | 2 | 0 | 0 | 0 |
| Lazzeri, 2b | 3 | 0 | 0 | 0 | Brucker, c | 2 | 0 | 0 | 0 |
| Gomez, p | 4 | 0 | 0 | 0 | Thomas, p | 2 | 0 | 0 | 0 |
| | | | | | Nelson, p | 1 | 0 | 0 | 0 |
| **Totals** | **36** | **5** | **8** | **5** | **Totals** | **28** | **1** | **1** | **1** |

| | | | | | | | |
|---|---|---|---|---|---|---|---|
| New York | 2 0 0 | 0 0 0 | 0 3 0 — 5 |
| Philadelphia | 0 0 0 | 0 1 0 | 0 0 0 — 1 |

Errors—Moses, Newsome, Brucker (2).
Doubles—Selkirk, Dickey, Rolfe, DiMaggio. Home run—Johnson.
Stolen bases—Selkirk (2). Left on base—New York 6, Philadelphia 2

| NEW YORK | IP | H | BB | K |
|---|---|---|---|---|
| Gomez (W) | 9 | 1 | 2 | 7 |

| PHILADELPHIA | IP | H | BB | K |
|---|---|---|---|---|
| Thomas (L) | 7 | 8 | 2 | 3 |
| Nelson | 2 | 0 | 0 | 2 |

*1937*

The 1937 All-star Game resulted in another American League victory, 8-3, and it was a New York Yankee production—Lou Gehrig doubled, homered, and drove in four runs, Red Rolfe tripled in what would be the winning run in the fourth, and Gomez allowed one hit in three shutout innings of work.

But then, the Yankees were stealing the show in the AL pennant race as well. They had moved into first place on May 24, and although they had to share the lead for one day with Chicago in early June, they were in control by the break, leading by 5½ games. Leading the charge were Gehrig (.371 at the midpoint of the season), Joe DiMaggio

(.361), and George Selkirk (.344). A nine-game winning streak that took place before and after the All-Star Game pretty much decided the race.

After the All-Star Game, Gomez won his first three starts, but then a combination of factors prevented him from winning for nearly a month. After two losses, his record dropped to 13-8, and he didn't get a decision his next time out on August 3. Four days later he got word that his mother was seriously ill in California, and he left the team to go to her bedside. He missed a turn, then rejoined the Yankees in Philadelphia on the August 13. Exhausted after a thirteen-hour flight, he lasted just 6⅓ innings and took the loss. Gomez chose to stay with the team instead of flying back home between starts. "She told me not to worry and not to fly back again," he told reporters.

An hour before his next start, on August 17, Gomez was called aside by McCarthy. The Yankee manager handed him a telegram that said his mother had died. Gomez went out and threw a three-hitter against Washington for his first victory since July 19, then left for the funeral.

After returning, Gomez won seven of his next eight decisions, three of them shutouts, including a four-hitter against Detroit on September 20 for his twentieth victory of the season. At that point in the season he had surrendered only 18 hits and struck out 30 in his last 36 innings, and had pitched 24 consecutive shutout innings. The Red Sox broke that streak in the first inning of his next start, but he won the game nevertheless, bringing his record to 21-10.

The Yankees clinched the pennant on September 23, giving them a week and a half to rest up before they played the New York Giants in the World Series. In the Series opener, on October 6 at Yankee Stadium, Gomez outdueled Carl Hubbell, allowing only six hits. The Yankees won 8-1 on the strength of a six-run sixth inning. The highlight, as far as Gomez was concerned, was his two walks in the inning. "Any of you guys know if two walks in an inning is a World Series record?" he asked reporters afterward.

The Yankees took the next two games easily, and the Giants won Game 4. That left it to Gomez to wrap things up in Game 5, and he didn't disappoint. Another complete game, another victory—his fourth in as many career Series starts—and another world championship for the Yankees. And the winning hit in Game 5 was delivered by Gomez— his infield single drove in Tony Lazzeri with the deciding run in the fifth.

It was a wonderful ending to a glorious season for Gomez. He led the American League in victories (21), strikeouts (194), earned-run average (2.33), shutouts (6), fewest hits allowed per game (7.53), and lowest opponents' batting average (.223). He even had a .200 average with twenty-one hits— both career highs.

In his five more years with the Yankees, Gomez would go 54-33. He wound up his

> "I want to thank all my teammates who scored so many runs, Joe DiMaggio, who ran down so many of my mistakes, and Johnny Murphy, without whose relief pitching I wouldn't be here."
>
> —LEFTY GOMEZ AT HIS HALL OF FAME INDUCTION IN 1972

career playing for Washington (with a record of 0-1) in 1943. He left baseball with an armload of records—he was 6-0 in World Series competition, the most wins without a loss; his 3-1 record is an All-Star Game record, as is the number of innings he pitched (6) in the 1935 contest; and he's still ranked in the top ten in most Yankee pitching categories.

Gomez, who died in 1989, never let all the fame and records go to his head, though. He often told a story to illustrate why: Returning to his hometown after the 1931 season, when he had gone 21-9, he was "feeling pretty good" about himself. The first man he met while walking through town put things into perspective, however, by saying, "Vernon, I can't recall seeing you around here very much lately. You been away for the summer?"

## Baseball News Of 1937

- Carl Hubbell's twenty-four-game winning streak was broken on May 31 when the New York Giants lost 10-3 to Brooklyn. It was his first loss since July 13, 1936.

- Cleveland pitcher Johnny Allen won his first fifteen games, then lost to Detroit 1-0 on the last day of the season.

- On June 15 Boston's Ben Chapman made seven putouts on seven consecutive fly balls.

- The Boston Bees signed Casey Stengel as manager.

- The Yankees' Bill Dickey hit grand slams on consecutive days—August 3 against Chicago and August 4 against St. Louis.

## Around The World In 1937

- On December 12 the U.S. gunboat *Panay* was sunk in Chinese waters by Japanese planes, killing two.

- Pulitzer Prizes were awarded to Margaret Mitchell for *Gone With the Wind*, to Allan Nevinis for *Hamilton Fish*, and to Moss Hart and George S. Kaufman for *You Can't Take It With You*.

- Franklin Roosevelt was inaugurated for a second term on January 20.

- The National Labor Relations Act of 1935 was upheld by the U.S. Supreme Court.

- Hundreds of American volunteers went to Spain to fight in the Spanish Civil War.

# 8
# Season of Glory

## Joe DiMaggio

### 1941

| AB | R | H | BA | OB% | 2B | 3B | HR | K/BB | RBI | BR | SB |
|----|----|----|------|------|----|----|----|-------|-----|----|----|
| 541 | 122 | 193 | .357 | .440 | 43 | 11 | 30 | 13/76 | 125 | 66 | 4 |

| | | G | PO | A | DP | E | FA | FR | | | |
|---|---|-----|-----|----|----|----|------|----|---|---|---|
| | | 139 | 385 | 16 | 5 | 9 | .978 | 10 | | | |

# 8

# Joseph Paul DiMaggio

**BORN**
November 25, 1914
Martinez, California

**DIED**
March 8, 1999
Hollywood, Florida

**HEIGHT**
6-2

**WEIGHT**
193

**THREW**
right hand

**BATTED**
right hand

New York Yankees
1936–1942
1946–1951

**HALL OF FAME**
1955

> "When he walked in the clubhouse,
> the lights flickered. Joe DiMaggio was a star."
>
> —Longtime Yankee clubhouse custodian Pete Sheehy

Forget for a moment, as if that were possible, what Joe DiMaggio did on the field, and think instead of the Joe DiMaggio aura. Tall, handsome, elegant, always meticulously dressed, he was the epitome of class. Quiet, zealously protective of his privacy, at times antiseptically distant, DiMaggio fostered an air of mystery.

George Steinbrenner has always preached about a Yankee image that he wants his players to live up to. No one, before or since, has fit that image better than Joe DiMaggio.

OK, now think about what he did on the field.

He was a great hitter, in terms of both power and average; defensively he was untouchable, covering center field with speed and grace; he was a smart player who didn't make mistakes; he was a team leader. He was a winner, pure and simple.

His accomplishments could fill a book—a lifetime .325 batting average with 361 homers and 1,537 RBIs over thirteen seasons; ten AL pennants and nine World Series championships in those thirteen years; a three-time AL Most Valuable Player; a member of the AL All-Star team every one of his thirteen seasons; election to the Hall of Fame in 1955.

And then there was the streak. "I believe there isn't a record in the books that will be harder to break," Ted Williams once said of DiMaggio's 56-game hitting streak of 1941, his greatest season. "It may be the greatest batting achievement of all."

When an athlete accomplishes something extraordinary, his career is often defined by that single feat. Roger Maris, for example, was an excellent all-around ballplayer, but he's remembered as the man who broke Babe Ruth's home run record. Lou Gehrig's prodigious feats are overshadowed by his consecutive-games-played streak. Bill Mazeroski was one of the finest second basemen of his generation, but to most fans he'll forever be the guy who hit the most dramatic home run in World Series history. Not so with DiMaggio. As impressive and perhaps unreachable as his hitting streak is, he is remembered as, simply, Joe DiMaggio. That says it all.

DiMaggio was born on November 25, 1914, in Martinez, California, which is just north of San Francisco. He was one of nine children born to fisherman Giuseppe DiMaggio and his wife, Rosalie. When Joe was one, the family moved to the North Beach section of San Francisco, where Joe developed into a top-notch sandlot and semipro ballplayer.

The two older DiMaggio boys, Tom and Mike, became fishermen like their father. Brother Vince, the next oldest, avoided the family business by signing with the Pacific Coast League's San Francisco Seals. Joe knew that was the path he wanted to follow as well—not only was he a natural baseball talent, he also tended to get seasick—and late in the 1932 season, he was asked to try out for the Seals.

The seventeen-year-old DiMaggio made an immediate impression, tripling in his first at-bat. He played three games at short for the Seals, performing well enough that he was offered a contract for 1933— $225 a month, a huge amount for a Depression-era teenager and twice what the average rookie made in the PCL.

It was money well spent. DiMaggio, assigned to play right field early in the season, led the league in RBIs (169), hit .340 with 28 homers, and had a 61-game hitting streak, a professional baseball record that still stands.

DiMaggio was baseball's most promising star, with every major-league club showing some interest. But it all nearly ended in 1934. Early in the season, after having dinner at his sister's, DiMaggio grabbed a jitney cab for the ride home to his parents' apartment. It was crowded and he was jammed in the back seat. His left foot had fallen asleep, and when he jumped out of the cab and put all

*The Jolter*

of his weight on the foot, something snapped. He had torn the cartilage in the knee, a far more serious injury then than now, and was hobbled the rest of the season. He wound up hitting .341 and drove in 69 runs in 101 games, 86 fewer than the year before, but the injury scared off most of the teams that had been salivating over the young prospect.

One team, however, remained interested. The Yankees offered the Seals $25,000 and five players for DiMaggio, provided that he passed a physical. After a Los Angeles orthopedist gave DiMaggio's knee the green light, the deal was made.

# Game of Glory • July 16, 1941

On July 16, DiMaggio's first-inning single off Cleveland's Al Milnar extends his hitting streak to 56 games. The streak would end the next day against the Indians.

| NEW YORK | AB | R | H | RBI | | CLEVELAND | AB | R | H | RBI |
|----------|----|----|----|-----|---|-----------|----|----|----|-----|
| Sturm, 1b | 5 | 0 | 0 | 0 | | Boudreau, ss | 4 | 1 | 1 | 0 |
| Rolfe, 3b | 4 | 0 | 0 | 0 | | Keltner, 3b | 4 | 0 | 1 | 0 |
| Henrich, rf | 4 | 1 | 0 | 0 | | Weatherly, cf | 3 | 0 | 0 | 0 |
| DiMaggio, cf | 4 | 3 | 3 | 0 | | Heath, rf | 4 | 1 | 2 | 1 |
| Gordon, 2b | 4 | 2 | 2 | 1 | | Trosky, 1b | 3 | 0 | 1 | 1 |
| Rosar, c | 5 | 1 | 3 | 5 | | Campbell, lf | 4 | 0 | 0 | 0 |
| Keller, lf | 3 | 3 | 2 | 1 | | Mack, 2b | 3 | 1 | 1 | 0 |
| Rizzuto, ss | 5 | 0 | 1 | 2 | | Desautels, c | 3 | 0 | 0 | 0 |
| Donald, p | 4 | 0 | 0 | 0 | | Walker, ph | 1 | 0 | 1 | 1 |
| | | | | | | Bell, ph | 1 | 0 | 0 | 0 |
| | | | | | | Milnar, p | 2 | 0 | 1 | 0 |
| | | | | | | Krakauskas, p | 1 | 0 | 0 | 0 |
| | | | | | | Rosenthal, ph | 1 | 0 | 0 | 0 |
| **Totals** | **38** | **10** | **11** | **9** | | **Totals** | **34** | **3** | **8** | **3** |

New York    2 0 0   1 4 0   0 1 2 — 10
Cleveland    1 1 0   0 0 1   0 0 0 — 3

Error—Trosky. Triple—Keller. Home run—Keller. Double play—New York.
Left on base—New York 8, Cleveland 7.

| NEW YORK | IP | H | BB | K |
|----------|----|----|----|----|
| Donald (W) | 9 | 8 | 4 | 5 |

| CLEVELAND | IP | H | BB | K |
|-----------|----|----|----|----|
| Milnar (L) | 5 | 8 | 4 | 3 |
| Krakauskas | 4 | 3 | 3 | 3 |

Time—2:17. Attendance—15,000 (est.)

*1941*

The Yankees thought DiMaggio needed another year of seasoning, so he played with the Seals in 1935. He was better than ever: a .398 average with 34 homers and 154 RBIs, 24 stolen bases in 25 attempts, and the PCL Most Valuable Player Award. Thus, the following spring, DiMaggio made the cross-country trip to the Yankees' training camp in Florida accompanied by fellow Bay Area Yankees Tony Lazzeri and Frank Crosetti.

Upon DiMaggio's arrival, the *New York World-Telegram* reported, "Here is the re-placement for Babe Ruth." This was a bit premature, to be sure. He started quickly—12 hits in his first 20 at-bats over five exhibition games—but then injured his left foot in a force play at second. For treatment, he used diathermic heat, but the lamp burned his foot, making matters worse.

By the time he was ready to play again, the season was sixteen games old. He debuted on May 3, 1936, as the Yankees' leftfielder, lining a single in his first at-bat and adding two more hits in a victory over St. Louis.

*A pensive DiMaggio at Comiskey Park's batting cage.*

(He moved to center field six weeks later and, for the next thirteen years, played it like he had invented it.) DiMaggio was a star right out of the gate: his averages for his first five years were .323, .346, .324, .381 and .352.

The Yankees won the World Series the first four years DiMaggio played for them, then finished a disappointing third in 1940, two games behind Detroit. But the next year, the Yankees returned to form. They won the American League pennant by a staggering 17 games, clinching on September 4. (They had all but wrapped things up in July, having won 25 of 29 games.) And in the World Series, they needed just five games to beat Brooklyn and win their ninth world championship.

But 1941 was not a glorious year just for the Yankees, it was also DiMaggio's best year, the year of his record hitting streak.

DiMaggio was an expert on such things. There was the 61-game streak for the Seals.

As a Yankee rookie, he hit safely in 18 games. In his second season he had a 22-gamer. In his third season, another streak of 23 games. And in spring training in 1941, he hit safely in the last 19 exhibition games, then in his first eight in the regular season, twenty-seven in a row. He was just warming up.

The streak began on May 15 at Yankee Stadium with a single off roly-poly White Sox left-hander Ed Smith. The next afternoon, he hit a triple and homer that helped the team defeat Chicago, bringing the fourth-place Yankees back to .500 at 15-15. DiMaggio was on his way.

During the first two weeks of the streak, DiMaggio rarely had more than one hit per game, and there wasn't a lot of media interest. But that changed as the streak continued into June and the nation began to take notice.

DiMaggio was already breaking records by the third week of June. He broke the Yankees' team record of 29 on June 17 with a bad-hop single against Chicago. On June 21 he hit in his thirty-fourth game, bettering the NL record of 33 held by Rogers Hornsby. On June 29 he hit in his forty-second game, a single off Washington's Red Anderson that broke George Sisler's AL record. And on July 2, he hit a three-run homer against Boston that brought his streak to 45 games, passing Wee Willie Keeler's all-time record of 44 games, set in 1898.

There were several close calls in June. In a five-game stretch from the June 13 to June 18, he had just one hit per game. On June 24 against St. Louis, he was hitless his first three at-bats. He stepped to the plate in the bottom of the eighth against Browns right-

> "He made the rest of the players look like plumbers."
>
> —CASEY STENGEL

hander Bob Muncrief and finally lined a 1-1 pitch to left field to bring his streak to 36 games. (Asked afterward why he didn't walk DiMaggio, Muncrief said, "That wouldn't have been fair. To him or to me. Hell, he's the greatest player I've ever seen.")

DiMaggio had his closest call of all on June 26. Batting against Browns pitcher Eldon Auker, he flied out in the second inning, was safe on an error in the fourth, and bounced out in the sixth. In the bottom of the eighth, with the Yankees leading 3-1, DiMaggio was scheduled to bat fourth.

The leadoff man popped out, and Red Rolfe walked. That brought Tommy Heinrich to the plate, with DiMaggio in the on-deck circle. Heinrich returned to the dugout to confer with McCarthy. He told his manager he wanted to bunt to ensure that there wouldn't be a double play that would end the inning and, in all probability, the streak. McCarthy agreed. Heinrich then laid down a perfect sacrifice bunt, moving Rolfe to second and giving DiMaggio a last chance.

"What DiMaggio did then impresses me still even after all these years," Robert W. Creamer wrote in his 1991 book *Baseball in '41*. "You'd think he would have waited at bat, taken a pitch or two to get his timing just right, to sound out the pitcher a little. Not at all. He swung at the first pitch and rifled the ball down the left-field line for a double. Oh, the cheers then!"

DiMaggio's streak was now at 38 games. He reached 40 on June 28. He made it to 50 on July 12 with a pair of hits against St. Louis. On July 15 he got two hits against Chicago's Smith, the man against whom the streak began. The next afternoon in Cleveland, DiMaggio—who hadn't struck out since June 8—had a double and two singles.

He was at 56 games and seemed unstoppable.

But the next night he was stopped. A crowd of 67,468 fans—the largest crowd ever to see a night game in the majors—packed Municipal Stadium. In his first at-bat, DiMaggio hit a sharp two-bouncer over third that Cleveland's Ken Keltner, playing on the edge of the outfield grass, speared before throwing him out. DiMaggio walked in the fourth; in the seventh he hit another smash that Keltner made a fine play on before throwing him out. In the eighth inning, facing reliever Jim Bagby, DiMaggio hit a sharp bouncer up the middle that shortstop Lou Boudreau fielded and tossed to second to begin a double play. For the first time in more than two months, DiMaggio took the collar.

When DiMaggio's hitting streak started, the Yankees were in fourth place, 5½ games out of first. When it ended they were ahead by six games. Over the 56 games, DiMaggio hit .408, with 91 hits, including 16 doubles, 4 triples and 15 home runs. He scored 56 runs in the 56 games and drove in 55. He struck out only seven times.

And he wasn't finished, either. After being stopped by the Indians, DiMaggio embarked on another streak, this one 16 games long, raising his average to .381.

DiMaggio finished his season at .357, third in the league, with 122 runs (second), 193 hits (third), 348 total bases (first), and

*Yankee pride and Yankee management: Joe McCarthy with Joe DiMaggio.*

125 RBIs (first). But as great as those numbers were, and as great a year as the Yankees had, 1941 will be remembered for the streak. "The strain of the streak was terrific," DiMaggio remembered years later.

When I hit in 61 games in a row my first year with San Francisco, nothing bothered me in those days. Besides, it happened in the minor leagues, and nobody paid much attention to me. There were no big crowds, no fans waiting outside the park, no writers interviewing me every day.

If I say it myself, that 56-game streak was a good trick. That's one job the boys are not going to beat while I'm around.

## Baseball News Of 1941

- Boston's Ted Williams hit .406—by going 6-for-8 on the final day of the season—the last major-leaguer to hit .400.

- On July 8 the NL's Arky Vaughan became the first player to hit two homers in an All-Star Game, but he was upstaged by Ted Williams, whose two-out, three-run homer in the bottom of the ninth gave the AL a 7-5 victory.

- On April 23 Phil Rizzuto's first major-league homer gave the Yankees a 4-2 victory over Boston.

- In his last game before going into the service, Hank Greenberg hit two homers in Detroit's 7-4 victory over the Yankees on May 6.

- Mel Ott hit his 400th homer and drove in his 1,500th run in the New York Giants' 3-2 victory over Cincinnati on June 1.

- On June 2, sixteen years to the day after he became a starter for the Yankees, Lou Gehrig died. He was 37.

## Around The World In 1941

- Germany invaded Russia on June 22.

- Japan attacked Pearl Harbor on December 7.

- On April 11 the Ford Motor Company signed its first contract with a labor union, settling a nine-day-old strike.

- The phrase "Praise the Lord and pass the ammunition" was uttered by Chaplain Howell M. Forgy aboard the U.S. cruiser *New Orleans* as it was attacked at Pearl Harbor.

- Wake Island fell to Japan on December 22 after a valiant fifteen-day stand by 400 U.S. Marines.

- Thanksgiving was moved to the last Thursday in November; the two previous years it had been the next-to-last Thursday.

# 9

# Season of Glory

# Ron Guidry

## 1978

| W | L | PCT. | IP | GS | CG | SH | SV | K/BB | OPP. BA | ERA |
|---|---|------|-----|-----|-----|-----|-----|--------|---------|------|
| 25 | 3 | .893 | 273.2 | 35 | 16 | 9 | 0 | 248/78 | .193 | 1.74 |

| | G | PO | A | DP | E | FA | ER/R | PR | DEF | |
|---|---|-----|-----|-----|-----|------|-------|-----|-----|---|
| | 35 | 14 | 44 | 1 | 2 | .967 | 53/61 | 57 | 2 | |

# Ronald Ames Guidry

**BORN**
August 28, 1950
Lafayette, Louisiana

**HEIGHT**
5–11

**WEIGHT**
160

**THREW**
left hand

**BATTED**
left hand

New York Yankees
1975–1988

*I*t's amazing what a few words of encouragement can do for a player. Take Ron Guidry, for example.

"If there's anybody in this league you can get out, let me know, and I'll let you pitch to him," Billy Martin, his manager, once told him.

"Guidry, you will never be able to pitch in this league," offered Yankee owner George Steinbrenner.

"Maybe you don't have what it takes. Maybe you're not mean enough," said Yankee president Gabe Paul.

With those enthusiastic endorsements in mind, Guidry set out to prove the experts wrong. And he did—again and again—over his fourteen-year career with the Yankees.

Ronald Ames Guidry was born on August 28, 1950, in Lafayette, Louisiana, the heart of Cajun country. An American Legion baseball star during his high school years, he enrolled at the University of Southwestern Louisiana in 1968 to study architecture. It was there that he was discovered by Yankee scout Atley Donald, on whose recommendation the team picked Guidry in the third round of the 1971 draft.

He devoted the next four years to the Ron Guidry Minor-League Tour, with stops in Johnson City, Tennessee, Ft. Lauderdale, Kinston, North Carolina, and West Haven, Connecticut. His four-year record was a lackluster 13-16, but the Yankees stuck with him, largely because he had a high strikeout-per-inning ratio and a fastball that belied his 5-foot-11-inch, 160-pound frame. What he didn't have, and what he needed, was another "out" pitch. He had had a serviceable curve during his Legion ball days, but somewhere along the line it had deserted him. That left him relying on his fastball, and no matter how hard a starting pitcher throws, eventually batters are going to catch on. And that's where 13-16 records come from.

Cloyd Boyer, a Yankee pitching coach, suggested to Guidry that he become a reliever during his stint in West Haven. The idea was that Guidry could come into a game in a tight spot, blow a fastball past a batter, and get out of the inning. Guidry managed just three saves and an ERA of 5.26 in 29 games as a reliever for West Haven. The key numbers, though, were 79 strikeouts in 77 innings. That helped get him promoted to Syracuse, the Yankees' top farm team, in 1975. After a successful first half there, he was called up to the parent club in late July. Guidry appeared in ten games that season, losing his only decision.

He had a good spring in 1976 but was sent down to Syracuse because the Yankees, loaded with high-priced pitching talent, simply had no room for him. A few weeks into the season, he was recalled, but after one bad outing, he found himself in Martin's doghouse. He sat on the bench, unused, frustrated, and discouraged, for forty-six days before the Yankees shipped him back to Syracuse on July 6.

Guidry had had enough. He and his wife, Bonnie, got into the car for the drive to Syracuse. Instead, he began driving to Lafayette. After an hour he pulled over and told her of his frustration, of how badly he felt he'd been treated. "Bonnie said, 'You know you can play major league baseball,'" he wrote in *Guidry*. "'When the time comes that YOU decide you can't, that's the time to go home. Not now. Don't let them destroy your ego the way they've been doing. You have to fight them.'" Guidry turned the car around and headed to Syracuse. His next month there was nothing short of spectacular: he allowed just 15 hits and had 50 strikeouts in 40 innings, posting a 0.68 ERA.

That earned him another recall to New York, where he experienced his epiphany, courtesy of the two wise men of the Yankee bullpen, Dick Tidrow and Sparky Lyle. They took Guidry aside and transformed him from a thrower into a pitcher. Tidrow instructed him on the art of pitching—how to set up a hitter, how to move the ball around, how to outsmart a batter—and Lyle taught him his slider, explaining the mechanics and working with him on the side almost daily, until he had mastered the pitch. With his 95-mile-an-hour fastball, Lyle's slider, and Tidrow's smarts, Ron Guidry was beginning to put all the pieces together.

Early in the 1977 season, he got his chance to show what he had learned. He had had a lousy spring—his ERA was over 10 at one point—but once the season began he pitched well in relief and was doing a good job out of the bullpen. On April 29, though, came the turning point. Pressed into service as a starter, he pitched 8⅓ shutout innings against Seattle. Lyle retired the last two hitters, preserving the 3-0 win, Guidry's first as a Yankee.

Working as a reliever and as a starter, Guidry finished 1977 with a 16-7 record. More important, he was 10-2 after the All-Star break, when the Yankees made a tre-mendous charge to capture the AL East flag (they won 28 of 34 from the beginning of August to mid-September, assisted by Guidry, who won eight straight games down the stretch). He won one game in the playoffs and another in the World Series, which the Yankees won in six games.

The Yankees began the 1978 season as the AL favorites, but pitchers Don Gullett, Andy Messersmith, and Catfish Hunter were soon out of the lineup (Gullett and Messersmith because of injuries, Hunter because of diabetes), putting the pitching staff on the spot. Guidry stepped in and was, simply, brilliant.

> "To look at me, you wouldn't believe I could throw as hard as I can. You don't, however, have to be well-built to throw a good fastball. You need strong legs, an efficient, compact windup, and a long arm that will supply a lot of leverage. I have all three."
>
> —RON GUIDRY IN *GUIDRY*, BY GUIDRY AND PETER GOLENBOCK

At the end of April, he was 2-0 in five starts, all solid, none headline-grabbers. But then he just kept getting better. And winning. And winning. By the end of May, he was 7-0 with an ERA under 2.00. On June 2 he struck out eleven A's in 8⅓ innings for No. 8; five days later came a complete-game six-hit win over Seattle; on June 12, it was Oakland's turn again as he fanned eleven and allowed just three singles in a 2-0 win that ran his record to 10-0.

The most spectacular victory of a spectacular season occurred on June 17 at Yankee Stadium. With a crowd of 33,162 cheering him on—it became the custom for fans to begin screaming and stomping whenever he got two strikes on a hitter—Guidry fanned eighteen Angels in a 4-0 victory. The performance broke the team record of 15 strikeouts shared by Bob Shawkey and Whitey Ford and the AL mark of 17 held by California's Frank Tanana. It also announced

# Game of Glory • June 17, 1978

On June 17 Guidry fans eighteen Angels to run his record to 11-0.

| CALIFORNIA | AB | R | H | RBI | | NEW YORK | AB | R | H | RBI |
|---|---|---|---|---|---|---|---|---|---|---|
| Grich, 2b | 4 | 0 | 1 | 0 | | White, lf | 4 | 1 | 1 | 0 |
| Miller, cf | 4 | 0 | 1 | 0 | | Munson, c | 4 | 1 | 2 | 0 |
| Chalk, ss | 4 | 0 | 1 | 0 | | Thomasson, cf | 4 | 1 | 2 | 2 |
| Rudi, 1b | 4 | 0 | 0 | 0 | | Blair, cf | 0 | 0 | 0 | 0 |
| Baylor, rf | 3 | 0 | 1 | 0 | | Jackson, rf | 4 | 1 | 1 | 1 |
| Jackson, 2b | 4 | 0 | 0 | 0 | | Chambliss, 1b | 4 | 0 | 1 | 0 |
| Rettenmund, rf | 3 | 0 | 0 | 0 | | Nettles, 3b | 4 | 0 | 1 | 1 |
| Downing, c | 2 | 0 | 0 | 0 | | Spencer, dh | 4 | 0 | 1 | 0 |
| Hampton, dh | 3 | 0 | 0 | 0 | | Stanley, ss | 3 | 0 | 0 | 0 |
| | | | | | | Doyle, 2b | 3 | 0 | 2 | 0 |
| Totals | 32 | 0 | 4 | 0 | | Totals | 34 | 4 | 11 | 4 |

| | | | | | | |
|---|---|---|---|---|---|---|
| California | 0 0 0 | 0 0 0 | 0 0 0 | — 0 | | |
| New York | 1 0 3 | 0 0 0 | 0 0 * | — 4 | | |

Left on base—California 4, New York 6. Triple—Thomasson.

| CALIFORNIA | IP | H | R | ER | BB | K |
|---|---|---|---|---|---|---|
| Hartzell (L, 1-5) | 2.1 | 8 | 4 | 4 | 0 | 1 |
| Brett | 5.2 | 3 | 0 | 0 | 0 | 4 |

| NEW YORK | IP | H | R | ER | BB | K |
|---|---|---|---|---|---|---|
| Guidry (W, 11-0) | 9.0 | 4 | 0 | 0 | 2 | 18 |

Wild pitch—Hartzell. Time—2:07. Attendance—33,162.

Time—2:07. Attendance—33,162 (est.)

*1978*

to the baseball world that Ron Guidry— 11-0, 1.45 ERA, winner of 21 of his last 22 decisions—was darned near unbeatable.

"I made good pitches and they couldn't hit them," he later said. "I made bad pitches, and they couldn't hit them either. I threw sliders in the dirt and they swung and missed. I threw fast balls in the sky and they swung and made out. Everything I threw, they swung at. And missed. They were so intent on *not* striking out that they did. That game established me in the hitters' minds. Guys started being defensive after that."

Sparky Lyle, in his book *The Bronx Zoo*, raved about his young teammate's performance that night. "I've been saying all year long that Guidry's the most impressive pitcher I've ever seen. He's more impressive than Seaver or Palmer or Ryan . . . You're sitting there watching the guy, and he's just winding up, throwing the ball, and the catcher's throwing it back to him, like they're playing catch, and before you know it, Jesus Christ, the ballgame is over, they've got three hits, and he's won 2 to nothing."

Guidry got his twelfth win on June 22, when the Yankees rallied for four runs in the ninth to beat Detroit 4-2. After a no-decision on June 27 (four runs and eight hits in six-plus innings) he got number 13 on July 2 in a 3-2 victory over the Tigers.

Guidry was scheduled to pitch once more

before the All-Star break. His arm was tired, and he considered asking Martin if he could skip a turn. But with the Red Sox running away in the AL East and with a certain feeling of invincibility, he decided to take the mound on July 7 in Milwaukee. Mistake. "When I went out there, I had nothing on the ball," he later said. Larry Hisle touched him for a two-run homer in the first. The Brewers added two more runs in the fourth, and another pair in the sixth, and Guidry was gone after six innings. The loss left him at 13-1 with a 1.99 ERA at the break (he worked just one-third of an inning in the All-Star Game—Yankee manager Billy Martin, who managed the the AL, wisely used him as little as possible).

By the end of July, Martin had been fired and Bob Lemon had replaced him. Guidry was 15-1, and the Yankees were a half-dozen games behind Boston in the pennant race. Guidry lost his first start in August, 2-1 to Baltimore, as a result of Doug DeCinces' two-run homer in the seventh, but, as in 1977, he was unbeatable down the stretch. He won seven in a row, including a three-hitter against Milwaukee on August 10, a four-hitter five days later against Oakland, and a five-hitter over Detroit on September 4 for his twentieth victory.

The Yankees won two of their next three games, moving to within four games of first and setting the stage for a crucial four-game series in Boston. With Guidry winning number 21 and the Yankees outscoring the Red Sox 42-9, New York swept the series and moved into a first-place tie with Boston.

The race continued until the last day of the season—and beyond. Guidry picked up his final loss of the season on September 20, when he was knocked out in the second inning of an 8-1 loss to Toronto. He came back with a two-hitter four days later in Cleveland and ran his record to 24-3 on the September 28, beating Toronto 3-1.

The Yankees and Red Sox both finished with 99-63 records. The AL East race would be decided by a one-game playoff at Fenway. Guidry, working on three days' rest, surren-

*Ron Guidry*

dered two runs in 6⅓ innings, but Bucky Dent's three-run homer in the top of the seventh and Goose Gossage's relief work carried the Yankees to a 5-4 victory and the AL East crown.

New York's opponent in the AL Championship Series was Kansas City, which won the AL West by five games. The Yankees won two of the first three games in the best-of-five series, and Lemon sent Guidry out to go for the clincher on October 7. He didn't let his manager down, surrendering just one run and seven hits in eight innings as the Yankees won 2-1 to advance to the World Series.

Guidry would make just one appearance in the Series, but it was crucial. The Dodgers had won the first two games, and if ever Lemon needed his stopper—15 of Guidry's 25 wins during the season had come after

Yankee losses—it was now. "A lot of people wondered how I could handle my first full season in the majors," Guidry told reporters on the eve of the game. "And I think I've showed them. I've always had confidence in myself. I think I've done my job well. I'm not tired, physically or mentally, and I think I can do the job again [in Game 3]."

And he did, but not as expected. From the first pitch, he realized he would not be overpowering on this night. So, he became a finesse pitcher. "When you learn to pitch, it comes naturally," he said of his change in approach. "You know when you don't have your best stuff to resort to something else." Taking something off his fastball, varying speeds, and hitting spots, he allowed eight hits. Assisted by Roy White (a home run in the first) and Graig Nettles (three outstanding defensive plays at third base to kill Dodger rallies in the fourth, fifth, and sixth innings), Guidry coasted to a 5-1 victory. Guidry's gutsy 137-pitch performance turned the tide. The Yankees swept the next three games to capture their second straight World Series.

Guidry's final numbers for 1978 were awesome. He led major-league pitchers in victories (25), winning percentage (.893), ERA (1.74), shutouts (9), fewest hits allowed per nine innings (6.15), and lowest opponents' batting average (.193). He won a number of postseason honors as well: He was the unanimous winner of the AL Cy Young Award, was voted the Associated Press Male Athlete of the Year, and won *Sport Magazine*'s Performer of the Year Award, and *The Sporting News*' Major League Player of the Year and Man of the Year Awards.

"Everything had gone right," he once observed about his spectacular season. "My fastball and slider both exploded, and I had good control over both pitches, and when I'd make a bad pitch, the batter would hit a long foul or my fielders would make great plays, and it was like being in heaven."

## Baseball News Of 1978

- Making his major-league debut, Baltimore pitcher Sammy Stewart struck out seven consecutive White Sox hitters on September 1.

- California outfielder Lyman Bostock was killed by a shotgun blast, an innocent victim of a domestic dispute, on September 23 in Gary, Indiana.

- The Pirates won twenty-four home games in a row. The Phillies ended Pittsburgh's winning streak on September 29.

- U.S. District Court Judge Constance Baker Motley ruled that female sportswriters cannot be barred from locker rooms.

## Around The World In 1978

- The United States and the People's Republic of China announced they would initiate full diplomatic relations in 1979.

- Among 1978's obituaries were those of Charles Boyer (on August 26, age 79), Edgar Bergen (September 30, age 75), Bruce Catton (August 28, age 78), Jack Oakie (January 23, age 74), and Norman Rockwell (November 9, age 84).

- Hannah H. Gray became the first woman university president in the United States (University of Chicago).

- The city of Cleveland became the first major U.S. city since the '30s to fail to meet its financial obligations when it defaulted on $15.5 million in short-term notes on December 15.

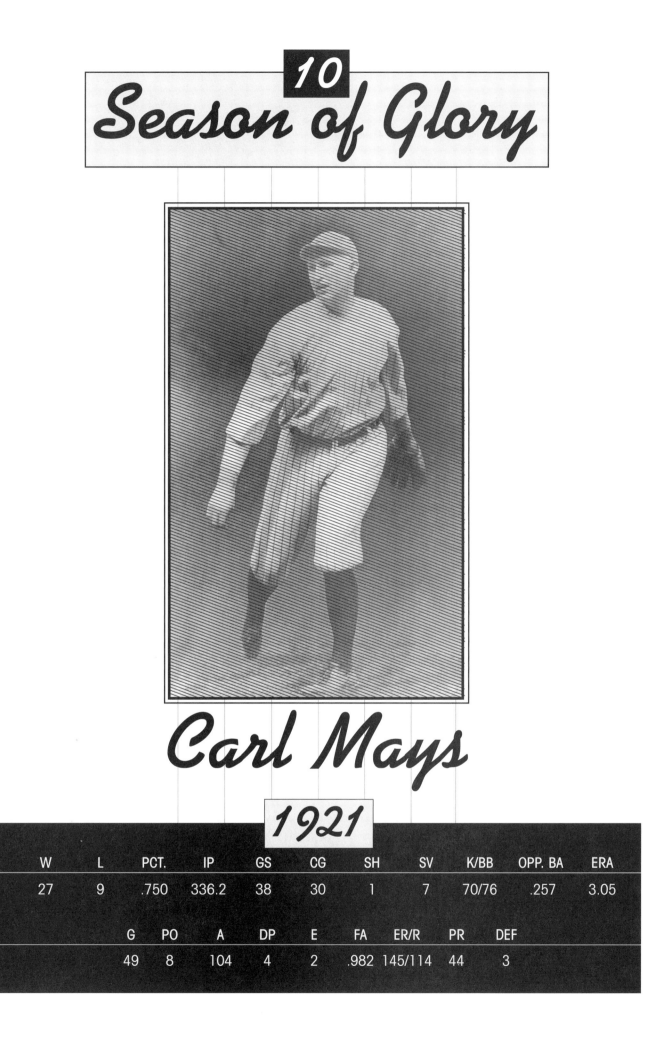

## Carl Mays

### 1921

| W | L | PCT. | IP | GS | CG | SH | SV | K/BB | OPP. BA | ERA |
|---|---|------|-----|-----|-----|-----|-----|-------|---------|------|
| 27 | 9 | .750 | 336.2 | 38 | 30 | 1 | 7 | 70/76 | .257 | 3.05 |

| | | G | PO | A | DP | E | FA | ER/R | PR | DEF |
|---|---|---|-----|-----|-----|-----|------|--------|-----|-----|
| | | 49 | 8 | 104 | 4 | 2 | .982 | 145/114 | 44 | 3 |

# 10

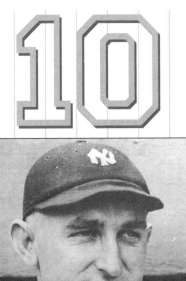

BORN
November 12, 1891
Liberty, Kentucky

DIED
April 4, 1971
El Cajon, California

HEIGHT
5-11½

WEIGHT
195

THREW
right hand

BATTED
left hand

New York Yankees
1919–1923

## 1921

# Carl William Mays

*B*ut for one pitch, Carl Mays would be remembered as one of the best players of his time, and he probably would have been elected to the Hall of Fame. He won 207 games, lost only 126, and had an earned-run average of 2.92 over his fifteen-year career. Despite those stats, including a career-best 27-9 season in 1921, Mays is best known for a fastball that caused the death of Cleveland Indians shortstop Ray Chapman on August 17, 1920.

Carl William Mays began his major-league career with the Boston Red Sox in 1915, when the twenty-three-year-old right-hander with the unorthodox delivery—he was a submarine-style pitcher whose knuckles nearly scraped the ground—went 6-5 with a league-leading seven saves. Over the next three seasons, he went 18-13, 22-9, and 21-13 for Boston. But his career took an abrupt turn in 1919.

Red Sox owner Harry Frazee had made a habit of sending talented players to the Yankees when he needed money to bail out other business ventures. Babe Ruth, Duffy Lewis, Ernie Shore, and Dutch Leonard had all been sent by Frazee to the cash-rich Yankees. (Later Wally Schang, Waite Hoyt, Red Ruffing, and even general manager Ed Barrow made the trip.)

The loss of so many talented players had turned the Red Sox from contenders into also-rans. And it didn't do much for Mays' disposition, which was prickly in even the best of times. Throughout his career Mays was notorious for not getting along with teammates, both in the minors and with Boston and in New York. "He was sulky. He was not congenial," said one anonymous teammate, quoted in Mike Sowell's fine 1989 book *The Pitch That Killed*. "You would ask him a question and he would brush you off. I was never on a club that a fellow was disliked as much as Mays."

His mood was particularly sour in 1919. He engaged in a preseason salary dispute with the Red Sox. Late in the spring, his home and virtually all his possessions were lost in a fire. And once the season started, his troubles continued on the field. During a Memorial Day game in Philadelphia, he threw a ball into the stands in response to hecklers. He hit a fan, who later swore out a warrant. Mays avoided the police and was later fined by the league (a fine team management reluctantly paid). During Mays's eight starts in June the Red Sox scored just seven runs. He further endeared himself to his teammates by accusing some of them of laying down when he was pitching.

Everything came to a head on July 13, 1919, in Chicago. Mays left the Red Sox's game against the White Sox after two innings, having surrendered four runs and five hits. He had also been hit in the head by a throw from his catcher, Schang, who was trying to nail a White Sox runner at second. The Red Sox's front-office incompetence, what he viewed as a lack of support from his teammates, and his own 5-11 record were too much for the volatile Mays. He left the dugout—one report stated he was in tears in the clubhouse—went to the team's hotel, checked out and returned to Boston. The next day he contacted Red Sox General Manager Barrow and told him he was quitting baseball.

Before the end of the month, Mays was sent to the Yankees for $40,000 and two sub-.500 pitchers. AL President Ban Johnson and several other owners objected to the deal. Johnson believed Mays should have been suspended for insubordination; other ball clubs didn't want to see the Yankees add yet another talented player. The dispute dragged on for two weeks before the American League board overruled Johnson and reinstated Mays—as a Yankee. That afternoon he made his debut with New York, going nine innings against Detroit and failing to get a decision (he was ejected by umpire Brick Owens for throwing his bat after objecting to a called third strike in the tenth inning).

Mays finished out the season with a 9-3 record and 1.65 ERA. The Yankees ran third behind Chicago and Cleveland.

In 1920 Mays continued to be one of the most successful pitchers in the league. But then on August 16 Mays threw a pitch in the fifth inning of a game against the first-place Indians that would haunt him for the rest of his career. The batter was Ray Chapman, one of the most popular players in the AL. A nine-year veteran with a .278 lifetime average, he was handsome, had a beautiful wife, and entertained teammates with his wonderful singing voice. Mays's first pitch to Chapman was a strike, the second a ball. Chapman, who liked to crowd the plate, edged even closer as Mays delivered the 1-1 pitch. Some witnesses said the pitch moved up and in on Chapman. Others said he

leaned over the plate and into the path of the pitch, a badly scuffed, dirty ball that would have been difficult to pick up. Still others said he froze. Years later, Mays told Jack Murphy of the *San Diego Union*,

> Chapman was the fastest baserunner in the league, he could fly. He liked to push the ball toward second or down the first-base line and run. I had to guard against this, of course.
>
> I knew that Chapman had to shift his feet in order to get into position to push the ball. I saw him doing this . . . and I threw my fastball high and tight so he would pop up.
>
> Chapman ran into the ball. If he had stayed in the batter's box, it would have missed him by a foot.

The ball hit Chapman on the side of the head with a resounding pop. Mays, thinking the ball had hit Chapman's bat, fielded it to throw to first. Chapman crumpled to the ground. After being given first aid in the

> "Carl Mays wasn't very popular, but when nobody else could win, Carl could. He was a great stopper."
>
> —FORMER TEAMMATE DUFFY LEWIS

field, he was taken to a hospital, where he underwent surgery. He never regained consciousness.

When Mays, who had secluded himself in a hotel room, learned of Chapman's death, he went to the district attorney's office, where he tearfully gave a statement, explaining the accident. Assistant District Attorney John Joyce ruled the beaning an accident and told Mays he would not be charged.

Others weren't as forgiving. Detroit and Boston players called for Mays to be expelled from baseball (Tiger shortstop Donie Bush offered to play the rest of the season for the Indians if the league would ban Mays from playing). The Senators and Browns threatened to strike if Mays was not punished.

# Game of Glory • September 25, 1921

In front of an estimated 40,000 hometown fans, Mays and his Yankee teammates defeat second-place Cleveland 21-7 on September 25 to retain a one-game lead in the AL race. It is his twenty-sixth win of the year—tops in the majors.

| CLEVELAND | AB | R | H | | NEW YORK | AB | R | H |
|---|---|---|---|---|---|---|---|---|
| Jamieson, lf-cf | 5 | 0 | 3 | | Miller, cf | 5 | 1 | 2 |
| Wambsganss, 2b | 5 | 0 | 0 | | Peckinpaugh, ss | 6 | 2 | 3 |
| Speaker, cf | 3 | 0 | 0 | | Ruth, lf | 3 | 1 | 1 |
| Johnston, 1b | 2 | 1 | 1 | | Fewster, lf | 1 | 2 | 1 |
| Smith, rf | 4 | 2 | 1 | | Meusel, rf | 6 | 3 | 3 |
| Gardner, 3b | 2 | 1 | 2 | | Pipp, 1b | 5 | 2 | 3 |
| Stephenson, 3b | 2 | 1 | 1 | | Ward, 2b | 6 | 2 | 2 |
| Sewell, ss | 4 | 0 | 1 | | McNally, 3b | 4 | 3 | 1 |
| Burns, 1b | 3 | 1 | 1 | | Schang, c | 3 | 2 | 1 |
| Clark, p | 2 | 0 | 0 | | DeVormer, c | 0 | 1 | 0 |
| O'Neill, c | 2 | 1 | 1 | | Mays, p | 5 | 2 | 3 |
| Shinault, c | 2 | 0 | 1 | | | | | |
| Caldwell, p | 0 | 0 | 0 | | | | | |
| Mails, p | 1 | 0 | 0 | | | | | |
| Graney, lf | 3 | 0 | 1 | | | | | |
| **Totals** | **40** | **7** | **13** | | **Totals** | **44** | **21** | **20** |

| | | | | | | | | |
|---|---|---|---|---|---|---|---|---|
| Cleveland | 0 0 0 | 4 1 0 | 0 0 2 — 7 | | | | | |
| New York | 0 5 2 | 8 0 3 | 1 2 * — 21 | | | | | |

Doubles—McNally, Mays, Jamieson (2). Triples—Meusel, Miller. Home runs—Meusel, Fewster. Stolen bases—Ward, DeVormer.

| CLEVELAND | IP | H | BB | K |
|---|---|---|---|---|
| Caldwell (L) | 1.1 | 5 | 1 | 1 |
| Mails | 2.2 | 9 | 4 | 2 |
| Clark | 4 | 6 | 3 | 0 |

| NEW YORK | IP | H | BB | K |
|---|---|---|---|---|
| Mays (W) | 9 | 13 | 5 | 3 |

Time—2:17. Attendance—15,000 (est.)

Cleveland manager Tris Speaker, though, announced that he would not hold Mays responsible.

Typically, Mays refused to look back. "I fooled [my critics]," he told sportswriter Murphy. "I went out and pitched the rest of the year. Why should I let it ruin the rest of my life? I had a wife and two children and they had to eat. I had to make a living. I had to provide for them."

Mays finished the season with a 26-11 record and a 3.06 ERA. The Yankees finished third, three games behind the Indians, who used Chapman's death as a rallying point on their way to the AL pennant and a World Series victory over Brooklyn.

A lesser competitor might have let the Chapman tragedy affect him. Not Mays. As good as he was in 1920, he was even better in 1921.

In the first game of the season, on April 13, Mays pitched a complete-game three-hitter, helping the Yankees defeat Philadelphia 11-1. Four days later he allowed his old Boston teammates only four hits, and on April 21 the Yankees beat the A's 6-1—bringing Mays's record to 3-0—thanks, in part, to a 4-for-4 day by Ruth, who by that point was 9 for 12 in support of Mays.

Mays' and the Yankees' luck ran out at the end of April. Committing seven errors, the Yankees lost to Washington 5-3, even though Mays allowed only four hits. And they lost to the Red Sox 2-1 despite the fact that Mays allowed just five hits.

With the Yankees struggling through April and early May—they hovered around .500 and were mired in the second division—Yankee manager Miller Huggins began using his ace in relief as well. On May 7, a day after he beat Washington to bring his record to 4-2, Mays worked an inning of relief against the Senators. He didn't miss his next regularly scheduled start,

*Carl Mays*

a 2-1, five-hit win over Detroit on May 10. He then pitched in relief on May 12 and May 13 in two more wins over the Tigers.

By the middle of the month, the Yankees were in second place and heading to Cleveland—their first visit to Cleveland since Chapman's death—for a three-game series with the first-place Indians. The Yankees won the opener 6-4 thanks to Ruth's three-run homer in the eighth and then moved into first place the next afternoon with an 8-2 rout of the Indians. The following day, Mays scattered nine hits, striking out three, in a 6-3 victory that brought his record to 6-2. The reaction from the stands during this game, as reported by *The New York*

# Comin' At You

Carl Mays had a reputation as a pitcher who liked to throw at opposing batters. He hit 89 men in his fifteen-year career (an average of .265 batters per 9 innings), not even in the top ten. Mays was, however, the only pitcher to kill a batter in the majors. Below is a list of the ten pitchers who hit the most batsmen:

| Pitcher | Hit Batsmen | Innings Pitched | Hit Batsmen per 9 Innings |
|---|---|---|---|
| Chick Fraser | 215 | 3,356 | 0.6 |
| Walter Johnson | 206 | 5,924 | 0.3 |
| Eddie Plank | 188 | 4,505 | 0.4 |
| Joe McGinnity | 184 | 3,441 | 0.5 |
| Jim Bunning | 160 | 3,759 | 0.4 |
| Don Drysdale | 154 | 3,432 | 0.4 |
| Howard Ehmke | 137 | 2,821 | 0.5 |
| Hooks Dauss | 121 | 3,391 | 0.4 |
| Jack Warhop | 114 | 1,424 | 0.8 |
| George Uhle | 113 | 3,120 | 0.4 |

*Times*, was almost as extraordinary as Mays' performance.

"The Cleveland fans showed their real sportsmanship when Mays went to bat for the first time in the second inning. He was greeted with applause that must have warmed the cockles of his heart. . . . There was not the least sign of ill-feeling."

Mays was 8-3 by the end of May, but the Yankees had fallen back into second place, behind the Indians. He lost a game on June 1 against the Senators, giving up five runs in the ninth, and then began a phenomenal six-week winning streak that would temporarily put the Yankees in first place.

He won six decisions in a row, improving his record to 14-4, and nailed down two other victories with strong relief appearances. His first loss in more than a month came on July 21, when the Indians shelled him in the third inning of a 17-8 rout that put Cleveland back into first place.

The Indians and Yankees stayed neck and neck through the rest of July and August. September began with the teams in a virtual dead heat, the Indians leading by .001. Mays won his first four decisions that month, im-proving his record to 24-8 and helping the Yankees move into first place by a half game after a double-header sweep of St. Louis on September 16.

In the final week of September, the Yankees and the Indians—who were only percentage points behind—played a five-game series in New York to determine the AL pennant. The Yankees won the opener 4-2 (assisted by Ruth, who went 3-for-3), but Cleveland won Game 2 to put the teams in a virtual tie again. Mays then took control of matters, earning his twenty-sixth win in the third game, a 21-7 rout, and working 1⅓ innings of shutout relief for the save—his seventh, best in the AL—in the fourth game, an 8-7 Yankee victory. New York finally won the AL pennant—setting the stage for the Yankees' first ever World Series—on October 1, and again Mays was the hero, beating the Red Sox 5-3.

At the end of his greatest season, Mays led the AL or shared the league lead in victories (27), winning percentage (.750), games (49), innings pitched (336), and saves (7). In addition, he had 49 hits—the most ever by a major-league pitcher in a single season—and batted .343 (he was also one of the best-fielding pitchers in the game). Yet the season would end in controversy for Mays because of his performance in the World Series against John McGraw's Giants.

In the Series opener on October 5, he pitched a nearly flawless game. He allowed five hits, four of them singles by Frankie Frisch, and didn't walk a batter as the Yankees took Game 1 by a score of 3-0. The teams split the next two games, putting Mays back on the mound on October 9 for Game 4. He went into the eighth coasting with a two-hitter and protecting a 1-0 lead. But the Giants bunched four quick hits to take a 3-1 lead, then added another run in the ninth, holding on for a 4-2 victory.

Again, the teams split the next two games, leaving the best-of-nine Series tied 3-3. And again, Huggins called on his ace for Game 7 on October 12. Once more, though, Mays failed. He surrendered single runs in the fourth and seventh—both Giant rallies aided by misplays by second baseman Aaron Ward—and lost 2-1. The Giants wrapped up the Series the next day with a 1-0 victory—a four-hitter by Art Nehf.

The controversy began when rumors started circulating that Mays had thrown Game 4—sportswriter Fred Lieb brought a man to Commissioner Kenesaw Mountain Landis who related the story of the supposed fix. The accusations seemed credible because Mays had defied Huggins and inexplicably served a fat changeup to the Giants' Irish Meusel that he rapped for a triple that turned Game 4 around. Nothing, though, was ever proved, but the allegations—along with his notoriety from the Chapman tragedy—shadowed Mays for the rest of his life.

"Was he throwing at Chapman that day? I wouldn't like to say," Yankee pitcher Bob Shawkey once said. "I don't know. It never seemed to bother him afterward, though. Nothing bothered him. He wasn't too popular with the boys. Down south in spring training the next year none of the regular players would mix with him. He corraled some of the younger players and told them, 'If you got to knock somebody down to win a ball game, do it. It's your bread and butter.' He says this after killing a man! That's the type he was."

Mays's Yankee career ended after the 1923 season, when Huggins finally had him waived. It may not have been the smartest of moves. In 1924 he went 20-9 for Cincinnati, while the Yankees finished second, just two games behind the Senators. So while Huggins had rid himself of a player he didn't particularly like, he probably cost himself a pennant.

Mays spent five seasons with the Reds before winding up his career in 1929 with McGraw's Giants. He spent the next twenty years as a scout for Milwaukee and Cleveland, and finished out his days living in Oregon and helping his nephew coach a high school baseball team. He died on April 4, 1971, remembered not as the star of the Yankee pitching staff of the early '20s, but as the man whose pitch killed Ray Chapman.

## Baseball News Of 1921

- Chewing gum magnate William Wrigley became the sole owner of the Chicago Cubs.

- Babe Ruth hit his 137th career home run, breaking Roger Connor's record.

- Ty Cobb got his 3,000th career hit on August 19 against Boston.

- Babe Ruth had a monster season: 59 homers, a .378 average, an .846 slugging percentage, 171 runs batted in, 144 walks, and 177 runs. He also pitched two games—and won both.

- Game 1 of the 1921 World Series between the Yankees and Giants was the first to be broadcast on radio.

## Around The World In 1921

- The state of war between Germany and the United States was declared at an end on July 2, and a peace treaty was signed on August 25.

- Popular songs of 1921 included "Blue Moon," "Look for the Silver Lining," and "I Never Knew."

- Postwar America suffered through a financial depression that lasted until early 1922.

- Samuel Gompers was re-elected president of the American Federation of Labor for the fortieth time.

- Armistice Day, November 11, was declared a legal holiday by President Warren Harding on November 5.

- Margaret Gorman, of Washington, D.C., was selected as the first Miss America on September 8.

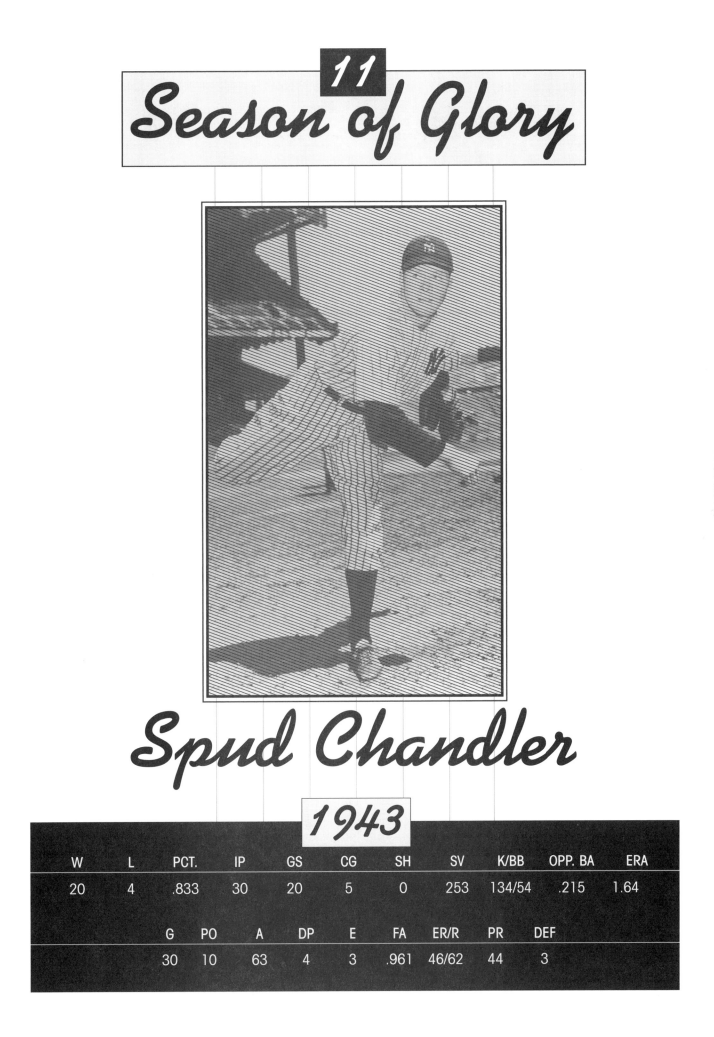

## 11
# Season of Glory

# Spud Chandler

## 1943

| W | L | PCT. | IP | GS | CG | SH | SV | K/BB | OPP. BA | ERA |
|---|---|------|-----|-----|-----|-----|-----|--------|---------|------|
| 20 | 4 | .833 | 30 | 20 | 5 | 0 | 253 | 134/54 | .215 | 1.64 |

| | G | PO | A | DP | E | FA | ER/R | PR | DEF |
|---|-----|-----|-----|-----|-----|------|-------|-----|-----|
| | 30 | 10 | 63 | 4 | 3 | .961 | 46/62 | 44 | 3 |

# Spurgeon Ferdinand Chandler

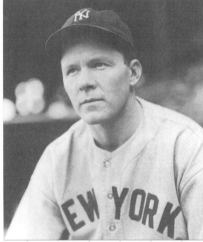

**BORN**
September 12, 1907
Commerce, Georgia

**DIED**
January 9, 1990
South Pasadena, Florida

**HEIGHT**
6-0

**WEIGHT**
181

**THREW**
right hand

**BATTED**
right hand

New York Yankees
1937–1947

**1943**

Dan Daniel, the respected *New York World-Telegram* columnist who covered the New York Yankees for so many years, asked his *Sporting News* readers, "Upon what meat hath this our Chandler fed, that he hath grown so great?" The question followed Spud Chandler's September 11, 1943, shutout victory over Boston, which raised his record to 19-3 and dropped his ERA to 1.71. Chandler went on to finish 20-4 and lead American League pitchers in five categories as the Yankees breezed to the AL pennant and the World Series championship.

To put Chandler's greatest season into perspective, it's instructive to look at the extraordinary events and circumstances of that wartime season. Let's start with something as fundamental as the ball itself. The 1943 version of the official baseball used in the majors was made with substitute rubber cement encasing a reclaimed cork-balata core. The dead-ball era was back. Less than two weeks, just 29 games, into the season, there were enough shutouts (11) and low-hit games to convince baseball's hierarchy that a change was needed. A reconstituted, peppier—though still sluggish—ball was quickly produced.

Wartime travel restrictions also meant fewer trips, hence, more double- headers. There were also many war-benefit games, plus exhibitions against armed services ball clubs. Clearly, wartime baseball was a different game that put a strain on pitching staffs.

That said, Chandler's achievement still stands out more than a half-century later.

Chandler graduated from the University of Georgia, where he participated in baseball, football, and track. The Yankees beat out the Chicago Cubs and St. Louis Cardinals for his services, and he spent 4½ years working his way through the minors before finally coming to the big club in 1937.

He went 7-4 in his rookie season, then was 14-5 in '38. He broke his leg in '39 and saw limited action (he was only 3-0, all in relief) then bounced back to go 34-16 over the next three years, setting the stage for his finest season as a Yankee.

The slider specialist opened and closed the season the same way— with shutouts. On April 24 he threw a one-hitter against Washington, winning 1-0, and he put the finishing touches on the Yankees' World Series victory with a 2-0 win over the Cardinals in Game 5. In between there were 19 other victories, four more shutouts, and nine one-run wins (four of them by 2-1 scores).

# The Wartime Wonders

By 1945, 5,400 of 5,800 professional ballplayers active during the 1941 season were in military service. This listing presents the top ten single-season performances from 1942 to '45 for position players and pitchers. They are ranked according to the rating system used in *Total Baseball*, Total Pitcher Index for the pitchers and Total Player Rating for the position players.

| Player, Team | Best Wartime Year | TPI | Record | Best Postwar Year Record/TPI |
|---|---|---|---|---|
| Dizzy Trout, Detroit | 1943 | 9.1 | 20–12 | 1946: 17–13, 5.6 |
| Hal Newhouser, Detroit | 1944 (MVP) | 7.8 | 29–9 | 1946: 26–9, 7.1 |
| Spud Chandler, NY (AL) | 1943 (MVP) | 5.7 | 20–4 | 1946: 20–8, 4.8 |
| Mort Cooper, St.Louis (NL) | 1942 (MVP) | 5.0 | 22–7 | 1946: 13–11, 0.6 |
| Bucky Walters, Cincinnati | 1944 | 4.7 | 23–8 | 1946: 10–7, 1.6 |
| Jim Tobin, Boston (NL) | 1943 | 4.7 | 14-14 | — |
| Jack Kramer, St.Louis (AL) | 1944 | 4.3 | 17-13 | 1946: 13-11, 1.2 |
| Rip Sewell, Pittsburgh | 1943 | 4.0 | 21-9 | 1948: 13-3, 1.1 |
| Ted Lyons, Chicago (AL) | 1942 | 4.0 | 14-6 | 1946: 1-4, 0.5 |
| Johnny Beazley, St.Louis (NL) | 1942 | 4.0 | 21-6 | 1946: 7-5, -1.2 |

## Position Players

| Player, Team | Best Wartime Year | TPR | Avg./RBI | Best Postwar Year | TPR | Avg./RBI |
|---|---|---|---|---|---|---|
| Ted Wiilliams, Boston (AL) | 1942 | 8.1 | .356/137 | 1946 | 7.9 | .342, 123 |
| Lou Boudreau, Cleveland | 1943 | 7.8 | .286/67 | 1948 | 6.9 | .355, 106 |
| George Stirnweiss, NY (AL) | 1945 | 7.2 | .309/64 | 1949 | 0.0 | .261, 11 |
| Stan Musial, St. Louis (NL) | 1943 (MVP) | 6.4 | .357/81 | 1951 | 6.4 | .355, 108 |
| Luke Appling, Chicago (AL) | 1943 | 6.0 | .328/80 | 1946 | 3.2 | .309, 55 |
| Eddie Lake, Boston (AL) | 1945 | 5.7 | .279/51 | 1948 | 0.2 | .263, 18 |
| Joe Gordon, NY (AL) | 1942 (MVP) | 5.4 | .322/103 | 1947 | 3.1 | .272, 93 |
| Tommy Holmes, Boston (NL) | 1945 | 5.4 | .352/117 | 1946 | 2.1 | .310, 79 |
| Stan Spence, Washington | 1944 | 5.2 | .316/100 | 1946 | 3.3 | .292, 87 |
| Stan Hack, Chicago (NL) | 1945 | 5.2 | .323/43 | 1946 | 1.6 | .285, 26 |

Chandler's ERA for the year was 1.64, tops in the AL. He was also first in wins, complete games (20), shutouts (5), and opponents' on-base percentage (.261). He had winning streaks of four, three, six, and seven games. In addition, his batting average was a respectable .258 and he hit two home runs, both in games he won.

Chandler was, without question, the most talented pitcher on an outstanding Yankee pitching staff, which led the league with a 2.95 ERA. On May 30, for example, he beat Cleveland 4-3—contributing a pair of hits to the attack—as New York took a one-game lead over Washington. On July 7 and 11, he posted back-to-back shutouts, running his record to 10-2. He got his fifteenth victory, against only three losses, on August 13, when he beat the Browns 4-0 in St. Louis. And on September 25, his twentieth victory—a 2-1 win over Detroit in fourteen innings—clinched the pennant.

# Game of Glory • October 11, 1943

On October 11, 1943, Chandler shuts out the Cardinals in Game 5 of the World Series, wrapping up another championship for the Yankees.

| NEW YORK | AB | R | H | PO | A | ST. LOUIS | AB | R | H | PO | A |
|---|---|---|---|---|---|---|---|---|---|---|---|
| Crosetti, ss | 4 | 0 | 1 | 0 | 5 | Klein, 2b | 5 | 0 | 1 | 3 | 1 |
| Metheny, rf | 5 | 0 | 1 | 1 | 0 | Garms, lf | 4 | 0 | 0 | 1 | 0 |
| Lindell, rf | 0 | 0 | 0 | 0 | 0 | Musial, rf | 3 | 0 | 0 | 1 | 0 |
| W. Johnson, 3b | 4 | 0 | 1 | 1 | 2 | W. Cooper, c | 2 | 0 | 1 | 6 | 0 |
| Keller, lf | 3 | 1 | 1 | 1 | 1 | O'Dea, c | 2 | 0 | 2 | 2 | 0 |
| Dickey, c | 4 | 1 | 1 | 7 | 0 | Kurowski, 3b | 4 | 0 | 2 | 3 | 3 |
| Etten, 1b | 3 | 0 | 1 | 11 | 1 | Sanders, 1b | 3 | 0 | 1 | 7 | 2 |
| Gordon, 2b | 2 | 0 | 0 | 6 | 6 | Hopp, cf | 4 | 0 | 0 | 1 | 0 |
| Stainback, cf | 3 | 0 | 1 | 0 | 0 | Marion, ss | 3 | 0 | 1 | 2 | 3 |
| Chandler, p | 3 | 0 | 0 | 0 | 2 | M. Cooper, p | 2 | 0 | 0 | 0 | 1 |
| | | | | | | Walker, ph | 1 | 0 | 1 | 0 | 0 |
| | | | | | | Lanier, p | 0 | 0 | 0 | 0 | 1 |
| | | | | | | Dickson, p | 0 | 0 | 0 | 1 | 0 |
| | | | | | | Litwhiler, ph | 1 | 0 | 1 | 0 | 0 |
| Totals | 31 | 2 | 7 | 27 | 17 | Totals | 34 | 0 | 10 | 27 | 11 |

| | | | | | | | | |
|---|---|---|---|---|---|---|---|---|
| New York | 0 0 0 | 0 0 2 | 0 0 0 | — 2 | 7 | 1 |
| St. Louis | 0 0 0 | 0 0 0 | 0 0 0 | — 0 | 10 | 1 |

Sacrifices—Marion, Garms, Stainback, Chandler. Home run—Dickey.
Runs batted in—Dickey (2). Double plays—New York 1, St. Louis 1.
Winning pitcher—Chandler. Losing pitcher—M. Cooper.
Strikeouts: Chandler 7, M. Cooper 6, Lanier 2.
Bases on balls—Chandler 2, M. Cooper 2, Lanier 2, Dickson 1.

Time—2:24. Attendance—33,872.

1943

The 1943 World Series, which pitted the Yankees against the Cardinals, gave Chandler another opportunity to display his skills. He won the opener—a complete-game seven-hitter—4-2. The Cardinals bounced back to take Game 2, but the Yankees won Games 3 and 4. Chandler wrapped things up in Game 5 with his ten-hit shutout, winning 2-0 with the help of Bill Dickey's two-run homer in the sixth. "I didn't have too good a stuff in that fifth game but I guess I was lucky," he once said. "I had what I call just average pitching. My control was a little shaky. My arm had gotten tired. I was just lucky to win 2-0."

Not surprisingly, Chandler won the postseason awards by a landslide. The Baseball Writers Association of America and *The Sporting News* named him AL MVP, and *The Sporting News* chose him Player of the Year.

Chandler played in only one game the next season before going into the service. He returned to the Yankees after the war, going

*Spud Chandler has the highest all-time winning percentage for pitchers with more than 100 victories.*

2-1 in 1945 and 20-8 with a 2.10 ERA in 1946. He was 9-5 with a 2.46 ERA in 1947, but that was the end of the road. Arm troubles had bothered him all season, and in the spring of '48, he called it quits at the age of forty.

It would be a mistake to attribute Chandler's spectacular 1943 season to the fact that he was facing wartime competition. His 109-43 career record is the highest winning percentage (.717) of any 100-game winner in major-league history. He had an impressive 2.84 career ERA and was a four-time AL All-Star, and when he retired he was in the top ten on the Yankees' all-time pitching list in winning percentage, shutouts, ERA, and complete games. War or no war, Spud Chandler was one of the game's best.

## Baseball News Of 1943

- The National Father's Day Commission voted Mel Ott of the Giants No. 1 Father of the Year.
- Cardinals pitcher Mort Cooper threw back-to-back one-hitters against Brooklyn and Philadelphia.
- Manager Joe Cronin pinch-hit 42 times for his Red Sox, getting 18 hits and an AL record five home runs.
- Carl Hubbell's 3-2 victory over the Pirates was the last of his career.
- Schoolboy Rowe of the Phillies hit a grand slam, becoming the first pitcher to hit one in both leagues.
- The Philadelphia A's lost twenty in a row.

## Around The World In 1943

- President Roosevelt dedicated the Jefferson Memorial.
- Race riots brought Detroit to a standstill.
- At the peak of the U.S. war effort, two million American women were employed.
- *Oklahoma!* opened on Broadway.
- U.S. Marines recaptured Guadalcanal.
- Gen. George Patton's troops stormed Sicily.

# 12

# Season of Glory

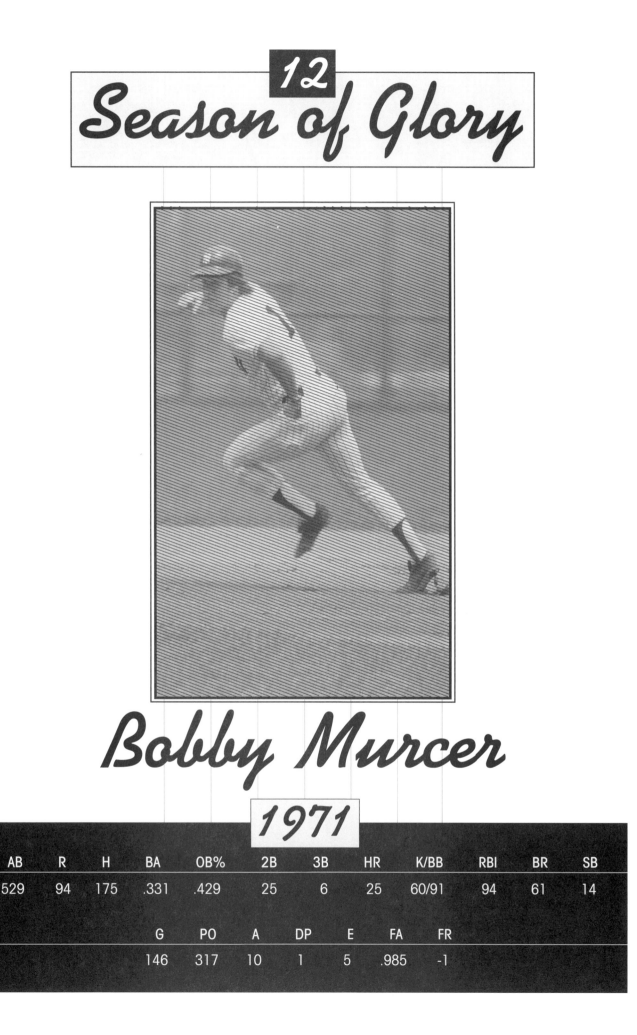

## Bobby Murcer

### 1971

| AB | R | H | BA | OB% | 2B | 3B | HR | K/BB | RBI | BR | SB |
|-----|----|-----|------|------|----|----|----|-------|-----|----|----|
| 529 | 94 | 175 | .331 | .429 | 25 | 6 | 25 | 60/91 | 94 | 61 | 14 |

| | | G | PO | A | DP | E | FA | FR | | | |
|--|--|-----|-----|----|----|---|------|----|--|--|--|
| | | 146 | 317 | 10 | 1 | 5 | .985 | -1 | | | |

# Bobby Ray Murcer

BORN
May 20, 1946
Oklahoma City, Oklahoma

HEIGHT
5-11

WEIGHT
180

THREW
right hand

BATTED
left hand

New York Yankees
1965–1974
1979–1983

*1971*

For more than four decades, the New York Yankees always had one player who epitomized their greatness. The line began with Ruth. Ruth begat Gehrig, Gehrig begat DiMaggio, DiMaggio begat Mantle. It was more than a great Yankee tradition; it was a great baseball tradition.

But on March 1, 1969, at the Yankees' spring training site in Florida, Mantle announced his retirement. And for the first time in a half-century, there was no one to step in as "The Man." In their search for someone to continue the line of succession, the media and fans focused on a twenty-two-year-old infielder, Bobby Murcer.

Bobby Ray Murcer was born on May 20, 1946, in Oklahoma City. He signed with the Yankees after he graduated from high school in 1964, and after two successful seasons in the Yankee farm system was a September recall in 1965, hitting .243 in 11 games. He was back in the minors in '66, but was called up again by the Yanks later that year and hit .174 in 21 games. Murcer spent the next two seasons in the army; when he got out and returned to the Yankees, he was twenty-three and had filled out to 5 foot-11 inches and 180 pounds.

Mantle's departure threw an unwelcome spotlight on the young infielder. But as unfair as it was, it was easy for people to make comparisons. Both were from Oklahoma; both first came to the Yankees as nineteen-year-old shortstops; both were signed by legendary Yankee scout Tom Greenwade; both could hit—and hit with power; and both could run.

Murcer created more buzz with his magnificent performance that spring. He hit .380 at training camp, then opened the season on a rampage: a homer and three RBIs in the opener, a .393 average through the first week of the season, and five homers in his first nine games. The press jumped all over it. Here was a worthy successor to Mantle and the rest.

But as even Murcer would have been the first to admit, he was no Mickey Mantle, offensively or defensively. He tailed off (only two homers in June and July as his average fell 40 points) and finished hitting .259; after a shaky start as the Yankees' third baseman (14 errors in 31 games), he was moved to right field.

Still, his final figures—146 hits, 82 runs, 26 homers, and 82 RBIs—were wonderful for a first-year regular. And they did nothing to lessen the pressure in 1970, when manager Ralph Houk moved him to center field, the old stomping grounds of Mantle and DiMaggio. But the real experts, the guys who had been there, cautioned about the burden Murcer was facing. "If he hits .300," DiMaggio commented, "there'll be guys who expect him to hit .350. If he hits .350, some people will say he could hit .400."

"If I didn't get to a fly ball, someone would invariably say that Joe would have caught it," Mantle said. "Or if I made a bad throw in a key situation, they'd say DiMag would have cut the runner down."

Much to his credit, though, Murcer withstood the pressure. He had another decent year in 1970 (.251, 23 homers, and 78 RBIs), but he still wasn't meeting anyone's expectations, including his own. "I really wasn't satisfied with my first two years in the majors," Murcer later said. "Maybe I wasn't another Mantle or DiMaggio, but I was certainly better than I had shown."

In 1971 Murcer decided to change his strategy. He knew he wasn't capable of hitting forty or fifty home runs in a season like other greats, and he realized that when he swung for the fences he was only striking out more and hitting for a lower average. So he decided to concentrate on just meeting the ball, hitting for average and getting on base. His strategy would work: 1971 would be Murcer's greatest season.

Bobby Murcer the contact hitter got off to another strong start in '71. He was 9-for-28 (.321) through the first week of the season, with no homers (he hit his first home run of the season in the Yankees' ninth game). By early May he was at .359, with just three homers. "I guess it took me a while to get smart," he later said. "There are certainly many things a ballplayer can do offensively besides hitting homers."

And Murcer was doing them: he poked a single through a drawn-in infield to give the Yankees a 2-1 victory in eleven innings against Chicago on May 8; he had two hits and a pair of RBIs to help beat Milwaukee 4-3 five days later; he had two more singles and two more runs batted in on May 21 in Cleveland; he scored from third on an infield grounder on May 25 against Detroit; and his three hits, two RBIs, and stolen base helped beat California on May 30. By the end of May Murcer had a batting average of .353 and was on a pace to get more than 230 hits and 100 RBIs.

His bat stayed hot through the first week of June. He went 11-for-28 (.393), hit three homers, and raised his average to .361. A hand injury suffered on June 9 in a collision with California pitcher Andy Messersmith slowed him through much of the rest of the month. Nevertheless, Murcer ended June with a .341 average.

The Yankees, on the other hand, weren't doing nearly as well. By June 30 they were in fifth place in the AL East, thirteen games behind Baltimore and all but out of the race.

> "He's one of the most class individuals I've been associated with."
>
> — GEORGE STEINBRENNER

Fortunately, July was a better month for both Murcer and the Yankees. He hit .429 during the first week of July to raise his average to almost .350. He played in the All-Star Game (this was the first of his five consecutive All-Star appearances), contributing a single to the AL's 6-4 victory.

Meanwhile, the Yankees won 13 of 17 games during one stretch, and on July 25, the team swept a double-header against Milwaukee to reach .500 for the first time since May 1. The hero of the day was Murcer. He had an RBI sacrifice fly in the first game and a pinch grand slam in the second. Still, the Yankees were only 53-55 when July ended, and hovered around the .500 mark for the rest of the season (they would finish fourth, 82-80).

Murcer continued playing well in August, entering the month with a .331 average and was at .321 when September began. And although Murcer was unable to play for more than a week because of a kidney ailment, he ended the season with a flourish, raising his average almost ten points in the last two

# Game of Glory • July 7, 1971

On July 7, the day after Murcer was passed over in the naming of the AL All-Star team, he gets four hits, three of them doubles. He gets the third double in the 11th and helps the Yankees beat Detroit.

| NEW YORK | AB | R | H | RBI | | DETROIT | AB | R | H | RBI |
|---|---|---|---|---|---|---|---|---|---|---|
| Clarke, 2b | 6 | 1 | 3 | 0 | | Rodriguez, 3b | 5 | 0 | 0 | 0 |
| Munson, c | 5 | 2 | 2 | 0 | | Taylor, 2b | 4 | 0 | 0 | 0 |
| Murcer, cf | 5 | 1 | 4 | 3 | | Kaline, rf | 5 | 0 | 1 | 0 |
| White, lf | 4 | 1 | 1 | 0 | | Horton, lf | 3 | 1 | 0 | 0 |
| Alou, 1b | 5 | 0 | 1 | 0 | | Freehan, c | 3 | 2 | 2 | 3 |
| Swoboda, rf | 0 | 0 | 0 | 0 | | Cash, 1b | 5 | 0 | 2 | 0 |
| Blomberg, rf | 5 | 0 | 0 | 1 | | Stanley, cf | 4 | 0 | 1 | 0 |
| Michael, ss | 5 | 0 | 2 | 1 | | Brinkman, ss | 4 | 0 | 0 | 0 |
| Kenney, 3b | 5 | 0 | 1 | 0 | | Kilkenny, p | 0 | 0 | 0 | 0 |
| Peterson, p | 3 | 0 | 0 | 0 | | Chance, p | 1 | 0 | 0 | 0 |
| Kekich, p | 2 | 0 | 1 | 0 | | Gutierrez, ph | 1 | 0 | 0 | 0 |
| | | | | | | Timmerman, p | 0 | 0 | 0 | 0 |
| | | | | | | Brown, ph | 1 | 0 | 0 | 0 |
| | | | | | | Scherman, p | 1 | 0 | 0 | 0 |
| | | | | | | Deheny, p | 0 | 0 | 0 | 0 |
| | | | | | | Niekro, p | 0 | 0 | 0 | 0 |
| | | | | | | Jones, ph | 1 | 0 | 0 | 0 |
| **Totals** | **45** | **5** | **15** | **5** | | **Totals** | **38** | **3** | **6** | **3** |

| | | | | | | | | |
|---|---|---|---|---|---|---|---|---|
| New York | 3 0 0 | 0 0 0 | 0 0 0 | 0 2 — 5 |
| Detroit | 0 1 0 | 0 0 0 | 2 0 0 | 0 0 — 3 |

Double plays—New York 1, Detroit 1. Left on base—New York 11, Detroit 9.
Doubles—Murcer 3, Clarke. Home runs—Freehan 2. Stolen base—Murcer.

| NEW YORK | IP | H | R | ER | BB | K |
|---|---|---|---|---|---|---|
| Peterson | 6 | 3 | 3 | 3 | 2 | 1 |
| Kekich (W, 2-4) | 5 | 3 | 0 | 0 | 4 | 2 |

| DETROIT | IP | H | R | ER | BB | K |
|---|---|---|---|---|---|---|
| Kilkenny | .1 | 3 | 3 | 3 | 1 | 0 |
| Chance | 4.2 | 5 | 0 | 0 | 1 | 2 |
| Timmerman | 2 | 0 | 0 | 0 | 0 | 1 |
| Scherman | 2 | 5 | 0 | 0 | 1 | 1 |
| Deheny (L, 0-2) | 1.2 | 2 | 2 | 2 | 1 | 0 |
| Niekro | .1 | 0 | 0 | 0 | 0 | 0 |

Hit by pitch—by Kekich (Freehan).

Time—3:17. Attendance—18,204.

Bobby Murcer

weeks to finish second in the AL at .331, which would be his career high. His final stats put him among the league leaders in almost every offensive category: his .429 on-base percentage was best in the league; his .543 slugging percentage was second; his 94 runs scored tied him for second; his 287 total bases placed him third; and his 94 RBIs tied him for fourth, as did his 91 walks and 175 hits.

Nevertheless, Murcer was traded after the 1974 season to San Francisco for Bobby Bonds—"the next Mantle for the next Mays," one paper called it—as the Yankees decided they needed a right-handed-hitting slugger. Murcer spent two years with the Giants, then 2½ years with the Cubs, and his last 4½ years with the Yankees before retiring during the 1983 season, his spot on the Yankee roster taken by a young infielder named Don Mattingly. The torch had been passed again.

## Baseball News Of 1971

- Batting helmets became mandatory.

- Boston's Carl Yastrzemski became the highest-paid player in history when he signed a three-year, $500,000 contract on February 17.

- Atlanta rookie infielder Leo Foster made a memorable major-league debut on July 9: He made an error on the first ball hit to him, hit into a double play in his first at-bat, and later hit into a triple play. Foster lasted five years in the majors, hitting .198.

- On June 19 the U.S. Supreme Court upheld the dismissal of Curt Flood's antitrust suit against baseball.

## Around The World In 1971

- On February 9 an earthquake in Southern California killed sixty-five people, including forty-seven at a VA hospital, and caused more than a half-billion dollars in damage.

- The U.S. Capitol was bombed on March 1 by radicals protesting the U.S. role in Vietnam.

- The U.S. voting age was lowered to eighteen.

- A riot at the state prison at Attica, New York, left forty-three people, including nine prison guards, dead after authorities launched an assault to retake the prison.

- *Fiddler on the Roof* became the longest-running Broadway musical with its 2,845th performance on July 21.

- The music world lost Louis Armstrong (July 6, age 71), Duane Allman (October 29, age 24), and Jim Morrison (July 3, age 27).

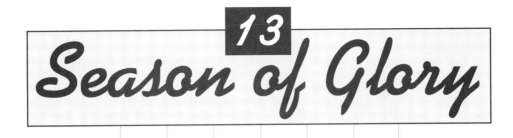

# 13
# Season of Glory

# Joe Gordon

## 1942

| AB | R | H | BA | OB% | 2B | 3B | HR | K/BB | RBI | BR | SB |
|---|---|---|---|---|---|---|---|---|---|---|---|
| 538 | 88 | 173 | .322 | .409 | 29 | 4 | 18 | 95/79 | 103 | 41 | 12 |

| | | | | G | PO | A | DP | E | FA | FR | | |
|---|---|---|---|---|---|---|---|---|---|---|---|---|
| | | | | 147 | 354 | 442 | 121 | 28 | .966 | 4 | | |

# 13

## Joseph Lowell Gordon

BORN
February 18, 1915
Los Angeles, California

DIED
April 14, 1978
Sacramento, California

HEIGHT
5–10

WEIGHT
180

THREW
right hand

BATTED
right hand

New York Yankees
1938–1943
1946

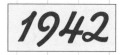

*T*ommy Henrich, the great Yankee outfielder of the 1930s and '40s, was once asked about his old teammate and friend Joe Gordon. Explaining what made Gordon special, Henrich recalled an incident involving manager Joe McCarthy.

"One day McCarthy was talking to some newspaper guys on the bench and he said, 'I'll take Gordon's kind of baseball and I'll show you why.' He called, 'Hey Joe, what are you hitting now?' 'I don't know,' Joe said. 'What's your fielding average,' McCarthy said. 'How the hell would I know?' Joe said. 'See what I mean?' McCarthy said. 'All he does is try to beat you.'"

And there were so many ways he could beat you—with his bat, with his glove, and with his influence on others.

"Gordon is a splendid player to have in the infield," wrote Daniel M. Daniel in *The Sporting News* in 1941. "He likes to be the teacher. He goes out of his way to tell [shortstop Phil] Rizzuto things he should have done. He spends a lot of time setting [first baseman Johnny] Sturm to rights."

Gordon was born in 1915 in Los Angeles and grew up in Portland, Oregon. He attended Southern Cal and later the University of Oregon. At Oregon he not only played shortstop on the baseball team, but also participated in gymnastics, which helps explain his derring-do in the field. ("[Gordon is] the most acrobatic fielder I have ever played with," Rizzuto once said. "The plays he could make off balance, throwing in midair or off one foot or lying down, unbelievable!")

The Yankees signed him out of Oregon and assigned him to their Oakland ball club in the Pacific Coast League for the 1936 season. The next year he was promoted to New York's top farm team, Newark of the International League. There, under orders from McCarthy, the 5-foot-10-inch, 180-pound Gordon was switched from shortstop to second base and groomed to replace Tony Lazzeri.

In less than one season, he made a believer out of Newark manager Oscar Vitt. "Gordon is going to be the greatest second baseman you ever saw," he told reporters one afternoon in New York. "I've seen Lajoie, Collins, Evers, Hornsby, Frisch, Lazzeri, and Gehringer, among others. I don't say this kid is better than them. All I'm saying is that someday he will be. He's better than anybody in the big leagues right now, with the exception of Gehringer, and he'll catch him in a year."

When the 1938 season began, Lazzeri had gone to the Chicago Cubs and Gordon was the Yankees' new second baseman. But Gordon

*Drawing a bead on a Yankee win: (left to right) Gehrig, Gordon, Heinrich, DiMaggio, and Dickey.*

struggled in the early weeks of the campaign and was benched in favor of Bill Knickerbocker. McCarthy gave him another chance in June, and he responded by winning his job back. He went on to a 25-homer, 97-RBI rookie season as the Yankees cruised to the 1938 pennant and a four-game sweep of the Cubs in the World Series. (He was 6-for-15 with six RBIs in the Series.)

By '39 Gordon had become a star—he had 28 homers, 111 RBIs, a .284 average, and an All-Star berth that year (the first of nine in his eleven-year career). He also played solidly in 1940. Gordon batted .276 with 24 homers and 87 RBIs in '41, his weakest season so far with the Yankees.

In 1942 Gordon made some adjustments, eliminating his uppercut, developing a more level swing, and being more selective at the plate. The changes worked. Through the first 12 games of the season—nine of them Yankee victories—Gordon hit .469 (22-for-47).

"I know I can't hit to right," the right-handed-hitting Gordon told *The Sporting News* after a week of the season, ". . . [but] I do know I should be a better hitter than my average for the past indicates. I'm picking my pitches better and not letting them sucker

> "Gordon can play anything, including the violin."
>
> —MANAGER JOE MCCARTHY

me with the high, fast one. But this is too early to be talking about averages . . . Just let me work at this thing a while."

Gordon was sidelined on April 29, when he hurt his back in a 3-1 loss to lowly St. Louis. The injury forced him to miss three games and ended his modest streak of 471

# Game of Glory • July 13, 1942

Gordon makes four of the Yankees' six hits and drives in a pair of runs in a 4-3 victory over Detroit on July 13.

| DETROIT | AB | R | H | RBI | | NEW YORK | AB | R | H | RBI |
|---|---|---|---|---|---|---|---|---|---|---|
| Hitchcock, ss | 5 | 0 | 1 | 0 | | Hassett, 1b | 4 | 1 | 0 | 0 |
| McCosky, lf | 3 | 1 | 0 | 1 | | Rolfe, 3b | 4 | 1 | 1 | 2 |
| Cramer, cf | 3 | 0 | 1 | 1 | | Henrich, rf | 3 | 1 | 0 | 0 |
| Higgins, 3b | 2 | 0 | 0 | 0 | | DiMaggio, cf | 4 | 1 | 1 | 0 |
| York, 1b | 4 | 0 | 0 | 0 | | Keller, lf | 3 | 0 | 0 | 0 |
| Ross, rf | 3 | 0 | 0 | 1 | | Gordon, 2b | 4 | 0 | 4 | 2 |
| Bloodworth, 2b | 4 | 0 | 0 | 0 | | Dickey, c | 0 | 0 | 0 | 0 |
| Tebbetts, c | 3 | 1 | 1 | 0 | | Rosar, c | 3 | 0 | 0 | 0 |
| Trout, p | 2 | 0 | 0 | 0 | | Rizzuto, ss | 1 | 0 | 0 | 0 |
| Harris, ph | 1 | 1 | 1 | 0 | | Gomez, p | 4 | 0 | 0 | 0 |
| Gorsica, p | 0 | 0 | 0 | 0 | | | | | | |
| Gehringer, ph | 1 | 0 | 0 | 0 | | | | | | |
| **Totals** | **31** | **3** | **4** | **3** | | **Totals** | **30** | **4** | **6** | **4** |

```
Detroit      1 0 0   0 0 0   2 0 0 — 3
New York     0 1 0   0 3 0   0 0 * — 4
```

Errors—Dickey, Tebbetts, Hitchcock. Doubles—Cramer, Gordon 2.
Home run—Rolfe. Stolen base—Tebbetts. Sacrifice—Rizzuto.
Left on base—New York 9, Detroit 7.

| NEW YORK | IP | H | BB | K |
|---|---|---|---|---|
| Gomez (W) | 9 | 4 | 5 | 7 |

Hit by pitcher—Cramer (by Gomez). Wild pitch—Gomez.

| DETROIT | IP | H | BB | K |
|---|---|---|---|---|
| Trout (L) | 6 | 5 | 5 | 3 |
| Gorsica | 2 | 1 | 1 | 1 |

Time—2:01. Attendance—8,026.

consecutive games, which had begun in 1939. Despite Gordon's injury and other early problems—Cleveland won thirteen straight at one point, pitcher Marius Russo's arm went bad, Joe DiMaggio couldn't find a consistent groove, and Rizzuto and Charlie Keller were both mired in slumps—the Yankees stayed at the top of the standings. After May 6 they remained in first place for the rest of the season.

New York solidified its hold on first dur-ing a mid-May tour through Cleveland, Detroit, St. Louis, and Chicago, winning five of seven games thanks largely to Gordon. After getting just two hits in the first two games of the trip—and hitting numerous long fouls—he made another adjustment. Teammate Red Branch suggested he use a heavier bat, which would slow down his swing and keep him from getting way in front of pitches. So he switched from a 33-ounce, 34-inch bat to a 36-ounce, 36- incher.

The results were dramatic: 12 hits in his next 20 at-bats. He hit .519 on the trip, raising his average to .393, a gain of 43 points. The trip also marked the start of a 29-game hitting streak for Gordon. By the time it ended, on June 14—he was 0-for-4 against Browns righty Johnny Niggeling—he led the AL with a .392 average.

With the Yankees turning another pennant race into a walkover—their lead was in double digits by the end of July, and they were able to clinch on September 14—attention turned to the AL batting race. Gordon's main competition early in the season was Boston's Bobby Doerr, but in early July Gordon slowed down—he was 10-for-43 (.233) over the first two weeks—and was passed by both Doerr and his Red Sox teammate Ted Williams. Doerr soon faded, leaving Gordon and Williams battling for the top spot well into August. "At first I thought I was hitting over my head, and the average would catch up with me," Gordon told reporters. "But I've kept it up over 100 games and figure that after four seasons in the league I've learned something."

On August 6 he had one hit in three at-bats, raising his average to .343. Meanwhile, Williams went hitless in three trips and dropped to second at .341. Gordon, though, had just one hit in his next three games and surrendered the batting lead once again. On August 25 he went 3-for-4, including a two-run homer in the eighth that helped New York win the game, moving past Williams once more. But Gordon had just one hit in his next four games and dropped out of the lead for good. Williams eventually won the AL batting title with a .356 average, while Gordon finished fourth at .322.

The Yankees' opponent in the World Series was St. Louis, which had won the NL pennant by two games. New York, the obvious favorite, won Game 1 by a score of 7-4, making the Yankees look like even more of a sure thing. But the ninth inning of that game may have been the turning point of the Se-

"The Flash"—Joe Gordon

ries. In the bottom of that inning, the Cardinals, who had been shut down for 8⅓ innings by Yankee starter Red Ruffing, rallied for four runs. "I'm sure those four runs we scored will serve as a tonic for my boys," Cardinals manager Billy Southworth predicted before the start of Game 2 the next day. "And I think you'll find us a steadier team."

Southworth couldn't have been more on the money. St. Louis swept the next four games, dethroning the Yankees. The Cardinals' success was due in no small part to their handling of Gordon, who hit a paltry .095

(2-for-21) and struck out seven times in the Series. "All right, boys," he told reporters after Game 5. "Put the horns and whiskers on me; I deserve 'em. I'm the goat all right."

His World Series failure aside, Gordon had a stellar season in 1942. He had 18 homers and 103 RBIs and anchored a defense that led the AL in fielding and double plays. The Baseball Writers Association of America and *The Sporting News* both voted him American League Most Valuable Player.

Gordon's numbers dropped in '43, his last year as the Yankees' regular second baseman. He went into the service in 1944 and '45, and appeared in just 112 games in '46. After that season, in which he hit .210, he was traded to Cleveland for pitcher Allie Reynolds.

The change did Gordon good. He hit .272 with 29 homers in '47, and .280 with 32 homers and 124 RBIs in 1948, leading the Indians to the AL pennant and a World Series victory over Boston. His playing career finally ended in 1950, when he embarked on a managerial career that led him first through the Pacific Coast League and then back to the American League, with stops in Cleveland, Detroit, and Kansas City. He eventually retired to Sacramento, spending his days hunting, fishing, golfing, and selling real estate part time. One morning in early April 1978, he suffered a heart attack. He recovered and was sent home from the hospital, but a few days later, on April 14, he suffered a second, fatal heart attack. He was sixty-three.

## Baseball News Of 1942

- Cleveland's Lou Boudreau, 24, was the youngest manager to begin a season in charge of a team.

- White Sox pitcher Ted Lyons, working only on Sundays, made just twenty appearances—all were complete games. He went 14-6.

- The Phillies and Athletics both finished last in their respective leagues for the third straight season.

- The Boston Braves' Paul Waner got his 3,000th hit, a single against Pittsburgh's Rip Sewell on June 19.

- Branch Rickey resigned as the St. Louis Cardinals' vice president and became president of the Brooklyn Dodgers.

## Around The World In 1942

- The Bataan Death March began on April 10, with American and Philippine prisoners forced to march 85 miles in six days. More than 5,200 Americans and many more Filipinos died along the way.

- The first American jet plane, the XP-59, was tested at Muroc Army Base in California on October 1.

- Wartime gas, sugar, and coffee rationing went into effect in the United States.

- Among the books published that year were *The Moon Is Down* by John Steinbeck, *The Robe* by Lloyd C. Douglas, *Go Down, Moses* by William Faulkner, and *See Here, Private Hargrove* by Marion Hargrove.

- The first sustained nuclear reaction was demonstrated by scientists at the University of Chicago on December 2.

# 14
## Season of Glory

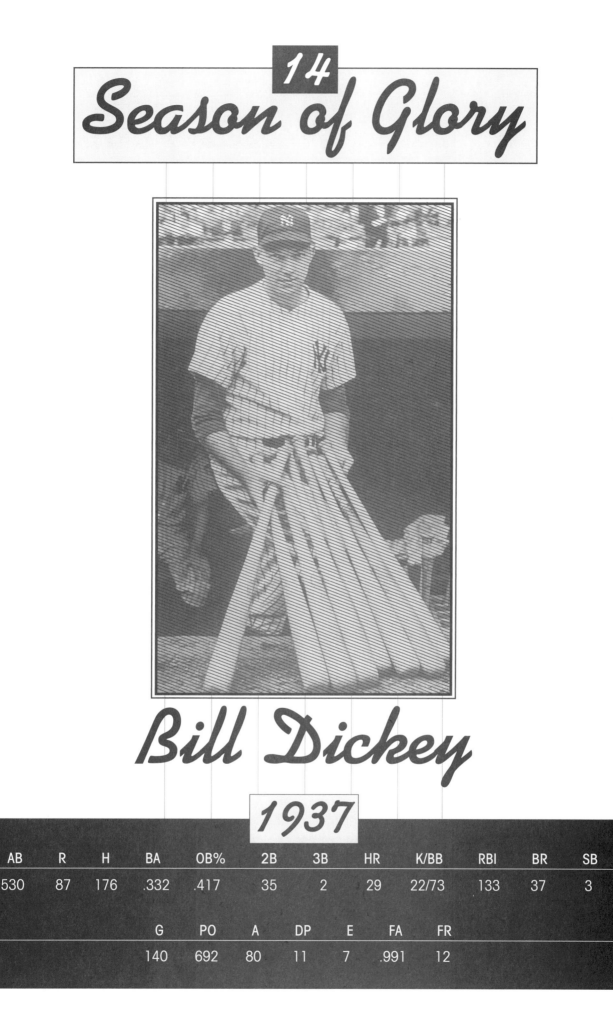

## Bill Dickey

## 1937

| AB | R | H | BA | OB% | 2B | 3B | HR | K/BB | RBI | BR | SB |
|-----|-----|-----|------|------|-----|-----|-----|-------|-----|-----|-----|
| 530 | 87 | 176 | .332 | .417 | 35 | 2 | 29 | 22/73 | 133 | 37 | 3 |

| | | | G | PO | A | DP | E | FA | FR | | |
|---|---|---|-----|-----|-----|-----|-----|------|-----|---|---|
| | | | 140 | 692 | 80 | 11 | 7 | .991 | 12 | | |

# 14

**BORN**
June 6, 1907
Bastrop, Lousiana

**DIED**
November 12, 1993
Little Rock, Arkansas

**HEIGHT**
6-1½

**WEIGHT**
185

**THREW**
right hand

**BATTED**
left hand

New York Yankees
1928–1943
1946

**HALL OF FAME**
1954

1937

# *William Malcom Dickey*

*W*as Bill Dickey the greatest catcher the game has ever known? Connie Mack thought so, as did Ed Barrow and Ty Cobb. He certainly had the stats. He hit over .300 eleven seasons and finished with a .313 lifetime average. He led the AL in fielding four times. One season he didn't allow a passed ball in 125 straight games. He was an eleven-time All-Star and caught more than 100 games for thirteen consecutive seasons, a remarkable figure for a catcher.

But maybe more important than the numbers were the intangibles. Dickey was a legendary leader: He was known for his knowledge of opposing batters and his ability to call a game, he was a quiet yet forceful presence in the clubhouse, and he was a team player who didn't let injuries keep him from the lineup. And to fans, he was the picture of Yankee class.

Dickey began his professional baseball career in the Southern League with Little Rock in 1925. The Yankees invited him to spring training in 1928, but he was optioned to Buffalo of the International League before the season began. He was shipped back to Little Rock later in the year, then the Yankees recalled him in August.

The twenty-one-year-old catcher was an obvious talent to all who saw him, but he needed work. Manager Miller Huggins had him change his hitting style—he had been swinging for the fences; Huggins converted him into a more slashing type of hitter—and Dickey himself spent hours improving his throwing accuracy. The effort paid off—he worked his way into the starting lineup in 1929 and stayed there for thirteen years.

Dickey hit .324 in 1929, .339 in 1930, and .327 in '31, the year he played 125 consecutive games without allowing a passed ball, made just three errors, and had a league-leading fielding percentage of .996. On a team dominated by the likes of Ruth, Gehrig (Dickey's roommate and close friend), Lazzeri, Combs, and other legends, Dickey quietly, dependably did his job, becoming the best catcher and clutch hitter in the game.

After winning the AL pennant by 13 games (and sweeping the Chicago Cubs in the World Series) in 1932, the Yankees hit a dry spell, with second-place finishes the next three seasons. They snapped out of it in a big way in 1936, with five players, including Dickey and rookie Joe DiMaggio, driving in more than 100 runs. That year, they won the pennant by an AL-record 19½ games and beat the Giants in the World Series in six games.

*Hall of Famer Bill Dickey knew what to do with lumber in his hands.*

Bill Dickey

# Game of Glory • June 20, 1937

Dickey's big game in the nightcap of a June 20 double-header against Chicago is the start of a 14-for-24 week.

| CHICAGO | AB | R | H | RBI | | NEW YORK | AB | R | H | RBI |
|---|---|---|---|---|---|---|---|---|---|---|
| Radcliff, lf | 4 | 0 | 0 | 0 | | Crosetti, ss | 4 | 2 | 2 | 0 |
| Kreevich, cf | 5 | 0 | 1 | 0 | | Rolfe, 3b | 5 | 0 | 1 | 1 |
| Walker, rf | 4 | 1 | 1 | 0 | | DiMaggio, cf | 4 | 1 | 1 | 1 |
| Bonura, 1b | 4 | 1 | 1 | 0 | | Gehrig, 1b | 4 | 1 | 3 | 0 |
| Appling, ss | 4 | 1 | 1 | 1 | | Dickey, c | 4 | 1 | 4 | 4 |
| Hayes, 2b | 4 | 1 | 1 | 1 | | Selkirk, rf | 4 | 0 | 0 | 0 |
| Piet, 3b | 4 | 0 | 1 | 0 | | Powell, lf | 3 | 1 | 0 | 0 |
| Rensa, c | 4 | 0 | 3 | 2 | | Heffner, 2b | 4 | 1 | 1 | 1 |
| Whitehead, p | 2 | 0 | 0 | 0 | | Pearson, p | 4 | 0 | 0 | 0 |
| Cain, p | 0 | 0 | 0 | 0 | | Murphy, p | 1 | 0 | 0 | 0 |
| Haas, ph | 1 | 0 | 0 | 0 | | | | | | |
| Dietrich, p | 0 | 0 | 0 | 0 | | | | | | |
| Rosenthal, ph | 1 | 0 | 0 | 0 | | | | | | |
| Totals | 37 | 4 | 9 | 4 | | Totals | 37 | 7 | 12 | 7 |

| | | | | | | | | |
|---|---|---|---|---|---|---|---|---|
| Chicago | 0 0 0 | 0 0 0 | 1 3 0 | — 4 |
| New York | 1 2 0 | 0 2 0 | 2 0 * | — 7 |

Errors—Piet, Crosetti. Doubles—Rensa, Bonura, Hayes.
Triples—Hefner, DiMaggio. Home run—Dickey. Stolen base—Crosetti.
Double plays—Chicago 1, New York 1. Left on base—Chicago 8, New York 7.

| CHICAGO | IP | H | R | ER | BB | K |
|---|---|---|---|---|---|---|
| Whitehead (L) | 6 | 9 | 5 | 5 | 0 | 3 |
| Cain | 1 | 3 | 2 | 2 | 0 | 0 |
| Dietrich | 1 | 0 | 0 | 0 | 1 | 2 |

| NEW YORK | IP | H | R | ER | BB | K |
|---|---|---|---|---|---|---|
| Pearson (W) | 7 | 5 | 0 | 0 | 2 | 0 |
| Murphy | 2 | 4 | 4 | 4 | 1 | 1 |

Hit by pitcher—Crosetti (by Whitehead).

Time: 2:08.

*1937*

Dickey and his teammates got off to a solid, if not spectacular, start in 1937. The Yankees were in and out of first place over the first three weeks of the season, and Dickey's average was just under .300. Then, his numbers began to slip. He tumbled to .229 by June 8, but the slump was only temporary. Over the next 15 games, Dickey hit .474 (27-for-57) with eight homers and 26 runs batted in as the Yankees, who had been tied for first with Detroit on June 8, won 11, lost 3, and tied 1, and took control of the AL pennant race. In six remarkable games between June 20 and 25, Dickey went 14-for-24 with six home runs and 17 RBIs. His average was .300 at the end of

June and .312 at the All-Star break (Dickey contributed two hits and an RBI to the AL's 8-3 victory).

The second half of the season was all New York. The Yankees won their first five games after the break, taking control of the pennant race. In early August second-place Chicago came to New York, five games out of first. The Yankees swept the series, led by Dickey. He was 6-for-14 in the four games, with an eighth-inning grand slam that enabled New York to win the second game 5-3, and a four-RBI afternoon in the third game, which the Yankees won 10-9. "The Yanks had to go into their ninth inning to win [Game 3]," wrote Edward Burns in the *Chicago Tribune*, "which was looked upon as something of a moral triumph." By the time the Sox left town, Dickey was up to .315 with 20 homers and 94 RBIs and the race had all but been conceded.

The Yankees cruised home by 13 games, and Dickey, who had been in the .230s over the first month, finished with a rush—11-for-18 in his last five games—to close at .332. While it was 30 points lower than his 1936 average, he had more hits, doubles, homers, and RBIs in 1937. He also had a spectacular defensive year, so, overall, 1937 was Dickey's finest season.

The Yankees' opponent in the '37 Series was again the New York Giants. This time it took only five games to subdue them. Dickey hit just .211 in the Series, but three of his hits were crucial: In Game 2, which the Yankees won 8-1, he singled during a four-run sixth and added an RBI single an inning later. In Game 3 he had an important RBI triple in a 5-1 victory.

Dickey spent four more seasons as the Yankees' star catcher, then became a part-timer in 1942. The next season he played in just 85 games, batting .351 and hitting the game-winning homer in Game 7 of the World Series. After two years in the service, he returned in 1946, ostensibly as a part-time player. But when manager Joe McCarthy resigned in May, Dickey took the reins. He stepped down in September, ending his illustrious major-league career.

> "I never shake Dickey off. I just let him pitch my games for me."
>
> —Yankee pitcher Ernie Bonham

Two seasons later Dickey returned as a Yankee coach and instructor. Among his best students were Yogi Berra, Elston Howard, and Tim McCarver. "He told me things I'd never heard before," McCarver once recalled. "He never talked about hitting. Once, he gave me a list of ten things a catcher must do. The one that stood out was to be the pitcher's best friend, to stand up to him when you thought he was wrong, and to pat him on the back when he was down."

Dickey, who was voted into the Hall of Fame in 1954, retired from baseball in 1960 and went to work for a securities firm in Little Rock. He retired in 1977 and died on November 12, 1993.

# Baseball News Of 1937

- Detroit's Gee Walker hit for the cycle on April 20 against Cleveland. He was the first player to hit for the cycle on Opening Day.

- The St. Louis Cardinals signed sixteen-year-old Stan Musial to his first professional contract.

- On May 25 Detroit player-manager Mickey Cochrane was beaned by New York's Bump Hadley. He spent more than a week in a coma and was unable to resume his playing career.

- Joe DiMaggio hit the first grand slam of his career on July 5 against Boston.

# Around The World In 1937

- The dirigible *Hindenburg* exploded as it approached its mooring in Lakehurst, New Jersey, on May 6.

- The Golden Gate Bridge was dedicated in San Francisco on May 27.

- The first coast-to-coast radio program was conducted by Herbert Morrison on the morning of the *Hindenburg* disaster.

- The U.S. Supreme Court ruled that a law establishing a minimum wage for women was constitutional.

- Labor unrest spread through the United States; more than 500,000 workers quit their jobs.

# Season of Glory

# Roger Peckinpaugh

## 1919

| AB | R | H | BA | OB% | 2B | 3B | HR | K/BB | RBI | BR | SB |
|----|---|---|-----|------|----|----|----|-------|-----|----|----|
| 453 | 89 | 138 | .305 | .390 | 20 | 2 | 7 | 37/59 | 33 | 10 | 10 |

| | | G | PO | A | DP | E | FA | FR | | | |
|--|--|---|----|---|----|---|-----|-----|--|--|--|
| | | 126 | 271 | 434 | 57 | 43 | .943 | 28 | | | |

# 15

# Roger Peckinpaugh

BORN
February 5, 1891
Wooster, Ohio

DIED
November 17, 1977
Cleveland, Ohio

HEIGHT
5-10½

WEIGHT
165

THREW
right hand

BATTED
right hand

New York Yankees
1913-1921

*1919*

"Murderers' Row": The words conjure up images of Ruth, Gehrig, Lazzeri, Combs, and Meusel in the late '20s. Or Mantle, Maris, Berra, Skowron, and Howard a generation later. But how about Peckinpaugh, Pipp, Baker, Bodie, and Lewis? Those men, members of the 1919 Yankees, were the original Murderers' Row, and they were given the nickname by Robert Ripley, believe it or not. (They also, along with their teammates, started the Yankee longball tradition.)

The team captain of the 1919 ball club was Peckinpaugh, an experienced team leader who, at twenty-eight, was in his prime. Peckinpaugh came to the Yankees in May of 1913 in a trade with Cleveland. The next year, in his first full season, he became the first player in Yankee history to play in every game of a season. And his leadership qualities so impressed owners William Devery and Frank Farrell that they made the twenty-three-year-old shortstop the team's manager for the final fourteen games of the season.

When Miller Huggins became Yankee manager in 1918, one of the first things he did was obtain second baseman Del Pratt from St. Louis. Peckinpaugh and Pratt became the anchor for a strong, smart veteran infield. With Wally Pipp at first and Frank "Home Run" Baker at third, the Yankee infield was formidable—each led the league in at least one defensive category. Still, the keys to the Yankee defense were Peckinpaugh and Pratt, especially the former.

A playing field-manager, Peckinpaugh had the kind of smarts Huggins—the old second baseman—appreciated. Peckinpaugh was skilled at playing opposing hitters and backing up Yankee pitchers according to their strengths and weaknesses. He was rarely out of position, went after anything hit in his direction (he usually got a glove on balls that most other shortstops wouldn't come close to, accounting for his seemingly high number of errors), and had a rifle arm.

Peckinpaugh had always been a defensive star, but in 1919 he took his game to another level when he led the team in hitting (.305), runs scored (89), and walks (59). The capstone of this season was a 29-game hitting streak in June and July that raised his average to over .380. (Not coincidentally, during that period the Yankees climbed past Chicago and Cleveland and into first place.) Peckinpaugh's streak, which stood as the team record until Joe DiMaggio hit in 56 straight games in 1941, began with a 2-for-3 day on June 11, when the Yankees beat Ty Cobb and Detroit 7-0.

# Game of Glory • July 29, 1919

On July 29 Peckinpaugh gets three hits in a somewhat suspicious rout of the White Sox. A week earlier Ed Cicotte had no trouble with the Yankees. In this game he was chased after five innings.

| NEW YORK | AB | H | PO | A | E | CHICAGO | AB | H | PO | A | E |
|---|---|---|---|---|---|---|---|---|---|---|---|
| Peckinpaugh, ss | 4 | 3 | 2 | 7 | 1 | J. Collins, rf, cf | 4 | 0 | 5 | 0 | 1 |
| Pipp, 1b | 5 | 2 | 10 | 0 | 0 | E. Collins, 2b, ss | 2 | 0 | 1 | 3 | 0 |
| Baker, 3b | 5 | 4 | 2 | 2 | 0 | Weaver, ss | 4 | 0 | 0 | 3 | 0 |
| Lewis, lf | 4 | 1 | 1 | 0 | 0 | Jackson, lf,rf | 4 | 1 | 0 | 0 | 0 |
| Pratt, 2b | 5 | 0 | 6 | 3 | 1 | Felsch, cf | 1 | 1 | 0 | 0 | 0 |
| Bodie, cf | 4 | 2 | 3 | 0 | 0 | Leibold, lf | 3 | 0 | 0 | 0 | 0 |
| Fewster, rf | 4 | 2 | 1 | 0 | 0 | Risberg, 1b | 4 | 1 | 10 | 1 | 0 |
| Hannah, c | 2 | 1 | 2 | 0 | 0 | McMullin, 3b | 4 | 0 | 3 | 1 | 0 |
| Ruel, c | 0 | 0 | 0 | 0 | 0 | Schalk, c | 2 | 1 | 1 | 0 | 0 |
| Thormahlen, p | 4 | 1 | 0 | 1 | 0 | Lynn, c | 2 | 1 | 4 | 2 | 0 |
| | | | | | | Cicotte, p | 1 | 1 | 0 | 2 | 0 |
| | | | | | | Danforth, p | 1 | 0 | 0 | 0 | 0 |
| | | | | | | Jenkins, ph | 1 | 0 | 0 | 0 | 0 |
| **Totals** | 37 | 16 | 27 | 13 | 2 | **Totals** | 34 | 6 | 24 | 12 | 1 |

| | | | | | | | | | | |
|---|---|---|---|---|---|---|---|---|---|---|
| Chicago | 0 0 0 | | 0 0 0 | | 0 0 0 | — | 0 | 6 | 1 |
| New York | 2 2 0 | | 4 0 0 | | 2 0 * | — | 10 | 16 | 2 |

Doubles—Peckinpaugh, Baker (2), Lewis, Risberg.
Triples—Bodie, Baker, Pipp. Stolen base—Peckinpaugh.
Double play—New York.
Bases on balls—Thormahlen 2, Cicotte 1, Danforth 1.
Strikeouts—Thormahlen 2, Cicotte 1, Danforth 2.
Winning pitcher—Thormahlen.
Losing pitcher—Cicotte.

1919

Two weeks later, Peckinpaugh had raised his average some 50 points. Then he got down to serious business. Between June 30 and July 6, he hit .442 (19 for 43) to climb to .382. His final hit in the streak, a single off Cleveland's Stan Covaleskie, came on July 9.

The 1919 Yankees were about more than just hitting, however. A fine pitching staff was led by Bob Shawkey (20-11, 2.72 ERA), who won 10 games in a row at one point, and Jack Quinn (15-14, 2.63).

In spite of having a talented team, the Yankees finished the season 7½ games behind the first-place Black Sox of Chicago. The Yankees finished the abbreviated season—it was trimmed to 140 games by owners who incorrectly assumed fans would be slow to return in the first postwar campaign—with an 80-59 record, a 20-game improvement over their record in 1918. And leading the way was Peckinpaugh, who raised his average 74 points and provided season-long leadership.

The Yankees' future looked bright. But no one knew just how bright. Shortly after Christmas 1919, the Yankees and their fans got the biggest gift of all: Babe Ruth, obtained in a deal with Boston. It would mark the beginning of a dynasty unlike any other in sports history.

Peckinpaugh would be part of the show for just two more seasons, however. After hitting .270 in 1920 and .288 in 1921, he was traded to Boston in a blockbuster deal that brought Everett Scott, Joe Bush, and Sam Jones to the Yankees. The Red Sox immediately sent Peckinpaugh to Washington, where he had five good seasons—including his MVP year in 1925—before winding up his career with the White Sox in 1927.

> "The Yankees at that time were what we used to call a joy club. Lots of joy and lots of losing. Nobody thought we could win and most of the time we didn't. But it didn't seem to bother the boys too much. They would start singing songs in the infield right in the middle of a game. There wasn't much managing to do outside of selecting the starting pitcher and hoping we didn't get beat too badly."
>
> —ROGER PECKINPAUGH, QUOTED IN *THE MAN IN THE DUGOUT* BY DONALD HONIG

## Baseball News Of 1919

- Fred Luderus of the Phillies played in his 479th consecutive game, breaking the major-league mark previously set by Eddie Collins. Luderus' streak ended at 533 games.
- White Sox outfielder Happy Felsch threw out four Boston base runners in one game, tying the AL record for outfield assists.
- Pitcher Bill Doak of the St. Louis Cardinals attached strips of leather between the thumb and forefinger of his glove, and the modern webbed glove was born.
- Baseball's National Commission recommended a best-of-nine World Series format, which was approved by owners.
- Among Babe Ruth's 29 home runs, which broke Ned Williamson's major-league record of 22 set in 1884, was a blast that cleared the right-field fence in Detroit's Navin Field, the longest homer ever hit there.

## Around The World In 1919

- The Post Office expanded its delivery system by initiating an air mail route between Chicago and New York.
- Massachusetts Governor Calvin Coolidge fired 1,117 striking policemen in Boston and replaced them with new officers.
- New York's thirty-four-story Municipal Building was opened.
- The American Legion, organized in Paris, held its first convention in St. Louis.
- A Wilkes-Barre, Pennsylvania, mine disaster claimed ninety-two lives.
- Booth Tarkington was awarded the Pulitzer Prize for Fiction for his novel, *The Magnificent Ambersons*.

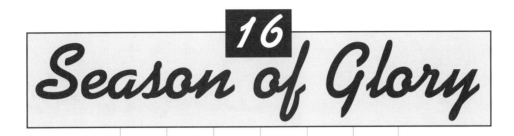

# Season of Glory

## Don Mattingly

### 1984

| AB | R | H | BA | OB% | 2B | 3B | HR | K/BB | RBI | BR | SB |
|-----|-----|-----|------|------|-----|-----|-----|-------|------|-----|-----|
| 603 | 91 | 207 | .343 | .386 | 44 | 2 | 23 | 33/41 | 110 | 46 | 1 |

| | | G | PO | A | DP | E | FA | FR | | | |
|---|---|-----|-------|-----|-----|-----|------|-----|---|---|---|
| | | 153 | 1,107 | 124 | 135 | 5 | .996 | 13 | | | |

BORN
April 20, 1961
Evansville, Indiana

HEIGHT
6-0

WEIGHT
175

THREW
left hand

BATTED
left hand

New York Yankees
1982–1995

# Donald Arthur Mattingly

On the August afternoon in 1997 when the Yankees retired Don Mattingly's number 23, Mattingly, unequivocally the team's best first baseman since Lou Gehrig, told the crowd: "I don't know what I did to deserve this." Talk about modesty. That was Don Mattingly. Never prone to self- promotion, never interested in grabbing the spotlight, never having an inflated opinion of his own worth, he simply went out and did his job—and did it well—with a blue-collar ethic that impressed fans, teammates, and opponents alike.

He hit .307 during his fourteen-year career as a Yankee, and was a six-time All-Star. Over his last six seasons, when he was hampered by a painful chronic back ailment, he still hit .286. For Mattingly, baseball was his business.

"I wanted the fans to know over the years everything I did was designed to keep everything strictly baseball for me," he told *The New York Times*' Murray Chass on the occasion of the retirement of his number. "I tried to stay away from doing too much stuff around town so when they thought of me, they thought of baseball, not a commercial or something that was going on with you because you became a celebrity." And that's exactly how things played out. Think of Don Mattingly, and you think of slashing line drives or nifty plays at first base, not candy bars, underwear ads, or appearances on the Home Shopping Network. "I'm not shy—I'm just not a ham," he once said.

Mattingly, born on April 20, 1961, in Evansville, Indiana, was Donnie Baseball before the media ever even heard of him. Quentin Merkle, who was Mattingly's high school baseball coach, once told a writer from *The New York Times* about watching Mattingly play as an eight-year-old. "Even then," Merkle said, "his swing was perfect."

Playing Babe Ruth League ball as a child, the ambidextrous Mattingly was a shortstop and third baseman. Later he switched to first base and threw left-handed exclusively. At Evansville's Reitz High School, he starred on the baseball (first base and pitcher), football (quarterback and defensive back), and basketball (point guard) teams. This big man on campus, though, was unassuming. "I didn't expect any special treatment at school for being an athlete," he told *Sports Illustrated* in a 1986 interview. "I never wore my letter sweater or anything like that."

Despite his obvious athletic skills, Mattingly was ignored during the first eighteen rounds of baseball's 1979 amateur draft, as teams figured he would accept one of the numerous college scholarships that he had been offered. Finally, after more than 400 other players had been drafted, the Yankees made him a nineteenth-round pick and signed him for a bargain $22,500 bonus.

Mattingly quickly moved through the Yankee farm system, hitting .349 for Class A Oneonta, New York, in 1979, .358 for Class A Greensboro, North Carolina, (where he was voted the South Atlantic League's MVP) in 1980, .316 for Double-A Nashville in 1981, and .315 for Triple-A Columbus the next season. He made the parent team at spring training in 1983 but was sent down with the season only weeks old. In June, though, he was brought back to stay. Playing primarily as a right-fielder, he hit .283 in 91 games that year.

After the 1983 season, Mattingly went to work to earn the full-time first base-man position. He hit .368 in winter ball in Puerto Rico and drove himself relentlessly to become a better fielder. New manager Yogi Berra, who had planned to use Mattingly as a fill-in in left and right and at first, gave him the first-base job. "I try to play first almost like a shortstop or second baseman plays his position," Mattingly once said in explaining how he handled first. "I know a lot of times people think, 'Oh, a first baseman kind of stands by the bag and gets what's hit at him and catches the throws.' But if I can play deep and cut off balls in the hole, that allows [second baseman] Willie [Randolph] to range more the other way. The more I can do, the more Willie can do."

Berra would not regret his decision. From almost the beginning of the 1984 season, Mattingly was a consistent hitter.

One of the Yankees' classiest ball players, Don Mattingly.

Through May and June, Mattingly led the way as the Yankees struggled to get out of last place. His 3-for-6 effort on May 10 helped the Yankees beat Cleveland and move past the Indians out of the cellar. He had a pair of five-hit games in June, which put him at .344.

# Game of Glory • October 1, 1984

On October 1, the final day of the 1984 season, Mattingly gets four hits to win the AL batting title, edging out teammate Dave Winfield .343 to .340.

| NEW YORK | AB | R | H | RBI |
|---|---|---|---|---|
| Moreno, cf | 3 | 0 | 2 | 1 |
| Mata, cf | 1 | 0 | 1 | 0 |
| Harrah, 2b | 3 | 1 | 0 | 1 |
| Hudler, 2b | 1 | 0 | 0 | 0 |
| Mattingly, 1b | 5 | 3 | 4 | 1 |
| Foli, 1b | 0 | 0 | 0 | 0 |
| Winfield, rf | 4 | 2 | 1 | 0 |
| Bradley, lf | 0 | 0 | 0 | 0 |
| Baylor, dh | 5 | 0 | 3 | 0 |
| Griffey, lf | 1 | 0 | 0 | 0 |
| Dayett, lf | 2 | 0 | 0 | 0 |
| Wynegar, c | 4 | 1 | 1 | 1 |
| Pagliarulo, 3b | 4 | 1 | 1 | 0 |
| Robertson, ss | 3 | 1 | 1 | 0 |
| **Totals** | **36** | **9** | **14** | **4** |

| DETROIT | AB | R | H | RBI |
|---|---|---|---|---|
| Kuntz, rf | 5 | 1 | 1 | 0 |
| Garbey, 1b | 4 | 0 | 2 | 1 |
| Laga, 1b | 1 | 0 | 0 | 0 |
| Herndon, lf | 1 | 0 | 1 | 0 |
| Simmons, lf | 1 | 0 | 0 | 0 |
| Parrish, dh | 4 | 0 | 0 | 0 |
| Lemon, cf | 4 | 0 | 2 | 0 |
| Bergman, rf | 0 | 0 | 0 | 0 |
| Brookens, 2b | 2 | 1 | 1 | 0 |
| Earl, 2b | 2 | 0 | 0 | 0 |
| Evans, 3b | 1 | 0 | 0 | 0 |
| Johnson, 3b | 2 | 0 | 0 | 0 |
| Castillo, c | 3 | 0 | 0 | 0 |
| Lowry, c | 3 | 0 | 0 | 0 |
| Baker, ss | 4 | 0 | 2 | 1 |
| **Totals** | **37** | **2** | **9** | **2** |

```
New York    3 0 1   3 2 0   0 0 * — 9
Detroit     0 1 0   0 0 0   1 0 0 — 2
```

Error—Lopez. Doubles—Baylor (2), Brookens, Mattingly (2), Lemon, Kuntz, Garbey, Mata. Sacrifice fly—Moreno. Double play—Detroit 1. Left on base—Detroit 9, New York 9.

| DETROIT | IP | H | R | ER | BB | K |
|---|---|---|---|---|---|---|
| O'Neal (L, 2-1) | 3.2 | 9 | 7 | 7 | 4 | 1 |
| Blair | 0.1 | 0 | 0 | 0 | 0 | 1 |
| Monge | 1.0 | 2 | 2 | 2 | 1 | 0 |
| Lopez | 1.0 | 1 | 0 | 0 | 0 | 0 |
| Scherrer | 1.0 | 1 | 0 | 0 | 0 | 1 |
| Hernandez | 1.0 | 1 | 0 | 0 | 0 | 0 |

| NEW YORK | IP | H | R | ER | BB | K |
|---|---|---|---|---|---|---|
| Rasmussen (W, 9-6) | 7.0 | 8 | 2 | 2 | 3 | 6 |
| Armstrong | 2.0 | 1 | 0 | 0 | 0 | 2 |

Wild pitch—O'Neal.

Time—2:35. Attendance—30,602.

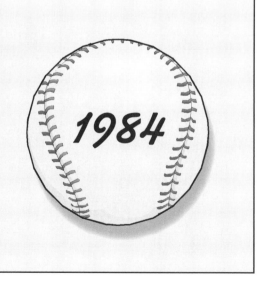

In 1997 Don Mattingly became the fifteenth Yankee to have his number (23) retired. The other fourteen are listed below.

| | | | |
|---|---|---|---|
| 1 | Billy Martin | 10 | Phil Rizzuto |
| 3 | Babe Ruth | 15 | Thurman Munson |
| 4 | Lou Gehrig | 16 | Whitey Ford |
| 5 | Joe DiMaggio | 32 | Elston Howard |
| 7 | Mickey Mantle | 37 | Casey Stengel |
| 8 | Bill Dickey and Yogi Berra | 44 | Reggie Jackson |
| 9 | Roger Maris | | |

The second half of the season turned into a two-man race for the league batting crown between Mattingly (.330 at the All-Star break) and teammate Dave Winfield (.370 at the break). Winfield began tailing off through July—he led Mattingly by just five points when the month ended—and the two went neck- and-neck down the stretch in August and September. Mattingly, on the strength of another five-hit day on August 25 against Seattle, moved into the lead, but August ended with Winfield ahead .352 to .350.

Winfield stayed points ahead through the first three weeks of September. Then, on September 21, Mattingly inched ahead by a point. Winfield, though, regained the lead on the 28th with a pair of hits against Detroit.

Their race came down to the last day of the season. Going into the final game, Winfield led .341 to .339. Winfield managed one hit in four at-bats and finished at .340, but Mattingly went 4-for-5, finishing at .343 and winning the crown.

Meanwhile, the Yankees wound up third at 87-75. They had an outstanding second half—they had the best record in the majors after the All-Star break—but they were never able to catch Detroit, which had gotten off to a 35-5 start.

In addition to leading the AL in hitting, Mattingly had 23 homers and drove in 110 runs. He also led the league in fielding percentage (.996) hits (207) and doubles (44).

Mattingly had five more outstanding seasons for the Yankees, hitting .324, .352, .327, .311, and .303, and leading the league in fielding during three of those years. In 1990, though, Mattingly, bothered by the bad back that would severely affect his production for the rest of his career, hit only .256 in just

> "I'm not flashy. I still don't think of myself as a great player. I think of myself as an everyday player. A worker type. Consistent. On time."
>
> —DON MATTINGLY IN THE JULY 9, 1984, EDITION OF *SPORTS ILLUSTRATED*

102 games. He held on through the 1995 season, but he was never again the hitter he had been.

Characteristically, Mattingly refused to feel sorry for himself.

"I was born with a congenital defect," he told *The New York Times* after he had retired. "If I hit too much, I got a pounding soreness. It was like a dead ache in my back.

"I hate talking about the back. It didn't really matter. I am who I am. I tried to make the best of it. I didn't want to talk about it. I didn't want sympathy from people. I didn't want to hear people say, 'How's your back?' Or, 'He's struggling because of his back.' So what? I was able to play for twelve or thirteen years, some of those years feeling pretty good, some of those years not feeling so good.

"I was still able to play in the major leagues, and I was very thankful for that."

## Baseball News Of 1984

- On Opening Day at Arlington Stadium in Texas, the Rangers confiscated the contents of picnic baskets, snacks, and lunches, enforcing their ban on food brought into the ballpark.

- Detroit's Jack Morris no-hit the White Sox 3-0 in Chicago in the Sox's home opener. It was the first no-hitter thrown by a Tiger pitcher in twenty-six years.

- On April 13 Montreal's Pete Rose doubled off the Phillies' Jerry Koosman for his 4,000th hit.

- *The Natural*, starring Robert Redford, was released.

- Forty-four-year-old Phil Niekro, signed by the Yankees as a free agent before the season, chalked up his 3,000th career strikeout on July 4.

- The Cubs obtained Rick Sutcliffe in a June 13 trade with Cleveland; he went on to win 16-of-17 decisions and carry the team to the NL East title, their first championship of any kind in nearly forty years.

## Around The World In 1984

- Ronald Reagan was re-elected president on November 6.

- Among the obituaries were those of Ansel Adams (April 22, age 82), Count Basie (April 26, age 79), Richard Burton (August 5, age 58), Truman Capote (August 25, age 59), Jackie "Uncle Fester" Coogan (March 1, age 69), William Powell (March 5, age 91).

- Donald Duck turned fifty on June 9.

- On October 11 Kathryn D. Sullivan became the first female U.S. astronaut to walk in space.

- A gunman killed twenty-one people in and near a fast-food restaurant in San Ysidro, California.

- The American Kennel Club turned one hundred years old on September 17.

- The first solo transatlantic balloon flight was completed on September 18 by Joe Kittinger.

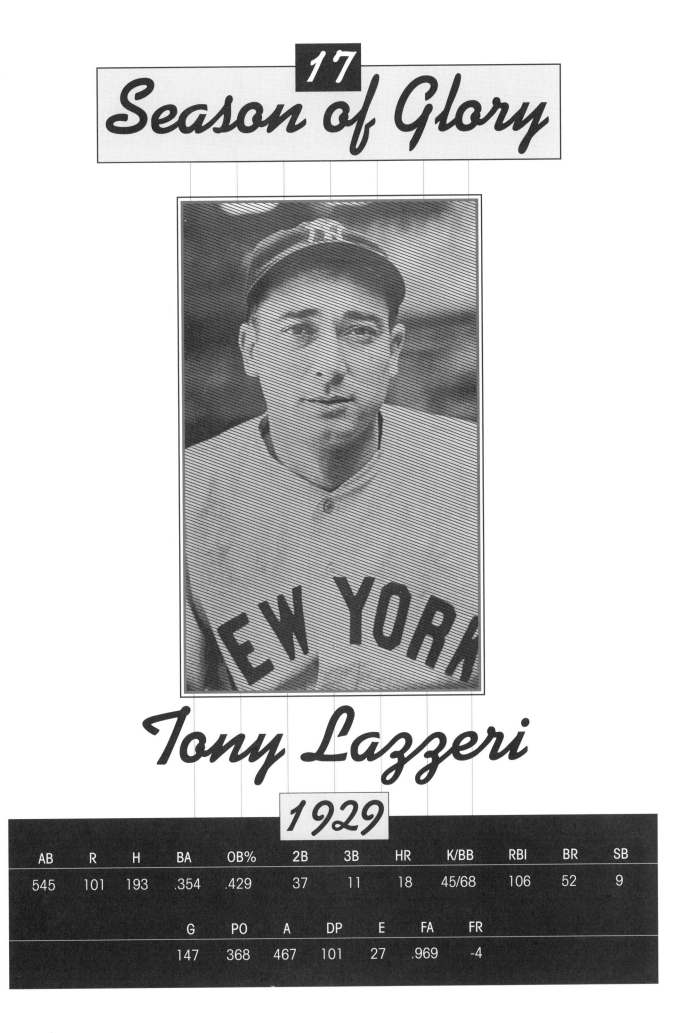

**17**

*Season of Glory*

*Tony Lazzeri*

**1929**

| AB | R | H | BA | OB% | 2B | 3B | HR | K/BB | RBI | BR | SB |
|-----|-----|-----|------|------|-----|-----|-----|-------|------|-----|-----|
| 545 | 101 | 193 | .354 | .429 | 37 | 11 | 18 | 45/68 | 106 | 52 | 9 |

| G | PO | A | DP | E | FA | FR |
|-----|-----|-----|-----|-----|------|-----|
| 147 | 368 | 467 | 101 | 27 | .969 | -4 |

BORN
December 6, 1903
San Francisco, California

DIED
August 6, 1946
Millbrae, California

HEIGHT
5–11½

WEIGHT
170

THREW
right hand

BATTED
right hand

New York Yankees
1926–1937

HALL OF FAME
1991

1929

# Anthony Michael Lazzeri

It was April 13, 1926, and Tony Lazzeri, a twenty-two-year-old rookie, had a great seat for the first major-league game he ever saw: He was the Yankees' starting second baseman. He made his debut in style, driving home Babe Ruth with the winning run in a 12-11 Yankee victory. The game was an auspicious one for Lazzeri, who would go on to a stellar fourteen-year major-league career.

Anthony Michael Lazzeri was born in San Francisco on December 6, 1903. His formal education ended when he went to work as a riveter at his father's boiler shop at the age of fourteen. A local sandlot star, the young shortstop was signed by a pro scout and played for Salt Lake City of the Pacific Coast League, where he hit 60 homers and drove in 222 runs in 200 games in 1925. The phenomenal season earned him a Yankee contract—New York purchased him from Salt Lake City for $75,000—and he was installed at second (Mark Koenig was already the team's shortstop) the following spring.

The Yankees had struggled through a disappointing 1925, finishing seventh, 28½ games out of first. Prospects for 1926 were uncertain at best. Manager Miller Huggins had a great outfield of Ruth, Combs, and Meusel and an adequate pitching staff. The big question was the infield. Joe Dugan was the best third baseman in the league. But Koenig, with just twenty-eight games of major-league experience, and Lazzeri, with none, were a cause for concern among fans. Huggins was concerned too.

Lazzeri was an immediate success. He batted .275, hit 18 homers (third best in the AL), and drove in 114 runs (tied for second) to anchor the bottom of the batting order. Defensively, his good range, strong arm, and sure glove solidified the right side of the infield. And, more important, he proved himself a leader on the field, a heads-up player who was almost a second manager.

Lazzeri also impressed the fans. He was a hero to the Italian-American population not only of New York, but of other American League cities as well. His nickname, "Poosh 'Em Up Tony," was a reference to his followers' calls for him to hit the ball into the seats.

He was also a favorite among his teammates. Although sportswriters considered him uncommunicative—his voice often had an angry quality, even when he was trying to be pleasant—he was a clubhouse favorite who loved to pull practical jokes. And he was a steadying influence, a mentor to rookies, and an inspiration to his fellow Yankees.

"Tony taught us what it meant to be a big-leaguer," Yankee pitch-

*Poosh 'em up!*

# Game of Glory • May 6, 1929

On May 6 Lazzeri gets three hits, two doubles, and a homer, helping the Yankees beat the White Sox 7-6 at Comiskey Park.

| NEW YORK | AB | R | H | RBI | | CHICAGO | AB | R | H | RBI |
|---|---|---|---|---|---|---|---|---|---|---|
| Combs, cf | 5 | 0 | 1 | 0 | | Metzler, lf | 6 | 0 | 1 | 0 |
| Koenig, 3b | 5 | 2 | 2 | 0 | | Kerr, 2b | 3 | 0 | 1 | 0 |
| Ruth, lf | 4 | 1 | 2 | 0 | | Redfern, 2b | 2 | 0 | 1 | 0 |
| Gehrig, 1b | 3 | 2 | 2 | 0 | | Kamm, 3b | 4 | 1 | 2 | 0 |
| Meusel, rf | 5 | 1 | 1 | 0 | | Clancy, 1b | 3 | 2 | 2 | 0 |
| Lazzeri, 2b | 5 | 1 | 3 | 0 | | Hoffman, cf | 4 | 2 | 1 | 0 |
| Durocher, ss | 3 | 0 | 1 | 0 | | Watwood, rf | 2 | 0 | 0 | 0 |
| Jorgens, c | 3 | 0 | 0 | 0 | | Reynolds, rf | 2 | 1 | 2 | 0 |
| Dickey, c | 1 | 0 | 0 | 0 | | Cissell, ss | 4 | 0 | 0 | 0 |
| Heimach, p | 4 | 0 | 1 | 0 | | Berg, c | 4 | 0 | 1 | 0 |
| Moore, p | 0 | 0 | 0 | 0 | | Weiland, p | 4 | 0 | 2 | 0 |
| Hoyt, p | 0 | 0 | 0 | 0 | | Thomas, p | 0 | 0 | 0 | 0 |
| Paschal, ph | 1 | 0 | 0 | 0 | | Shires, ph | 1 | 0 | 1 | 0 |
| | | | | | | Redfern, ph | 0 | 0 | 0 | 0 |
| | | | | | | Crouse, ph | 1 | 0 | 0 | 0 |
| **Totals** | **39** | **7** | **13** | **0** | | **Totals** | **40** | **6** | **14** | **0** |

| | | | | | | | | |
|---|---|---|---|---|---|---|---|---|
| New York | 0 1 0 | 1 0 0 | 0 1 0 4 — 7 |
| Chicago | 0 1 0 | 0 0 0 | 0 2 0 3 — 6 |

Doubles—Berg, Lazzeri (2). Triples—Koenig, Reynolds.
Home runs—Lazzeri, Meusel. Sacrifices—Durocher, Clancy.
Double plays—Chicago 2, New York 1.

| NEW YORK | IP | H | BB | K |
|---|---|---|---|---|
| Helmach (W) | 9.1 | 13 | 1 | 4 |
| Moore | 0 | 1 | 1 | 0 |
| Hoyt | .2 | 0 | 0 | 0 |

| CHICAGO | IP | H | BB | K |
|---|---|---|---|---|
| Weiland (L) | 9.1 | 11 | 4 | 8 |
| Thomas | .2 | 2 | 0 | 0 |

Hit by pitcher—by Helmach (Kamm).

Time—2:35.

ing star Lefty Gomez once recalled. "What was expected of us, and how we had to behave. He taught us what it meant to be a Yankee." Lazzeri followed his rookie season by playing a key role in the legendary Murderers' Row ball club of 1927: He had a .309 average, 18 homers, and 102 RBIs. He raised his average to .332 in 1928, another championship season, setting the stage for his most successful season—1929.

Lazzeri started slowly, hitting just .257 in April, but he soon found his groove. His first

# Have Your Pencils and Scorecards Ready . . .

On April 16, 1929, the Yankees became the first team to permanently add numbers on the backs of players' uniforms. Here's that day's lineup and numbers:

| Uniform No. | Player | Pos. |
| --- | --- | --- |
| 1 | Earle Combs | CF |
| 2 | Mark Koenig | 3B |
| 3 | Babe Ruth | RF |
| 4 | Lou Gehrig | 1B |
| 5 | Bob Meusel | LF |
| 6 | Tony Lazzeri | 2B |
| 7 | Leo Durocher | SS |
| 8 | Johnny Grabowski | C |
| 9 | George Pipgras | P |

really splendid day was May 5, when he tripled home two runs in the sixth and homered in the eighth of an 8-3 victory over Chicago. The next afternoon he had two doubles and a homer in another win. He went 11-for-27 over the last week of May—he hit .371 for the month—and was at .341 by the beginning of June. It turned out to be his month. Highlights that month included a three-run homer in an 8-1 victory over Chicago on June 1; a 14-for-28 streak in the first week that raised his average to .368; two hits in a June 19 win over Boston that gave him a .486 average for the month and a .392 mark for the season; and a 9-for-18 stretch to close out a .416 month and leave him at .377, 38 points behind AL batting leader Jimmie Foxx.

The Yankees had moved into first place with a victory in St. Louis on May 7, but fell out of the lead a week later when Philadelphia passed them. Although they played well through June and July, they couldn't catch the first-place A's. In fact, despite playing .702 ball through those two months, they actually lost 4½ games in the standings. The coup de grace came in late August, when the Yankees lost five in a row—three of them shutouts in St. Louis—to fall thirteen games out of first place. They would finish in second place, a distant 18 games behind the A's.

Lazzeri kept up his onslaught in July and August, hitting .324 and .308, respectively, and headed into the final month of the sea-

*Miller Huggins, diminutive Yankee Generalissimo.*

son at .353, some 20 points behind Foxx. In September, however, tragedy struck the ball club, prematurely ending Lazzeri's season.

As the Yankees struggled over the summer, Huggins had let himself get run down. He developed an infection—an ugly red blotch, later diagnosed as a carbuncle, appeared under his left eye—that quickly turned into blood poisoning. His condition deteriorated rapidly, and on September 25 the fifty-year-old Huggins died.

The Yankees were playing a home game

against Boston the day Huggins died. In the sixth inning the news arrived. The team was devastated, especially Lazzeri, whom Huggins, an old second baseman, had tutored at the new position when he first joined the Yankees in '26. Lazzeri finished the

> "He was a tremendous player, a great clutch player. He had ice water in his veins. He not only was a great ballplayer, he was a great man."
>
> —FORMER TEAMMATE FRANK CROSETTI

game—he had four hits—but not the season. He accompanied Huggins' body to Cincinnati, serving as a pallbearer at the funeral, then returned home to San Francisco, badly shaken by the death of his friend.

Lazzeri ended the season with a .354 average (he hit .367 in September), 18 homers, and 106 RBIs. He would hit .300 only twice more in another eight seasons in pinstripes. After the 1937 season, the Yankees, seeking to make room for young Joe Gordon at second base, released Lazzeri, who had lost a couple of steps and who had been bothered by a string of nagging injuries. (He finished his Yankee career with a .293 average.) Interestingly, his release came just days after he hit .400 in the 1937 World Series, which the Yanks won in five games. He was picked up by the Chicago Cubs—his solid performance helped them to the 1938 pennant—then split 1939 between the Brooklyn Dodgers and New York Giants. Midway through the season, the Giants released him, ending his major-league playing career after fourteen seasons.

After managing in the minors over the next five years, Lazzeri left baseball for good in 1943. Three years later he had an epileptic seizure and fell down a flight of stairs in his Millbrae, California, home. His body was found the next day. He was just forty-two.

## Baseball News Of 1929

- Detroit's George Uhle pitched 20 innings against the White Sox on May 24 in Chicago. He left for a pinch runner and got credit for the win. The loser? Ted Lyons, who went all 21 innings for the Sox.

- On July 5 the Polo Grounds in New York became the first major-league ballpark in which a public address system was used.

- Philadelphia's Chuck Klein hit four homers in the Phillies' 9-6, 10-inning victory over Pittsburgh on July 10.

- The Yankees bought Lefty Gomez from San Francisco (Pacific Coast League) on November 14.

- Twenty-year-old Mel Ott hit 42 homers for the Giants, becoming the youngest player ever to hit 40 in a season.

## Around The World In 1929

- Stock prices hit an all-time high on September 3, then began a slow decline that culminated with a crash on October 29, Black Tuesday. The Great Depression had begun.

- The first Academy Awards were presented on May 16. The first Best Picture was *Wings*.

- Seven members of mobster Bugs Moran's gang were gunned down in a Chicago garage on February 14, the St. Valentine's Day Massacre.

- The first flight over the South Pole was completed by Lt. Comdr. Richard E. Byrd on November 29.

# 18

# Season of Glory

# Wilcy Moore

## 1927

| W | L | Pct. | IP | GS | CG | SH | SV | K/BB | Opp. BA | ERA |
|---|---|------|-----|----|----|----|----|------|---------|-----|
| 19 | 7 | .731 | 213 | 12 | 6 | 1 | 13 | 75/59 | .234 | 2.26 |

| | | GP | PO | A | DP | E | FA | ER/R | PR | DEF |
|---|---|----|----|----|----|----|-----|------|----|-----|
| | | 50 | 18 | 89 | 1 | 1 | .991 | 54/68 | 37 | 8 |

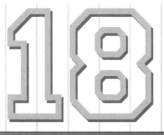

# William Wilcy Moore

**BORN**
May 20, 1897
Bonita, Texas

**DIED**
March 29, 1963
Hollis, Oklahoma

**HEIGHT**
6-0

**WEIGHT**
195

**THREW**
right hand

**BATTED**
right hand

New York Yankees
1927–1929
1932, 1933

**1927**

*H*umphrey Bogart and Sidney Greenstreet were marvelous in *The Maltese Falcon*. But Peter Lorre almost stole the show as the weasley Joel Cairo. Judy Garland gave a bravura performance in *The Wizard of Oz*. But the film wouldn't have been nearly as good without Margaret Hamilton's Wicked Witch. Likewise, Babe Ruth and Lou Gehrig were the headliners for the 1927 Yankees. But the supporting cast, players like Wilcy Moore, helped make the ball club arguably the greatest ever assembled.

To carry the film-baseball comparison a step further, Moore's story reads like something from the imagination of a second-rate screenwriter. The scenario: A thirty-year-old bumpkin from the cotton fields of Oklahoma is discovered by the American League champion Yankees and invited to spring training. He makes the team and helps the ball club win a world championship. Even by Hollywood standards, that's a bit too corny. But it's the true tale of Wilcy Moore, the first great relief pitcher in Yankee history.

It all began in 1926, when Ed Barrow, the Yankees' ever vigilant general manager, read about Moore, who had burned up the South Atlantic League with a 30-4 record for Greenville. He was 20-1 at one point, winning 17 in a row, and won 27 of 29 over another stretch. Barrow purchased Moore's contract for a reported $3,500 and told him to report to spring training the following spring.

Yet this was no fireballing young phenom, a second coming of Walter Johnson. Moore was a journeyman right-hander who had bounced around the minors for six unremarkable seasons. What had made Moore a new man in 1926 was an injury to his upper arm he had suffered in the 1925 season. After the injury healed he discovered he could no longer throw overhand. He began throwing sidearm, giving a decidedly average sinker a different rotation and more movement. Voila—a star was born at the age of twenty-nine.

Moore made an immediate good impression on his new teammates, both on the field—that sinker was something to behold—and off. He was old enough and wise enough to be considered one of the senior members of the ball club, and his happy-go-lucky approach to life endeared him to the other Yankees, especially Ruth. (Moore's new teammates also noticed that he was unable to swing a bat—he tore the cover off the ball to the tune of a .102 career average. Ruth bet Moore $500 that he would not get three hits during the '27 season. Moore sur-

# The Start of Something Big

When Wilcy Moore was piling up thirteen saves in 1927, he never could have dreamed how the role of the reliever would evolve over the years. Here's a look at how Yankee relief pitching developed:

| Name | Year | IP | W-L | ERA | Saves | Team Saves | League Saves |
|------|------|------|------|------|-------|------------|--------------|
| Clark Griffith | 1906 | 59.2 | 2-2 | 3.02 | 2 | 5 | 32 |
| Bob Shawkey | 1916 | 276.2 | 24-14 | 2.21 | 8 | 17 | 100 |
| Wilcy Moore | 1927 | 213.0 | 19-7 | 2.28 | 13 | 20 | 116 |
| Johnny Murphy | 1939 | 61.1 | 3-6 | 4.40 | 19 | 26 | 121 |
| Joe Page | 1949 | 135.1 | 13-8 | 2.59 | 27 | 36 | 136 |
| Luis Arroyo | 1961 | 119.0 | 15-5 | 2.19 | 29 | 39 | 289 |
| Sparky Lyle | 1972 | 107.2 | 9-5 | 1.92 | 35 | 39 | 372 |
| Rich Gossage | 1980 | 99.0 | 6-2 | 2.27 | 33 | 50 | 457 |
| Dave Righetti | 1986 | 106.2 | 8-8 | 2.45 | 46 | 58 | 524 |
| John Wetteland | 1996 | 63.2 | 2-3 | 2.83 | 43 | 52 | 536 |

prised Ruth—and probably himself as well—by getting six. He purchased two plow mules with his winnings for his farm back in Oklahoma, naming them "Babe" and "Ruth.")

Although he quickly fit in with the other players, Moore still had to prove to Barrow and manager Miller Huggins that he belonged. During the early part of the 1927 season, Huggins used him exclusively in relief. His record during his first thirteen appearances was 4- 2. His first start was May 28; he lost 3-2 to Washington. Two days later, Moore picked up a victory in relief in Philadelphia. He then won his next five decisions, not losing until mid-July.

Moore's biggest, and busiest, month was August, when he went 5-1 in two starts and nine relief appearances covering 43⅔ innings. Among the highlights were a complete-game 6-3 victory over the Senators on August 13, back-to-back wins out of the bullpen on August 17 and August 18 in Chicago, and victories in relief on August 18 and August 26 in Detroit.

The workload didn't seem to bother Moore. He won 15 of his last 18 decisions, finishing with a 19-7 record (three of the losses came in relief). His thirteen saves tied him with Washington's Garland Braxton for the American League lead, and he led the league in relief wins (13), fewest hits allowed

per nine innings (7.82), ERA (2.28), and opponents' batting average (.234).

The Yankees, meanwhile, were building a huge lead, clinching the pennant on September 13 and finishing with a 110-44 record. Leading the way, of course, were Ruth (60 homers, 164 RBIs, .356 average)

"There has been no more valuable player on the Yanks this season than Mr. Wilcy Moore. Without him the Yanks would not have made a joke of the American League race. Moore has come to the rescue of many a game that was about to die on the Yanks' hands."

—RICHARD VIDMER, IN THE NEW YORK TIMES

and Gehrig (47 homers, 218 hits, 175 RBIs, .373 average). But the supporting players—Earle Combs hit .356, Bob Meusel .337, and Tony Lazzeri .309—helped boost the team's batting average to .307. What's more, the Yankees had an excellent pitching staff, including Waite Hoyt (22-7, 2.63), Urban Shocker (18-6), Herb Pennock (19-8), Dutch Ruether (13-6), George Pipgras (10-3), and. of course, Moore.

# Game of Glory • October 5, 1927

Moore saves Waite Hoyt's victory in Game 1 of the World Series.

| NEW YORK | AB | H | PO | A | Pittsburgh | AB | H | PO | A |
|---|---|---|---|---|---|---|---|---|---|
| Combs, cf | 4 | 0 | 4 | 0 | L. Waner, cf | 4 | 1 | 1 | 0 |
| Koenig, ss | 4 | 1 | 2 | 2 | Barnhart, lf | 5 | 1 | 3 | 0 |
| Ruth, rf | 4 | 3 | 5 | 0 | P. Waner, rf | 4 | 3 | 3 | 0 |
| Gehrig, 1b | 2 | 1 | 9 | 2 | Wright, ss | 2 | 1 | 1 | 5 |
| Meusel, lf | 3 | 0 | 2 | 0 | Traynor, 3b | 4 | 1 | 1 | 2 |
| Lazzeri, 2b | 4 | 1 | 2 | 5 | Grantham, 2b | 3 | 0 | 5 | 3 |
| Dugan, 3b | 3 | 0 | 0 | 0 | Harris, 1b | 4 | 1 | 8 | 2 |
| Collins, c | 2 | 0 | 3 | 0 | Smith, c | 4 | 0 | 4 | 1 |
| Hoyt, p | 3 | 0 | 0 | 0 | Kremer, p | 2 | 1 | 0 | 0 |
| Moore, p | 1 | 0 | 0 | 1 | Miljus, p | 1 | 0 | 1 | 2 |
| | | | | | Brickell, ph | 1 | 0 | 0 | 0 |
| Totals | 30 | 6 | 27 | 10 | Totals | 34 | 9 | 27 | 15 |

| | | | | | |
|---|---|---|---|---|---|
| New York | 1 0 3 | 0 1 0 | 0 0 0 — 5 | | |
| Pittsburgh | 1 0 1 | 1 0 0 | 0 1 0 — 4 | | |

Doubles—P. Waner, Kremer, L. Waner, Koenig, Lazzeri.
Triples—Gehrig. Sacrifice—Dugan. Sacrifice flies—Wright (2), Gehrig.
Double plays—New York 1, Pittsburgh 1.

| NEW YORK | IP | H | BB | K |
|---|---|---|---|---|
| Hoyt | 7.1 | 8 | 1 | 2 |
| Moore | 1.2 | 1 | 0 | 0 |

| PITTSBURGH | IP | H | BB | K |
|---|---|---|---|---|
| Kremer | 5 | 5 | 3 | 1 |
| Miljus | 4 | 1 | 1 | 3 |

Time—2:40.

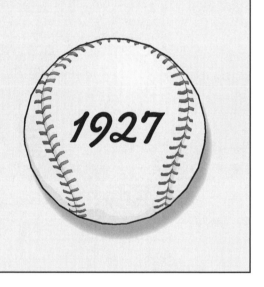

Not surprisingly, the 1927 World Series was no nail-biter. Even before Game 1, at Pittsburgh's Forbes Field, the Yankees had already won the psychological war, as Ruth, Gehrig, and player after player laced batting practice line drives into the seats while the Pirate players watched in awe. After this, the games themselves were a mere formality.

New York won the opener 5-4 as Moore saved the victory for Hoyt. Pipgras and Pennock shut the Pirates down in Games 2 and 3. And Moore got the start—and win—in the decisive Game 4.

Moore returned home to Oklahoma some $11,000 richer—two Yankee bonuses, the money from his bet with Ruth, and his World Series share more than made up for his paltry $1,800 salary—but he did not have a great off-season. He fell off a barn and injured his pitching arm again. He saw limited action in 1928, going 4-4. Eventually the Yankees traded him to Boston, where he spent a season and a half before returning to New York, where he finished his career in 1933.

# Baseball News Of 1927

- Ban Johnson, founder of the American League, resigned as league president on October 17 and was succeeded by Cleveland Indians president Ernest Barnard.

- The Yankees-Athletics season opener on April 12 featured thirteen future Hall of Famers.

- Ty Cobb got the 4,000th hit of his career on July 18 at Navin Field in Detroit—as a Philadelphia Athletic.

- Philadelphia's Lefty Grove shut out the Yankees 1-0 on September 3; it was the only time the Yankees were shut out in 1927.

- Eighteen-year-old Mel Ott got his first major-league homer, an inside-the-park job on July 27. It would be the only inside-the-park homer in his career.

# Around The World In 1927

- American Charles Strite invented the pop-up toaster.

- The first talkie, *The Jazz Singer* with Al Jolson, opened.

- The Ford Motor Company replaced the Model T with the sportier Model A.

- A tornado ripped through St. Louis, leveling 1,000 homes, killing eighty-seven and injuring 1,500 in five minutes.

- The largest crowd ever to see a football game—123,000—watched Notre Dame defeat Southern Cal 7-6 at Chicago's Soldier Field.

- Alexander Alekhine of France defeated Cuba's Jose Capablanca to become the world chess champion.

# 19

# Season of Glory

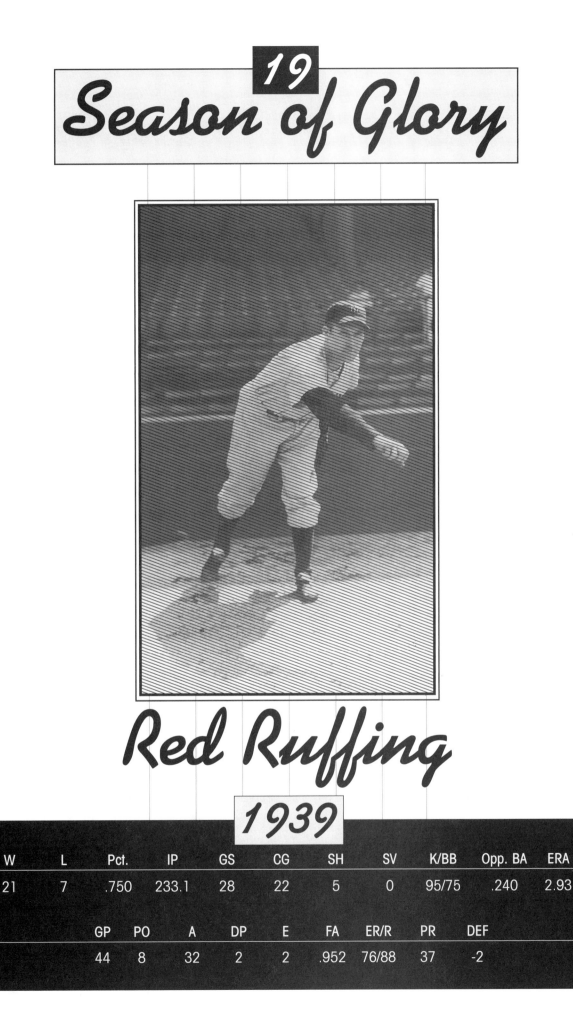

## Red Ruffing

### 1939

| W | L | Pct. | IP | GS | CG | SH | SV | K/BB | Opp. BA | ERA |
|---|---|------|-----|----|----|----|----|------|---------|-----|
| 21 | 7 | .750 | 233.1 | 28 | 22 | 5 | 0 | 95/75 | .240 | 2.93 |

| | | | GP | PO | A | DP | E | FA | ER/R | PR | DEF |
|---|---|---|----|----|---|----|---|----|------|----|----|
| | | | 44 | 8 | 32 | 2 | 2 | .952 | 76/88 | 37 | -2 |

# 19 Charles Herbert Ruffing

BORN
May 3, 1904
Granville, Illinois

DIED
February 17, 1986
Mayfield Heights, Ohio

HEIGHT
6-1½

WEIGHT
205

THREW
right hand

BATTED
right hand

New York Yankees
1930–1942
1945–1946

HALL OF FAME
1967

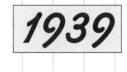

*I*f ever a guy was in the wrong place at the wrong time, it was Red Ruffing. He started his major-league career in 1924 with the Boston Red Sox, and over the next 6½ seasons, he was one of the losingest pitchers in the majors. He lost 18 games in 1925, 15 in '26, and 13 in '27. And those were his good years with Boston. He lost 25 games in 1928 and 22 in 1929, both league-leading figures. It looked like he was in for another long year when he started the 1930 campaign with three straight losses that dropped his career record to 39-96.

Still, there were those who recognized Ruffing's talent. One of them was Yankee manager Bob Shawkey, who pushed general manager Ed Barrow to make a deal for Boston's hard-luck right-hander. "He was pitching all with his arm," Shawkey later said in an interview, "and his arm would get tired, he'd lose some of his stuff and we would get to him.

"So we got Ruffing and I worked with him about ten days to get him to throw more with his body—the same way Chief Bender had worked with me when I was a rookie with the Athletics. Ruffing became a winner after that . . ."

A reborn Ruffing finished out the 1930 season by going 15-5 for the Yankees. He was 16-14 and 18-7 his next two years. Clearly, he had turned things around, and not just because of Shawkey's tinkering. Backed by the powerful Yankee lineup, helped by a strong defense, and pitching in spacious Yankee Stadium, Ruffing became the greatest right-hander in team history. He won twenty games for four consecutive seasons (1936-39), a feat no other Yankee has surpassed.

Fittingly, his greatest season came in 1939, which was also a memorable year for the Yankees, for New York City, and in baseball history. The Yankees would win their fourth consecutive World Series in 1939. New York City hosted the World's Fair—attended by thirty-three million people—that year. Nineteen thirty-nine was also chosen as the year to celebrate the 100th anniversary of the invention of baseball and to dedicate the Hall of Fame.

Into all this stepped the thirty-five-year-old Ruffing. He started his most memorable season by outdueling Boston's Lefty Grove 2-0 on opening day, April 20, in New York. He would also win his next six games, winning the 200th game of his career on May 25 against Detroit. Not a bad milestone for a pitcher who, at one time, seemed to be headed for 200 career losses in record time.

And Ruffing was getting plenty of help from his teammates. For

# They Can Hit, Too

Below is a list of the top ten hitting pitchers in the majors in 1939. They are ranked according to their Pitcher's Hitting Index (PHI), which rates pitchers as hitters according to a sabermetric formula. The formula takes into consideration the pitcher's offensive contribution and its impact on team performance. The formula also takes into consideration batting order, game situations, runs produced, and the performance of the team itself, and is designed to rate a pitcher's ability to score runs, advance runners, or drive them in. An average pitcher rates from 0-3; 4-8 is excellent; 9-14 is outstanding (in the following charts, G indicates the number of games played as a pitcher).

| Player, Team | G | H | Avg. | W-L | PHI |
|---|---|---|---|---|---|
| Bucky Walters, Cincinnati | 39 | 39 | .325 | 27-11 | 13 |
| Curt Davis, St. Louis (NL) | 49 | 40 | .381 | 22-16 | 12 |
| Joe Bowman, Pittsburgh | 37 | 33 | .344 | 10-14 | 12 |
| Red Ruffing, NY (AL) | 28 | 35 | .307 | 21-7 | 9 |
| Chubby Dean, Philadelphia (AL) | 54 | 27 | .351 | 5-8 | 8 |
| Monte Pearson, NY (AL) | 22 | 17 | .321 | 12-5 | 6 |
| Ted Lyons, Chicago (AL) | 21 | 18 | .294 | 14-6 | 4 |
| Al Milnar, Cleveland | 37 | 20 | .253 | 14-12 | 4 |
| Steve Sundra, NY (AL) | 24 | 13 | .265 | 11-1 | 4 |
| Bill Lohrman, NY (NL) | 38 | 14 | .233 | 12-13 | 4 |

## Red Ruffing's Top Five Seasons

| Year, Team | G | H | Avg. | W-L | PHI |
|---|---|---|---|---|---|
| 1930 (Boston-NY) | 34 | 40 | .364 | 15-8 | 18 |
| 1936 (NY) | 33 | 37 | .291 | 20-12 | 16 |
| 1935 (NY) | 30 | 37 | .339 | 16-11 | 14 |
| 1932 (NY) | 35 | 38 | .306 | 18-7 | 14 |
| 1941 (NY) | 23 | 27 | .303 | 15-6 | 12 |
| Lifetime | 624 | 521 | .269 | 273-225 | 143 |

Continued on page 125

example, on May 2 in Detroit—the day, coincidentally, that Lou Gehrig took himself out of the lineup—the Yankees hammered the Tigers 22-2. Five days later New York had 15 runs and 19 hits in a rout of Chicago. On May 14, Ruffing allowed just four hits as the Yankees beat the A's 10-0 in Philadelphia.

The Yankees continued to pound other teams throughout the summer. They beat St. Louis in New York 14-1 (Ruffing allowed just three hits), massacred the A's in Philadelphia 21-0 (the most lopsided

"Some of the young guys on the Yankees used to kid me about going to bed at 7:30 p.m. after running all day. But as the years went by, I noticed I was still up there and they were forgotten."

—RED RUFFING

Ruffing starts the Yankees' 1939 season with a win, outdueling Boston's Lefty Grove on April 20.

| BOSTON | AB | H | RBI | PO | A | NEW YORK | AB | H | RBI | PO | A |
|--------|-----|-----|-----|-----|-----|----------|-----|-----|-----|-----|-----|
| Cramer, cf | 4 | 1 | 0 | 2 | 0 | Crosetti, ss | 4 | 0 | 0 | 0 | 0 |
| Vosmik, lf | 4 | 2 | 0 | 3 | 0 | Rolfe, 3b | 4 | 0 | 0 | 0 | 2 |
| Foxx, 1b | 4 | 0 | 0 | 5 | 0 | Powell, lf | 4 | 3 | 1 | 4 | 0 |
| Cronin, ss | 4 | 0 | 0 | 2 | 1 | DiMaggio, cf | 2 | 1 | 0 | 3 | 0 |
| Tabor, 3b | 4 | 1 | 0 | 0 | 1 | Gehrig, 1b | 4 | 0 | 0 | 6 | 0 |
| Williams, rf | 4 | 1 | 0 | 3 | 0 | Dickey, c | 3 | 2 | 1 | 7 | 0 |
| Doerr, 2b | 4 | 1 | 0 | 4 | 3 | Gallagher, rf | 3 | 0 | 0 | 3 | 0 |
| Desautels, c | 3 | 0 | 0 | 5 | 1 | Gordon, 2b | 3 | 1 | 0 | 4 | 3 |
| Nonnenkemp, ph | 1 | 0 | 0 | 0 | 0 | Ruffing, p | 3 | 0 | 0 | 0 | 3 |
| Grove, p | 2 | 1 | 0 | 0 | 1 | | | | | | |
| Peacock, ph | 1 | 0 | 0 | 0 | 0 | | | | | | |
| Totals | 35 | 7 | 0 | 24 | 7 | Totals | 30 | 7 | 2 | 27 | 8 |

```
Boston      0 0 0   0 0 0   0 0 0 — 0 7 2
New York    0 1 0   0 1 0   0 0 * — 2 7 1
```

Doubles—Williams, Dickey, Tabor, Vosmik.
Triple—Powell.
Home run—Dickey. Errors—Cronin, Foxx, Gehrig.
Double plays—Boston (2).
Left on base—New York 6, Boston 9.
Bases on balls—Grove 2, Ruffing 1.
Strikeouts—Grove 5, Ruffing 5.

Time—1:47. Attendance—30,278.

*1939*

shutout in Yankee history), and hammered the White Sox in Chicago 16-4. They eventually won the pennant by 17 games over second-place Boston and 64½ games over last-place St. Louis.

Ruffing finished the season at 21-7 with a 2.93 ERA. He came in second in the league in wins, winning percentage (.750), and opponents' on-base percentage (.301). He ranked first in shutouts (5), third in complete games (22) and fourth in fewest hits per game (8.14). What's more, Ruffing contributed a respectable number of hits (35) and had an outstanding batting average (.307) that season. (He was perhaps the best hitting pitcher in the game's history. He hit .300 or better in eight seasons and finished with a lifetime .269 average, 36 homers, 98 doubles, and 273 RBIs.)

Ruffing's achievements earned him a spot on *The Sporting News*' All-Star team for the third consecutive year. In addition, Ruffing was the starting pitcher for the AL in the 1939 All-Star Game.

After helping the Yankees sweep the 1939 World Series (against the Reds), Ruffing had three more successful seasons in New York. He went to war, at age thirty-eight, in 1942. He returned from the service in July 1945, going 7-3 the rest of the season. He was 5-1 when the Yankees released him late in the '46 season, and he finished his career with the White Sox in 1947, going 3-5 and winding up his career with a 273-225 record.

# They Can Hit, Too *(continued from page 123)*

In the history of the game, only 25 pitchers have rated a 15 or over:

| Player, Team | Year | G | H | Avg. | W-L | PHI |
|---|---|---|---|---|---|---|
| Guy Hecker, Louisville (AA) | 1884 | 75 | 94 | .297 | 52-20 | 28 |
| Bob Caruthers, St. Louis (AA) | 1886 | 44 | 106 | .334 | 30-14 | 26 |
| Jim Whitney, Boston (NL) | 1882 | 49 | 81 | .323 | 24-21 | 23 |
| Al Spalding, Boston (NL) | 1875 | 72 | 107 | .312 | 54-5 | 22 |
| Don Drysdale, Los Angeles (NL) | 1965 | 44 | 39 | .300 | 23-12 | 22 |
| Rynie Wolters, NY Mutuals (NS) | 1871 | 32 | 51 | .370 | 16-16 | 20 |
| Wes Ferrell, Boston (AL) | 1935 | 41 | 52 | .347 | 25-14 | 20 |
| Red Ruffing, Boston-NY (AL) | 1930 | 34 | 40 | .364 | 15-8 | 18 |
| Warren Spahn, Milwaukee | 1958 | 38 | 36 | .333 | 22-11 | 18 |
| John Ward, Providence (NL) | 1879 | 65 | 104 | .286 | 44-18 | 17 |
| Charlie Ferguson, Phil. (NL) | 1885 | 48 | 72 | .306 | 26-20 | 17 |
| Babe Ruth, Boston (AL) | 1917 | 41 | 40 | .325 | 24-13 | 17 |
| Walter Johnson, Washington | 1925 | 30 | 42 | .433 | 20-7 | 17 |
| Bob Lemon, Cleveland | 1950 | 44 | 37 | .272 | 23-11 | 17 |
| Scott Stratton, Louisville (AA) | 1890 | 54 | 61 | .323 | 34-15 | 16 |
| Claude Hendrix, Pittsburgh | 1912 | 39 | 39 | .322 | 24-9 | 16 |
| Jack Bentley, NY (NL) | 1923 | 31 | 38 | .427 | 13-8 | 16 |
| George Uhle, Cleveland | 1923 | 54 | 52 | .361 | 26-16 | 16 |
| Schoolboy Rowe, Phil. (NL) | 1943 | 27 | 36 | .300 | 14-8 | 16 |
| Tony Mullane, Toledo (AA) | 1884 | 66 | 97 | .276 | 36-26 | 15 |
| Dave Foutz, St. Louis (AA) | 1887 | 36 | 151 | .357 | 24-12 | 15 |
| Pete Conway, Detroit (NL) | 1888 | 45 | 46 | .275 | 31-14 | 15 |
| Adonis Terry, Brooklyn | 1890 | 44 | 101 | .278 | 26-15 | 15 |
| Jack Stivetts, Boston (NL) | 1892 | 47 | 71 | .296 | 33-14 | 15 |
| Red Lucas, Cincinnati | 1927 | 37 | 47 | .313 | 18-11 | 15 |

# Baseball News Of 1939

- The American League's first night game was played at Philadelphia's Shibe Park on May 16, with the Indians beating the A's 8-3 with a five-run ninth.
- The Cincinnati-Brooklyn contest of August 26 was the first game to be telecast, with Bill Stern doing the broadcast over New York's W2XBS.
- The White Sox staged the first twi-night double-header, losing both games to the Indians.
- Americans celebrated baseball's centennial with the June 12 dedication of the Hall of Fame.
- Carl Stotz and George Bebble formed the Little League in Williamsport, Pennsylvania.
- The Cincinnati Reds won their first pennant since 1919.

# Around The World In 1939

- Trans World Airline's *Dixie Clipper* inaugurated transoceanic passenger flights to Europe.
- Sylvan Goodman introduced the first shopping cart in an Oklahoma City grocery store.
- Irving Berlin composed "God Bless America."
- John Steinbeck published *The Grapes of Wrath*.
- Bobby Riggs won the U.S. Open and Wimbledon.
- A tidal wave killed 200,000 in northern China.
- Italy invaded Albania, Russia invaded Finland, and Germany invaded Czechoslovakia and Poland.

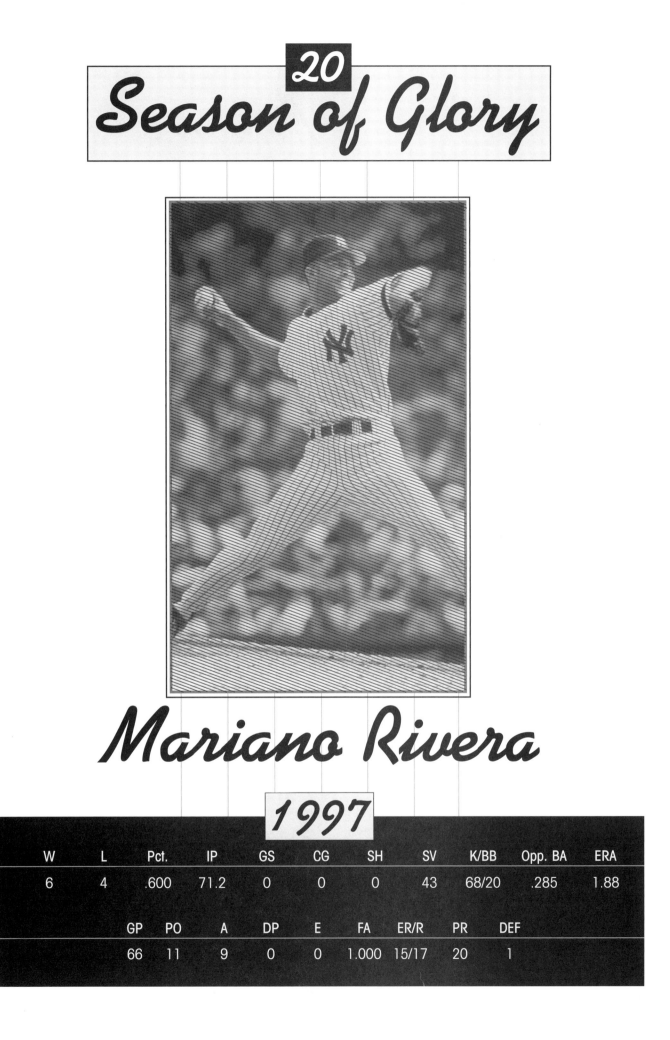

# 20
# Season of Glory

## Mariano Rivera

## 1997

| W | L | Pct. | IP | GS | CG | SH | SV | K/BB | Opp. BA | ERA |
|---|---|------|------|----|----|----|----|------|---------|-----|
| 6 | 4 | .600 | 71.2 | 0 | 0 | 0 | 43 | 68/20 | .285 | 1.88 |

| GP | PO | A | DP | E | FA | ER/R | PR | DEF |
|----|----|---|----|---|------|------|----|-----|
| 66 | 11 | 9 | 0 | 0 | 1.000 | 15/17 | 20 | 1 |

# Mariano Rivera

**BORN**
November 29, 1969
Panama City, Panama

**HEIGHT**
6-2

**WEIGHT**
168

**THREW**
right hand

**BATTED**
right hand

New York Yankees
1995–

*M*innesota Twins manager Tom Kelly figured out a way to handle Mariano Rivera. "The kid throws too hard for us," Kelly said after the Yankee reliever won two games in relief in one 1996 series against the Twins. "He's too good for this league. I say we ban him from baseball."

In '96 Rivera was the game's premier setup man, helping the Yankees win the world championship. In 1997 he inherited an even more important role, as the team's closer, and responded with his greatest season.

Rivera was signed by the Yankees in 1988, when he was nineteen. He played for Class A Tampa the following year, performing stunningly. He allowed just one earned run in 52 innings of work—an ERA of 0.17—and posted a 5-1 record. He had just one start, but it was remarkable: he pitched a seven-inning no-hitter against Bradenton.

The next season Rivera played for Class A Greensboro, splitting his time between starting and relieving. His record was just 4-9, but he had a 2.75 ERA with 123 strikeouts in 114⅔ innings. During the next two seasons, which he split among Greensboro, Ft. Lauderdale, and Tampa, he was plagued by injuries, including elbow problems that required surgery. He bounced back in 1994 and, used exclusively as a starter, had a combined 10-2 record with a 3.09 ERA at Columbus, Albany, and Tampa.

Rivera split '95 between Columbus and the Yankees, who used him as a starter and reliever. His stats weren't impressive—5-3 with a 5.51 ERA—but he showed promise. (In the second game of the AL Championship Series, for example, he pitched 3⅓ shutout innings to defeat Seattle.)

Everything fell into place for Rivera in 1996, when the Yankees won their twenty-third world championship. As the best setup man in the game that season, Rivera retired 30 of the first 31 men he faced in 1996, and during one stretch in April and May, he pitched 14 hitless innings. He had 27 holds that season, worked 107⅔ innings (tops in the majors), and finished 8-3 with a 2.09 ERA (he finished third in the Cy Young Award voting).

Rivera and closer John Wetteland were a practically unbeatable tandem that season: The Yankees were 87-1 in games they led after eight innings and 79-1 in games they led after seven. But this wasn't to be a lasting relationship. Just days after the World Series victory, Wetteland, who had forty-three saves and was the Series MVP, signed a free-agent

**1997**

Mariano Rivera

contract with Texas, and Rivera inherited the closer job.

He played great in his first game of the 1997 season, getting four outs on April 5 for his first save. But then he struggled: on April 11 he gave up a game-tying homer to Mark McGwire in the ninth inning in a game the Yankees eventually lost; he suffered his first loss on the April 15 when he surrendered a two-run double to California's Jim Leyritz in the ninth; and by April 19 he had blown three of his first six save opportunities. He wasn't alone; the Yankee bullpen blew leads in eight of the team's first ten games. In spite of his shaky performance, Rivera remained optimistic. "There's nothing we can do about Wetteland being gone," Rivera said. "Why even think about it? We've been through

# Game of Glory • July 3, 1997

Another day at the office for Rivera: On July 3 he strikes out the side in the ninth for his twenty-seventh save of the season, tops in the AL.

| NEW YORK | AB | R | H | RBI |
|---|---|---|---|---|
| Jeter, ss | 5 | 0 | 1 | 0 |
| Boggs, 3b | 5 | 0 | 1 | 0 |
| Williams, cf | 3 | 0 | 0 | 0 |
| Martinez, 1b | 4 | 1 | 1 | 0 |
| O'Neill, rf | 4 | 0 | 1 | 0 |
| Fielder, dh | 4 | 1 | 1 | 0 |
| Curtis, lf | 2 | 1 | 2 | 1 |
| Girardi, c | 4 | 0 | 3 | 1 |
| Kelly, 2b | 2 | 0 | 0 | 1 |
| Totals | 33 | 3 | 10 | 3 |

| TORONTO | AB | R | H | RBI |
|---|---|---|---|---|
| Nixon, cf | 3 | 0 | 1 | 0 |
| Merced, rf | 4 | 1 | 2 | 0 |
| Carter, lf | 4 | 0 | 0 | 0 |
| Delgardo, 1b | 4 | 0 | 1 | 1 |
| Sprague, 3b | 4 | 0 | 0 | 0 |
| Green, dh | 3 | 0 | 0 | 0 |
| O'Brien, c | 4 | 0 | 2 | 0 |
| Gonzalez, ss | 3 | 0 | 0 | 0 |
| Garcia, 2b | 3 | 0 | 0 | 0 |
| Totals | 32 | 1 | 6 | 1 |

| | | | | | | |
|---|---|---|---|---|---|---|
| New York | 0 1 0 | 1 0 1 | 0 0 0 — 3 |
| Toronto | 0 0 0 | 0 0 1 | 0 0 0 — 1 |

Error—Nixon. Doubles—Curtis, Girardi, Delgado, O'Brien (2). Sacrifice fly—Curtis, Kelly. Double play—Toronto. Left on base—New York 8, Toronto 7.

| NEW YORK | IP | H | R | ER | BB | K |
|---|---|---|---|---|---|---|
| Wells (W, 9-4) | 7.1 | 5 | 1 | 1 | 3 | 6 |
| Nelson | 0.1 | 0 | 0 | 0 | 0 | 1 |
| Stanton | 0.1 | 0 | 0 | 0 | 0 | 1 |
| Rivera (S, 27) | 1.0 | 1 | 0 | 0 | 0 | 3 |

| TORONTO | IP | H | R | ER | BB | K |
|---|---|---|---|---|---|---|
| Williams (L, 3-8) | 5.0 | 8 | 3 | 3 | 1 | 4 |
| Spoljaric | 1.0 | 1 | 0 | 0 | 1 | 1 |
| Quantrill | 1.2 | 1 | 0 | 0 | 1 | 1 |
| Plesac | 0.1 | 0 | 0 | 0 | 0 | 0 |

Time—2:54. Attendance—31,227.

*1997*

some tough games, and we just have to work through something like this." And that's just what he and his teammates did.

By the end of April, he had seven saves, and they kept coming in May and June, often in dramatic fashion. He fanned Texas's Juan Gonzalez in the ninth with the bases loaded to preserve a 5-4 victory on May 8; he worked a perfect ninth on May 24 against Boston and got his first win when Charlie

Hayes hit a two-run homer in the bottom of the inning; on June 6 he worked a perfect ninth to save a win over Milwaukee; he repeated the feat the next day; he got his twentieth save on June 11 against Chicago; and on June 25 he got his twenty-fifth save—and third of the series—against Detroit.

By the second half of the season, the Yankee bullpen found itself. Jeff Nelson, Mike

Stanton, and Graeme Lloyd filled the setup role that Rivera had been so good at in '96. And Rivera proved to be Wetteland's equal as a closer—there was no better right-handed reliever in the game. He finished with a 6-4 record, 1.88 ERA, and 43 saves.

The defending world champions couldn't even win their division in 1997, finishing second to Baltimore in the AL East despite winning four more games than they did in '96. New York's opponent in the first round of the playoffs was Cleveland, and the Yankees seemed to have matters in hand. They led the best-of-five series two games to one, had a 2-1 lead with two outs in the bottom of the eighth in the fourth game, and Rivera was on the mound. Four more outs, and the Yankees would be in the second round. But Sandy Alomar, Jr., shattered that dream with a dramatic homer

> "Rivera just doesn't let anybody get on base."
>
> —YANKEES MANAGER JOE TORRE

that tied the score. The Indians went on to win the game with a run in the ninth, then beat the Yankees the next day to end the Yankees' hopes of once again winning the championship.

# Baseball News Of 1997

- Nellie Fox, Tom Lasorda, and Willie Wells, Jr., were elected to the Hall of Fame by the veterans committee.
- For the first time in baseball history, the salary of one player (Chicago's Albert Belle, at $10 million) exceeded the payroll for an entire team (the Pittsburgh Pirates, $9,071,667).
- The Cubs set a record for the worst start in NL history, losing their first fourteen games.
- Toronto's Roger Clemens won his first eleven decisions.
- Interleague play started.
- Texas' Bobby Witt became the first AL pitcher to hit a home run in twenty-five years when he connected off Los Angeles' Ismael Valdes on June 30.

# Around The World In 1997

- Thirty-nine members of the Heaven's Gate sect committed suicide on March 26.
- Scottish scientists announced that they had successfully cloned a living creature, a sheep named Dolly.
- On February 4, the jury in a civil case against O. J. Simpson found him guilty in the deaths of his ex-wife and her friend.
- After a seven-month journey, the U.S. spacecraft *Pathfinder* landed on Mars on July 4.
- Diana, Princess of Wales, was killed in a Paris car crash on August 31.
- Among the obituaries that year were those of William Brennan (July 24, age 91), Jacques Cousteau (June 25, age 87), Deng Xiaoping (February 19, age 92), James Dickey (January 19, age 73), George Fennenan (May 29, age 77), Jimmy Stewart (July 2, age 89), Red Skelton (September 17, age 84), Mother Teresa (September 5, age 87), and Robert Mitchum (July 1, age 79).

# 21

# Season of Glory

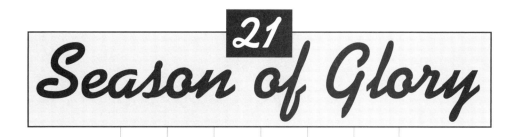

# Goose Gossage

## 1978

| W | L | Pct. | IP | GS | CG | SH | SV | K/BB | Opp. BA | ERA |
|---|---|------|-----|----|----|----|----|------|---------|-----|
| 10 | 11 | .476 | 134.1 | 0 | 0 | 0 | 27 | 122/59 | 187 | 2.01 |

| | GP | PO | A | DP | E | FA | ER/R | PR | DEF | |
|---|----|----|----|----|----|-----|------|----|-----|---|
| | 63 | 6 | 12 | 0 | 3 | .857 | 30/41 | 24 | -1 | |

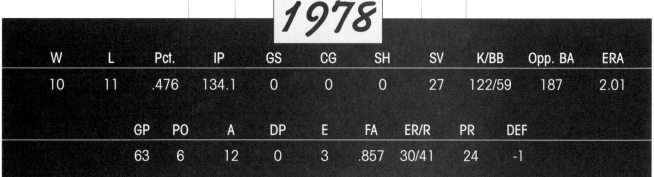

# Richard Michael Gossage

**BORN**
July 5, 1951
Colorado Springs, Colorado

**HEIGHT**
6-3

**WEIGHT**
217

**THREW**
right hand

**BATTED**
right hand

New York Yankees
1978-83
1989

*I*t was April 13, 1978, at the Yankees' home opener, and pregame player introductions were being made. Reliever Rich "Goose" Gossage, who had been signed as a big-money free agent the previous November, heard his name over the public address system and trotted out of the dugout. The crowd reaction was instant and unanimous. Boos. Loud boos.

As he jogged to the first-base line and stood next to teammate Ken Holtzman, the cacophony of boos was almost deafening. "They ain't yelling 'Goose,'" Holtzman said. Tough crowd. Welcome to New York.

Although Gossage was the losing pitcher in two of the Yankees' first five games, he thought the crowd's reaction was unfair—the season wasn't even a week old. Angry and hurt, Gossage determined to prove himself as a player that year. "I took my hat off and I said to myself, I'm going to turn all those boos into cheers," he later recalled. Gossage would, indeed, prove himself to Yankee fans before the season—his greatest season—was over. He'd be a key player in one of the most exciting pennant races ever, the start of a stellar seven-year career in New York.

Richard Michael Gossage was born on July 5, 1951, in Colorado Springs, one of six children born to Jack and Susanne Gossage. His first exposure to professional baseball was watching *The Game of the Week* on television. This being the late '50s and early '60s, more often than not, one of the teams featured was the Yankees. They soon became Gossage's favorite team.

When Gossage was just a kid, he began developing the competitive spirit—and blazing fastball—that would later become his trademarks over a twenty-two-year major-league career. He loved to play catch with his older brother, Jack Jr., who would constantly push Gossage to throw harder. "He'd keep telling me, 'Can't you throw any harder than that?'" Gossage recalled. "And I'd be busting my gut trying to throw the ball harder, trying to hurt him."

By the time he'd reached high school, the 6-foot-2-inch right-hander was overpowering his competition. He passed up several college basketball scholarship offers to sign with the Chicago White Sox, who picked him in the ninth round of the June 1970 draft.

Gossage played out the 1970 season with Sox farm teams in Sarasota and Appleton, Wisconsin, going 0-3 in 13 games. The following season, though, he dominated the Midwest League, going 18-2 with a 1.83 ERA for Appleton. As a result, he was promoted to the White Sox the next year, where he was made a reliever.

Gossage considered being moved to relief a demotion, however, and it took him a while to adjust. Worse, after a strong rookie season (7-1 in 36 games), the Sox tried to teach him to throw a breaking ball. This distracted him so much that he lost some of the zip off his fastball and became a decidedly average pitcher. He was sent back to the minors several times in 1973 and '74.

In 1975, Gossage managed to get back on track. His stats were spectacular that year: a 9-8 record, a 1.84 ERA and a league-leading 26 saves for the fifth-place Sox. That fifth-place finish cost manager Chuck Tanner his job, and new manager Paul Richards decided to move Gossage back into the starting rotation for 1976. It was a disaster: a 9-17 record for the last-place Sox.

Tanner, meanwhile, was named manager of the Pittsburgh Pirates for the 1977 season. He soon traded for Gossage, who, reinstated to the bullpen, went 11-9 with 26 saves and the second-best ERA (1.62) in the league. He also set a National League record for strikeouts by a reliever (151).

What made Gossage such a great reliever? His fastball, obviously, had a lot to do with it. And he did develop a pretty good curve. Just as important, though, was his persona on the mound. According to his teammate Dave Winfield, Gossage was a "fearful competitor" and a sight to behold, "sweating and spitting, fuming and flailing and hurling." Moreover, he was "always on an even keel," according to Pirate reliever Kent Tekulve. "He's the kind of guy who could leave the park after the game was over, and go out for a couple of beers, and sitting there at the bar, you couldn't tell whether he won or lost," Tekulve said.

Gossage became a free agent after the 1977 season. When the Yankees offered him a $3.6 million, six-year deal (he had earned $46,000 with the Pirates in '77), Gossage was bound for New York, where, according to the plan, he and lefty Sparky Lyle—the 1977 Cy Young Award winner—would give the Yankees the best bullpen in baseball.

The Yankees opened the 1978 season on April 8 at Texas, and Gossage made his Yankee debut in relief of Ron Guidry in the eighth. In the ninth, with the score tied 1-1,

*One of baseball's great intimidators, Yankee bullpen ace Goose Gossage*

he hung a curve to Richie Zisk ("right at my nose"), who lined the 0-2 pitch through a twenty-mile-an-hour wind into the seats for a 2-1 Ranger victory. Four days later in Milwaukee, Gossage made his next appearance, surrendering a game-tying homer to Larry Hisle and two more runs in a 5-3 loss to the Brewers. For this George Steinbrenner was paying $3.6 million? No wonder Gossage got such a warm welcome the next day at Yankee Stadium.

# *Game of Glory* • *October 2, 1978*

On October 2 Gossage pitches 2⅔ innings to save a 5-4 victory over Boston in the playoff game that gave the Yankees the AL East championship.

| NEW YORK | AB | R | H | RBI |
|---|---|---|---|---|
| Rivers, cf | 2 | 1 | 1 | 0 |
| Blair, cf | 1 | 0 | 1 | 0 |
| Munson, c | 5 | 0 | 1 | 1 |
| Piniella, rf | 4 | 0 | 1 | 0 |
| Jackson, dh | 4 | 1 | 1 | 1 |
| Nettles, 3b | 4 | 0 | 0 | 0 |
| Chambliss, 1b | 4 | 1 | 1 | 0 |
| White, lf | 3 | 1 | 1 | 0 |
| Doyle, 2b | 2 | 0 | 0 | 0 |
| Spencer, ph | 1 | 0 | 0 | 0 |
| Stanley, 2b | 1 | 0 | 0 | 0 |
| Dent, ss | 4 | 1 | 1 | 3 |
| Totals | 35 | 5 | 8 | 5 |

| BOSTON | AB | R | H | RBI |
|---|---|---|---|---|
| Burleson, ss | 4 | 1 | 1 | 0 |
| Remy, 2b | 4 | 1 | 2 | 0 |
| Rice, rf | 5 | 0 | 1 | 1 |
| Yastrzemski, lf | 5 | 1 | 2 | 2 |
| Fisk, c | 3 | 1 | 1 | 0 |
| Lynn, cf | 4 | 0 | 1 | 1 |
| Hobson, dh | 4 | 0 | 1 | 0 |
| Scott, 1b | 4 | 0 | 2 | 0 |
| Brohamer, 3b | 1 | 0 | 0 | 0 |
| Bailey, ph | 1 | 0 | 0 | 0 |
| Duffy, 3b | 0 | 0 | 0 | 0 |
| Evans, ph | 1 | 0 | 0 | 0 |
| Totals | 36 | 4 | 11 | 4 |

| | | | | | | | | |
|---|---|---|---|---|---|---|---|---|
| New York | 0 0 0 | 0 0 0 | 4 1 0 | — 5 |
| Boston | 0 1 0 | 0 0 1 | 0 2 0 | — 4 |

Doubles—Rivers, Munson, Scott, Burleson, Remy. Home runs—Dent, Yastrzemski, Jackson. Stolen bases—Rivers 2. Sacrifices—Brohamer, Remy. Left on base—New York 9, Boston 9.

| NEW YORK | IP | H | R | ER | BB | K |
|---|---|---|---|---|---|---|
| Guidry (W, 25-3) | 6.1 | 6 | 2 | 2 | 1 | 5 |
| Gossage (S, 27) | 2.2 | 5 | 2 | 2 | 1 | 2 |

| BOSTON | IP | H | R | ER | BB | K |
|---|---|---|---|---|---|---|
| Torrez (L, 16-13) | 6.2 | 5 | 4 | 4 | 3 | 4 |
| Stanley | .1 | 2 | 1 | 1 | 0 | 0 |
| Hassler | 1.2 | 1 | 0 | 0 | 0 | 2 |
| Drago | .1 | 0 | 0 | 0 | 0 | 0 |

Passed ball—Munson.

Time—2:52. Attendance—32,925.

Gossage continued to struggle during the rest of the first half of the season. For a couple of months, it seemed as if he was unable to win a game without losing one. Still, by the All-Star break, his ERA was just over 2.00 and he led the league in saves (12). That earned him a berth on the AL team, but he turned in another lackluster performance. Called in with the game tied 3-3 in the eighth, he gave up a leadoff triple, wild-pitched home what would be the winning run, and then got roughed up for three more runs. "You don't want to do what I did tonight in front of sixty million people," he told reporters afterward. "This hurts."

The Yankees were also in trouble as the second half of the season started. They had stumbled out of the gate but were in second place (just three games behind Boston) at the end of May. Between late May and mid-June, though, they lost 20 of 25, and by July 1 they were 9 games out of the lead and sliding. The low point came on July 19, when they found themselves 14 games back.

Manager Billy Martin took the fall, and on July 24, with the Yankees in fourth place at 52-43, he stepped down. (Martin resigned a day after he blasted both Jackson and Steinbrenner—"One's a born liar, and the other's convicted"—in the press.) Taking over was Bob Lemon, who had been fired by the White Sox less than a month earlier.

Slowly, the Yankees climbed back in the race. They won seven in a row at the end of August, moving to within 6½ games of the lead. Gossage picked up his twentieth save of the season on August 31 with two perfect innings, preserving Ron Guidry's nineteenth win against just two losses. The Yankees then won five of their next seven games, pulling within four games of the lead as they traveled to Fenway Park for a big series against first-place Boston.

The Yankees shocked the Red Sox in the series opener on September 7, winning 15-3. The blitz continued the next day—a 13-2 rout—and the next (7-0) and the next, when New York beat Boston 7-4 to put the teams in a tie for first at 86-56.

"I don't think we intimidated them," said Gossage, who worked three innings in the fourth game for his twenty-third save. "But I'm sure we hurt their morale. We stung the ball from the first night, and it was kind of a steamroller effect."

The flattened Red Sox would lose 9 of 10 before they recovered and got back in the race. The two teams battled to the final days of the season, the Yankees holding a one-game lead from September 23 until the last day of the season, when the Yankees lost to Cleveland 9-2 while the Red Sox were beating Toronto 5-0, necessitating a one-game playoff on October 2.

"I went to bed the night before thinking I could see me facing [Carl] Yastrzemski for the final out," Gossage later recalled. He was on the money, as it turned out.

The Red Sox took an early 2-0 lead against Guidry, who didn't have it this afternoon. But the Yankees came back; by the seventh they were ahead 3-2 thanks to Bucky Dent's now-famous home run. They added another run in the inning for a 4-2 lead that Gossage inherited when he came on in the bottom of the seventh with a man on and two out. He escaped that jam, then got an insurance run on a Jackson homer in the top of the eighth. But in the bottom of the inning the Red Sox rallied, scoring a pair of runs to pull within 5-4. After six months and 162 games, the championship would be determined in one inning.

In the ninth, with men on first and second, Gossage faced Jim Rice, the Red Sox' hitter at .315. Gossage retired him on a long fly for the second out, the tying run moving

"The Goose was the best reliever I ever saw. He had the ability to throw 100 miles an hour, and throw strikes, low strikes. He came off as being a tough guy. But he was very sensitive. The guilt worried him. That's what made him a great pitcher."

—Dave Righetti in the April 18, 1995; Chicago Tribune

to third. Then, up stepped the man of Gossage's dreams, Yastrzemski. "I felt like I was facing a firing squad," Gossage told Newsday in a 1983 interview. "Then it came to me. I asked myself, 'What's the worst thing that can happen to me?' I had an answer. I'll be in the mountains of Colorado tomorrow. I guess to some it might sound silly, but it was like the weight of the world came off my shoulders. . . . Suddenly I could breathe."

Yaz took the first pitch low for ball one. Gossage then delivered the pitch Yastrzemski was looking for, a fastball inside. He tried to pull it but was overpowered. He swung late and hit a soft pop to Graig Nettles at third. The Yankees had won the AL East.

"I didn't want to go home by losing on a hanging curve," the Goose told reporters. "I had been going with fastballs, so I stayed with fastballs. There isn't a man in the world I want to face less than Yaz in that situation. He's murder. That's the toughest couple innings I've ever pitched in my life."

But Gossage wasn't done yet. In the American League Championship Series against Kansas City, he got a victory in Game 3 with three innings of relief, then saved the Game 4 clincher for Guidry with an inning of hitless relief.

And in the World Series against the Los Angeles Dodgers, Gossage helped the Yanks win a crucial Game 4 (the Dodgers were leading the Series two games to one). Gossage came on in the ninth with the score tied 3-3. Relying exclusively on his fastball, he retired all six men he faced, fanning two. The Yankees pushed a run across in the bottom of the tenth for the victory, gaining the momentum that would carry them through the rest of the Series. The Yankees romped in Game 5, 12-2, then wrapped up the Series in Game 6 with a 7-2 win to which Gossage contributed two shutout innings.

Gossage finished the Series having al-lowed just one hit over six shutout innings, a victory and a 0.00 ERA. He finished the season with a league-best 27 saves, a 2.01 ERA and a 10-11 record. Gossage was voted AL Fireman of the Year and Rolaids Relief Man of the Year.

Gossage's second season with New York was a disappointment—he got into a club-house scuffle with teammate Cliff Johnson, injured his thumb, and was just 5-3 after missing twelve weeks. He had four more full seasons with the Yankees, averaging 26 saves, before signing as a free agent with San Diego. His career would take him to Chicago, San Francisco, the Yankees again briefly, Texas, Japan, Oakland, and Seattle. He finally retired in April 1995 after twenty-two years.

Late in his career, with the end of the road in sight, Gossage was asked how he would like to be remembered. He thought for a second. He simply said, "I gave them their money's worth."

## Baseball News Of 1978

- Joe McCarthy, who won eight pennants and seven World Series in twenty-four years as manager of the Yankees and Cubs, died at ninety on January 3.
- Cincinnati's Pete Rose got the 3,000th hit of his major-league career, a single off Montreal's Steve Rogers on May 5.
- On June 4 the Baltimore Orioles selected eighteen-year-old high school senior Cal Ripken Jr. in the second round of the draft.
- San Francisco's Willie McCovey hit the 500th homer of his career on June 30 off Atlanta's Jamie Easterly.
- Pete Rose hit in forty-four consecutive games between June 14 and August 1. His streak was ended by Atlanta pitchers Larry McWilliams and Gene Garber.

## Around The World In 1978

- Production of the neutron bomb was deferred by President Carter on April 7.
- Margaret Brewer became the first female general in the Marines on May 11.
- The Love Canal area of Niagara Falls, New York, was declared unsafe for human habitation because of toxic waste and was declared a disaster area on August 7.
- San Francisco mayor George Moscone and city supervisor Harvey Milk were shot to death at City Hall on November 27 by a former city supervisor.
- A mass suicide of members of the People's Temple in Guyana on November 18 left more than 900 dead, including more than 200 children.

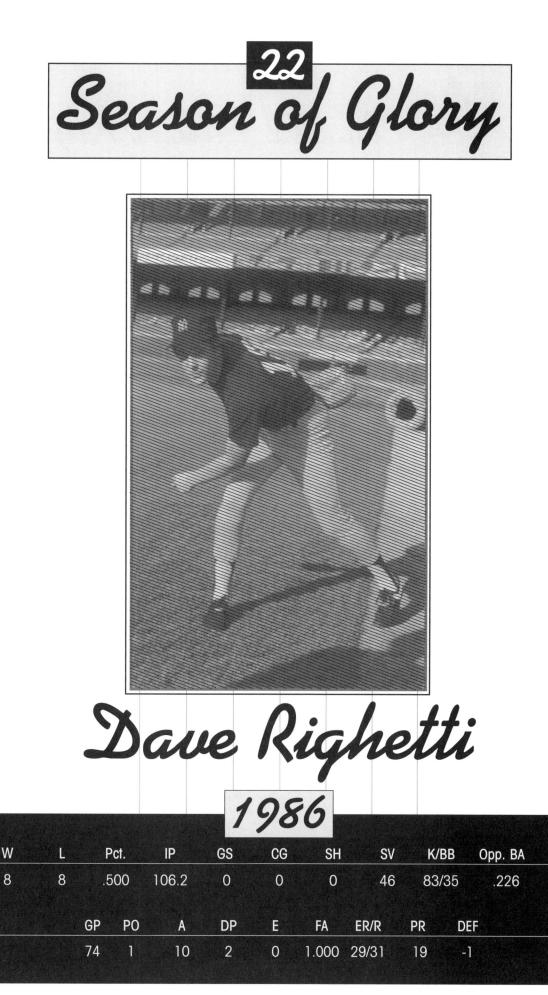

# 22
# Season of Glory

# Dave Righetti

## 1986

| W | L | Pct. | IP | GS | CG | SH | SV | K/BB | Opp. BA | ERA |
|---|---|------|------|----|----|----|----|------|---------|-----|
| 8 | 8 | .500 | 106.2 | 0 | 0 | 0 | 46 | 83/35 | .226 | 2.45 |

| | | GP | PO | A | DP | E | FA | ER/R | PR | DEF |
|---|---|----|----|---|----|----|----|------|----|-----|
| | | 74 | 1 | 10 | 2 | 0 | 1.000 | 29/31 | 19 | -1 |

# 22

# David Allan Righetti

BORN
November 28, 1958
San Jose, California

HEIGHT
6–3

WEIGHT
198

THREW
left hand

BATTED
left hand

New York Yankees
1979–1990

1986

It may not have been the highlight of Dave Righetti's greatest season, but was darn near the most entertaining moment. It was June 1986, and the Yankees were chasing the Toronto Blue Jays in the American League East. Righetti, who was 1981 AL Rookie of the Year, who pitched a no-hitter in 1984, and who was one of the top closers in the game, was struggling despite having sixteen saves.

In the opener of a three-game series in Toronto on June 19, he surrendered the winning hit to the Jays' Damaso Garcia in the tenth inning; it was the Yankees' fifth loss in a row. The next day, Toronto papers quoted Yankees owner George Steinbrenner as saying Righetti was responsible for the team's problems.

Then on June 20, Righetti surrendered a game-tying grand slam to George Bell in the ninth inning. When plate umpire Don Denkinger threw a new ball to Righetti, he turned and in defiance and frustration fired it over the right-field fence. He got a nice cheer from the Toronto crowd. Even his manager was impressed. "It reminded me of me as a player," said Lou Piniella.

Ironically, the 1986 season would turn out to be Righetti's finest. That year he broke the major-league record for saves with 46. But Steinbrenner's remarks would haunt him for many months; Righetti later said that he was unable to enjoy his greatest season—even when he broke the record—because the criticism had hurt him so.

Righetti had experienced similar highs and lows during his early Yankee career.

He was traded to the Yankees by the Texas Rangers after the 1978 season in a nine-player deal and made his major-league debut in September, 1979. Sent back to the minors in 1980, he struggled at Triple-A Columbus (6-10, 4.63 ERA), but found himself in '81 and was called up early in the season. "I was in a groove from Columbus already [5-0]," he later recalled, "and so when I got to New York they kind of let me alone."

Relying on a good fastball and a wicked curve, the big left-hander went 8-4 with a 2.06 ERA and 89 strikeouts in 105 innings. Righetti was the obvious choice for the AL Rookie of the Year Award. But he was back on the rollercoaster in 1982; with a 5-5 record he was sent back to Columbus in June. He was later recalled and finished out the season with an 11-10 record and 3.79 ERA.

Righetti was back on top in 1983—his 14-8 record included a July 4 no-hitter against Boston at Yankee Stadium—or so he thought. Toward

*Lefty "Rig" Righetti fired a July the Fourth firecracker at the Boston Red Sox in 1980 to earn a 4-0 no-hitter.*

*Dave Righetti* **141**

# Game of Glory • October 1, 1986

On October 1, Righetti saves both games of a double-header, giving him 46 for the season and breaking Kansas City's Dan Quisenberry's record of 45.

**SECOND GAME**

| NEW YORK | AB | R | H | RBI | | BOSTON | AB | R | H | RBI |
|---|---|---|---|---|---|---|---|---|---|---|
| Washington, cf | 4 | 0 | 2 | 1 | | Owen, ss | 2 | 0 | 0 | 0 |
| Randolph, 2b | 4 | 1 | 2 | 1 | | Romero, 3b | 4 | 0 | 0 | 0 |
| Mattingly, 1b | 5 | 1 | 1 | 1 | | Henderson, cf | 4 | 0 | 0 | 0 |
| Easler, dh | 4 | 0 | 3 | 0 | | Rice, lf | 3 | 0 | 0 | 0 |
| Winfield, rf | 4 | 0 | 0 | 0 | | Greenwell, lf | 1 | 0 | 0 | 0 |
| Pasqua, lf | 4 | 1 | 3 | 0 | | Baylor, 1b | 4 | 0 | 0 | 0 |
| Pagliarulo, 3b | 3 | 0 | 0 | 0 | | Evans, dh | 3 | 1 | 1 | 0 |
| Skinner, c | 4 | 0 | 0 | 0 | | Armas, rf | 2 | 0 | 1 | 0 |
| Tolleson, ss | 3 | 0 | 0 | 0 | | Romine, rf | 2 | 0 | 1 | 0 |
| | | | | | | Sax, c | 4 | 0 | 1 | 0 |
| | | | | | | Stapleton, 2b | 3 | 0 | 1 | 1 |
| **Totals** | **36** | **3** | **11** | **3** | | **Totals** | **32** | **1** | **5** | **1** |

```
New York    1 1 0    0 0 0    0 1 0 — 3
Boston      0 0 0    0 1 0    0 0 0 — 1
```

Error—Washington. Doubles—Washington, Easler, Pasqua. Home runs—Randolph, Mattingly. Double play—Boston. Left on base—New York 9, Boston 7.

| NEW YORK | IP | H | R | ER | BB | K |
|---|---|---|---|---|---|---|
| Rasmussen (W, 18-6) | 6.1 | 5 | 1 | 1 | 2 | 4 |
| Fisher | 2.1 | 0 | 0 | 0 | 1 | 2 |
| Righetti (S, 46) | .1 | 0 | 0 | 0 | 0 | 0 |

| BOSTON | IP | H | R | ER | BB | K |
|---|---|---|---|---|---|---|
| Nipper (L, 10-12) | 7 | 8 | 2 | 2 | 2 | 4 |
| Schiraldi | 2 | 3 | 1 | 1 | 1 | 1 |

Hit by pitch—by Schiraldi (Washington).

Time—2:32. Attendance—34,290.

*1986*

the end of the season, Yankee manager Yogi Berra and coaches Sammy Ellis and Jeff Torborg made a suggestion: They wanted Righetti to consider becoming a reliever. That was not what he wanted to hear. Not only would Righetti have to go to the bullpen, he'd be replacing a hero—Goose Gossage, who'd saved 150 games over the six previous seasons and had signed with San Diego.

With a little prodding from Berra and teammate Ron Guidry, Righetti agreed to the change. And it was the best move he ever made. In 1984 he saved 31 games and had a 2.34 ERA, in 1985 he had 29 saves, a 12-7 record, and a 2.78 ERA.

Righetti's 1986 season started slowly. He blew nine of his first 26 save opportunities as the Yankees, who had been in first place

## Ups and Downs

Dave Righetti was the AL Rookie of the Year in 1981, yet the Yankees sent him to the minors the next season. That's not that unusual. From 1950 to 1998, seventeen Rookies of the Year were sent down because of ineffectiveness or rehab within two years of winning the honor.

| Player | ROY season | Sent down | Player | ROY season | Sent down |
|---|---|---|---|---|---|
| Walt Dropo | 1950 | 1951 | Chris Sabo | 1988 | 1989 |
| Joe Black | 1952 | 1954 | Jerome Walton | 1989 | 1990 |
| Albie Pearson | 1958 | 1960 | Sandy Alomar, Jr. | 1990 | 1991 |
| Willie McCovey | 1959 | 1960 | David Justice | 1990 | 1991 |
| Mark Fidrych | 1976 | 1978 | Pat Listach | 1992 | 1993 |
| Butch Metzger | 1976 | 1978 | Bob Hamelin | 1994 | 1995 |
| Joe Charboneau | 1980 | 1981 | Marty Cordova | 1995 | 1997 |
| Dave Righetti | 1981 | 1982 | Todd Hollandsworth | 1996 | 1997 |
| Ron Kittle | 1983 | 1985 | | | |

as late as May 14, fell off the pace (they would finish five games behind Boston).

He reached the All-Star break with 19 saves—he pitched an inning in the game, which the AL won 3-2—but then began picking up save after save.

He got his thirtieth on August 22 and his fortieth on September 15. During one period he converted 25 consecutive save opportunities. This streak ended on September 23, when he let Baltimore score in the ninth to tie the game. But he ended up with a victory when the Yankees pushed a run across in the tenth.

With less than two weeks left in the season, the record of 45 saves, set by Dan Quisenberry in 1982 and tied by Bruce Sutter in '84, was within sight. "When I had nineteen at the All-Star break, I figured I'd have thirty-eight saves and a bad stomach," Righetti told reporters. "I knew I had a chance at the Yankee record [35 by Sparky Lyle in 1972]. To be thinking of 45 saves is kind of ridiculous."

Righetti got his forty-second save on September 24, his forty-third on September 30 with 2⅓ perfect innings of work, and his forty-fourth on October 2. He was one save short of the record going into the last day of the season, October 4, on which the Yankees were scheduled to play a double-header in Boston.

In the first game, he pitched two uneventful innings, tying the save record with the help of two double plays. In the nightcap, the Yankees took a 3-1 lead into the ninth. With two out and a right-handed hitter coming up,

> "It's a fear factor. You're afraid because you've got it all on your shoulders. You don't want to lose this man's game, the team's game. You can't let your teammates down."
>
> —DAVE RIGHETTI IN THE APRIL 18, 1995, *CHICAGO TRIBUNE*

Piniella replaced right-hander Brian Fisher with lefty Righetti, ignoring the percentages to give him a chance at the record. It worked— Righetti got Dave Sax to pop up, ending the game and giving him his forty-sixth save.

"He's been tremendous all year," Piniella said in defense of his decision. "He's pitched in quite a few games where he didn't get a save and we didn't win the game. He deserved this."

"I don't care what anybody thinks," Righetti told reporters who asked about the circumstances surrounding the final save.

"There's been too many heartaches, and the biggest one of all was the day Boston clinched and we were ten games out. This has been a great day for me."

Righetti would have many more great days—he had 117 saves over the next four seasons—before leaving the Yankees after the 1990 season. Over the next few years, he played for San Francisco, Toronto, and Chicago. He retired in 1995.

## Baseball News Of 1986

- Boston's Roger Clemens struck out twenty batters in a 3-1 victory over Seattle April 29 at Fenway Park.
- The Cubs fired ball girl Marla Collins after it was revealed that she posed nude for *Playboy*.
- Houston's Mike Scott no-hit San Francisco 2-0 on September 25. The victory gave the Astros the NL West championship.
- The Phillies' Mike Schmidt set a major-league record by leading his league in homers for an eighth time.
- This was the first season in baseball history that every team in the majors drew more than one million fans.
- Minnesota pitcher Bert Blyleven surrendered fifty homers, a major-league record.
- Pete Rose retired after twenty-four seasons and 4,256 hits.
- Obituaries: Former Indians pitcher Mike Garcia (January 1, age 62), Hall of Fame pitcher Red Ruffing (February 17, age 81), former manager and general manager Paul Richards (May 4, age 77), White Sox pitcher Ted Lyons (July 25, age 85), Tiger legend Hank Greenberg (September 4, age 75), Vince DiMaggio (October 3, age 75), and former Tiger first baseman Norm Cash (October 12, age 51).

## Around The World In 1986

- The space shuttle *Challenger* exploded seventy-four seconds after liftoff on January 28, killing all seven astronauts aboard.
- On July 2, the U.S. Supreme Court ruled that affirmative action programs were constitutional.
- Vanilla was reported to be the nation's favorite flavor of ice cream.
- The NCAA adopted the three-point field goal.
- Robert Penn Warren became the first official poet laureate of the United States on February 26.
- Television coverage of Senate proceedings began on June 1.
- The Oreo turned seventy-five.
- Among the obituaries were those of Desi Arnaz (December 2, age 69), Broderick Crawford (April 26, age 74), Benny Goodman (June 13, age 77), Cary Grant (November 29, age 82), Gordon McRae (January 24, age 64), Ray Milland (March 10, age 81), Georgia O'Keeffe (March 6, age 98), Kate Smith (June 17, age 79), and L. Ron Hubbard (January 24, age 71).

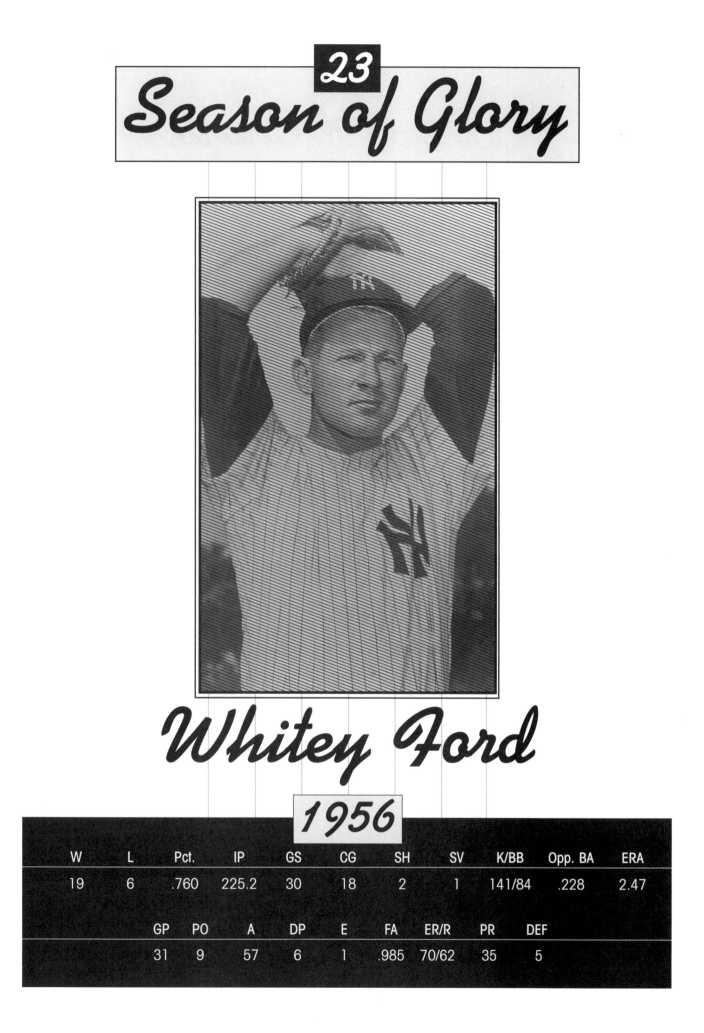

**23**

## Season of Glory

# Whitey Ford

## 1956

| W | L | Pct. | IP | GS | CG | SH | SV | K/BB | Opp. BA | ERA |
|---|---|------|-----|-----|-----|-----|-----|--------|---------|------|
| 19 | 6 | .760 | 225.2 | 30 | 18 | 2 | 1 | 141/84 | .228 | 2.47 |

| | | GP | PO | A | DP | E | FA | ER/R | PR | DEF |
|---|---|-----|-----|-----|-----|-----|------|-------|-----|-----|
| | | 31 | 9 | 57 | 6 | 1 | .985 | 70/62 | 35 | 5 |

# Edward Charles Ford

**BORN**
October 21, 1928
New York City, New York

**HEIGHT**
5–10

**WEIGHT**
181

**THREW**
left hand

**BATTED**
left hand

New York Yankees
1950
1953–1967

**HALL OF FAME**
1974

*W*hitey Ford was the greatest pitcher ever to wear Yankee pin-stripes. No argument. Case closed. Look at the evidence:

- A ten-time All-Star, he won 236 games and had a 2.75 ERA over his sixteen-year Yankee career.
- He has the highest winning percentage (.690) of major-league pitchers who have won more than 200 games.
- He holds Yankee records for victories, games started (438), innings pitched (3,171), strikeouts (1,956), and shutouts (45).

Not convinced yet? Listen to some witnesses:

- Ralph Terry: "Whitey was a master. It was like watching a pitching textbook in the flesh."
- Bud Daley: "It always seemed to me that Whitey was throwing half-speed. He never broke a sweat. I never saw a guy who made pitching look so easy."
- John Blanchard: "The best thing [about catching Ford] was that you never had to think that much because Whitey was calling the game. You didn't have to worry about going to the mound to settle him down because it seemed he never got upset."
- Joe DeMaestri: "Whitey was incredible. He not only knew where his pitch was going, he knew where the guy was going to hit it. He'd tell you to move a couple of steps to your left, and the guy would hit the ball right at you. I couldn't believe it."
- Mickey Mantle: "I don't care what the situation was, how high the stakes were—the bases could be loaded and the pennant riding on every pitch, it never bothered Whitey. He pitched his game. Cool. Crafty. Nerves of steel."

Edward Charles Ford was, simply, a master of his craft. He had a good assortment of pitches, he changed speeds, he fielded his position well, and, perhaps most important, he was serious and unshakeably confident on the mound. He was a money pitcher if ever there was one, and his teammates loved him.

Ford was born on October 21, 1928, and grew up in Queens. As a high school first baseman, the seventeen-year-old left-hander impressed

Yankee scouts at a 1946 tryout. They signed him later that year, converted him to a pitcher, and assigned him to their minor-league system the following season.

After 3½ years in places like Edenton, North Carolina; Butler, Pennsylvania; Norfolk, Virginia; Binghamton, New York; and Kansas City, Missouri; Ford was called up in June 1950. He was a sensation, winning 9 of 10 decisions and helping the Yankees hold off Detroit to win the American League pennant by three games.

There would be no baseball heroics for Ford over the next two seasons—he was drafted and spent two years in the service. But when he returned in 1953, Ford showed that his rookie year was no fluke. He won his first seven decisions that season, finishing 18-6 with a 3.00 ERA and firmly establishing himself as the team's ace.

Ford went 16-8 and 18-7 the next two years,

They called him "slick" . . . and for good reason.

but both seasons ended in disappointment. In 1954 the Yankees finished second to Cleveland, and in '55 they won the AL pennant but were beaten by Brooklyn in the World Series. That World Series loss not only motivated the Yankees to win the world championship in 1956, it proved to be a learning experience for Ford. "[Brooklyn's Johnny] Podres mixed up all his pitches exceptionally well and had our hitters way off stride," Ford said of the Dodger left-hander who won two games and held the Yankees to just two earned runs over eighteen innings in the '55 Series. "Our hitters kept looking for his fastball most of the time and he kept coming in with his change. It got me to thinking if Podres could stop a free-swinging club like the Yankees with a good changeup, I might be able to use that same kind of pitch against a team like the Cleveland Indians, who generally go for the long ball."

That was Whitey Ford. He'd won 52 games over the previous three seasons and was one of the top pitchers in baseball, and he was still looking for ways to improve his game.

When the Yankees opened the 1956 season on April 17 in Washington, Don Larsen, and not Ford, was the starting pitcher. Ford

# Game of Glory • September 10, 1956

On September 10 Ford outduels Chuck Stobbs, thanks to two unearned runs, and fans eleven to help the pennant-bound Yankees reduce their magic number to eight.

| WASHINGTON | AB | R | H | RBI | NEW YORK | AB | R | H | RBI |
|---|---|---|---|---|---|---|---|---|---|
| Yost, 3b | 3 | 0 | 2 | 0 | Bauer, rf | 4 | 0 | 1 | 0 |
| Fitzgerald, c | 4 | 0 | 1 | 0 | Carey, 3b | 3 | 0 | 0 | 0 |
| Runnells, 1b | 4 | 0 | 1 | 0 | Mantle, cf | 4 | 0 | 0 | 0 |
| Sievers, lf | 4 | 0 | 0 | 0 | Berra, c | 3 | 0 | 1 | 0 |
| Lemon, rf | 1 | 0 | 0 | 0 | Skowron, 1b | 4 | 0 | 1 | 0 |
| Oravetz, rf | 3 | 0 | 0 | 0 | Collins, 1b | 0 | 0 | 0 | 0 |
| Olson, cf | 2 | 0 | 0 | 0 | McDougald, 2b | 2 | 1 | 1 | 0 |
| Plews, 2b | 0 | 0 | 0 | 0 | Howard, lf | 2 | 1 | 0 | 0 |
| Roig, 2b,ss | 4 | 1 | 2 | 0 | Hunter, ss | 3 | 0 | 1 | 2 |
| Valdivielso, ss | 2 | 0 | 0 | 0 | Ford, p | 3 | 0 | 0 | 0 |
| Killebrew, 2b | 1 | 0 | 0 | 0 | | | | | |
| Stobbs, p | 2 | 0 | 0 | 0 | | | | | |
| Courtney, ph | 0 | 0 | 0 | 1 | | | | | |
| Chakales, p | 0 | 0 | 0 | 0 | | | | | |
| Totals | 30 | 1 | 6 | 1 | Totals | 28 | 2 | 5 | 2 |

| | | | | | | |
|---|---|---|---|---|---|---|
| Washington | 0 0 0 | 0 0 0 | 0 1 0 — 1 | | | |
| New York | 0 0 0 | 0 0 0 | 2 0 * — 2 | | | |

Errors—FitzGerald, Yost, Roig. Double—Roig. Triples—Roig, Hunter. Stolen base—Roig. Sacrifices—McDougald, Carey. Sacrifice fly—Courtney. Double plays—New York 2. Left on base—Washington 6, New York 6.

| NEW YORK | IP | R | ER | H | BB | K |
|---|---|---|---|---|---|---|
| Ford (W, 17-5) | 9 | 1 | 1 | 6 | 3 | 11 |

| Washington | IP | R | ER | H | BB | K |
|---|---|---|---|---|---|---|
| Stobbs (L, 15-11) | 7 | 2 | 0 | 4 | 1 | 5 |
| Chakales | 1 | 0 | 0 | 1 | 1 | 0 |

Attendance—17,851. Time—2:15.

*1956*

had had an OK spring, but he had injured his ankle when he stepped in a hole in the outfield before an exhibition game in New Orleans. So manager Casey Stengel decided to save his ace for the Yankees' home opener, on April 20 against Boston. It was a classic 1950s-era Yankee victory: Ford pitched a complete-game five-hitter, Mantle hit a three-run homer, and the Yankees cruised to a 7-1 win.

It was also the start of another season-opening streak for Ford. He won his next five decisions, running his record to 6-0 and allowing just five earned runs through 54 innings (0.83 ERA). The streak ended on May 22 in Detroit, when Tiger catcher Red Wilson hit a two-run homer in the bottom of the ninth to beat Ford and the Yankees 3-2.

He bounced back in his next outing, blanking Boston 2-0. But his luck didn't last.

Ford had to leave his next start—a 6-3 loss—after just 4⅓ innings because of a blister on his finger. He lasted just five innings, surrendering six runs, in his next outing, a 9-0 loss to Chicago that left him at 7-3.

He seemed to be on track in his next appearance, allowing just four hits (all in one inning) in a 4-2 win over the White Sox on June 12. His next outing, though, ended early because of back pain (he allowed the Indians two hits and walked four in just 1⅔ innings). He lasted just one inning in a 14-2 loss to the White Sox on June 24 (part of a four-game Sox series sweep that moved them within one game of the first- place Yankees) that left him at 8-4.

Ford next sandwiched four victories around a disappointing All-Star appearance (two runs, three hits and a walk in an inning of work in the NL's 7-3 win) to improve to 12-4. By the end of July, he was 14-4 with a 2.40 ERA.

Meanwhile, the Yankees were finally taking control of the AL race. They had moved into first on May 16, but they were closely followed by the White Sox and Indians. They won five straight before the break and six in a row after it—three over Cleveland and two over Chicago—which all but decided the issue. The Yanks went 23-6 in July and ended the month with a nine-game lead over the second-place Indians.

In August Ford was once again bogged down by injuries. He was struck on the little finger of his left hand by a Ray Boone linedrive in the first inning of a loss to Detroit on August 3. He was out until August 15, when he left a game against Boston because of shoulder trouble (he didn't get a decision). That injury cost him two turns, and he didn't pitch again until August 31, when he got his fifteenth win by working 7⅓ innings against Washington. Ford won his next four outings to run his record to 19-5. He had one last chance—against Baltimore—to win his twentieth game (something he had never done before).

Whitey, meet Charlie Beamon. Beamon was a twenty-one-year-old right-hander the Orioles called up from Vancouver. Making his major-league debut, he allowed only four hits (two by Ford), winning 1-0. The run came in the third, scoring on a wild pitch by Ford.

Stengel gave Ford another chance to win his twentieth: He could start the season finale against Boston on September 30 on just three days' rest. It was a major concession for Stengel. He was a firm believer in the five-man rotation and insisted his pitchers get four days of rest between starts. That explains why Ford didn't win twenty until 1961, the year Stengel was replaced by Ralph Houk, who used a four-man rotation, giving Ford at least another half-dozen starts a year. Ford, though, declined Stengel's offer, saying he preferred to get the extra rest before the start of the World Series.

In the Series opener, on October 3 at

> "(Working every fourth day) didn't shorten my career. Working more made me a better pitcher. It's too bad it didn't happen earlier, but who could argue with Casey? He won five World Series in a row."
>
> —WHITEY FORD

Ebbets Field, the Dodgers knocked Ford out after three innings and went on to a 6-3 victory. He came back three days later, going the distance in a 5-3 victory that gave the Yankees a two-games-to-one lead. The pitching hero of the Series, of course, was Larsen, whose perfect game in Game 5 put the Yankees up three games to two and provided the spark that carried them to their seventeenth world championship.

Ford's Series stats were hardly impressive—1-1, 5.25 ERA, 14 hits in 12 innings of work—and they were hardly represtative of his typical postseason work. When he left baseball, Ford held an amazing number of World Series pitching records: most wins (10), most games pitched (22), most games started (22), most innings pitched (146), most strikeouts (94), most opening game starts (8), and most consecutive scoreless innings (33⅓).

Ford continued to consistently win for the

Yankees for another nine seasons. In 1964 he developed circulation problems in his left arm and underwent surgery. He had one more successful season, winning 16 games in 1965, then went 2-5 and 2-4 in '66. He announced his retirement in May 1967.

When he left, a Yankee era was over. "I always considered Whitey the consummate pro," Tony Kubek once said. "Ellie Howard called him 'the Chairman of the Board,' and it was an apt nickname. Whitey was in control of every pitch and every situation."

"They used to always say that 'as Mantle goes, so go the Yankees,'" Mantle once recalled. "I guess I thought I was an inspirational leader and all that crap, but we all knew that the real leader of the Yankees was Whitey."

## Baseball News of 1956

- The Pirates' Dale Long homered in eight consecutive games. His streak ended on May 29 when he went 0-for-4 against the Dodgers' Don Newcombe.

- The Dodgers' Jackie Robinson chose to retire rather than report to the Giants, to whom he was traded after the season. And Bob Feller called it a career after eighteen years with the Indians.

- Three minor-leaguers hit sixty or more home runs: Dick Stuart (66) for Lincoln, Nebraska, of the Western League; Ken Guettler (62) for Shreveport, Louisiana, of the Texas League; and Edward Kennedy (60) for Plainview, Texas, of the Southwestern League.

- Boston's Ted Williams hit his 400th home run (on July 17 vs. the Athletics), Brooklyn's Pee Wee Reese got his 2,000th hit (on July 21 vs. the Cardinals), and Brooklyn's Roy Campanella got his 1,000th hit (on April 19 vs. the Phillies).

## Around The World In 1956

- On November 13 the U.S. Supreme Court ruled that laws providing for segregation on buses and streetcars were unconstitutional.

- Albert Woolson, the last surviving veteran of the Union Army, died on August 2 at the age of 109.

- The first transcontinental helicopter flight was completed by an army H-21 helicopter on August 24. It flew nonstop from San Diego to Washington in thirty-seven hours.

- After an IRS investigation, Hans Paul, headwaiter at the Waldorf-Astoria in New York, was indicted for not reporting tips averaging $500,000 to $1 million a year. He was fined $7,500 and sentenced to four months in prison.

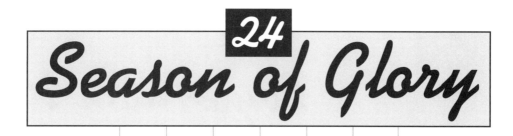

# Season of Glory

24

# Roy White

1971

| AB | R | H | BA | OB% | 2B | 3B | HR | K/BB | RBI | BR | SB |
|---|---|---|---|---|---|---|---|---|---|---|---|
| 524 | 86 | 153 | .292 | .399 | 22 | 7 | 19 | 66/86 | 84 | 40 | 14 |

| | | G | PO | A | DP | E | FA | FR |
|---|---|---|---|---|---|---|---|---|
| | | 147 | 306 | 8 | 1 | 0 | 1.000 | 10 |

# 24

# Roy Hilton White

BORN
December 27, 1943
Los Angeles, California

HEIGHT
5-10

WEIGHT
172

THREW
right hand

BATTED
both

New York Yankees
1965–1979

*1971*

Every team needs a Roy White. During his fifteen-year Yankee career, he played first base, second base, third base and the outfield and served as a designated hitter. A switch-hitter, he always hit for average. He was a superb team player, whether that meant laying down a bunt to move a runner or pulling off a hit-and-run flawlessly; he was respected and liked by his teammates and the media.

"He's a professional," Yankee manager Bill Virdon said of White. "I don't say that about a lot of people."

"Every year you read where they're going to trade Roy White," teammate Sparky Lyle once said, "but they can't, they can't afford to trade the guy until they can come up with someone who's going to be as consistent as he is, and there are very few of those around."

White was signed by the Yankees in 1962 when he was just eighteen. After 3½ years in the minors, he was called up at the end of the 1965 season and played in 14 games. In 1966, as a backup for Mickey Mantle, Roger Maris, and Tom Tresh, he played in 115 games and batted .225. Over the next few seasons, he would earn a reputation for consistency and professionalism.

In the mid- and late '60s, several members of the Yankees old guard left the team—Maris departed in '66, Mantle during spring training in '69, and Tresh midway through that season. That left White and Bobby Murcer as the anchors of the Yankee outfield. White did not disappoint. He became the Yankees' regular left-fielder in 1968, hitting .267 with 17 homers. In 1969 and '70, he hit .290 and .296, respectively, setting the stage for 1971, his greatest season.

He got off to a slow start that year, hitting just .269 in the first eight contests. A twisted ankle sidelined him for a couple of games, then he returned to the lineup on April 20. He went 2-for-3, hitting his third homer of the season that day, then went 2-for-5 the next day and 3-for-3 with his fourth homer of the season in his next game. A 3-for-6 performance the following day, including another homer and a pair of RBIs, boosted his average above .300.

White was one of the few bright spots as the Yankees struggled through May. His two-run double beat Milwaukee on May 2; he tripled home Murcer and later scored in a three-run first during a May 7 victory over Chicago; he had three hits on May 12 to lead the Yankees to a victory that brought them to the .500 mark; he heated up in the last week of May, going 9-for-19 (.474) between May 21 and 26, and ended the month hitting .293. He also contributed in other ways; for

*Roy White, consummate professional.*

# Game of Glory • July 18, 1971

On July 18 White has two hits and steals home to help the Yankees complete a sweep of Chicago.

| CHICAGO | AB | R | H | RBI | | NEW YORK | AB | R | H | RBI |
|---|---|---|---|---|---|---|---|---|---|---|
| Hershberger, cf | 3 | 0 | 0 | 0 | | Clarke, 2b | 4 | 0 | 0 | 0 |
| Lolich, rf | 4 | 0 | 0 | 0 | | Kenney, 3b | 3 | 1 | 2 | 0 |
| Reichardt, lf | 4 | 0 | 0 | 0 | | Murcer, cf | 2 | 1 | 0 | 0 |
| Melton, 3b | 4 | 0 | 0 | 0 | | White, lf | 2 | 3 | 2 | 2 |
| May, 1b | 3 | 0 | 0 | 0 | | Blomberg, rf | 1 | 0 | 1 | 0 |
| Andrews, 2b | 3 | 1 | 1 | 1 | | Swoboda, rf | 2 | 1 | 0 | 0 |
| Egan, c | 3 | 0 | 0 | 0 | | F. Alou, 1b | 4 | 0 | 1 | 2 |
| Alvarado, ss | 3 | 0 | 0 | 0 | | Gibbs, c | 4 | 0 | 0 | 0 |
| Bradley, p | 2 | 0 | 0 | 0 | | Baker, ss | 2 | 0 | 0 | 0 |
| Hinton, p | 0 | 0 | 0 | 0 | | Kekich, p | 3 | 0 | 0 | 0 |
| Forster, p | 0 | 0 | 0 | 0 | | | | | | |
| Johnson, p | 0 | 0 | 0 | 0 | | | | | | |
| Totals | 29 | 1 | 1 | 1 | | Totals | 27 | 6 | 6 | 4 |

| | | | | | | | | | |
|---|---|---|---|---|---|---|---|---|---|
| Chicago | 0 0 0 | 0 1 0 | 0 0 0 | — 1 |
| New York | 2 0 0 | 1 0 0 | 0 3 * | — 6 |

Error—Kenney. Double play—Chicago. Left on base—Chicago 3, New York 6. Doubles—Blomberg, White. Home runs—White, Andrews. Stolen bases—Kenney, White, F. Alou. Sacrifices—Blomberg, Kekich.

| CHICAGO | IP | H | R | ER | BB | K |
|---|---|---|---|---|---|---|
| Bradley (L, 8-8) | 5.1 | 4 | 3 | 3 | 2 | 4 |
| Hinton | 1.2 | 0 | 0 | 0 | 1 | 2 |
| Forster | 0.0 | 1 | 2 | 2 | 1 | 0 |
| Johnson | 1.0 | 1 | 1 | 1 | 1 | 0 |

| New York | IP | H | R | ER | BB | K |
|---|---|---|---|---|---|---|
| Kekich (W, 4-4) | 9.0 | 1 | 1 | 1 | 1 | 5 |

Hit by pitcher—by Bradley (White); by Kekich (Morales); by Forster (White).

Time—2:20. Attendance—35,004.

example, he had 38 walks in the Yankees' first 48 games.

By June 1 the Yankees were 21-26, eight games out of first and all but out of the AL East race. By the end of June, they were 13 games back and dead in the water.

A hamstring pull on June 18 kept White out of the lineup for eight days, and when he returned it was only as a pinch-hitter. He resumed full-time play on July 3—his two-

run homer in the sixth off Luis Tiant helped the Yanks beat Boston 2-1—and went 10-for-37 over the next week.

He started the second half of the season with a .296 average and lots of momentum. He contributed two hits and some impressive baserunning in a victory over Chicago on July 17, he hit a two-run homer and stole home against the White Sox the next day, and he had a pair of hits and two runs scored in a double-header sweep of Milwaukee on July 25 that put the Yankees at .500 for the first time since they were 16-16 on May 1.

It wasn't much to celebrate. By the end of August, the Yankees were buried, 17½ games out of first, and White was in the .270s. He played better in September, hitting .407 over the last week of the season to wind up at .292.

In addition to contributing 153 hits, 19 home runs, 84 RBIs, 86 walks and a .469 slugging average to the Yankee offense, White was perfect in the field: He had a 1.000 fielding percentage. He was the complete player, and without his help, the Yankees' dismal season would have been a disaster.

White spent eight more years with the Yankees, leaving in 1979 to play in Japan. He spent four years there before retiring as a player in 1982.

> "I'm more or less a pessimistic guy. I don't get too excited, in general, when I'm in a hot streak. . . . I know how easy it is to go bad because I've gone bad in the past. Basically, I guess, I'm a very humble person."
>
> —ROY WHITE IN THE JUNE 18, 1970, *CHICAGO TRIBUNE*

## Baseball News Of 1971

- Minnesota's Harmon Killebrew hit the 500th and 501st homers of his career on August 10 in a 4-3 Twins loss to Baltimore.
- Chicago's Billy Williams and Pittsburgh's Bill Mazeroski both got their 2,000th career hit on the same day, August 17.
- Ernie Banks got his 512th, and last, career homer on August 24 against Cincinnati at Wrigley Field.
- The Senators left Washington for Texas, ending seventy-one years of baseball in the nation's capital.

## Around The World In 1971

- The U.S. Supreme Court overturned Muhammad Ali's 1967 conviction for draft evasion.
- The first legal off-track betting system in the United States began operation in New York.
- Amtrak, the national passenger rail service, got rolling May 1.
- The use of busing to end racial segregation in schools was declared constitutional by the Supreme Court on April 20.
- A U.S. table tennis team was invited to China—Ping-Pong diplomacy, if you will.
- Golf great Bobby Jones died on December 18, at age 69.

# 25
# Season of Glory

## Sparky Lyle

### 1977

| W | L | Pct. | IP | GS | CG | SH | SV | K/BB | Opp. BA | ERA |
|---|---|------|-----|-----|-----|-----|-----|-------|---------|------|
| 13 | 5 | .722 | 137 | 0 | 0 | — | 26 | 68/33 | .257 | 2.17 |

| | GP | PO | A | DP | E | FA | ER/R | PR | DEF |
|---|-----|-----|-----|-----|-----|------|-------|-----|------|
| | 72 | 2 | 22 | 0 | 2 | .923 | 41/33 | 27 | -1 |

# 25

## Albert Walker Lyle

BORN
July 22, 1944
DuBois, Pennsylvania

HEIGHT
6-1

WEIGHT
192

THREW
left hand

BATTED
left hand

New York Yankees
1972–1978

*1977*

Gene Michael found a mouse hidden in his jockstrap—while he was wearing it. Yogi Berra discovered that the tube of toothpaste he had borrowed actually contained White Heat, a rubbing ointment—but only well after he'd started brushing. Rich Gossage, who was careless enough to fall asleep on the team bus, was on the receiving end of a hotfoot that set his Earth Shoes on fire. Sparky Lyle, the man who perfected the art of leaving his butt-print on clubhouse birthday cakes, carried lockerroom pranks to a new level.

Although Lyle was a jokester off the field, he was a pitcher to be reckoned with on it. His almost-unhittable slider made him the American League's top relief pitcher in the mid-'70s. For six consecutive seasons (1972 to 1977), the left-handed Lyle led the Yankees in saves. He led the American League in saves in 1972 (35) and '76 (23), and in 1977 he was at his best with 26 saves, 13 victories and the Cy Young Award as he helped the Yankees to their first world championship in fifteen years.

Lyle began his career in the Baltimore Orioles' organization, pitching for Bluefield, West Virginia, in 1964. Soon he was promoted to Double-A Appleton, Wisconsin, and after the season he was drafted by the Boston Red Sox. He suffered through a miserable 1965 campaign at Double-A Winston-Salem. It was the first year he'd been pitching in relief, and he wasn't very effective. The team was lousy, and he didn't get along with his manager, Bill Slack. It was, he later would say, the low point of his career.

But during spring training in 1966, Lyle met the man who would change his life: Ted Williams. Williams, who was working as a Red Sox coach, took Lyle aside and suggested he try throwing a slider, the pitch, Williams said, that had given him the most trouble when he was a player. "I was in awe of Williams," Lyle recalled in his 1979 book *The Bronx Zoo*, written with Peter Golenbock. "He knew more about hitting than anyone alive. When Ted Williams told me something, I listened . . ." Williams told Lyle how the pitch broke and what it was supposed to do. He left the rest, the mechanics, to Lyle.

Lyle worked on the pitch that season at Pittsfield, Massachusetts, experimenting with different ways of holding the ball and different releases. By the time the 1967 season started, he had been promoted to the Red Sox's top farm team, Toronto, and he had learned to control his slider, which he threw about 80 percent of the time. He was brought up to the parent club after less than half a season and appeared in 27 games (he had five saves) in the Red Sox's 1967 championship season.

After four more full, productive seasons in Boston, where he averaged 16 saves a year, Lyle was traded to the Yankees. Lyle was never a favorite of Red Sox manager Eddie Kasko—let's call it a personality clash—and after a blowup in spring training in March 1972 that started when Lyle was fined for being overweight, the deal was made.

Before spring training was over, Lyle had convinced Yankee manager Ralph Houk to let him be his go-to guy, a reliever who could handle left- and right-handed batters equally well, à la Rich Gossage or Mike Marshall. Lyle didn't let Houk down: He had 35 saves, a 9-5 record, and a 1.92 ERA in 59 appearances.

Lyle was a steady performer during the next four seasons. In 1976, helped by Lyle's league-leading 23 saves and a 2.26 ERA, the Yankees won the AL East and made it to the World Series, only to be swept by Cincinnati.

*Sparky Lyle lit up The Bronx Zoo.*

Then, in 1977, Yankee owner George Steinbrenner signed free agent Reggie Jackson. Perceived as an arrogant, overpaid prima donna, Jackson was resented and disliked by his new teammates. Not even a practical joker like Lyle could lighten the tense atmosphere in the Yankee clubhouse.

Yet Lyle was able to divorce himself from off-the-field distractions and concentrate on the job at hand: winning ballgames. He started his greatest season with an impressive performance on Opening Day, pitching two hitless innings of relief to protect Catfish Hunter's 3-0 victory over Milwaukee. He picked up his first victory of the season on April 27, pitching four innings against Baltimore. Even more noteworthy was his

May 17 performance, when he pitched 6⅔ shutout innings and got the win in Oakland.

By mid-June, the personality conflicts among Yankee teammates began to affect the entire team's performance. During a three-game series in Boston, a dugout confrontation between manager Billy Martin and Jackson nearly turned into fisticuffs. The Red Sox swept the series, leaving the Yankees reeling. This ballclub, though, had too much talent to fold up. Slowly, the Yankees righted themselves. Sometimes the victories were ugly and sometimes they were thrilling, but by the end of June, after a three-game sweep of Boston, the Yankees were within one game of first place.

By July 5, the midpoint of the season, Lyle

# Game of Glory • October 8, 1977

Lyle pitches 5⅓ shutout innings and picks up the win in Game 4 of the 1977 AL Championship Series.

| NEW YORK | AB | R | H | RBI | | KANSAS CITY | AB | R | H | RBI |
|---|---|---|---|---|---|---|---|---|---|---|
| Rivers, cf | 5 | 2 | 4 | 1 | | Poquette, lf | 3 | 0 | 0 | 0 |
| Nettles, 3b | 5 | 0 | 2 | 1 | | Zdeb, lf | 2 | 0 | 0 | 0 |
| Munson, c | 4 | 1 | 1 | 2 | | McRae, dh | 3 | 1 | 2 | 0 |
| Jackson, rf | 3 | 0 | 0 | 0 | | Brett, 3b | 4 | 0 | 2 | 1 |
| Blair, rf | 1 | 0 | 1 | 0 | | Cowens, rf | 3 | 0 | 0 | 0 |
| Piniella, lf | 5 | 0 | 2 | 1 | | Mayberry, 1b | 2 | 0 | 0 | 0 |
| Johnson, dh | 4 | 0 | 1 | 0 | | Wathan, 1b | 2 | 0 | 0 | 0 |
| R. White, pr | 0 | 0 | 0 | 0 | | Porter, c | 4 | 0 | 0 | 0 |
| Chambliss, 1b | 4 | 0 | 0 | 0 | | Otis, cf | 3 | 1 | 0 | 0 |
| Randolph, 2b | 4 | 2 | 1 | 0 | | Patek, ss | 4 | 2 | 3 | 1 |
| Dent, ss | 3 | 1 | 1 | 1 | | F. White, cf | 3 | 0 | 1 | 2 |
| Totals | 38 | 6 | 13 | 6 | | Totals | 33 | 4 | 8 | 4 |

| | | | | | | | | | |
|---|---|---|---|---|---|---|---|---|---|
| New York | 1 2 1 | 1 0 0 | 0 0 1 | — 6 | | | | | |
| Kansas City | 0 0 2 | 2 0 0 | 0 0 0 | — 4 | | | | | |

Doubles—Rivers, Dent, Munson, Patek, F. White, Piniella.
Triples—Patek, Brett. Sacrifice—Dent. Sacrifice flies—F. White, Munson.
Errors—Patek, Mayberry. Double plays—New York 1, Kansas City 1.
Left on base—New York 8, Kansas City 6.

| NEW YORK | IP | H | R | ER | BB | K |
|---|---|---|---|---|---|---|
| Figueroa | 3.1 | 5 | 4 | 4 | 2 | 3 |
| Tidrow | 0.1 | 1 | 0 | 0 | 1 | 0 |
| Lyle (W) | 5.1 | 2 | 0 | 0 | 0 | 1 |

| KANSAS CITY | IP | H | R | ER | BB | K |
|---|---|---|---|---|---|---|
| Gura (L) | 2.0 | 6 | 4 | 4 | 1 | 2 |
| Pattin | 6.0 | 6 | 2 | 1 | 0 | 0 |
| Mingori | 0.1 | 0 | 0 | 0 | 0 | 0 |
| Bird | 0.2 | 1 | 0 | 0 | 0 | 0 |

*1977*

had already pitched 75 innings—the most he'd ever worked in any previous season was 114—and his arm was getting tired. But New York's starters were consistently running into trouble, putting a burden on Lyle and fellow reliever Dick Tidrow. "My arm doesn't hurt, but I've only got so much left in it," Lyle told reporters after a Yankee victory on July 5, a game he entered in the fifth inning and finished up.

On July 19, Lyle got bounced around in the All-Star Game, a 7-5 National League victory, and two days later he blew a save (which happened only seven times that season) in a loss to Milwaukee.

That defeat, plus another one the following day, appeared to spell the end of Martin's regime. Rumors were flying for days that Martin was out; Steinbrenner let his manager hang by a thread. What may have saved Martin's job was a 5-4 victory over Baltimore on July 26, in which Lyle got the save. Mar-

## Putting It All Together

By 1977 New York had assembled a team of players that was "all that money could buy," as baseball historian David Neft wrote in his *Sports Encyclopedia Baseball*. Below is a chronology of New York's player acquisitions in the half-dozen years leading up to the team's 1977 world championship season.

1972: Obtained Sparky Lyle from Boston

1973: Obtained Graig Nettles (Cleveland) and Fred Stanley (San Diego)

1974: Obtained Lou Piniella (Kansas City) and Chris Chambliss and Dick Tidrow (Cleveland)

1975: Signed Catfish Hunter (free agent)

1976: Obtained Mickey Rivers and Ed Figueroa (California), Willie Randolph and Dock Ellis (Pittsburgh), and Oscar Gamble (Cleveland); and signed Reggie Jackson and Don Gullett (free agents)

1977: Obtained Paul Blair (Baltimore), Bucky Dent (Chicago White Sox), Mike Torrez (Oakland), and Cliff Johnson (Houston)

tin was able to hold on for another week, when the Yankees finally began their charge. Starting in early August, they won 40 of 50 games, passing the Red Sox and Orioles to move into first place.

Lyle was the key man down the stretch. He earned his seventeenth and eighteenth saves of the season on August 17 and 18, respectively. On August 29, 30, and 31, he won three consecutive games in relief, tying a league record.

The Yankees went on to win the AL East by 2½ games and defeat Kansas City in the ALCS. Lyle, who finished the season with a 13-5 record, a 2.17 ERA, and 26 saves, was again the hero, pitching 9⅓ innings over four of the five AL Championship Series games. He earned two masterful victories: In Game 4, he came on in the fourth inning and finished up, allowing just two hits; and in the decisive Game 5, he pitched 1⅓ scoreless innings.

The World Series star in 1977 was Jackson, who hit his three memorable home runs in consecutive at-bats in Game 6 to help New York defeat the Dodgers. Lyle's contribution was modest, but important nonetheless. He worked 4⅔ innings over two games and picked up one victory, in Game 1.

Lyle didn't have much time to enjoy the

Yankees' world championship and the Cy Young Award he received for his contributions that year. Before the 1978 season, the Yankees signed reliever Rich Gossage. Lyle knew no team needed two closers and that his days were numbered. He feuded with Steinbrenner over his contract, he didn't like the way he was used out of the bullpen (he finished the year with only nine saves), and he spent much of the '78 season in a funk. He went, in the words of teammate Graig

"I'm not the emotional type, and I've had so many ups and downs during my career that by next week this thing will be history to me, but I feel that on this one day, at least, I can be excited and proud and even fart in public if I want. I was on a team that won the pennant and the World Series, despite enough crap to last an entire career, and now that I've won the Cy Young Award everyone can say that Sparky Lyle was an important part of that team."

—Sparky Lyle's reaction to winning the 1977 Cy Young Award

Nettles, "from Cy Young to sayanora in one season." In November he was traded to Texas, and he never regained his All-Star form.

Lyle finished his career in 1982, with 238 saves, a 99-76 record, and a 2.88 ERA. He also left behind a lot of memories. "Sparky's record speaks for itself, stands on its own and immortalizes him as one of baseball's great all-time relief pitchers," sports writer Phil Pepe wrote after Lyle's performance in the 1977 ALCS. "But it's Sparky the man, and Sparky the clown, that endeared him for all time to his teammates and those fortunate enough to have covered him as baseball writers."

## *Baseball News Of 1977*

- The Montreal Expos inaugurated Olympic Stadium on April 15, which replaced tiny Jarry Park, their home between 1969 and 1976.
- The Braves retired Hank Aaron's jersey number, 44.
- Dennis Eckersley of the Cleveland Indians finally gave up a hit—a home run by Seattle's Ruppert Jones on June 1—after 22⅓ pitching consecutive hitless innings.
- The Braves' Gary Matthews, Biff Pocoroba, and Pat Rockett pulled off a triple steal against the Padres on September 11.
- Tom Lasorda debuted as the Dodgers' manager with a 5-1 win over the Giants on April 7.

## *Around The World In 1977*

- A collision between two airliners in the Canary Islands killed 582 people.
- Alex Haley was awarded a special Pulitzer Citation for *Roots*.
- *Star Wars, Close Encounters of the Third Kind* and *Saturday Night Fever* were America's most popular movies.
- Jerome Drayton of Toronto won the Boston Marathon.

# From 26 to 50
## An Outstanding Supporting Cast

*T*he great Yankees discussed in the second half of this book, from Charlie Keller at number 26 to happy-go-lucky reliever Joe Page at number 50, are only a shade less brilliant than players in the top twenty-five. Providing four more victories in their best season than the league-average player contributed in the same season, the vast majority of these Yankees are from the second half of the twentieth century.

Eight of these men, including Roger Maris, Clete Boyer, Mel Stottlemyre, Yogi Berra, and Elston Howard, provided power and pitching finesse in the '50s and '60s, which ensured Yankee domination in American League and World Series play during those decades. The '70s and '80s are represented by other familiar names: Reggie Jackson, Dave Winfield, Thurman Munson and Graig Nettles. And as we entered the twenty-first century, Derek Jeter, Bernie Williams, Paul O'Neill, and Andy Pettitte were there to carry the torch.

# 26

# Season of Glory

# Charlie Keller

## 1942

| AB | R | H | BA | OB% | 2B | 3B | HR | K/BB | RBI | BR | SB |
|-----|-----|-----|------|------|-----|-----|-----|--------|------|-----|-----|
| 544 | 106 | 159 | .292 | .417 | 24 | 9 | 26 | 61/114 | 108 | 49 | 14 |

| | | G | PO | A | DP | E | FA | FR | |
|---|---|-----|-----|-----|-----|-----|------|-----|---|
| | | 152 | 321 | 10 | 1 | 5 | .985 | 0 | |

# Charles Ernest Keller

BORN
September 12, 1916
Middletown, Maryland

DIED
May 23, 1990
Frederick, Maryland

HEIGHT
5-11

WEIGHT
185

THREW
right hand

BATTED
left hand

New York Yankees
1939–1943
1945–1949
1952

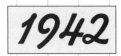

*C*harlie Keller was another of those talented young ballplayers who came to the Yankees like clockwork every year in the late '30s. Joe DiMaggio arrived on the scene in 1936, Tommy Henrich in '37, Joe Gordon in '38, and Keller in '39.

Keller was signed by the Yankees after he graduated from the University of Maryland in 1937. Assigned to their Newark ball club, the slugging outfielder led the International League in hitting (.353) in his first season and was named minor-league player of the year by *The Sporting News*. In 1938 he hit .365, and the Yankees welcomed him to the big club in the spring of 1939.

Dubbed "the next Babe Ruth" by the press—he also picked up the nickname "King Kong," which he detested—Keller was an immediate success in New York, batting .334 in his rookie season and hitting .438 with three homers in the Yankees' World Series sweep against Cincinnati. He hit just 11 home runs that season, though, so Yankee manager Joe McCarthy worked with Keller to get him to pull the ball more so he could take advantage of the short right-field dimensions (his long drives had been dying in center and left-center). The tutoring paid off; Keller hit 21 homers in 1940 (he also led the league in walks at 106). He increased his home run total to 33 in '41, battling Ted Williams down the stretch for the record that year before finishing second to the Red Sox star by four, and added 122 runs batted in. In just three seasons, the young Keller—he would be only twenty-five on Opening Day in 1942—had become one of the game's greatest sluggers.

Keller suffered an ankle injury late in the '41 campaign and took things slowly the next spring, not appearing in a game until the Yankees were a week into their exhibition schedule. For the most part, the first month was a struggle for Keller and several of his teammates. DiMaggio, Phil Rizzuto, and Keller weren't hitting, and pitcher Marius Russo and second baseman Gordon (hitting .407) suffered injuries. Still, the Yankees stayed competitive and were in third place at 10-5, only two games behind Cleveland, on May 1.

The Yankees moved into first for good on May 6—it was a fairly suspenseless pennant race as they waltzed home nine games ahead of Boston—but Keller continued to struggle.

He had a big day on May 23 in Washington, when he had three hits to help beat the Senators 8-4. Still, he had gone 2-for-33 in his previous eight games, which had dropped his average to .183.

Looking for help, he sought out Ty Cobb when the Yankees were in

*Charlie Keller, along with Joe DiMaggio and Tommy Heinrich, comprised the famed Yankee outfield of the '40s.*

# Game of Glory • July 26, 1942

On July 26 Keller hits his thirteenth and forteenth homers to carry the Yankees to a 5-2 victory over Detroit.

| NEW YORK | AB | R | H | RBI |
|---|---|---|---|---|
| Hassett, 1b | 5 | 0 | 2 | 1 |
| Rolfe, 3b | 5 | 0 | 2 | 0 |
| Henrich, rf | 5 | 0 | 2 | 0 |
| DiMaggio, cf | 5 | 0 | 0 | 0 |
| Keller, lf | 4 | 2 | 2 | 2 |
| Gordon, 2b | 3 | 1 | 0 | 0 |
| Rizzuto, ss | 4 | 2 | 2 | 0 |
| Hemsley, c | 5 | 0 | 2 | 1 |
| Ruffing, p | 3 | 0 | 0 | 1 |
| Totals | 39 | 5 | 12 | 5 |

| DETROIT | AB | R | H | RBI |
|---|---|---|---|---|
| Bloodworth, 2b | 4 | 0 | 1 | 0 |
| Cramer, cf | 4 | 1 | 1 | 0 |
| McCosky, lf | 4 | 1 | 3 | 0 |
| York, 1b | 3 | 0 | 1 | 1 |
| Harris, rf | 3 | 0 | 0 | 0 |
| Higgins, 3b | 4 | 0 | 0 | 1 |
| Tebbetts, c | 3 | 0 | 0 | 0 |
| Hitchcock, ss | 3 | 0 | 1 | 0 |
| Gehringer, ph | 1 | 0 | 0 | 0 |
| Trout, p | 2 | 0 | 0 | 0 |
| Rose, ph | 1 | 0 | 0 | 0 |
| Benton, p | 0 | 0 | 0 | 0 |
| Totals | 32 | 2 | 7 | 2 |

| | | | | | | | | |
|---|---|---|---|---|---|---|---|---|
| New York | 0 1 0 | | 1 0 1 | | 0 2 0 | — 5 | | |
| Detroit | 0 0 0 | | 0 0 2 | | 0 0 0 | — 2 | | |

Error—Bloodworth. Doubles—Bloodworth, Rolfe, Henrich. Home runs—Keller (2). Stolen bases—Rizzuto, Gordon. Sacrifice—Harris. Left on base—New York 12, Detroit 6.

| NEW YORK | IP | R | ER | H | BB | K |
|---|---|---|---|---|---|---|
| Ruffing (W, 10-5) | 9 | 2 | 2 | 7 | 2 | 0 |

| DETROIT | IP | R | ER | H | BB | K |
|---|---|---|---|---|---|---|
| Trout (L) | 7 | 3 | 3 | 9 | 1 | 4 |
| Benton | 2 | 2 | 2 | 3 | 4 | 1 |

Passed ball—Tebbetts. Attendance—26,341.

Time—2:17. Attendance—15,000 (est.)

*1942*

Detroit on May 16. Whatever Cobb told him didn't help; he had just one hit in his next 23 at-bats and told reporters he had never been in a worse slump. At least his manager was nonchalant about it. He told *The Sporting News*, "Oh, every slump is the worst and players never can remember anything to match it. But it all comes out in the wash. Then, somehow or other, our club gets into the World Series."

McCarthy knew what he was talking about. Keller began to come around at the end of May—he had two hits and a pair of runs batted in against Boston on May 26, and three more hits in a Memorial Day victory over Washington—and was up to .237 by the beginning of June. He raised his average to .254 by the end of June and to .257 on August 1, then hit .339 in August to bring his average to .279. Among the highlights that month were a three-run homer, his seventeenth of the year, on August 8 to help beat Philadelphia; a grand slam in the ninth inning on August 12 that beat Boston 8-4; and an 8-for-17 series with two homers against Boston (part of a 16-for-35 stretch that got him to .286). Keller also played well in September, finishing with a .292 batting average and in the top five in the American League in runs (106), homers (26), total bases (279), runs batted in (108), bases on balls (114), on-base percentage (.417), and slugging average (.513).

Unfortunately, Keller would not be able to add a World Series championship to his list of accomplishments that year. Although the Yankees were favored to beat the Cardinals (after all, they had won five of the previous six World Series, McCarthy's teams had won 24 of 28 Series games, and they had never lost two in a row), they lost their momentum after Game 1, losing four in a row to St. Louis. Keller hit two home runs in the Series, a two-run homer in Game 2 and a three-run shot in Game 3.

Keller also had a successful 1943 season (31 homers, 86 RBIs, and a .271 average). He served in the military the next two years and returned to play for the Yankees in 1946. In what would be his last full season, he hit 30 homers, drove in 101 runs, and batted

> "I never cared for big league ball. That is, I hated the travel. I didn't want to be away from home. I never liked any of that. I didn't want to leave my family for spring training and I disliked every road trip during the year."
>
> —CHARLIE KELLER IN 1960

.275. He suffered a back injury in 1947 that required surgery, and Keller was never again the feared slugger of old.

After the operation he spent two more seasons in pinstripes, hitting a combined nine homers in 143 games. He was released after the 1949 season and signed with Detroit, where he spent two seasons, primarily as a pinch-hitter (he played the outfield in only 14 games). He returned to the Yankees for two games late in the 1952 season—he struck out in his only at-bat—and retired after the season with a .286 career average and 189 home runs in 1,170 games.

After retiring, he became a successful harness horse breeder at his farm, Yankeeland, near Frederick in western Maryland. He died from cancer on May 23, 1990, at the age of 73.

## Baseball News Of 1942

- *The Pride of the Yankees*, starring Gary Cooper as Lou Gehrig, was released.

- Jackie Robinson and pitcher Nate Moreland asked for tryouts with the White Sox at the team's spring training camp in Pasadena, California. Manager Jimmie Dykes was impressed, but told the two black players he was unable to sign them.

- The American League won the All-Star Game by a score of 3-1 in New York thanks to homers by Lou Boudreau and Rudy York.

- Yankee shortstop Phil Rizzuto and second baseman Joe Gordon executed seven double plays (an American League record) in a 2-0 loss to Boston on August 14.

# *Around The World In 1942*

- Bombers under the command of Maj. Gen. Jimmy Dolittle attacked Tokyo on April 18. This was the first U.S. offensive against Japan in World War II.

- The Office of War Information was established to control dissemination of news and propaganda in the United States.

- Pulitzer Prizes were awarded to Ellen Glasgow for *In This Our Life*, Forrest Wilson for *Crusader in Crinoline*, Margaret Leech for *Reveille in Washington*, and William Rose Benet for *The Dust Which is God*.

- On August 7 U.S. Marines landed on Guadalcanal.

- Among the obituaries were those of John Barrymore (May 29, age 60), Carole Lombard (January 16, age 32) and Grant Wood (February 12, age 50).

- On March 17 officials of the AFL and CIO agreed there would be no strikes for the duration of the war.

# 27

# Season of Glory

# Russ Ford

## 1910

| W | L | Pct. | IP | GS | CG | SH | SV | K/BB | Opp. BA | DEF | ERA |
|---|---|------|-----|----|----|----|----|------|---------|-----|-----|
| 26 | 6 | .813 | 299.2 | 33 | 29 | 8 | 1 | 209/70 | .188 | -3 | 1.65 |

| | | | GP | PO | A | DP | E | FA | ER/R | PR | DEF |
|---|---|---|----|----|---|----|---|-----|------|-----|-----|
| | | | 36 | 7 | 63 | 4 | 7 | .921 | 55/69 | 34 | -3 |

# Russell William Ford

**BORN**
April 25, 1883
Brandon, Manitoba, Canada

**DIED**
January 24, 1960
Rockingham, North Carolina

**HEIGHT**
5-11

**WEIGHT**
175

**THREW**
right hand

**BATTED**
right hand

New York Yankees
1909–1913

*1910*

*W*ith low-hit, low-run games the rule, base-to-base offense the prevailing strategy, and league earned-run averages under 3.00, baseball in the early years of the twentieth century was clearly a pitcher's game. The pitchers who dominated the dead-ball era—Christy Mathewson, Cy Young, Three-Finger Brown, Ed Walsh, Grover Cleveland Alexander, Eddie Plank, Chief Bender—still appear in the record books nearly a century later. In 1910, a new name joined the list of pitching stars: Russ Ford.

Ford had appeared in one game in 1909—an inauspicious debut, allowing four hits and walking four in three innings of work on April 28—and when the Yankees (still officially the Highlanders) made their way north the following spring, Ford was brought along. Manager George Stallings' ballclub was a question mark for 1910; they had finished fifth the year before, and on paper the pitching staff was decidely average. Once the season started, though, the Yankees showed surprising strength, thanks in large part to their unheralded twenty-seven-year-old rookie Ford.

He made an immediate impression on April 21 with a brilliant 1-0 victory over the pennant-bound Philadelphia A's. By May 23 he had three shutouts, and by mid-June he was 8-1.

Among opposing hitters, the word was that Ford threw a spitter. That was inaccurate. The secret to the right-hander's success was his emery ball: He had a small piece of emery board in his glove, which he used to scuff the ball.

Thanks in large part to Ford's success, the Yankees showed surprising strength during the first half of the season, challenging Connie Mack's A's for first place. On July 4, though, Ford was outdueled by Philadelphia's Jack Coombs—only his second loss of the year—and the A's began to slowly pull away, eventually winning the pennant by 14½ games ahead of the Yankees.

Not coincidentally, as the A's were taking command in the pennant race, Ford was struggling. He lost four more games over the next month and was 14-6 after losing to Detroit on August 4. Then, however, he regained his touch and went on to one of the greatest seasons of any Yankee pitcher.

Over the next two months, he won twelve straight to close out the season. His streak—the third longest in Yankee history—began on August 9 with a three-hit shutout of St. Louis. Four days later he outdueled Chicago ace Doc White, winning 1-0 and allowing only four hits. He

*Master of the emory ball, pitcher Russell Ford won 48 games in his first two Yankee seasons.*

# Game of Glory • April 21, 1910

On April 21 Ford stifles the pennant-bound A's in Philadelphia, allowing only five hits in a 1-0 Yankee victory.

| NEW YORK | R | H | P | A | E | | PHILADELPHIA | R | H | P | A | E |
|---|---|---|---|---|---|---|---|---|---|---|---|---|
| Hemphill, cf | 0 | 1 | 1 | 0 | 0 | | Hartsel, lf | 0 | 1 | 1 | 0 | 0 |
| Wolter, rf | 1 | 1 | 0 | 0 | 0 | | Oldring, cf | 0 | 1 | 4 | 0 | 0 |
| Chase, 1b | 0 | 1 | 9 | 0 | 0 | | Collins, 2b | 0 | 2 | 3 | 3 | 0 |
| Cree, lf | 0 | 0 | 0 | 0 | 0 | | Baker, 3b | 0 | 0 | 2 | 3 | 1 |
| Gardner, 2b | 0 | 0 | 3 | 3 | 0 | | Davis, 1b | 0 | 0 | 12 | 2 | 0 |
| Foster, ss | 0 | 0 | 2 | 1 | 0 | | Murphy, rf | 0 | 1 | 1 | 0 | 0 |
| Austin, 3b | 0 | 1 | 0 | 1 | 0 | | McInnes, ss | 0 | 0 | 1 | 4 | 0 |
| Sweeney, c | 0 | 0 | 12 | 2 | 0 | | Livingston, c | 0 | 0 | 3 | 2 | 0 |
| Ford, p | 0 | 0 | 0 | 2 | 1 | | Morgan, p | 0 | 0 | 0 | 5 | 1 |
| Totals | 1 | 4 | 27 | 9 | 1 | | Totals | 0 | 5 | 27 | 19 | 2 |

```
New York        1 0 0    0 0 0    0 0 0 — 1
Philadelphia    0 0 0    0 0 0    0 0 0 — 0
```

Doubles—Wolter. Sacrifices—Cree, Chase, Wolter.
Double plays—New York (2).
Stolen bases—Wolter, Hartsel, Collins.
Strikeouts—Ford 9, Morgan 3.

Time—1:50.

*1910*

continued his shutout streak on August 19, beating St. Louis 6-0.

Ford's shutout streak ended on August 23, but he continued to pitch masterfully, defeating Detroit. Cleveland, Philadelphia, Boston and Washington. He finished the season by beating Philadelphia 3-1 on October 6. giving him a 26-6 record for the year. (Technically, the streak ended when Ford lost to Mathewson and the Giants in the postseason New York city series. Officially, the streak ended when he lost his first decision in 1911.)

While Ford's numbers were impressive in 1910—he had a 26-6 record, a 1.65 ERA, and eight shutouts—he didn't lead the American League in any major pitching categories (don't forget the aforementioned competition of Coombs, Bender, Walsh, Alexander et al.). He was second in wins, winning percentage (.813), opponents' batting average (.188), and opponents' on-base percentage (.245). He was also third in shutouts and fourth in innings pitched (299⅔) and strikeouts (209). And his hits-per-nine-innings ratio of 5.83 was the best in the AL.

Ford was by far the top pitcher on the Yankee staff that year, leading the club in eight categories. He was also the ace in 1911, going 21-11 with a 2.27 ERA. But he slumped to 13-21 and 13-18 records the following two seasons, then jumped to the Federal League, where he played for two seasons, until the league folded. He never made it back to the majors.

# Unstoppable

Between August 9 and October 6, Russ Ford was unbeatable, winning a rookie-record twelve consecutive games.

| Date | Opponent | Record | Comment |
| --- | --- | --- | --- |
| August 9 | St. Louis | 15-6 | Three-hit shutout |
| August 13 | Chicago | 16-6 | Four-hit shutout |
| August 19 | St. Louis | 17-6 | Third shutout in a row |
| August 23 | Detroit | 18-6 | Scoreless streak ends at 30 innings |
| August 29 | Cleveland | 19-6 | Beats Cy Young; also triples |
| September 5 | Philadelphia | 20-6 | Beats Cy Morgan |
| September 10 | Boston | 21-6 | Beats Ed Cicotte in Boston |
| September 13 | Boston | —— | Gets save in relief |
| September 17 | St. Louis | 22-6 | Holds Browns to one run |
| September 22 | Cleveland | 23-6 | Outduels George Kahler 2-1 |
| September 29 | Detroit | 24-6 | Gets 10 runs to work with |
| October 1 | Washington | 25-6 | A 3-1 win |
| October 6 | Philadelphia | 26-6 | Beats Jim Dygert; also triples |

# Baseball News Of 1910

- The White Sox's Ed Walsh led the AL with a 1.26 ERA, yet still lost 20 games for the punchless Sox.

- Philadelphia Athletics pitcher Jack Coombs won 18 of 19 games between July and September. He finished the season with 13 shutouts, then a major-league record.

- The major leagues drew 3.4 million spectators.

- Comiskey Park, the $750,000 "Baseball Palace of the World," opened in Chicago on July 1. The White Sox lost to St. Louis 2-0.

- Dode Paskert of Cincinnati stole second, third, and home in the ninth inning of a game against Boston.

# Around The World In 1910

- The Boy Scouts of America were founded in Washington, D.C.

- Arizona and New Mexico became states.

- In Los Angeles, a Wright biplane was flown to a record height of 11.47 feet.

- William Howard Taft became the first president to throw out the ceremonial first pitch, at Washington's home opener.

- Japan annexed Korea.

- The American Hotel and Motel Association was founded.

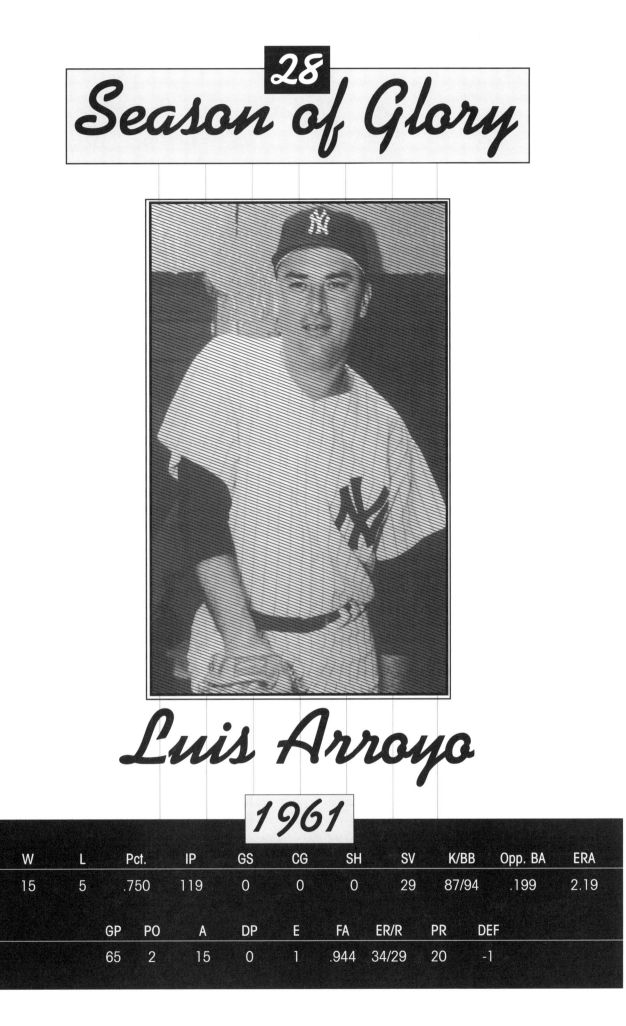

## 28
## Season of Glory

## Luis Arroyo

## 1961

| W | L | Pct. | IP | GS | CG | SH | SV | K/BB | Opp. BA | ERA |
|---|---|------|-----|----|----|----|----|------|---------|-----|
| 15 | 5 | .750 | 119 | 0 | 0 | 0 | 29 | 87/94 | .199 | 2.19 |

| | | | GP | PO | A | DP | E | FA | ER/R | PR | DEF |
|---|---|---|----|----|---|----|----|-----|------|-----|-----|
| | | | 65 | 2 | 15 | 0 | 1 | .944 | 34/29 | 20 | -1 |

# Luis Enrique Arroyo

BORN
**February 18, 1927**
**Penuelas, Puerto Rico**

HEIGHT
**5–8**

WEIGHT
**190**

THREW
**left hand**

BATTED
**left hand**

**New York Yankees**
**1960–1963**

**1961**

The 1961 Yankees were one of the most devastating teams ever assembled, with Mantle, Maris, Berra, Howard, Ford, Skowron and the rest all taking turns in the spotlight. But here's a vote for another hero, Luis Arroyo, often forgotten when fans talk about those slugging world champions. Without the portly left-handed reliever, Tony Kubek once said, "the 1961 Yankees would not have been a great team."

Arroyo, nicknamed "Yo-Yo" by manager Casey Stengel, who couldn't pronounce his name, was one of the most colorful characters in baseball. His tastes ran to Panama hats, flashy clothes, and huge cigars. He had begun his professional career in 1948, and after fifteen teams he was overjoyed to be in New York, where he had the time—and season—of his life.

A mediocre (18-22) pitcher with three major-league teams over four seasons, he had been sent to Jersey City by the Cincinnati Reds during the 1960 season. After a strong showing against the Yankees' Richmond farm team, they made a deal to bring him to New York. "All I know is that the Yankees pulled me out of Jersey City, and, believe me, I never thought I'd see New York," he told Kubek in Kubek's book, *Sixty-One*. Relying on a wicked screwball, Arroyo appeared in 29 games, all in relief, in 1960 and went 5-1 with a career-best 2.88 ERA and seven saves.

The Yankees started slowly in 1961, seemingly unsure under the direction of their new manager, Ralph Houk. Detroit, which had one of its finest seasons in the history of the franchise in 1961, jumped into first place early, and the two teams went back and forth through most of the campaign. Arroyo, too, started slowly. He was only 3-3 with eight saves on July 1.

In his first appearance after the All-Star break, on July 13 in Chicago, Arroyo allowed one hit in three innings as the Yankees beat the White Sox, 6-2, to move past Detroit and into first by percentage points. Two days later he allowed two hits in one inning of work but got the win when the Yankees scored a run in the tenth.

That season, Arroyo was often rescued by the Yankees' late-inning heroics. "I'd hold them for an inning, then Roger or Mickey would hit a homer, and I'd get the win," he remembered. On July 18 Mantle's homer in the eighth gave Arroyo his fifth victory. On July 22 Arroyo helped himself win when he doubled in a three-run ninth. On August 4 it was John Blanchard's turn to bail Arroyo out, hitting a three-run homer in the last of the ninth. And on August 8, Maris singled home a run in the tenth, helping Arroyo to his tenth victory of the season.

Arroyo, meanwhile, was returning the favors by bailing out Whitey Ford. Throughout his Yankee career, Ford had followed Stengel's regimen, working every fifth day. But when Houk succeeded Stengel for 1961, he implemented a four-man rotation. It would mean Ford's first twenty-victory season—and a lot of work for Arroyo.

"[When Houk] saw the slightest hint of fatigue in his little left-hander, he picked up the phone and dialed 1-900-LOUIE," Bob Cairns wrote in *Pen Men*. "The call to rescue came so often that when asked about his own efforts that year, Ford said, 'I'll have a good season as long as Louie's arm holds out.'"

Ford and Arroyo were a great team. By the end of April, Arroyo had relieved Ford twice, winning one game and saving another with two innings of work. As the season wore on, Houk brought him in more and more frequently to spell Ford. One typical appearance came on June 6 against Minnesota. Ford was cruising with a 7-0 lead in the eighth. He had retired eleven in a row before a walk, double and single brought in two runs. Houk called on Arroyo. He threw one pitch to Zoilo Versalles, who grounded into a double play to end the inning. A 1-2-3 ninth wrapped up the victory for Ford.

Ford picked up his twentieth victory—and fourteenth in a row—on August 10, again with the help of his little buddy. Pitching in the hottest weather of the season, Ford lasted only seven innings against the Los Angeles Angels. He turned a 3-1 lead over to Arroyo, who worked two shutout innings to save the victory for Ford, the tenth time he'd done it that season.

The Yankees managed to stay just ahead of Detroit during much of the second half

*Gifted Hispanic reliever, Luis Arroyo.*

of the season. On September 1 the Yankees began a three-game series in New York against the Tigers, who were only 1½ games

# Game of Glory • September 17, 1961

On September 17 Arroyo win his fifteenth game of the season when the Yankees beat Detroit 6-4 thanks to Roger Maris's homer in the twelfth inning.

| NEW YORK | AB | R | H | RBI | | DETROIT | AB | R | H | RBI |
|----------|----|----|----|-----|---|---------|----|----|----|-----|
| Richardson, 2b | 6 | 0 | 2 | 0 | | McAuliffe, ss | 6 | 1 | 2 | 0 |
| Kubek, ss | 5 | 2 | 2 | 0 | | Bruton, cf | 6 | 0 | 1 | 0 |
| Maris, rf | 4 | 1 | 2 | 3 | | Kaline, rf | 5 | 1 | 2 | 0 |
| Mantle, cf | 4 | 0 | 0 | 0 | | Colavito, lf | 5 | 0 | 3 | 0 |
| Berra, lf | 5 | 0 | 0 | 0 | | Cash, 1b | 5 | 0 | 2 | 1 |
| Blanchard, c | 5 | 0 | 0 | 0 | | Boros, 3b | 1 | 0 | 0 | 1 |
| Howard, ph-c | 1 | 0 | 0 | 0 | | Brown, c | 3 | 0 | 0 | 0 |
| Skowron, 1b | 4 | 2 | 2 | 1 | | Maxwell, ph | 1 | 1 | 1 | 0 |
| Boyer, 3b | 5 | 1 | 1 | 2 | | Roarke, c | 1 | 0 | 0 | 0 |
| Stafford, p | 3 | 0 | 0 | 0 | | Wood, 2b | 6 | 1 | 1 | 1 |
| Arroyo, p | 2 | 0 | 0 | 0 | | Wertz, ph | 1 | 0 | 0 | 0 |
| | | | | | | Bunning, p | 3 | 0 | 0 | 0 |
| | | | | | | Morton, ph | 1 | 0 | 0 | 0 |
| | | | | | | Fox, p | 1 | 0 | 0 | 0 |
| | | | | | | Aguirre, p | 0 | 0 | 0 | 0 |
| | | | | | | Regan, p | 0 | 0 | 0 | 0 |
| | | | | | | Osborne, ph | 1 | 0 | 0 | 0 |
| **Totals** | **44** | **6** | **9** | **6** | | **Totals** | **46** | **4** | **12** | **3** |

| | | | | | | | | | | |
|---|---|---|---|---|---|---|---|---|---|---|
| New York | 0 1 0 | 2 0 0 | 1 0 0 | 0 0 2 — 6 | | | | | | |
| Detroit | 1 0 1 | 0 0 0 | 0 2 0 | 0 0 0 — 4 | | | | | | |

Error—Skowron. Double—Maxwell. Triple—Maris.
Home runs—Skowron, Boyer, Maris. Double plays—New York 2.
Left on base—New York 9, Detroit 14.

| NEW YORK | IP | H | R | ER | BB | K |
|----------|-----|----|----|----|----|----|
| Stafford | 7.1 | 10 | 4 | 3 | 5 | 2 |
| Arroyo (W, 15-4) | 4.2 | 2 | 0 | 0 | 3 | 6 |

| DETROIT | IP | H | R | ER | BB | K |
|---------|-----|----|----|----|----|----|
| Bunning | 8 | 5 | 4 | 4 | 4 | 9 |
| Fox (L, 4-2) | 3.2 | 4 | 2 | 2 | 2 | 1 |
| Aguirre | 0 | 0 | 0 | 0 | 0 | 0 |
| Regan | .1 | 0 | 0 | 0 | 0 | 0 |

Hit by pitcher—by Bunning (Skowron).

Time—3:46. Attendance—44,219.

*1961*

behind the Yanks. When they left they were 4½ back and fading, thanks in large part to Arroyo.

The day before the series started, Arroyo received a letter containing a death threat. He went to Houk, who increased the number of security guards in the stands. Still, it didn't completely settle Arroyo's nerves. "I wondered how they could watch everybody, but I wasn't going to ask out," he later said.

In the opener the teams battled through eight scoreless, tense innings. Arroyo was called in to relieve Bud Daley in the ninth. "Ralph flipped me the ball and said, 'Luis, you better get them out or *I'll* kill you.' I know Ralph was trying to make a joke, but I was very scared." He held back Detroit in the ninth, then ended up with the win when Bill Skowron singled home Ellie Howard in the bottom of the inning.

The next afternoon, with a gametime temperature of 96°, Arroyo again was the hero. He relieved Ralph Terry in the bottom of the seventh and struck out three of the four men he faced. In the bottom of the eighth, he led off with a single, raced to third on a hit by Bobby Richardson, then scored the winning run on a single by Kubek. A homer by Maris, his second of the day and fifty-third of the season, was icing on the cake.

Arroyo wasn't as sharp the next day. He came on in the eighth with a 4-2 lead, but frittered it away and soon found himself down 5-4 in the bottom of the ninth. But Mantle and Howard rescued him by hitting homers, as the Yankees won 8-5 for a sweep of the series.

The victory, which ran Arroyo's record to 13-3, was his eleventh in a row. He won his twelfth straight on September 10, but his streak ended on September 14—his first loss since June 19—when he failed to protect a 3-0 eighth-inning lead against the White Sox and lost 4-3. The defeat snapped the Yankees' thirteen-game winning streak, but the loss was hardly decisive—they finally won their twenty-sixth American League pennant on September 20.

In a season dominated by Maris and Mantle's pursuit of Babe Ruth's home run record, the World Series against Cincinnati was almost an afterthought. The Yankees won it in five games, with Arroyo getting the win in Game 3 thanks to a Maris homer in the top of the ninth.

Arroyo's final numbers for '61—a 15-5 record, a league-best 29 saves, and a 2.19

> "(Yankee president) Dan Topping called me the bartender because he said that's what I looked like. All I know is when I walked up to the Yankee dressing room for the first time, they wouldn't let me in. The guard didn't believe I was a player until he called someone in the front office to check with them. I was five foot eight and over two hundred pounds, and it wasn't exactly all muscle."
>
> —LUIS ARROYO QUOTED IN *SIXTY-ONE*, BY TONY KUBEK AND TERRY PLUTO

ERA in 65 games—earned him Fireman of the Year honors from *The Sporting News*. Unfortunately, he was never able to come close to repeating his magical 1961 season. The Yankees asked him not to play winter ball after the 1961 campaign, fearing he was wearing himself out. So instead of pitching and staying in shape, Arroyo let himself go. He reported to spring training in 1962 overweight and out of shape. Early in the season, pitching on a cold day in Detroit, he hurt his arm and was never the same. He was 1-3 with seven saves in 1962 and just 1-1 with no saves in '63, his last season as a player. After working as a manager and general manager in Mexico for ten seasons, he went back to work for the Yankees as a scout, covering his native Puerto Rico.

# Baseball News Of 1961

- Roger Maris broke Babe Ruth's thirty-four-year-old record when he hit 61 home runs. He earned American League MVP honors but little respect.

- The Yankees won 109 games in capturing the AL pennant.

- Cubs owner Philip K. Wrigley decided to have his team run not by a manager, but by an eight-man "college of coaches." Leading off the rotation: Vedie Himsl.

- In his major-league debut, on April 11, Carl Yastrzemski singled in his first at-bat.

- Willie Mays hit four home runs in a 14-4 Giants victory over the Braves on April 30 in Milwaukee.

# Around The World In 1961

- John F. Kennedy was sworn in as the United States' thirty-fifth—and youngest— president on January 20.

- Some 1,500 anti-Castro Cuban exiles attempted to invade Cuba; they were routed in what became known as the Bay of Pigs invasion.

- Henry Miller's *Tropic of Cancer*, first published in 1934, finally became available in the United States after years of obscenity battles.

- Newton Minnow called television "a vast wasteland."

- Alan Shepard Jr. became the first American in space, making a successful suborbital flight aboard *Freedom Seven* on May 5.

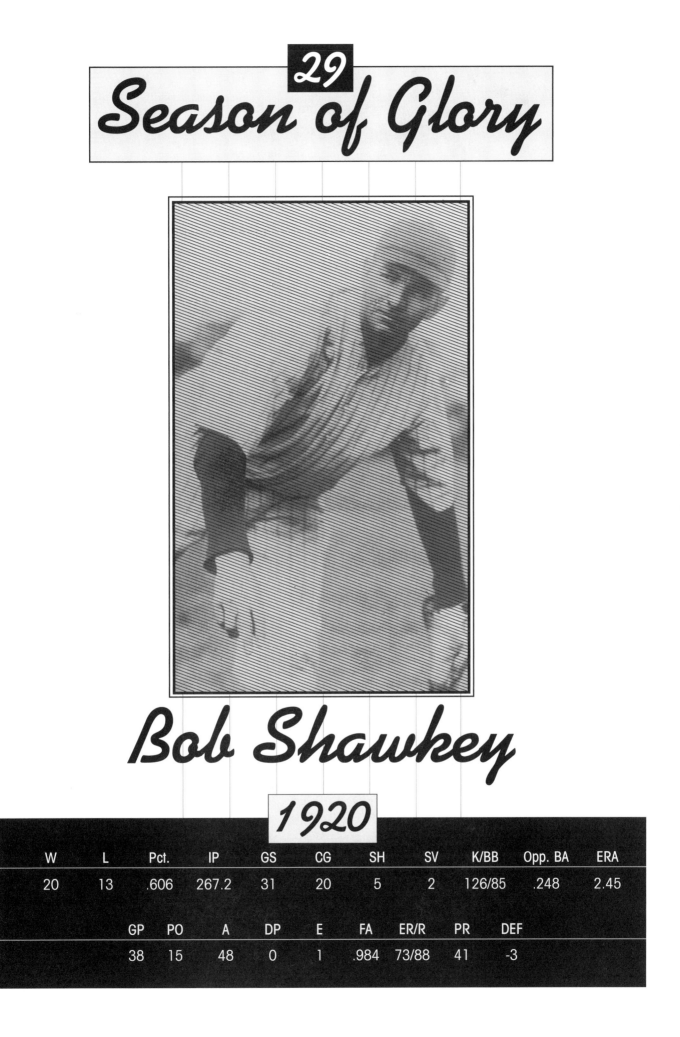

## 29
# Season of Glory

# Bob Shawkey

## 1920

| W | L | Pct. | IP | GS | CG | SH | SV | K/BB | Opp. BA | ERA |
|---|---|------|-----|-----|-----|-----|-----|------|---------|-----|
| 20 | 13 | .606 | 267.2 | 31 | 20 | 5 | 2 | 126/85 | .248 | 2.45 |

| | GP | PO | A | DP | E | FA | ER/R | PR | DEF |
|---|-----|-----|-----|-----|-----|-----|------|-----|-----|
| | 38 | 15 | 48 | 0 | 1 | .984 | 73/88 | 41 | -3 |

# 29 James Robert Shawkey

**BORN**
December 4, 1890
Sigel, Pennsylvania

**DIED**
December 31, 1980
Syracuse, New York

**HEIGHT**
5–11

**WEIGHT**
168

**THREW**
right hand

**BATTED**
right hand

New York Yankees
1915–1927

*1920*

*U*ntil his death in 1980 at the age of 90, Bob Shawkey was a living piece of New York Yankee history. He was the ace of the pitching staff during their first glorious era in the 1920s, won 20 or more games four times and won 168 games over thirteen seasons. He was the starting pitcher in the first game played at Yankee Stadium—his three-hitter on April 18, 1923, helped beat Boston 4-1. Fifty years later he threw out the first pitch at the stadium's golden anniversary day, and he did the same three years later when the refurbished stadium reopened. He took over as Yankee manager after Miller Huggins died in 1929. And he was Babe Ruth's golfing buddy.

Don't think, though, that Shawkey was merely carried along by the historical events going on around him. The intense and fiercely competitive right-hander, though often overlooked, was an integral part of the Yankees' success.

Shawkey started his career with Connie Mack's Philadelphia A's in 1913. In July 1915 the Yankees purchased his contract for a reported $85,000. That was a lot of money back then, but considering that the Yankees would build their pitching staff around him, it was a bargain.

During his first full season in New York, Shawkey went 24-14. He slumped to 13-15 in 1917 as the punchless Yankees fell to sixth place, then went 1-1 in 1918 before going into the service. He returned in 1919 to go 20-13 with a 2.72 ERA. It was a tremendous year, a year that set the stage for his remarkable season in 1920.

Before examining Shawkey's finest year, it's instructive to look at what else was going on in baseball in 1920. The spitball and all other such pitches were outlawed; further, umpires were instructed to take dirty, scuffed balls from play and replace them with new balls. These rules were to the hitter's advantage and—along with a juiced-up ball—helped make 1920 a hitter's year.

The biggest hitter of all, of course, was Babe Ruth, the man who would become the most prominent player during baseball's long-ball era. Ruth came to the Yankees on January 3, 1920, in that historic trade with the Red Sox. Although Ruth's first season in pinstripes was memorable (he hit 54 homers), his first game as a Yankee was hardly the stuff of legend. And Shawkey was the one who suffered. On April 14 Ruth misplayed Joe Dugan's line drive to right field in the eighth inning, letting the A's score two runs for a 3-1 victory over Shawkey and the Yankees.

Shawkey lost his next two outings—3-2 to Boston and 2-1 to the

*Stylish Bob Shawkey, Yankee staff ace in the early '20s.*

# Game of Glory • July 23, 1920

On July 23 Bob Shawkey beats the Indians 6-3 to help the Yankees move into first place.

| CLEVELAND | AB | R | H | RBI | | NEW YORK | AB | R | H | RBI |
|---|---|---|---|---|---|---|---|---|---|---|
| Jameson, lf | 4 | 0 | 1 | 0 | | Peckinpaugh, ss | 4 | 1 | 1 | 0 |
| Chapman, ss | 5 | 2 | 3 | 1 | | Pipp, 1b | 3 | 1 | 1 | 0 |
| Speaker, cf | 4 | 0 | 2 | 1 | | Pratt, 2b | 4 | 1 | 1 | 0 |
| Smith, rf | 4 | 1 | 1 | 0 | | Ruth, lf | 3 | 2 | 2 | 0 |
| Gardner, 3b | 4 | 0 | 2 | 0 | | Meusel, rf | 4 | 1 | 0 | 0 |
| Wambsganss, 2b | 4 | 0 | 0 | 0 | | Bodie, cf | 4 | 0 | 2 | 0 |
| Johnson, 1b | 4 | 0 | 1 | 1 | | Ward, 3b | 4 | 0 | 0 | 0 |
| O'Neill, c | 2 | 0 | 1 | 0 | | Ruel, c | 4 | 0 | 1 | 0 |
| Thomas, c | 1 | 0 | 1 | 0 | | Shawkey, p | 3 | 0 | 0 | 0 |
| Morton, p | 2 | 0 | 0 | 0 | | Mogridge, p | 0 | 0 | 0 | 0 |
| Uhle, p | 0 | 0 | 0 | 0 | | | | | | |
| Niehaus, p | 0 | 0 | 0 | 0 | | | | | | |
| Graney, ph | 1 | 0 | 0 | 0 | | | | | | |
| Caldwell, ph | 1 | 0 | 0 | 0 | | | | | | |
| Burns, ph | 1 | 0 | 0 | 0 | | | | | | |
| Totals | 37 | 3 | 12 | 3 | | Totals | 33 | 6 | 8 | 0 |

| | | | | | | | | |
|---|---|---|---|---|---|---|---|---|
| Cleveland | 1 0 0 | 0 0 0 | 0 2 0 | — 3 |
| New York | 0 0 0 | 3 0 1 | 2 0 * | — 6 |

Doubles—Speaker, Pipp. Triples—Chapman (2).
Home runs—Ruth, Peckinpaugh. Stolen base—Pipp.

| NEW YORK | IP | R | H | BB | K |
|---|---|---|---|---|---|
| Shawkey | 8.1 | 3 | 12 | 0 | 3 |
| Mogridge | 0.2 | 0 | 0 | 1 | 0 |

| CLEVELAND | IP | R | H | BB | K |
|---|---|---|---|---|---|
| Morton | 6.0 | 3 | 5 | 1 | 8 |
| Uhle | 0.2 | 1 | 2 | 0 | 0 |
| Niehaus | 1.1 | 2 | 1 | 0 | 0 |

Time—2:20. Umpires—Chill and Moriarity.

A's—then won his first game, with Ruth's help (he hit his first home run as a Yankees) on May 1. He lasted only six innings in his next start, losing to Washington, but then began an eleven-game winning streak that lasted until July 28, when he dropped a 1-0 heartbreaker to St. Louis and Urban Shocker.

Perhaps the most interesting game of the streak was on May 27, when Shawkey got into a fight with home plate umpire George Hildebrand. The Yankees led 3-0 in the fourth. Shawkey walked Boston's Wally Schang with the bases loaded, forcing in a run. Shawkey's teammates protested Hildebrand's call on Ball 4, to no avail. After the next batter, pitcher Harry Harper, was called out on strikes, Shawkey bowed and tipped his hat to the ump in mock respect. Hildebrand ordered Shawkey out of the game, and the Yankee pitcher charged the ump, who defended himself by hitting Shawkey in the head with his mask several times, opening a bloody gash. Shawkey was escorted off the field and later slapped with a suspension that cost him several starts in July.

Shawkey won his last four decisions in June, served his suspension, and then won his next two starts, including a 6-3 decision over Cleveland on July 23—with help from Ruth's thirty-third homer—that moved the Yankees into first place, percentage points ahead of the Indians. By the end of July, the Yankees were back in second and Shawkey was in the midst of a three-game losing streak that left him 12-7. A month later he was 15-9 and the Yankees had slipped to third place, just two games out of first.

In September, Shawkey kept the Yankees in the race. His 13-3 victory over Detroit on the September 14, in fact, moved New York 6 percentage points ahead of Cleveland and into first place. But after an 8-3 loss in Chicago on September 16, which, coincidentally was the day the Black Sox scandal broke in the press— the Yankees dropped out of the lead for good. Shawkey split his last four decisions, closing out the Yankees' season on September 29 with a 9-4 victory—his twentieth—over Philadelphia in eleven innings.

In this season of hitters—AL players hit 369 homers, 129 more than the year before, and that year more than thirty players hit .300—Shawkey led the league with a 2.45 ERA, more than a run better than the league average (only five AL pitchers under 3.00). Among his twenty victories were five shutouts, two of them three-hitters. He was also second in the league in strikeouts per game (2.94) and in shutouts.

The Yankees won the AL pennant each

"Several years ago (Miller) Huggins discussed with me the possibility of something happening to him and frequently mentioned several men in the employ of the Yankees whom he thought most suitable to carry on his methods if ever he had to step down. . . . "(There was a player) whom Huggins mentioned repeatedly the last year as one whom he thought excellently fitted for carrying on his ideas if he had to quit. His name was Bob Shawkey, and Bob Shawkey, gentlemen, is the new manager of the Yankees."

—YANKEES OWNER JACOB RUPPERT, NAMING BOB SHAWKEY TO SUCCEED THE LATE MILLER HUGGINS ON OCTOBER 17, 1929

of the next three years, thanks in large part to Shawkey, who averaged 18 wins over those three seasons. His Yankee playing career ended after the 1927 season, but Shawkey remained a Yankee for the rest of his life, as a coach, manager, and fan.

# Baseball News Of 1920

- Nihon Undo Kyokai became Japan's first professional baseball club.
- Tris Speaker set a record for consecutive hits (11) on July 10.
- The St. Louis Cardinals moved to their new home, Sportsman's Park.
- In three successive days in May, the Dodgers played 58 innings, tying the Braves (in 26 innings) and losing to the Phillies (in 13) and Braves (in 19).
- Rube Foster and other black team owners formed the Negro National Baseball League, which debuted on May 2.
- George Sisler set a record for hits in a single season (257).
- Runs batted in and the sacrifice fly became official statistics.
- Ed Barrow left the Red Sox to become the Yankees' general manager.

# Around The World In 1920

- The great Gansu earthquake in China killed more than 100,000 people.
- Sprinter Charles Paddock won the 100 meters in 10.8 seconds at the Olympic Games in Antwerp, Belgium.
- Best sellers *Main Street*, by Sinclair Lewis, and *This Side of Paradise*, by F. Scott Fitzgerald, were published.
- William E.B. Du Bois was the Springarn Medal winner.
- The American yacht *Resolute* won the Americas Cup.
- The Federal Bar Association was founded in Washington, D.C.

**30**

*Season of Glory*

*Yogi Berra*

*1956*

| AB | R | H | BA | OB% | 2B | 3B | HR | K/BB | RBI | BR | SB |
|---|---|---|---|---|---|---|---|---|---|---|---|
| 521 | 93 | 155 | .298 | .381 | 29 | 2 | 30 | 29/65 | 105 | 31 | 3 |

| | | G | PO | A | DP | E | FA | FR | |
|---|---|---|---|---|---|---|---|---|---|
| | | 140 | 732 | 11 | 15 | 11 | .986 | 6 | |

# 30 Lawrence Peter Berra

**BORN**
May 12, 1925
St. Louis, Missouri

**HEIGHT**
5-8

**WEIGHT**
194

**THREW**
right hand

**BATTED**
left hand

New York Yankees
1946–1963

**HALL OF FAME**
1972

*W*ith his "Yogi-isms" and an appearance that could be described, at best, as rumpled, Yogi Berra has long been considered as something of a comic figure. But nothing could be further from the truth. Lawrence Peter Berra was a gifted athlete with an astute mind, a baseball innovator, good natured, loyal to his friends, and a dedicated family man. And he was one great ballplayer. "He seemed to be doing everything wrong, yet everything came out right," Mel Ott once observed. "He stopped everything behind the plate and hit everything in front of it."

Berra grew up in the Hill, the Italian section of St. Louis, where his athletic feats were legendary. No matter what sport the neighborhood kids were playing—football, soccer, baseball—Yogi was always the first person picked when teams were choosing up sides. "Yogi Berra . . . was always the one you wanted with you. He was the best at baseball, the best at football, even the best at pitching horseshoes," Joe Garagiola, his boyhood pal, recalled in *The Wit and Wisdom of Yogi Berra*, written by Phil Pepe in 1974.

Garagiola and Berra grew up across the street from each other on Elizabeth Avenue in St. Louis (Berra was "Lawdie" back then; a friend later gave him the nickname "Yogi"). They were nearly inseparable. Until baseball came calling. The hometown Cardinals offered both of them contracts. But Garagiola also got a $500 signing bonus. When the Cardinals refused to offer Berra the same amount, he turned down the contract and went back to his job in a shoe factory. "He felt he deserved to get as much as I did," Garagiola said. "In his mind and heart he knew he was the better ballplayer. And I knew it, too."

The Yankees knew it too. Their bullpen coach, Johnny Schulte, lived in the St. Louis area and sought out the young outfielder from the Hill. He offered Berra a $500 signing bonus and Berra accepted the contract. He was assigned to Norfolk, then was called to serve in the navy. After his discharge in 1946, he was sent to the Yankees' top farm club in Newark, where he hit 15 homers in 77 games and had a .314 batting average. He was promoted to the parent club in the last week of season.

By the time Berra arrived in the majors, he was in the process of being converted into a catcher. He played as both an outfielder and catcher in 1947 and '48, then found a permanent home behind the plate in 1949. With his quick feet and strong arm, Berra had the prerequisites for the job. And with Bill Dickey helping him, everything else fell into place.

Tom Meany, in *The Magnificent Yankees*, described Dickey's first impressions of Berra after new Yankee manager Casey Stengel asked him to work with the twenty-three-year-old catcher before the start of the 1949 season:

Dickey got his first look at Berra at Miller Huggins Field in St. Petersburg in spring training in 1949. It was about the third day of training and Yogi worked behind the plate in batting practice for about fifteen minutes. Dickey parked his car, tied his dog to a fire hydrant and settled into some sort of trance as he watched Berra. . . .

There was a moment of concentrated silence by Dickey and then a smile. 'That Berra has the makings of a good catcher,' he said. 'I can't say a great one but I wouldn't be surprised if he is even that some day. Right now he does just about everything wrong but I was warned about that. But nobody told me that he could move—really hurry—and that's the main idea. I believe I can get him to throw all right once he learns where to throw the ball from.'

Dickey worked endlessly on his project, and it paid off as Berra quickly developed into one of the best catchers in baseball. (He also became something of an innovator when he introduced the catching technique of placing the index finger outside the catcher's mitt; that created an air pocket in the mitt that provided an extra cushion of protection.) Berra hit .277 (with a .989 fielding percentage in 109 games behind the plate) in 1949. In the following years he just got better: He had a .322 average with 28 homers and 124 RBIs in 1950, won an MVP award the following season, received a second MVP award in 1954, and was awarded a third in 1955.

*Yogi Berra and Bill Dickey*

Yogi Berra, the kid from the Hill, became the highest-paid Yankee when he signed a $56,000 contract in 1956. Both Berra and the Yankees got the 1956 season off to a good start when they beat Washington 10-4 in their April 17 opener. Berra went 4-for-4 (a homer, double and two singles) with five runs batted in, and Mickey Mantle hit two massive homers. At the end of the month, the Yankees were in first and Berra was hitting .325. Over the next two weeks Berra had a 13-game hitting streak, which raised his average to .353 (he was stopped on May 12 by Baltimore's Don Ferrarese).

Berra and Mantle carried the ballclub through most of May. At the midpoint of the month, Mantle was hitting .400 and Berra .330 (the Yankee infield was mired in a dreadful slump—second baseman Billy Martin was hitting .179, shortstop Gil McDougald's average was .227, third baseman Andy Carey was batting .200, and first baseman Moose Skowron was hitting .289. But with Mantle (on his way to a Triple Crown season) and Berra picking up the slack, the Yankees were able to stay in first place.

# Game of Glory • July 25, 1956

On July 25 Berra and the Yankees snap a five-game losing streak by routing Chicago 10-1.

| NEW YORK | AB | R | H | RBI | | CHICAGO | AB | R | H | RBI |
|---|---|---|---|---|---|---|---|---|---|---|
| Bauer, rf | 5 | 2 | 2 | 0 | | Minoso, lf | 4 | 0 | 0 | 0 |
| McDougald, ss | 3 | 2 | 2 | 1 | | Fox, 2b | 3 | 0 | 1 | 0 |
| Mantle, cf | 5 | 0 | 1 | 0 | | Philley, rf | 4 | 1 | 1 | 0 |
| Berra, c | 4 | 3 | 3 | 3 | | Lollar, c | 2 | 0 | 0 | 0 |
| Skowron, 1b | 5 | 2 | 2 | 1 | | Doby, cf | 4 | 0 | 1 | 1 |
| Siebern, lf | 4 | 1 | 1 | 2 | | Dropo, 1b | 4 | 0 | 0 | 0 |
| Carey, 3b | 4 | 0 | 0 | 0 | | Hatfield, 3b | 4 | 0 | 0 | 0 |
| Coleman, 2b | 4 | 0 | 1 | 0 | | Aparicio, ss | 3 | 0 | 0 | 0 |
| Ford, p | 4 | 0 | 0 | 0 | | Donovan, p | 2 | 0 | 1 | 0 |
| | | | | | | LaPalme, p | 0 | 0 | 0 | 0 |
| | | | | | | Phillips, ph | 1 | 0 | 0 | 0 |
| | | | | | | Kinder, p | 0 | 0 | 0 | 0 |
| **Totals** | **38** | **10** | **12** | **7** | | **Totals** | **31** | **1** | **4** | **1** |

```
New York    0 0 0    0 2 2    0 3 3 — 10
Chicago     0 0 0    1 0 0    0 0 0 —  1
```

Errors—Skowron, Hatfield, Aparicio. Sacrifice fly—Berra.
Doubles—Mantle, Berra (2), Skowron. Triple—Siebern.
Stolen base—Bauer. Double plays—Chicago 1, New York 1.
Left on base—Chicago 6, New York 5.

| NEW YORK | IP | H | R | ER | BB | K |
|---|---|---|---|---|---|---|
| Ford (W, 14-4) | 9 | 4 | 1 | 1 | 3 | 4 |

| CHICAGO | IP | H | R | ER | BB | K |
|---|---|---|---|---|---|---|
| Donovan (L, 4-6) | 5 | 6 | 4 | 4 | 1 | 3 |
| LaPalme | 3 | 2 | 3 | 2 | 2 | 2 |
| Kinder | 1 | 4 | 3 | 3 | 0 | 1 |

Wild pitches—Donovan, LaPalme. Time—2:45. Attendance—34,745.

Time—2:17. Attendance—15,000 (est.)

*1956*

In late May, Berra pulled a muscle in his side and had to sit out for a week, but by then the team was finally beginning to come around, ending May 6½ games ahead of the pack. Berra was hitting .341 (44-for-129) when May ended, and he raised his average another ten points by the middle of June. Soon after, however, he experienced one of the worst slumps of the season—he was 0-for-23 at one point. His average plunged to .296 by July 1, and by the All- Star break, he was at .281 and falling. Finally, by mid-

month, Stengel had had enough, benching Berra and his .275 average. The summer heat and a number of double-headers had simply worn him down.

Berra got his second wind in early August, raising his average to nearly .300. He experienced a slight slump in late August, then rebounded in September. After a nineteen-game hitting streak in the final weeks of the season, he reached the .300 mark. Berra slowed down in the last week of the season, finishing with a .298 average, 30 homers (third in the league),

105 RBIs (fifth in the AL), and a .986 fielding average. He reached several milestones along the way:

- On September 14 Berra hit his twenty-ninth home run of the season—and the 236th of his career, passing Gabby Hartnett for most homers by a catcher.
- On September 18 against Chicago, he singled home Martin in the ninth inning to tie the score at 2. Two innings later, Mantle hit his fiftieth homer to give the Yankees the AL pennant.
- On September 23 he went 2-for-5 in a victory over Boston. His three runs batted in put him over the 1,000-RBI mark for his career.

The 1956 World Series was a rematch of the previous year's Series, when the Yankees lost to Brooklyn in seven games. The Dodgers won the first two games, Berra's grand slam in Game 2 notwithstanding, then New York rallied to win Game 3 (Yogi contributed two hits and an RBI), Game 4 (he had an RBI single), and Game 5, in which Yankee pitcher Don Larsen threw the only perfect game in World Series history. (Afterward, home plate umpire Babe Pinelli was asked about Larsen's stuff. He responded, "[Larsen had] great courage and a great catcher, Yogi Berra, who directed all 97 of his pitches without a mistake.")

The Series, though, was far from over. Brooklyn rebounded to win Game 6, 1-0 in 10 innings, behind Clem Labine, setting the stage for the decisive game, on October 10 at Ebbets Field. The suspense lasted less than an inning. In the top of the first, Berra homered, with a man on base, to get the Yankees off and running. He added a second two-run homer in the third, as New York waltzed home a 9-0 winner.

Berra's homers in Game 7 were important to him for personal as well as professional reasons. On the night before Game

"We practiced baseball all day long. We'd chip in and buy a 75-cent baseball at a drugstore. We'd bat all day. By the time it got dark, that baseball was ruined but we'd had plenty of practice. Yogi and I would get there early in the morning. It was only a couple of blocks to home but we'd pack a couple of sandwiches so we wouldn't have to leave for lunch. And when it was getting dark, the one we'd have to drag away was Yogi. He'd be yelling, 'one more turn, one more turn.'"

—JOE GARAGIOLA, ON HIS CHILDHOOD PAL YOGI BERRA, IN THE JANUARY 25, 1956, EDITION OF *THE SPORTING NEWS*

6, he had called his mother in St. Louis. She suffered from diabetes and had had a leg amputated about a week earlier. "She asked me to hit a home run [in Game 6]," he explained. "I tried my darndest, but I couldn't do it. So I got two today."

Yogi Berra, dutiful son, finished the Series with a .360 average (9-for-25). It was the third straight Series in which he led all hitters. He also had the most total bases (20), home runs (3) and RBIs (10, a Series record).

Berra would never again be as productive as he was in 1956. His batting average dropped 47 points in 1957, and although he improved his average in '58 and '59, his run production continued to decline. After two more mediocre seasons, he became a part-time player for the Yankees for two seasons.

Following the 1963 World Series, he announced his retirement as a player. He left the playing field with an armload of records, including most homers by a catcher (313), most consecutive errorless games by a catcher (149), most consecutive chances without an error (950), most World Series (14), and most Series hits (71). He was eventually elected to the Hall of Fame. He had come a long way from the Hill.

## Baseball News Of 1956

- Connie Mack, longtime owner and manager of the Philadelphia Athletics, died on February 8. He was 93.

- American League umpire Ed Rommel became the first ump to wear glasses while working a game, April 17 in Washington.

- Cubs third baseman Don Hoak struck out six times against six pitchers in the Cubs' 6-5 loss to the Giants May 2 at Wrigley Field.

- Cincinnati fans stuffed the All-Star ballot box, electing Reds players to every starting position for the game. Commissioner Ford Frick unstuffed it and replaced two of the Reds.

## Around The World In 1956

- In the worst commerical airline disaster to date, 128 persons were killed when two airliners collided and crashed into the Grand Canyon on June 30.

- Dwight Eisenhower was re-elected president in a landslide victory over Adlai Stevenson. He carried forty-one states.

- The Salk anti-polio vaccine went on the market on August 1.

- The Nobel Prize in physics was awarded to William Shockley, Walter Brattain, and John Bardeen for their discovery of the transistor effect in semiconductors and the development of the transistor.

- Actress Grace Kelly married Prince Rainier of Monaco on April 19.

- The Ringling Bros. and Barnum & Bailey Circus performed its last show under the big top. Rising costs forced the circus to move performances into permanent structures.

# 31
## Season of Glory

## Reggie Jackson

### 1980

| AB | R | H | BA | OB% | 2B | 3B | HR | K/BB | RBI | BR | SB |
|---|---|---|---|---|---|---|---|---|---|---|---|
| 514 | 94 | 154 | .300 | .399 | 22 | 4 | 41 | 122/83 | 111 | 51 | 1 |

| | | G | PO | A | DP | E | FA | FR | | | |
|---|---|---|---|---|---|---|---|---|---|---|---|
| | | 143 | 174 | 3 | 0 | 7 | .962 | -2 | | | |

BORN
May 18, 1946
Wyncote, Pennsylvania

HEIGHT
6-0

WEIGHT
200

THREW
left hand

BATTED
left hand

New York Yankees
1977–1981

HALL OF FAME
1993

*1980*

# Reginald Martinez Jackson

*I*t was May 4, 1980, and Reggie Jackson was facing Minnesota left-hander Jerry Koosman in the fourth inning of a scoreless game. A Koosman fastball knocked Jackson down; it was the third time he'd found himself in the dirt in as many games. He picked himself up, got back in the box, and slammed Koosman's next pitch some 450 feet into the center-field seats. "Maybe they're trying to intimidate me," Jackson said afterward. "I'm glad to do well when there's a challenge. . . . I guess some people still feel they have to put me through the test."

At times it seemed Jackson's life was one long test. The test began in in Wyncote, Pennsylvania, where Jackson grew up. Although he lived with his father and two siblings in the upper-class Philadelphia suburb of Cheltenham (his parents divorced when he was young), his family was far from wealthy. His father, a dry cleaner and tailor, worked long hours supporting his children; consequently, Reggie learned quickly to be self-sufficient. "My dad was up and out of the house very early," Jackson told Bill Gutman for his book *At Bat*, "so I had to get up, wash, get dressed and get over to school by myself. I rarely ate any breakfast during the week because we didn't have much in the house. Dad didn't get home some nights until ten or eleven, and that's when we ate supper.

"There were a lot of tough times when he had to do anything he could to support us, but he always kept something on the table and we never starved."

Jackson survived those tests and became a star athlete—he played baseball, track and football—at Cheltenham High School. By his senior year, he had received nearly four dozen college scholarship offers from schools such as Notre Dame, Penn State, Syracuse, and Michigan State. He chose Arizona State, which promised to let him play both baseball and football.

He was a member of the Sun Devils' freshman football team in 1964, playing defensive back and running back. His scholarship stipulated that he couldn't play baseball as a freshman, but he worked out with the team. ASU baseball coach Bobby Winkles, later a major-league manager, could only watch. And wait. "I knew he was a great prospect and would really help our club," Winkles later said. "We had Sal Bando, Rick Monday and Duffy Dyer that year, but I had a hunch a couple of them might sign [with pro teams] and leave after the season, so I really looked forward to getting Reggie full time the next year."

Winkles' hunch was correct—Bando and Monday signed with Charley Finley's Kansas City A's after the season. The next spring, Jackson, taking over Monday's position in center field, was the Sun Devils' star, hitting .327 with 9 doubles, 6 triples, 15 homers (a school record), and 65 RBIs in 52 games. Great numbers, but not great enough to convince the New York Mets, who had the first pick in the 1966 major-league draft, to choose him (they went for catcher Steve Chilcott). The Kansas City A's, picking second, grabbed Jackson. After two days of negotiations with Finley in Chicago, Jackson signed for $75,000, plus $2,000 a semester to cover his college education and a new maroon Pontiac. Total value: about $85,000.

He spent 1966 and most of the '67 season playing in the A's farm system. He was called up late in '67 (he hit .178 in 35 games) and in 1968 the A's moved to Oakland, where Jackson established himself as one of the game's most exciting players. Before the start of the '76 season, Finley—desperate to cut his payroll and worried about losing Jackson to free agency—traded him to Baltimore.

He had a terrific season with the Orioles, hitting 27 homers and driving in 91 runs in just 134 games—he missed four weeks at the start of the season because of a contract holdout. His numbers made Jackson the most attractive player of that season's free-agent crop. And George Steinbrenner didn't fail to take notice.

Steinbrenner was one of the first owners to recognize that baseball is as much entertainment as it is sport. A winning team puts fannies in the seats, but so does a big splash in the media. He wanted Jackson. And Jackson wanted New York, a town that would

*Reggie Jackson*

feed his ego, a place where he could be a star, on the field and off. "I've got to admit," he wrote in his autobiography, *Reggie*, "that hot lady called New York and that smoothie Steinbrenner swept me off my feet."

Steinbrenner first offered $2 million over five years; Jackson wanted $3 million. Later, during a final negotiating session on Novem-

# Game of Glory • July 10, 1980

On July 10 Jackson hits a home run and a double (with the bases loaded) in a 13-5 rout of Texas.

| NEW YORK | AB | R | H | RBI | TEXAS | AB | R | H | RBI |
|---|---|---|---|---|---|---|---|---|---|
| Randolph, 2b | 3 | 2 | 2 | 1 | Rivers, cf | 4 | 1 | 1 | 0 |
| Murcer, lf | 5 | 2 | 2 | 1 | Wills, 2b | 5 | 0 | 1 | 0 |
| Nettles, 3b | 3 | 2 | 1 | 2 | Oliver, lf | 5 | 1 | 1 | 0 |
| Soderholm, 3b | 1 | 0 | 0 | 0 | Bell, 3b | 4 | 2 | 2 | 0 |
| Jackson, rf | 5 | 2 | 3 | 4 | Zisk, rf | 4 | 1 | 3 | 2 |
| Lefebvre, rf | 0 | 0 | 0 | 0 | Ellis, dh | 5 | 0 | 2 | 1 |
| Gamble, dh | 4 | 1 | 1 | 1 | Staub, 1b | 4 | 0 | 0 | 1 |
| Piniella, dh | 1 | 0 | 0 | 0 | Sundberg, c | 3 | 0 | 2 | 1 |
| Spencer, 1b | 5 | 1 | 1 | 1 | Harrelson, ss | 2 | 0 | 0 | 0 |
| Jones, cf | 2 | 1 | 0 | 0 | Frias, ss | 2 | 0 | 0 | 0 |
| Brown, cf | 1 | 0 | 0 | 0 | | | | | |
| Cerone, c | 2 | 1 | 0 | 1 | | | | | |
| Oates, c | 1 | 0 | 0 | 0 | | | | | |
| Dent, ss | 5 | 1 | 2 | 2 | | | | | |
| Totals | 39 | 13 | 12 | 13 | Totals | 38 | 5 | 12 | 5 |

| | | | | | | | | |
|---|---|---|---|---|---|---|---|---|
| New York | 10 0 2 | 0 0 0 | 0 0 1 — 13 | | | | | |
| Boston | 0 1 0 | 1 2 0 | 0 0 1 — 5 | | | | | |

Errors—Oliver, Harrelson, Jackson, Dent. Doubles—Jackson, Bell, Ellis. Home runs—Nettles, Jackson, Spencer, Zisk. Sacrifice—Randolph. Double plays—New York 2. Left on base—New York 5, Texas 10.

| NEW YORK | IP | H | R | ER | BB | K |
|---|---|---|---|---|---|---|
| Guidry (W, 10-4) | 6 | 10 | 4 | 4 | 2 | 3 |
| Lollar (S, 1) | 3 | 2 | 1 | 1 | 2 | 0 |

| TEXAS | IP | H | R | ER | BB | K |
|---|---|---|---|---|---|---|
| Jenkins (L, 7-7) | .1 | 5 | 8 | 8 | 3 | 0 |
| Lyle | 2.2 | 5 | 4 | 4 | 0 | 0 |
| Medich | 2 | 1 | 0 | 0 | 1 | 1 |
| Kern | 2 | 0 | 0 | 0 | 1 | 2 |
| Johnson | 1 | 1 | 1 | 1 | 0 | 0 |

Time—2:41. Attendance—34,463.

*1980*

ber 29, 1976, at the Hyatt in Chicago, Steinbrenner proposed $2.96 million, writing his offer on a hotel napkin. "At the bottom of that Hyatt napkin I wrote to George, 'I will not let you down. Reginald M. Jackson,' " he recalled in his autobiography.

While Steinbrenner was pleased to see Jackson go to spring training in 1977 as a Yankee, Reggie was hardly welcomed by his new teammates—his big salary, his big ego, and his predictions that he'd make the Yankees winners rubbed a lot of players the wrong way. And manager Billy Martin, who had no shortage in the ego department himself, was no Reggie fan either. To make matters worse, Jackson was quoted in Sport magazine as saying that he was "the straw that stirs the drink" and that "it all [came] back to [him]." He also insulted teammate Thurman Munson in the article, saying, "Munson thinks he can be the straw that stirs the drink, but he can only stir it bad." Jackson has long claimed he was misquoted.

Needless to say, the first few weeks of Jackson's first season in New York were not easy: In essence, he was facing another test, maybe the biggest of his life. And when he got into a near-brawl with Martin in the dugout in June—on national television, yet—his challenge became even greater. Again, Jackson rose to the occasion, finishing the season with 32 homers and leading the team in RBIs (110), doubles (39), walks (75) and slugging percentage (.550). He capped it all with a "Reggie moment", hitting three consecutive first-pitch homers in Game 6 of the World Series, carrying the Yankees to their first world championship since 1962.

In 1978, the Yankees won another World Series, this one

*Reggie Jackson, as productive as he was talented—and outspoken.*

without Martin, who resigned in July after the team fell 14 games off the pace. Jackson, who had hit .274 with 27 homers and 97 RBIs in the regular season, again took the Mr. October role in the Series, hitting .391 with two homers.

The 1979 season was disappointing and tragic for the Yankees. They got off to a slow start, prompting the return of Martin as manager. But on August 2, any chance they had in the pennant race ended when Munson died in a plane crash. The team went through the motions over the last two months, winding up fourth in the AL East, 13½ games back.

Jackson, who had led the Yankees in homers (29), RBIs (89) and slugging (.544) in '79, became the team's undisputed leader with the death of Munson. Another test. And in 1980 he responded with his greatest season.

Martin, who had made peace with Jackson during the '79 campaign, wasn't back in '80. He had gotten into another brawl—this time it was with a marshmallow salesman in a bar—shortly after the season ended and was again fired by Steinbrenner. His replacement was Dick Howser, a much respected baseball lifer who'd been a Yankee player and coach for more than a dozen years.

*Three of the Yankees' great stars of the '80s tip their "bonnets" with Reggie Jackson. (left to right) Dave Winfield, Tommy John, Goose Gossage, and Reggie.*

Howser earned Jackson's respect and gratitude when he assigned Reggie to the cleanup spot in the lineup and left him there. Martin usually made Jackson bat fifth, or lower, which irritated him. Jackson always believed that if he was consistently allowed to bat fourth, all would be right with the world. Or at least Reggie's world.

It took a while for Howser's decision to pay off. Jackson struggled at first and was hitting just .206 at the end of April. Around the middle of May, he began to come around—he had two hits in four at-bats in a victory over Texas on May 16 and a 3-for-4 game in another win the next day—and he raised his average to .268 by the end of the

month. Meanwhile the Yankees were leading the AL East by 4½ games.

May 31 was an especially eventful day for Jackson. First, he hit a two-run homer in the 11th inning to beat Toronto 8-6. Then, around 2 the next morning, as he was heading to a favorite restaurant, Jackson got into an altercation on the street that ended with a man firing a gun in the direction of Jackson and two others. No one was injured. Just part of New York's charm.

Jackson, for the most part, confined his flair for the dramatic to the baseball field for the rest of 1980. He hit his 10th homer of the year on June 7 beat Seattle 1-0; his one-out homer in the ninth two days later against the Angels sent the game into extra innings (the Yankees eventually won); he had eight hits and eight RBIs over a three-game span against the Angels a week later; and he had raised his average to .310 by June 20.

By the end of June, the Yankees led the AL East with a 47-25 record, best in the majors, and Jackson, bothered by a hamstring injury, was hitting .272. He was at .289 at the All-Star break—he contributed a hit in the AL's annual loss—and closed out the month with a rush (10-for-23 with three homers and six RBIs in his last seven games) to end July with a .306 average and 29 homers.

In early August Jackson reached a career milestone: his 400th home run. He hit it on August 11 against Chicago at Yankee Stadium, fifty-one years to the day that Babe Ruth hit his 500th career homer in the same ballpark. It came off Britt Burns and took some pressure off Jackson and the Yankees, who had seen their big lead in the AL East steadily shrink.

The Yankees had a seemingly comfortable 7½-game lead heading into August, but Baltimore mounted a charge, winning eight in a row and coming to within a half-game of first place on August 22. The Orioles then lost four of their next six games and were 1½ back at the end of the month. Slowly, the Yankees pulled away, leading the East by 2½ on September 4, by 3½ three days later, by 5 games on September 14. The Orioles crept back within three games of the lead in the final days of the season, but would get no closer.

The Yankees won the AL East pennant on October 4 with a 5-2 victory over Detroit. The highlight of the game was Jackson's three-run homer, the 410th of his career and forty-first of the season. The hit, and another hit in Game 2 that day, put him at .298 going into the last day of the season. That day, Jackson opened the second inning with a triple. The hit raised his average to .300. He came out of the game at that point, concluding the only .300 season of his major-league career. He later said that hitting .300 was "a milestone of which I was very proud. It's funny, but that was a big deal for me. Even with all the other accomplishments it meant something—it was another barrier I was able to jump over."

The American League Championship Series pitted the Yankees against Kansas City.

> "The crazy times really began after Reggie announced that he was the straw that stirred the drink, and of course Billy (Martin) right away wanted Reggie to know that he, Billy, was the straw. And all the while, there was George (Steinbrenner), sitting in his office thinking he was stirring the drinks. I'll tell you, for a couple of years there, there was an awful lot of stirring going on. Something crazy was going on every day."
>
> —FORMER TEAMMATE GRAIG NETTLES IN *BALLS*, WITH PETER GOLENBOCK

The Royals swept the series, ending Jackson's greatest season. He finished with 41 homers, 111 RBIs, 94 runs, 83 walks, and that .300 average.

Jackson's numbers fell drastically in 1981, a season marred by a players' strike. He hit just .237 with 15 homers in a 94-game season marked by a series of confrontations between him and Steinbrenner. After opting for free agency, Jackson signed with California the following January. He spent five seasons with the Angels before winding up his career with the A's in 1987. Jackson later worked as a special adviser to Steinbrenner and, in 1993, had his jersey number (44) retired by the Yankees.

# Baseball News Of 1980

- Players went on strike during spring training, canceling the last eight days of camp.

- On July 4 the Reds' Cesar Geronimo became Nolan Ryan's 3,000th strikeout victim. In 1974 he had been Bob Gibson's 3,000th victim.

- Ace Astros pitcher J.R. Richard suffered a stroke during a July 30 workout. He underwent surgery and attempted a comeback, but his career was over.

- Baseball innovator Charley Finley, unable to keep up with escalating salaries, sold the Oakland A's for $12.7 million.

- Rickey Henderson broke Ty Cobb's single-season stolen-base record of 96 by stealing 100.

# Around The World In 1980

- The United States boycotted the Summer Olympics in Moscow in protest of the Soviet Union's invasion of Afghanistan.

- Ronald Reagan unseated Jimmy Carter as president.

- Race riots in Miami in May left fourteen dead and more than 300 injured.

- John Lennon was shot and killed outside his New York apartment building by a former mental patient on December 8.

- The U.S. Supreme Court ruled that organisms created in a lab through genetic engineering can be patented.

- Twenty-two members of a U.S. amateur boxing team died in a plane crash in Poland on March 14. In all, eighty-seven people died in the crash.

# 32
# Season of Glory

# Elston Howard

# 1961

| AB | R | H | BA | OB% | 2B | 3B | HR | K/BB | RBI | BR | SB |
|----|---|---|----|-----|----|----|----|------|-----|----|----|
| 446 | 64 | 155 | .348 | .390 | 17 | 5 | 21 | 65/28 | 77 | 33 | 0 |

| | | | G | PO | A | DP | E | FA | FR | | |
|--|--|--|---|----|---|----|---|----|----|--|--|
| | | | 129 | 713 | 44 | 12 | 4 | .993 | 7 | | |

# 32

# Elston Gene Howard

**BORN**
February 23, 1929
St. Louis, Missouri

**DIED**
December 14, 1980
New York City, New York

**HEIGHT**
6-2

**WEIGHT**
200

**THREW**
right hand

**BATTED**
right hand

New York Yankees
1955–1967

*1961*

Elston Howard was the first African-American to wear Yankee pin-stripes; the first black Most Valuable Player in the American League; and the AL's first black coach. However, for a time, it appeared that he might not even get an opportunity to crack the majors, much less be a pioneer and a star. Black professional athletes faced enormous obstacles in those days, and Howard was no exception. Yet through it all, he maintained his dignity and stayed focused on playing baseball.

Elston Gene Howard was born in St. Louis on February 23, 1929, the son of a high school principal and a dietician. In high school he excelled in baseball, football, and basketball, and after he graduated in 1947, he turned down numerous college scholarship offers to pursue a professional baseball career. He was playing for the Kansas City Monarchs in the Negro Leagues when the Yankees signed him in July, 1950. They assigned him to Muskegon, Michigan, of the Class A Central League, where he played outfield—he was fast and had a great arm—and caught. He spent the next two seasons in the military, returning to pro ball with Triple-A Kansas City in 1953.

At spring training in 1954, manager Casey Stengel told Howard that the Yankees wanted him to concentrate on his catching skills. "He assured me that I'd have a better chance, a better career there than as an outfielder," Howard once told sportswriter Tom Meany. Howard got extensive training from coach Bill Dickey, then was assigned to Toronto of the International League for 1954.

Some observers were suspicious that by making Howard a catcher, the Yankees were trying to keep him in the minors, as the team had plenty of quality catchers already. One writer told Howard he didn't think the Yankees were serious about giving him a chance. "I told him he was wrong," Howard recalled in a *New York Times* interview in 1963. "I knew I wasn't getting a runaround, and later events proved how right I was."

Howard didn't think he was prepared to be a major-league catcher either. "I wasn't disappointed," he told Meany about being assigned to Toronto. "I knew I was far from ready and that I had to get experience, put the things Bill had been hammering into my head to work."

He proved to be a good student. He turned in a league MVP performance in Toronto, hitting .330, with 22 homers and 109 RBIs. After the season the Yankees purchased his contract from Toronto. Howard made his Yankee debut on April 14, 1955, appearing in 97 games in his rookie season—in 75 of them as an outfielder, seven as a catcher, and the rest as a pinch-hitter—and hitting a respectable .290. "I realized from the start that I was second string to a man [Yogi Berra] who was a cinch to be elected to the Hall of Fame someday," Howard once recalled. "When I broke in, Yogi and [Roy] Campanella were the best there were. Thank God I was able to play more than one position. That's what kept me going, the ability to fill in at first base and the outfield."

He was also able to handle the pressure and problems that he experienced when he traveled with his white teammates. During spring training in Florida, for example, he wasn't allowed to stay at the same hotel as his teammates. He often had to eat his meals on the team bus. And the problems didn't end once the season started and the ballclub returned north. "I remember that Ellie couldn't stay with the rest of us at the hotel in Kansas City," Yankee pitcher Bob Turley said in Tony Kubek's book *Sixty-One*. "The Yankees put him up with a local black family."

Howard's numbers slipped the next two seasons, but he still made valuable contributions to the team. In 1958, Howard hit .314 and was the hero in the Yankees' World Series victory over Milwaukee, making a great catch in left field and turning it into a double play to turn the tide in Game 5, contributing two hits to a Yankee victory in Game 6, then driving in the winning run in the eighth inning of the deciding seventh game. Then, in 1960, Stengel used him primarily as a catcher (he played only one game as an outfielder). "That's when I came into my own," Howard explained. "I love to catch."

Stengel was fired after the Yankees lost the 1960 World Series to Pittsburgh, and new manager Ralph Houk—an old catcher himself—wanted Howard and John Blanchard to get some time behind the plate. Berra's most productive days were behind him (he agreed to play left field), and the

*Ellie Howard—a pro's pro.*

pitchers liked having Howard behind the plate. He was active, talking and keeping their minds on the task at hand. And where Berra liked to position himself deep in the box, Howard moved much closer to the plate. It gave pitchers the feeling that they didn't have to throw as far, something Whitey Ford has said helped him. Howard aided Ford in another way as well.

"Ellie Howard would catch my pitch, and then he'd go to work," Ford told Kubek. "On the outside of his right shinguard, he had a

# Game of Glory • June 4, 1961

Howard's bases-loaded double in the first inning of a game on June 4 gets the Yankees started on their way to a 10-1 victory over Chicago.

| NEW YORK | AB | R | H | RBI |
|---|---|---|---|---|
| Boyer, 3b | 5 | 0 | 0 | 1 |
| Kubek, ss | 6 | 1 | 2 | 2 |
| Maris, rf | 4 | 2 | 2 | 1 |
| Mantle, cf | 3 | 1 | 1 | 1 |
| Cerv, lf | 4 | 2 | 1 | 0 |
| Skowron, 1b | 5 | 1 | 0 | 0 |
| Howard, c | 4 | 1 | 3 | 3 |
| Richardson, 2b | 5 | 1 | 1 | 0 |
| Stafford, p | 5 | 1 | 0 | 0 |
| **Totals** | **41** | **10** | **10** | **8** |

| CHICAGO | AB | R | H | RBI |
|---|---|---|---|---|
| Aparicio, ss | 5 | 0 | 1 | 0 |
| Fox, 2b | 4 | 0 | 1 | 0 |
| Covington, rf | 4 | 1 | 2 | 1 |
| Sievers, 1b | 2 | 0 | 1 | 0 |
| Minoso, lf | 4 | 0 | 0 | 0 |
| Smith, 3b | 4 | 0 | 1 | 0 |
| Landis, cf | 3 | 0 | 0 | 0 |
| Lollar, c | 4 | 0 | 0 | 0 |
| Pierce, p | 0 | 0 | 0 | 0 |
| Kemmerer, p | 1 | 0 | 0 | 0 |
| Pizarro, p | 0 | 0 | 0 | 0 |
| Martin, ph | 1 | 0 | 0 | 0 |
| Staley, p | 0 | 0 | 0 | 0 |
| Robinson, ph | 1 | 0 | 0 | 0 |
| Lown, p | 0 | 0 | 0 | 0 |
| Torgeson, ph | 1 | 0 | 1 | 0 |
| **Totals** | **34** | **1** | **7** | **1** |

| | | | | | | | | | | |
|---|---|---|---|---|---|---|---|---|---|---|
| New York | 4 | 0 | 1 | 4 | 0 | 0 | 0 | 0 | 1 | — 10 |
| Chicago | 0 | 0 | 0 | 0 | 0 | 0 | 0 | 1 | 0 | — 1 |

Errors—Aparicio, Lollar, Lown 3. Double—Howard.
Home runs—Maris, Covington. Left on base—New York 10, White Sox 10.

| NEW YORK | IP | H | R | ER | BB | K |
|---|---|---|---|---|---|---|
| Stafford (W, 2-2) | 9.0 | 7 | 1 | 1 | 4 | 3 |

| CHICAGO | IP | H | R | ER | BB | K |
|---|---|---|---|---|---|---|
| Pierce (L, 1-5) | 0.2 | 1 | 4 | 0 | 3 | 0 |
| Kemmerer | 2.2 | 4 | 5 | 4 | 0 | 1 |
| Pizarro | 1.2 | 3 | 0 | 0 | 0 | 0 |
| Staley | 2.0 | 0 | 0 | 0 | 2 | 1 |
| Lown | 2.0 | 2 | 1 | 0 | 1 | 2 |

Wild pitch—Pierce.

Time—2:33. Attendance—28,362.

*1961*

rivet which he had sharpened. I never could see exactly how he would do this, but he'd catch the ball and scrape it against that rivet right before he threw it back to me."

The doctored ball, and a mudball Howard provided for Ford—after a pitch he'd pretend to lose his balance while sqatting, then would brace himself with his right hand, all the while rubbing the ball in the dirt—helped Ford to a 25-4 record and Cy Young Award.

## Fall Classics

Elston Howard homered in his first World Series at-bat, putting him on a list with twenty-two other players who have accomplished the feat.

| Player, Team | Year | Player, Team | Year |
|---|---|---|---|
| Joe Harris, Washington | 1925 | Gene Tenace, Oakland | 1972 |
| George Watkins, St. Louis (N) | 1930 | Jim Mason, New York (A) | 1976 |
| Mel Ott, New York (N) | 1933 | Doug DeCinces, Baltimore | 1979 |
| George Selkirk, New York (A) | 1936 | Amos Otis, Kansas City | 1980 |
| Dusty Rhodes, New York (N) | 1954 | Bob Watson, New York (A) | 1981 |
| **Elston Howard, New York (A)** | **1955** | Jim Dwyer, Baltimore | 1983 |
| Roger Maris, New York (A) | 1960 | Mickey Hatcher, Los Angeles | 1988 |
| Don Mincher, Minnesota | 1965 | Jose Canseco, Oakland | 1988 |
| Brooks Robinson, Baltimore | 1966 | Bill Bathe, San Francisco | 1989 |
| Jose Santiago, Boston | 1967 | Eric Davis, Cincinnati | 1990 |
| Mickey Lolich, Detroit | 1968 | Ed Sprague, Toronto | 1993 |
| Don Buford, Baltimore | 1969 | | |

But Ford was just a small part of the Yankee machine in 1961.

The Yankees got off to a slow start. It wasn't until May that Houk settled on the batting order that would go down in history as one of the Yankees' most devastating: Richardson, Kubek, Maris, Mantle, Berra, Howard, Skowron, and Boyer. Yet Howard wasn't waiting for the rest of the guys to catch up: He was hitting .370 at the end of April, raised his average to .400 in mid-May, and led the league at .386 as the month drew to a close. On a team packed with stars, he was able to grab the spotlight with regularity: A bases-loaded double in the first inning on June 4 got the Yankees started to a 10-1 victory against Chicago; a 4-for-7 afternoon the next day paced a sweep of Minnesota; two hits and an RBI in the seventh inning helped beat Cleveland on June 15 and put the Yankees into first place; key home runs on June 25 and July 2 helped provide victories; two hits, four RBIs and three runs scored helped the Yankees beat Boston 14-3 on July 7 to regain first place.

At the All-Star break, Howard was at .369, tops in the AL. He appeared in the All-Star Game, coming in as a defensive replacement in the ninth.

The Yankees started the second half as they had spent much of the first, fighting the Detroit Tigers for the lead. Detroit led by a half game at the break, but New York moved ahead by percentage points by winning two of three

> "Elston exemplified the Yankee class of the 1950s and 1960s. Class was the way to describe the guy. He epitomized the Yankee tradition. Everybody in baseball respected the guy."
>
> —DICK HOWSER

in a series in Chicago. (Among the highlights of the series was a mammoth home run by Howard on July 15. The ball cleared two decks at the 390-foot mark in left-center, hit the roof once, bounced across 34th Street, and came to a stop some 60 feet from the outside wall of the ballpark. It traveled 490 feet according to the Sox's engineering department.) They solidified their grip on first with a nine-game winning streak in early August, during which Howard went 13-for-27 (.481). Detroit closed the gap to 1½ games again as August ended, but New York then swept a three-game series against the Tigers as part of a twelve-game winning streak—Howard went 21-for-44 (.477) during the streak—to gain control for good. When the streak ended on September 12, Howard led the league at .365, five points ahead of his nearest competitor, Detroit's Norm Cash.

While the Yankees coasted to the pennant—they clinched on September 20—Howard and Cash's batting race went down to the wire. Cash took the lead on September 27, .355 to .353, when he got two hits against Kansas City. He went 9 for 18 over the last week, finishing at .361; Howard was hitless in 14 at-bats in his last week, finishing at .348.

The Yankees made short work of Cincinnati in the World Series, winning their nineteenth world championship in five games. Howard made his most significant contribution to the series in Game 1 when he led off the bottom of the fourth inning with a home run that sent Ford to a 2-0 victory.

Howard, who was 5-for-20 in the Series, ended the season with 155 hits, 21 homers, 77 RBIs, and a .549 slugging percentage in 129 games. He had five more strong seasons for the Yankees (he was chosen AL MVP in 1963)—then was traded in 1967 to Boston, where he helped the Red Sox win the pennant. He played part time for the Red Sox in '68 and retired after that season with a lifetime .274 average.

The Yankees hired Howard as a coach in 1969. He was successful in his new job, yet he was unable to achieve his last great dream—to manage the Yankees. "He did resent the fact that he never got the chance [to manage]," his widow once remarked. "Elston wondered why he had to be better than everyone else, why he had to be a superman to manage a baseball team."

Howard spent ten years coaching for the Yankees. Then, in 1979, a serious heart ailment kept him out of the game for the entire year. In early 1980 he was named an aide to owner George Steinbrenner, but in December of that year, he succumbed to heart disease at the age of 51.

## Baseball News Of 1961

- Eddie Gaedel, the midget whom Bill Veeck signed in 1951 for one memorable at-bat, died in Chicago on June 18 of injuries sustained when he was mugged. He was 36.

- Ty Cobb died on July 17, at the age of 74.

- Warren Spahn, age 40, no-hit the Giants on April 28 and won his 300th game on August 11. He finished 1961 leading the NL in victories (21), complete games (21), and ERA (3.01).

- The Phillies lost twenty-three straight games between July 28 and August 20.

- William "Dummy" Hoy, a deaf-mute who played fourteen years in the majors and had a lifetime .287 average, died at age 99 on December 15.

## Around The World In 1961

- East Berlin was sealed off by East German and Soviet guards on August 13 by what came to be known as the Berlin Wall.

- A U.S. passenger plane was hijacked to Cuba on July 24; Cuban officials turned it over to UN officials.

- A plane crash killed seventy-four army recruits near Richmond, Virginia, on November 8.

- President Kennedy signed a bill that provided $600 million in aid to Latin America.

- Gary Cooper died on May 13 at the age of 60.

- Ernest Hemingway committed suicide.

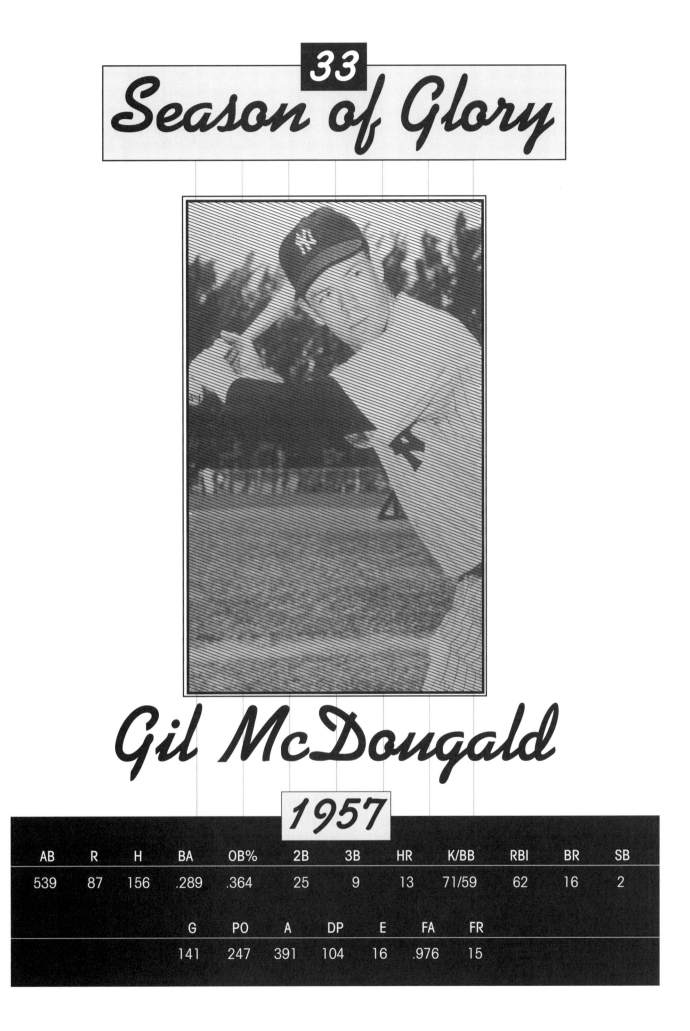

# 33
# Season of Glory

## Gil McDougald

### 1957

| AB | R | H | BA | OB% | 2B | 3B | HR | K/BB | RBI | BR | SB |
|-----|-----|-----|------|------|-----|-----|-----|-------|-----|-----|-----|
| 539 | 87 | 156 | .289 | .364 | 25 | 9 | 13 | 71/59 | 62 | 16 | 2 |

| | | G | PO | A | DP | E | FA | FR | | | |
|---|---|-----|-----|-----|-----|-----|------|-----|---|---|---|
| | | 141 | 247 | 391 | 104 | 16 | .976 | 15 | | | |

**33**

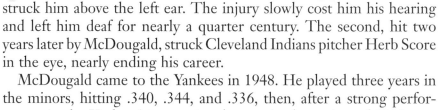

# Gilbert James McDougald

BORN
May 19, 1928
San Francisco, California

HEIGHT
6-1

WEIGHT
180

THREW
right hand

BATTED
right hand

New York Yankees
1951–1960

**1957**

*T*wo line drives. Gil McDougald's career, his life, were determined by two line drives. The first, hit during batting practice in 1955, struck him above the left ear. The injury slowly cost him his hearing and left him deaf for nearly a quarter century. The second, hit two years later by McDougald, struck Cleveland Indians pitcher Herb Score in the eye, nearly ending his career.

McDougald came to the Yankees in 1948. He played three years in the minors, hitting .340, .344, and .336, then, after a strong performance in the Yankees' instructional camp in the spring of 1951, was called up by New York. On Opening Day, he was the starting third baseman. He made a huge splash on May 3, when he drove in six runs in one inning—he had a two-run triple and a grand slam—during a 17-3 victory in St. Louis.

Midway through his rookie season, McDougald was switched to second base. He produced no matter where manager Casey Stengel put him. That year he hit .306—he was the only Yankee that season with a batting average above .300—and was chosen American League Rookie of the Year.

Over the next five seasons, he played almost every position in the infield for Stengel. He was the regular third baseman in 1952 and '53, the regular second baseman the next two seasons, and the regular shortstop in '56 and '57. He was solid offensively, hitting .279 his first six seasons, and steady defensively, three times leading the AL in double plays—at three different positions.

for all his contributions to the team (the Yankees won the pennant five of the first six years he played for them), he was largely overlooked. He was Rookie of the Year in 1951, but fellow rookie Mickey Mantle got all the press. He hit .311 in 1956 and finished second in the MVP voting, but again Mantle got all the press, for his Triple Crown season. It would take a near tragedy to burn McDougald's name into the minds of fans around the country.

Early in his career, the right-handed-hitting McDougald had used a strange, wide batting stance. Feet spread wide apart, his left toe would point at the mound and his chest faced the pitcher straight-on. He held his hands high, with the bat drooping downward. Eventually, pitchers learned to pitch him away. Stengel then altered his stance, and McDougald turned into a dangerous line-drive hitter.

The 1957 season began with the Yankees favored to win their third straight AL pennant. McDougald started fast, hitting .390 in April.

*Versatile Gil McDougald, whose infield play and steady stickwork helped pace the Yankees during the '50s.*

*Gil McDougald* **211**

# Game of Glory • June 5, 1957

On June 5 McDougald drives in five runs with two homers and a single in consecutive at-bats in the Yankees' 13-3 rout of Cleveland.

| NEW YORK | AB | R | H | RBI | | CLEVELAND | AB | R | H | RBI |
|---|---|---|---|---|---|---|---|---|---|---|
| Bauer, rf | 4 | 1 | 1 | 0 | | Raines, 3b | 4 | 0 | 1 | 0 |
| McDougald, ss | 5 | 2 | 3 | 5 | | Maris, lf | 4 | 1 | 1 | 0 |
| Mantle, cf | 5 | 2 | 3 | 0 | | Colavito, rf | 3 | 0 | 0 | 0 |
| Kubek, cf | 0 | 0 | 0 | 0 | | Wertz, 1b | 4 | 0 | 1 | 1 |
| Berra, c | 1 | 0 | 0 | 0 | | Smith, cf | 3 | 0 | 1 | 0 |
| Slaughter, lf | 4 | 1 | 1 | 0 | | Carrasquel, ss | 4 | 1 | 2 | 1 |
| Skowron, 1b | 5 | 4 | 4 | 3 | | Strickland, 2b | 4 | 0 | 0 | 0 |
| Howard, lf-c | 5 | 2 | 2 | 0 | | Hegan, c | 3 | 1 | 1 | 1 |
| Carey, 3b | 5 | 1 | 2 | 4 | | Wynn, p | 1 | 0 | 0 | 0 |
| Richardson, 2b | 4 | 0 | 0 | 0 | | Aguirre, p | 0 | 0 | 0 | 0 |
| Shantz, p | 5 | 0 | 0 | 0 | | McLish, p | 1 | 0 | 0 | 0 |
| | | | | | | Avila, ph | 1 | 0 | 0 | 0 |
| | | | | | | Pitula, p | 0 | 0 | 0 | 0 |
| **Totals** | **43** | **13** | **16** | **12** | | **Totals** | **32** | **3** | **7** | **3** |

| | | | | | | | | | |
|---|---|---|---|---|---|---|---|---|---|
| New York | 0 0 0 | 4 7 1 | 0 1 0 | — 13 |
| Detroit | 1 0 0 | 0 1 0 | 1 0 0 | — 3 |

Errors—McDougald, Carrasquel. Doubles—Howard, Slaughter, Skowron.
Home runs—McDougald (2), Mantle, Hegan, Carrasquel, Skowron.
Stolen base—Bauer. Double plays—New York 2, Cleveland 1.
Left on base—Cleveland 4, New York 5.

| NEW YORK | IP | R | ER | H | BB | K |
|---|---|---|---|---|---|---|
| Shantz (W, 6-1) | 9 | 3 | 3 | 7 | 2 | 5 |

| CLEVELAND | IP | R | ER | H | BB | K |
|---|---|---|---|---|---|---|
| Wynn (L, 6-6) | 4 | 6 | 6 | 7 | 1 | 4 |
| Aguirre | 0 | 5 | 3 | 4 | 0 | 0 |
| McLish | 3 | 1 | 1 | 3 | 1 | 2 |
| Pitula | 2 | 1 | 1 | 2 | 0 | 1 |

Wild pitch—Shantz.

Attendance—22,221. Time—2:38.

On May 1, in the fourth inning of a game against Detroit, McDougald hit a smash up the middle that struck Tiger pitcher Frank Lary in the hip. The injury was just a bad bruise, but it was enough to knock Lary out of the game. Six days later in Cleveland, Score wouldn't be as fortunate.

In the top of the first, McDougald ripped a liner that caught Score directly in the face. The impact of the ball shattered several bones and opened a gash was opened over his right eye. He was also bleeding profusely from his nose and mouth. "I didn't see the ball until it got a foot or two from my face,"

212    Seasons of Glory

Score told reporters. "Then I saw too much of it." "I heard the thud of the ball hitting his head and then saw him drop and lie there, bleeding, and I froze," McDougald told Ira Berkow of *The New York Times* in 1994. "Someone hollered for me to run to first. When Score was taken off the field on a stretcher, I was sick to my stomach. I didn't want to play anymore."

Score was rushed to a hospital—the Indians rallied to win 3-2—and McDougald was disconsolate. After the game, sitting in the locker room with a towel over his head, he was in tears, telling reporters he would quit baseball if Score lost his eye. A day later, doctors determined Score wouldn't lose his sight, but his vision was affected. He was in the hospital for three weeks, and he didn't return to the field until the following season. Even then, he was never the same. Score, who had been 36-19 over his first two seasons, altered his pitching motion—some people said he didn't follow through as he had before the accident—and began having arm troubles. He went 17-26 over the next five seasons, then retired.

McDougald wasn't the same again either. He stopped taking the ball up the middle, so he was no longer as much of an offensive threat. Still, he tried not to let the accident destroy his season. "Funny thing, as bad as I felt, I went on a hitting spree," he told Berkow, referring to an 8-for-16 stretch in his next four games that brought his average to .297. "I can't explain it."

Meanwhile, New York was trailing first-place Chicago. The teams met in a three-game series at Comiskey Park June 11-13. The Yankees won two games, and leading the way was McDougald, who was 6-for-14 in the series, and Mantle, who had a pair of homers.

The Yanks kept chipping away, finally moving into first on June 22. Chicago regained the lead three days later, but New York moved in front again, this time to stay, winning a double-header against Philadelphia on the June 30. Again, it was McDougald who led the way—he hit .407 during that hectic last week of June.

He kept up the heroics during the first week of July. His two-run double in the eleventh on July 2 helped beat Baltimore 6-4, and he had a 7-for-13 series in Washington, including a two-run homer in the ninth to win Game 3 and give the Yankees a series sweep. At the All-Star break, McDougald was at .312 and the Yankees had a 2½-game lead over Chicago.

They weren't able to finally put away the White Sox until late August. The teams met for another three-game series in Chicago, which the Yankees swept. New York now led by 6½ games, and the race was all but over. New York clinched on September 23 and coasted home by eight games.

McDougald finished his season with a .289 average, 13 homers, 62 RBIs, 25 doubles, and a league-best nine triples. The Yankees led the league in double plays, with McDougald again playing a major role in that success.

The '57 Series pitted the Yankees against the Milwaukee Braves. It went the full seven games, the Braves winning behind the pitching of three-time winner Lew Burdette, the hitting of Hank Aaron (.393, three home runs), and the defense of outfielder Wes Covington (a spectacular catch on a McDougald drive in Game 5) and third baseman Eddie Mathews, who turned Bill Skowron's bases-loaded smash into a Series-ending force in Game 7.

McDougald spent three more years with the Yankees. Before the 1960 campaign, he told Stengel he intended to retire after the season. "I just got tired of the travel and the attitude of the baseball people," he once recalled. "I started at $5,500 a year with the Yankees, and then was making $37,500 at the end. But they acted like they owned you and . . . were giving you the moon and the stars."

He went into business for himself, first owning a dry-cleaning business, then a building maintenance company. He also coached Fordham's baseball team for seven years. He gave that up when his hearing deteriorated to the point that he could no longer hear the crack of the bat.

Fortunately, McDougald's story has a happy ending. In late 1994 he underwent a cochlear implant, a relatively new procedure. The operation was a success, and by early 1995 Gil McDougald could hear again.

## Baseball News Of 1957

- For the second time in his career, Boston's Ted Williams lost the AL MVP Award by one vote (this time to repeat winner Mickey Mantle).

- On April 18, Indians rookie Roger Maris hit his first major-league home run, a grand slam against Detroit.

- Yankee scout Paul Krichell, who discovered Lou Gehrig, Tony Lazzeri, Phil Rizzuto, Whitey Ford, Red Rolfe, Charlie Keller, and Vic Raschi, among others, died at 74 on June 4.

- The New York Giants decided to move to San Francisco, and the Brooklyn Dodgers pulled up stakes and went to Los Angeles.

- Ted Williams, age 39, hit .388, becoming the oldest player to win a batting title.

## Around The World In 1957

- The Soviet Union launched the first satellite, *Sputnik*, on October 4.

- Among the obituaries were those of Humphrey Bogart (January 14, age 57), Jimmy Dorsey (June 12, age 53), Oliver Hardy (August 7, age 55), and Laura Ingalls Wilder (February 10, age 90).

- Underground atomic bomb testing began near Las Vegas on September 19.

- Massachusetts Senator John F. Kennedy won a Pulitzer Prize for *Profiles in Courage*.

- U.S. Surgeon General Leroy E. Burney announced that a link between cigarette smoking and lung cancer had been established by scientists.

- The world's longest suspension bridge, the Mackinac Straits Bridge in Michigan, opened for traffic on November 1.

**34**

*Season of Glory*

*Phil Rizzuto*

1950

| AB | R | H | BA | OB% | 2B | 3B | HR | K/BB | RBI | BR | SB |
|----|---|---|----|----|----|----|----|----|----|----|----|
| 617 | 125 | 200 | .324 | .418 | 36 | 7 | 7 | 39/92 | 66 | 25 | 12 |

| | | G | PO | A | DP | E | FA | FR | | | |
|--|--|---|----|---|----|---|----|----|--|--|--|
| | | 155 | 301 | 452 | 123 | 14 | .982 | 9 | | | |

# 34 Phillip Frances Rizzuto

BORN
**September 25, 1917**
**Brooklyn, New York**

HEIGHT
**5-6**

WEIGHT
**160**

THREW
**right hand**

BATTED
**right hand**

**New York Yankees**
**1941–1942**
**1946–1956**

HALL OF FAME
**1994**

*1950*

The Sultan of Swat . . . The Iron Horse . . . The Yankee Clipper . . . Mr. October . . . King Kong . . . The Commerce Comet . . . Scooter. Scooter? Okay, so maybe Phil Rizzuto's nickname didn't have the same panache as those of other Yankee greats. But make no mistake, Rizzuto's contributions to the Yankees were a major factor in the team's success in the 1940s and '50s. No less an authority than Ted Williams once said that if Rizzuto had played for Boston, the Red Sox, not the Yankees, would have been the dominant team of that era.

Rizzuto was born in Brooklyn in 1917, the third of four children of a streetcar conductor and his wife. Baseball was his love from childhood—his dad gave him his first glove when he was four, and his mom made him his first uniform when he was eight. Despite his size he developed into a top-notch outfielder on the sandlots of Brooklyn and Queens. In high school he switched to the infield—not only because he was small, but also because he was quick.

In the summer of 1936, still a few months shy of his nineteenth birthday, Rizzuto tried out for the Dodgers, Cardinals, and Giants. All rejected him because of his size. The Yankees, though, knew talent when they saw it—especially head scout Paul Krichell—and offered Rizzuto a minor-league contract after a five-day tryout camp at Yankee Stadium.

Rizzuto's professional career almost ended before it got off the ground. The next year, playing for Class D Bassett, Virginia, he suffered a leg injury that eventually became gangrenous. For a time he was in danger of losing the leg, but he recovered and went on to a spectacular minor-league career. He posted a .336 average at Class B Norfolk in 1938 and hit .316 and .347 for Kansas City, the Yankees' top farm team, the next two seasons (that's also where he picked up the "Scooter" nickname, from teammate Billy Hitchcock). He was named American Association MVP and minor-league player of the year after the 1940 season, and earned an invitation to the Yankees' spring camp in 1941. He played so well that spring that he earned a spot with the parent club, and he became the team's regular shortstop, supplanting the legendary Frank Crosetti.

Over his next eleven seasons—he was in the service from 1943 to '46—Rizzuto established himself not only as the top shortstop in the American League, but also as the best shortstop to ever play for the Yankees. He was smooth on defense, twice leading the league in fielding; he hit for average, not power, could hit to all fields, and was an

*Slick-fielding Yankee fielder, Scooter Rizzuto, a Hall of Famer.*

# Game of Glory • September 28, 1950

Rizzuto's tenth-inning single on September 28—his fourth hit of the day—lifts the Yankees past Philadelphia and assures them of atleast a tie for the AL pennant.

| NEW YORK | AB | R | H | RBI |
|---|---|---|---|---|
| Woodling, lf | 4 | 1 | 1 | 0 |
| Henrich, ph | 1 | 0 | 1 | 1 |
| Mapes, rf | 1 | 1 | 1 | 0 |
| Rizzuto, ss | 6 | 3 | 4 | 2 |
| Berra, c | 6 | 1 | 2 | 1 |
| DiMaggio, cf | 5 | 0 | 2 | 0 |
| Mize, 1b | 4 | 0 | 2 | 2 |
| Hopp, 1b | 1 | 0 | 0 | 0 |
| Brown, 3b | 0 | 0 | 0 | 0 |
| Johnson, 3b | 3 | 1 | 1 | 0 |
| Bauer, rf-lf | 4 | 0 | 1 | 0 |
| Coleman, 2b | 4 | 1 | 2 | 1 |
| Raschi, p | 4 | 0 | 1 | 0 |
| Reynolds, p | 1 | 0 | 0 | 0 |
| **Totals** | **44** | **8** | **18** | **7** |

| PHILADELPHIA | AB | R | H | RBI |
|---|---|---|---|---|
| Lehner, lf | 4 | 0 | 1 | 1 |
| Valo, rf | 3 | 0 | 0 | 0 |
| Fain, 1b | 5 | 0 | 0 | 0 |
| Chapman, cf | 5 | 0 | 0 | 0 |
| Hitchcock, 2b | 4 | 1 | 1 | 0 |
| Suder, 3b | 4 | 1 | 1 | 0 |
| Joust, ss | 3 | 2 | 2 | 2 |
| Tipton, c | 3 | 2 | 2 | 2 |
| Hooper, p | 0 | 0 | 0 | 0 |
| Moses, ph | 1 | 0 | 0 | 1 |
| Murray, p | 0 | 0 | 0 | 0 |
| Shantz, p | 3 | 0 | 1 | 0 |
| **Totals** | **35** | **6** | **8** | **6** |

| | | | | | | | | | |
|---|---|---|---|---|---|---|---|---|---|
| New York | 2 2 1 | 0 0 0 | 0 1 0 | 2 — 8 |
| Philadelphia | 0 4 0 | 1 0 0 | 0 0 1 | 0 — 6 |

Doubles—Mize, Woodling, Mapes, Rizzuto. Triple—Rizzuto.
Home runs—Joost, Tipton. Sacrifices—Lehner, Johnson.
Double plays—New York 1, Philadelphia 1.
Left on base—New York 13, Philadelphia 4.

| NEW YORK | IP | H | BB | K |
|---|---|---|---|---|
| Raschi | 8.1 | 3 | 4 | 5 |
| Reynolds (W, 16-12) | 1.2 | 0 | 0 | 1 |

| PHILADELPHIA | IP | H | BB | K |
|---|---|---|---|---|
| Hooper | 2 | 5 | 2 | 0 |
| Murray | .2 | 3 | 0 | 1 |
| Shantz (L, 8-14) | 7.1 | 10 | 1 | 2 |

Hit by pitch—by Shantz (Coleman).

Time—2:47. Attendance—2,273.

expert bunter; he stole bases; he was smart, seeming always to make the right play; and he was durable, the kind of guy who could be counted on every day. In short, he was a complete ballplayer. "For a little fellow to beat a big fellow he has to be terrific," manager Joe McCarthy once said of his shortstop. "He has to have everything, and Rizzuto's got it."

Not everyone saw that, though. Take the

Phil Rizzuto made another kind of history on February 16, 1950, when he appeared as the first mystery guest on the first telecast of *What's My Line?* Other highlights of the show: The first guest was a Stork Club hat-check girl, the second was a veterinarian and the third was a diaper deliveryman. Panelists were poet Louis Untermeyer, columnist Dorothy Kilgallen, former New Jersey Gov. Harold Hoffman and psychiatrist Richard Hoffman. The host? Why, the inimitable John Charles Daly, of course.

1949 season, for example. That year he led the world champion Yankees in hits (169), runs (110), total bases (220), doubles (22), triples (7) and stolen bases (18). He also had the fewest errors (29 in 792 chances) of any shortstop in the AL. But despite these stats and the fact that he carried the team early in the season while Joe DiMaggio recovered from surgery, he was largely ignored by fans in the All-Star voting. After the season he finished a distant second to Ted Williams in the MVP voting. He would just have to turn it up a notch. And he did in 1950, his greatest season.

It wasn't until the fourth game of the season that Rizzuto got his first hit, an RBI double in a 14-7 victory over Washington in the Yankees' home opener on April 21. But then he quickly found a hitting groove that he'd never experienced before as a Yankee—he went 12-for-18 over the next week and was at .339 by the end of May. And the hits were meaningful: A 3-for-6 afternoon on May 11 against St. Louis helped the Yankees move into second place; a 4-for-6 effort on May 16 against the Browns helped lift the team into first place; and five hits in a double-header sweep against Cleveland five days later.

In the field he was flawless. He didn't make his first error until June 8, when he fumbled a hard grounder by Detroit's Bob Swift. It ended a 59-game streak that had begun September 17, 1949, during which he had handled 288 chances without an error.

Rizzuto again was carrying the Yankees. DiMaggio was mired in what would be the worst slump of his career—he didn't get above .250 until June—first baseman Tommy Henrich was out with a knee injury, and other veterans were showing their age. It was up to Scooter to keep the Yankees competitive, and he was more than equal to the task.

Unlike previous years, 1950 was a year in which Rizzuto was rewarded by the fans for his hard work. Thanks to a big push by Yankee fans, he outdistanced Boston's Vern Stephens by a 6-to-1 margin in the New York-area All-Star balloting and was chosen to his first All-Star team. He proved he be-

> "He may not have been bigger than most of the bat boys who served during his long career, but for skill, spirit and resourcefulness, he ranked among the giants."
>
> —EDITORIAL IN *THE SPORTING NEWS*, SEPTEMBER 5, 1956

longed, getting a pair of hits and playing all fourteen innings of the game, which the AL lost 4-3. (The game was more notable for the broken elbow Ted Williams suffered while hitting the wall in the first inning; the injury sidelined him until September 7 and probably cost the Red Sox the pennant.)

The second half of the season turned into a battle between the Yankees and Tigers. July ended with Detroit just 2 percentage points ahead, but the Tigers opened August by sweeping a three-game series against the Yankees—Rizzuto managed just one hit—to increase their lead to 2½ games. On August 30 the Yankees won both games of a double-header against Cleveland, (Rizzuto contributed five hits), which put New York back on top, but the Tigers regained the lead by the first week of September. The two teams squared off in a three-game series in Detroit starting September 14. The Yankees won two games (with Rizzuto going 6-for-13 to raise his average to .329) to retake first.

The Yankees would never lose the lead again, though the race remained close for the rest of the season. They clinched at least a tie for the AL pennant on September 28 when Rizzuto's RBI single in the tenth inning sparked an 8-6 victory over Philadelphia. New York backed into the title the next day thanks to a Detroit loss.

The following day, Rizzuto wrapped up his season with a single in a 6-5 win over Boston, his 200th hit of the year. He finished second in hits, runs (125), and stolen bases (12), and third in doubles (36). He led AL shortstops in fielding (.982) and wound up with a team-high .324 batting average. And although he had an unproductive World Series—with just two hits in the Yankees' four-game sweep of the Phillies—there would be no ignoring Rizzuto's accomplishments. He was voted MVP and was named Player of the Year by *The Sporting News*.

Rizzuto would never again come within 50 points of his 1950 batting average. He played four more years as the Yankees' regular shortstop and was relegated to part-time duty in 1955. His career ended when he was waived on August 25, 1956—Oldtimers Day at Yankee Stadium. The next year he became a Yankee broadcaster, and—Holy cow!—was elected to the Hall of Fame in 1994.

## Baseball News Of 1950

- Red Sox utilityman Billy Goodman won the AL batting crown with a .354 average. He is the only player ever to win a batting title without having a regular position.

- Luke Appling, who hit .311 in twenty years with the White Sox, announced his retirement.

- Joe DiMaggio got his 2,000th hit on June 20 in Cleveland.

- Whitey Ford made his Yankee debut, allowing seven hits, six walks, and five earned runs in $4\frac{2}{3}$ innings on July 1 in Boston.

- After sixty-seven years in baseball, Connie Mack retired at the age of 87.

- On November 4 Grover Cleveland Alexander died at age 63.

## Around The World In 1950

- The Korean War began on June 25.

- The average blue-collar worker in America earned $60.53 a week.

- The U.S. Census Bureau announced that the U.S. population was 150,697,361.

- A minimum wage of 75 cents an hour took effect on January 24.

- Illiteracy in the U.S. reached a new low of 3.2 percent.

- Man O' War was voted the top racehorse of the first half of the twentieth century.

- On January 31 President Truman authorized the development of the hydrogen bomb.

- The first National Basketball Association championship was won by the

- Minneapolis Lakers, who beat the Syracuse Nationals four games to two in the final series.

# 35

# Season of Glory

# Paul O'Neill

## 1994

| AB | R | H | BA | OB% | 2B | 3B | HR | K/BB | RBI | BR | SB |
|-----|-----|-----|------|------|-----|-----|-----|-------|-----|-----|-----|
| 368 | 68 | 132 | .359 | .464 | 25 | 1 | 21 | 56/72 | 83 | 47 | 5 |

| | | G | PO | A | DP | E | FA | FR | | |
|--|--|-----|------|-----|-----|-----|------|-----|--|--|
| | | 99 | 203 | 7 | 0 | 1 | .995 | 2 | | |

# 35

## Paul Andrew O'Neill

**BORN**
February 25, 1963
Columbus, Ohio

**HEIGHT**
6-4

**WEIGHT**
215

**THROWS**
left hand

**BATS**
left hand

New York Yankees
1993-present

*1994*

For baseball fans the 1994 season was the best of times and the worst of times. It was the year of the hitter, as Frank Thomas, Jeff Bagwell, Ken Griffey, Jr., Tony Gwynn, Kenny Lofton, and others turned the offense up a notch. But what might have been a summer to savor was marred by one of the most unpleasant events in baseball history—a season-ending strike that began on August 12.

Chief among those who suffered because of the strike were the Yankees, who would have undoubtedly won the AL East, and their talented right-fielder, Paul O'Neill. In the 103 games O'Neill played before the curtain came down prematurely on the 1994 season, he hit .359 (best in the American League), with 21 homers and 83 RBIs. He led the team in batting, hits, total bases, homers, runs, walks, and intentional walks. Add to those numbers his defensive prowess—he made only one error, had a .995 fielding average, never missed the cutoff man and always threw to the right base—and it's obvious how big his 1994 season was.

O'Neill was born into a baseball family; his father, Charles, was a minor-league pitcher. After O'Neill graduated from high school in 1981, he was signed by the Reds. He hit .315 in his first year of pro ball, with Billings, Montana, of the Pioneer League, progressed through the Reds' farm system and played briefly for Cincinnati in '85 and '86, then came up to the parent club to stay in '87. After the 1992 season, when he hit .246, O'Neill was traded to the Yankees for Roberto Kelly.

In New York O'Neill adjusted his game. He stopped trying to hit home runs and learned to go with the pitch, meet the ball, and hit it into the wide open spaces of Yankee Stadium's outfield. Further, he learned to hit lefties, which had been a problem in Cincinnati (in 1994, for example, he hit .305 versus left-handers, .380 versus righties). His work paid off: He hit .311 in his first year season in New York, with 20 homers and 75 RBIs.

O'Neill began the 1994 season in grand fashion, getting two hits in four at-bats in an Opening Day victory over the Texas Rangers (it was the first of forty multiple-hit games for him that season, tops in the AL). In his next 46 at-bats, O'Neill had 23 hits, and by the end of April his batting average was .448, the highest mark registered by any Yankee in April since Bill Skowron hit .451 in 1956. By the end of May—he was hitting .441 with a .534 on-base percentage—O'Neill was made the Yankees' regular right-fielder (he had been platooned for the first month and a half by manager Buck Showalter, who still

*Paul O'Neill, sweet-swingin' Yankee outfielder.*

# Game of Glory • April 25, 1994

O'Neill goes 5-for-5 on April 25, raising his average to .490 and leading a romp over California.

| CALIFORNIA | AB | R | H | RBI | | NEW YORK | AB | R | H | RBI |
|---|---|---|---|---|---|---|---|---|---|---|
| Polonia, lf | 5 | 1 | 2 | 0 | | Easley, 3b | 3 | 0 | 1 | 0 |
| Boggs, 3b | 4 | 2 | 2 | 2 | | Curtis, cf | 4 | 0 | 1 | 0 |
| Mattingly, 1b | 4 | 2 | 1 | 1 | | Salmon, rf | 4 | 0 | 0 | 0 |
| Stanley, 1b | 0 | 0 | 0 | 0 | | Davis, dh | 4 | 1 | 2 | 0 |
| Tartabull, dh | 3 | 1 | 0 | 0 | | Jackson, lf | 3 | 0 | 0 | 0 |
| O'Neill, rf | 5 | 1 | 5 | 2 | | Edmonds, lf | 1 | 0 | 0 | 0 |
| G. Williams, pr,cf | 0 | 0 | 0 | 0 | | Perez, 1b | 4 | 0 | 0 | 0 |
| Nokes, c | 4 | 1 | 1 | 5 | | Turner, c | 3 | 0 | 1 | 0 |
| Leyritz, c | 1 | 0 | 0 | 0 | | Fabregas, ph | 1 | 0 | 1 | 1 |
| B. Williams, cf | 4 | 1 | 1 | 1 | | Hudler, 2b | 4 | 0 | 1 | 0 |
| Boston, ph, rf | 0 | 0 | 0 | 0 | | Owen, ss | 3 | 0 | 0 | 0 |
| Velarde, ss | 4 | 1 | 1 | 0 | | | | | | |
| Kelly, 2b | 3 | 1 | 1 | 0 | | | | | | |
| Totals | 37 | 11 | 14 | 11 | | Totals | 34 | 1 | 7 | 1 |

```
New York       2 0 5   0 0 3   1 0 *  — 11 14 1
California      0 0 0   0 0 0   0 0 1  —  1  7 3
```

Doubles—Polonia, Velarde. Home runs—B. Williams, Nokes.
Stolen base—O'Neill. Errors—Salmon, Jackson, Hudler, Kelly.
Lefton base—California 8, New York 9.

| CALIFORNIA | IP | H | R | ER | BB | K |
|---|---|---|---|---|---|---|
| Leiter (L, 2-1) | 5 | 8 | 7 | 7 | 2 | 3 |
| Sampen | 1 | 4 | 4 | 4 | 3 | 1 |
| Lewis | 2 | 2 | 0 | 0 | 1 | 0 |

| NEW YORK | IP | H | R | ER | BB | K |
|---|---|---|---|---|---|---|
| Key (W, 3-1) | 7 | 3 | 0 | 0 | 2 | 4 |
| Wickman | 2 | 4 | 1 | 1 | 0 | 3 |

Time—3:18. Attendance—14,782.

*1994*

doubted O'Neill's ability to play consistently well).

During June, O'Neill experienced his first slump of the season. He hit just .273 that the month (throw out June, and his season average was .390). But he worked his way out of the slump on an early-July West Coast trip, going 16-for-31 in series against Seattle, Oakland, and California. By the All-Star break, he was at .382.

O'Neill was back on track only briefly. He struggled through another wretched slump—0-for-22—in late July, the longest hitless stretch of his career. His average was down to .354.

On July 31 he was 3-for-4 against Cleveland, which signaled the end of his hitting slump. From that day until the premature end of the season, both he and the Yankees—in the middle of a 20-5 stretch—were nearly unstoppable.

The Yankees, meanwhile, had moved into

## Select Company

Paul O'Neill's .359 batting average in 1994 was the highest of any Yankee since Mickey Mantle hit .365 in 1957. Here's where O'Neill stood that year among his major-league peers in three selected batting categories:

| Batting Average | | On-Base Percentage | | Batting Runs | |
|---|---|---|---|---|---|
| Gwynn, SD | .394 | Thomas, Chi. (AL) | .494 | Thomas, Chi. (AL) | 74.0 |
| Bagwell, Hou. | .368 | **O'Neill, NY (AL)** | **.464** | Bagwell, Hou. | 71.2 |
| **O'Neill, NY (AL)** | **.359** | Bagwell, Hou. | .461 | Belle, Cleve. | 56.0 |
| Belle, Cleve. | .357 | Gwynn, SD | .458 | Bonds, SF | 49.9 |
| Thomas, Chi. (AL) | .353 | Belle, Cleve. | .442 | **O'Neill, NY (AL)** | **46.8** |

first place in mid-May and had held on to the top spot during most of the season. By the time the players went on strike, they had an impressive 70-43 record and a 6½-game lead over the rest of the pack. And although there may have been no postseason, there were plenty of postseason honors for the team. Pitcher Jimmy Key (17-4, 3.27) was the AL Cy Young Award winner, Showalter was manager of the year, and Don Mattingly and Wade Boggs won Gold Gloves. And with O'Neill's batting crown, it turned out to be a season that Yankee fans will remember, strike or no strike.

## Baseball News Of 1994

- Texas' Kenny Rogers threw the fourteenth perfect game in major-league history, beating California 4–0.

- The Cleveland Indians retired Larry Doby's number, 14, to honor him for breaking the American League's color barrier in 1947.

- Chicago Bulls star Michael Jordan quit basketball to try his hand at baseball.

- For the first time since 1904, there was no World Series.

- The major leagues were divided into three divisions each, and the playoffs were expanded to include a wild-card team.

## Around The World In 1994

- Nelson Mandela became the first black president of South Africa.

- The Channel Tunnel linking France and England was opened.

- A rail disaster in Angola killed more than 300 people.

- The United States lifted its trade embargo against Vietnam.

- An earthquake measuring 6.8 on the Richter Scale struck Los Angeles, killing sixty-one.

- The film *Forest Gump* and its star, Tom Hanks, both won Oscars.

# 36
# Season of Glory

## Graig Nettles

### 1976

| AB | R | H | BA | OB% | 2B | 3B | HR | K/BB | RBI | BR | SB |
|-----|-----|-----|------|------|-----|-----|-----|-------|-----|-----|-----|
| 583 | 88 | 148 | .254 | .330 | 29 | 2 | 32 | 94/62 | 93 | 24 | 11 |

| | | G | PO | A | DP | E | FA | FR | | | |
|---|---|-----|-----|-----|-----|-----|------|-----|---|---|---|
| | | 158 | 137 | 383 | 30 | 19 | .965 | 17 | | | |

# 36

BORN
August 20, 1944
San Diego, California

HEIGHT
6-0

WEIGHT
186

THREW
right hand

BATTED
left hand

New York Yankees
1973–83

*1976*

# Graig Nettles

*M*ost fans, when asked to name the best third baseman of the 1970s, choose Brooks Robinson, or George Brett, or Mike Schmidt. But what about Graig Nettles? He hit 390 home runs in his career (only twenty-four players have hit more in the history of baseball) he was a fielding wizard, and he was a student of the game. So any discussion of the best third basemen would have to include the man his teammates called "Puff."

"It takes a lot of courage to play third," he once explained. "A lot of balls go off your chest and sometimes off your head. Some players don't want to put up with that."

Former teammate Sparky Lyle agreed. "I'd say that without him at third base, my years on the Yankees would not have been half as productive as they were," he wrote in *The Bronx Zoo*. "He's probably the number one factor in my success . . . You ought to see some of the balls hit down to him when I'm pitching. He dives, makes unbelievable plays, half in defense of his life, half just in defense."

Nettles was born on August 20, 1944, in San Diego, where he played baseball and basketball in high school. He attended college at San Diego State, his parents' alma mater, where he was discovered by the Minnesota Twins. After his junior year in 1965, Nettles signed a $15,000 Twins contract. He played two years in the minors, then was called up to the Twins at the end of the 1967 season.

Although Nettles played in only three games that year with the Twins, he learned a valuable lesson about self-control and sportsmanship during that time. After Minnesota lost the pennant by one game, Nettles observed how a veteran team handled adversity. "They were down that we had lost," he recalled, "but there was no crying, no temper tantrums. They accepted it and were very gentlemanly about it."

Nettles' education continued during the next season when the Twins promoted him to Triple-A Denver, where Billy Martin was the manager. According to Nettles, Martin's management style was brutal. "[Martin] jumped all over me," Nettles wrote in *Balls*, co-authored with Peter Golenbock. "He would yell and scream at me. He yelled and screamed whenever a player made a mistake. . . . I never had a manager do that." But Martin got his point across, browbeating his young players into making the right plays and not making mistakes. It was another lesson that stuck with Nettles.

When Martin was promoted to manage the Twins for 1969, he took Nettles with him. He played in 96 games, primarily as an outfielder,

*Graig Nettles*

# Game of Glory • September 29, 1976

Nettles hits two homers—one a grand slam—two doubles, and drives in six runs on September 29 as the Yankees clinch a tie for the AL East title.

| NEW YORK | AB | R | H | RBI |
|---|---|---|---|---|
| Locklear, dh | 3 | 1 | 1 | 1 |
| Tovar, dh | 2 | 0 | 0 | 0 |
| White, cf | 2 | 2 | 1 | 0 |
| Murray, cf | 2 | 0 | 0 | 0 |
| Nettles, 3b | 5 | 4 | 4 | 6 |
| Chambliss, 1b | 4 | 0 | 2 | 0 |
| May, lf | 2 | 0 | 0 | 2 |
| Gamble, rf | 2 | 0 | 0 | 0 |
| Piniella, rf | 2 | 0 | 0 | 0 |
| Hendricks, c | 4 | 1 | 1 | 0 |
| Healy, c | 0 | 0 | 0 | 0 |
| Alomar, 2b | 3 | 1 | 0 | 0 |
| Mason, ss | 4 | 0 | 0 | 0 |
| **Totals** | **35** | **9** | **9** | **9** |

| BOSTON | AB | R | H | RBI |
|---|---|---|---|---|
| Burleson, ss | 4 | 1 | 1 | 0 |
| Doyle, 2b | 4 | 2 | 1 | 0 |
| Baker, ph | 1 | 0 | 0 | 0 |
| Heise, 2b | 0 | 0 | 0 | 0 |
| Miller, cf | 5 | 1 | 3 | 2 |
| Yastrzemski, 1b | 4 | 0 | 0 | 0 |
| Cooper, dh | 5 | 0 | 1 | 1 |
| Rice, lf | 4 | 0 | 1 | 1 |
| Evans, rf | 1 | 0 | 0 | 0 |
| Darwin, rf | 3 | 0 | 0 | 0 |
| Whitt, c | 3 | 0 | 0 | 0 |
| Fisk, c | 1 | 0 | 0 | 0 |
| Hobson, 3b | 4 | 2 | 2 | 1 |
| **Totals** | **39** | **6** | **9** | **5** |

| | | | | | | | | | |
|---|---|---|---|---|---|---|---|---|---|
| New York | 2 5 0 | 0 1 0 | 1 0 0 | — 9 |
| Boston | 0 0 2 | 0 2 0 | 1 1 0 | — 6 |

Errors—Burleson, Alomar (2), Mason. Doubles—White, Nettles (2), Miller. Triple—Hobson. Home runs—Nettles (2). Sacrifice flies—May (2). Left on base—New York 3, Boston 8.

| YANKEES | IP | H | R | ER | BB | K |
|---|---|---|---|---|---|---|
| Hunter (W, 17-15) | 7 | 8 | 5 | 2 | 1 | 5 |
| Lyle | 2 | 1 | 1 | 1 | 1 | 2 |

| BOSTON | IP | H | R | ER | BB | K |
|---|---|---|---|---|---|---|
| Tiant (L, 21-12) | 1.2 | 5 | 7 | 7 | 2 | 0 |
| Jones | 6.2 | 4 | 2 | 2 | 0 | 3 |
| Willoughby | 1 | 0 | 0 | 0 | 0 | 0 |

Time—2:25. Attendance—23,980.

hitting .222. That winter, Martin and Nettles both had changes of address—Martin was fired and Nettles was traded to Cleveland. He spent three seasons as the Indians' regular third baseman, averaging 24 homers and 73 RBIs and batting .250. He also developed into a solid defensive third baseman. The Yankees took notice, and in November 1972 they obtained him and Gerry Moses for Charlie Spikes, Rusty Torres, Jerry Kenney and John Ellis.

Nettles paid immediate dividends, averaging 22 homers and 82 RBIs during his first three seasons and developing into the AL's best fielding third baseman. He was great at going to his right, so he cheated a little and played farther off the line than most third basemen, enabling him to make more plays going into the hole. He also had a strong and accurate arm—and those baseball instincts.

Hopes were high for 1976. The Yankees were returning home to a refurbished Yankee Stadium, Billy Martin, who replaced Bill Virdon midway through the 1975 campaign, would have a full season as manager, and the team had obtained several players who would form the nucleus of the championship teams of the late '70s.

Nettles, a notoriously slow starter, didn't get his first hit of the 1976 season until the Yankees' fourth game. At the end of April, Nettles had a disappointing .143 average and had just one homer and five RBIs. He began to improve around the first two weeks of May, going 4-for-13 in a series at California, and hitting two homers in consecutive games against Detroit.

The most excitement in the first two months came on May 20 against defending AL East champion Boston, with Nettles in the middle of it. In the sixth inning, Yankee runner Lou Piniella crashed into Red Sox catcher Carlton Fisk. The two began shoving, and soon both teams were involved in the brawl. Nettles picked Red Sox pitcher Bill Lee out of the crowd and went after him. He tossed Lee to the ground, injuring his shoulder and rendering him virtually useless for the rest of the season.

Nettles warmed up as summer progressed. He finally passed the .200 mark on June 11, when he had two homers and five RBIs in a 7-5 victory over Texas. He hit .360 during the last week of June, raising his average to .226. And in his first four games after the All-Star break, all Yankee victories, he was 9-for-19 (.474) with seven RBIs, raising his average to .237.

Nettles and the Yankees, who had been in first place since April, cruised through July, August, and September. They captured the AL East on September 25 and wound up finishing 10½ games ahead of Baltimore. And Nettles finally climbed above .250 with a spectacular day on September 29—two home runs (one a grand slam), two doubles, five RBIs, and four runs scored in a 9-6 win over Boston. He finished the soeason at .254, with a league-leading 32 homers and career-high 93 RBIs.

The Yankees' AL Championship Series opponent in 1976 was Kansas City, which had battled with Oakland for the AL West

pennant until the final days of the season. New York defeated the Royals in five games. Nettles contributed two homers, both in Game 4, which the Yankees lost, and was 4-for-17 for the series.

There'd be no Yankee heroics in the World Series, however. They were swept in four games by Cincinnati, with Nettles managing just three hits and two RBIs in the Series. Nevertheless, Nettles remembers his 1976 season with fondness. "It was fun baseball," he wrote in *Balls*. "We ran away with the division, and I had more fun playing baseball than anytime before or since. We had a set lineup, everyone knew exactly what his role was, Billy was clearly in charge, and everything clicked like it was supposed to."

> "Some kids dream of joining the circus, others of becoming a major league baseball player. I have been doubly blessed. As a member of the New York Yankees, I have gotten to do both."
>
> —THE OPENING WORDS OF GRAIG NETTLES' BOOK, *BALLS*

After seven more productive seasons with the Yankees, Nettles, approaching his 40th birthday and with his best days behind him, was traded to his hometown San Diego Padres. He hit twenty homers, helping the Padres to win the 1984 NL pennant. After two more years in San Diego, he went to Atlanta in 1987 and concluded his twenty-two-year career with Montreal the next season. What kept him going all those years, until he was forty-four? One passage in *Balls* perhaps explains it.

"What I love about the game of baseball is that whether you win or lose, it's still so much fun. You go out on the field, and you're using your body to do something that you love to do. You learn it when you're four or five, and you're able to do it until you're in your forties, and every day is different and exciting and something to look forward to."

# Baseball News Of 1976

- The baseball world was captivated by Detroit Tiger rookie pitcher Mark "the Bird" Fidrych, who, when he wasn't manicuring the mound or talking to baseballs, found time to win nineteen games.

- Owners locked players out of spring training over a lack of a Basic Agreement. Commissioner Bowie Kuhn overruled the owners and ordered them to open the camps.

- Yankee Thurman Munson was named team captain—the team's first since Lou Gehrig.

- Well-known personalities who died that year included Dan Bankhead, the first black pitcher to play in the majors (May 2), Hall of Fame outfielder Max Carey (May 30), 1950 NL MVP Jim Konstanty (June 11), former pitcher Lon Warneke (June 23), Red Sox owner Tom Yawkey (July 9), Hall of Fame Yankee outfielder Earle Combs (July 21), Hall of Fame pitcher Red Faber (September 25), ex-Pirates pitcher Bob Moose (October 9), former Pirate manager Danny Murtaugh (December 2), and Texas infielder Danny Thompson (December 10).

- Dodgers manager Walter Alston won his 2,000th game on July 17 against the Cubs.

- Milwaukee's Hank Aaron hit the 755th and last homer of his career on July 20 against the Angels' Dick Drago.

- White Sox pitchers Blue Moon Odom and Francisco Barrios joined forces to no-hit the A's on July 28.

# Around The World In 1976

- Former Georgia Gov. Jimmy Carter was elected president on November 2.

- *Roots*, by Alex Haley, was published.

- Industrialist Armand Hammer bought the painting *Juno* for $3.25 million, the highest price ever paid for a Rembrandt painting.

- Among the obituaries that year were those of Howard Hughes (April 5, at age 72), J.P. Getty (June 6, age 83), Chicago Mayor Richard J. Daley (December 20, age 74), Busby Berkeley (March 14, age 80), Lee J. Cobb (February 11, age 64), Johnny Mercer (June 25, age 66), Man Ray (November 18, age 86) and Paul Robeson (January 23, age 77).

- Red Dye No. 2 was banned after researchers determined in was carcenogenic.

- Production of convertibles by U.S. automakers ended.

- America celebrated its bicentennial.

- Citizen Band radios became the rage.

- The National Basketball Association and the American Basketball Association merged.

**37**

# Season of Glory

## Andy Pettitte

### 1997

| W | L | Pct. | IP | GS | CG | SH | SV | K/BB | Opp. BA | ERA |
|---|---|------|----|----|----|----|----|----|------|---------|-----|
| 18 | 7 | .680 | 240.1 | 233 | 35 | 4 | 1 | 166/65 | .256 | 2.88 |

| | | GP | PO | A | DP | E | FA | ER/R | PR | DEF |
|---|---|----|----|---|----|---|----|------|----|----|
| | | 35 | 9 | 43 | 5 | 5 | .962 | 86/77 | 45 | 2 |

# 37 Andrew Eugene Pettitte

**BORN**
June 15, 1972
Baton Rouge, Louisiana

**HEIGHT**
6-5

**WEIGHT**
235

**THROWS**
left hand

**BATS**
right hand

New York Yankees
1995–present

*1997*

A defining moment in the career of pitcher Andy Pettitte occurred during the fifth game of the 1996 World Series. With the Series tied at two games apiece, Pettitte was battling Atlanta ace John Smoltz. The young Yankee left-hander went into the bottom of the sixth protecting a 1-0 lead. Smoltz was on second with nobody out, and the Braves' Mark Lemke was trying to bunt the potential tying run to third. Pettitte bare-handed Lemke's bunt and fired to third, catching Smoltz. The next man up, Chipper Jones, tapped back to the mound, and Pettitte started a 1-4-3 double play to end the inning.

Those two plays, happening only a minute apart, not only tested the twenty-four-year-old pitcher in a high-pressure situation, but they also helped the Yankees win the game and take the lead in the World Series. Speaking to the media afterward, Pettitte said, "We have a special thing going on here. I think we're destined to win this thing." Without realizing it, Pettitte had also defined his own career, a very special thing.

Pettitte was chosen by the Yankees in the twenty-second round of the June, 1990 free-agent draft, but chose to attend San Jacinto (Texas) Junior College. He was eventually signed by the Yankees as a free agent in 1991. He was 42-20 in four years in the minors, relying on a good sinker and breaking pitches and the excellent control that would become his trademark. In 1995 he was promoted to the parent club and went 12-9. Pettitte really shined in 1996, when he won 21 games, helped the Yankees beat Atlanta in the World Series, and was runner-up for the Cy Young Award. That 1996 world championship season would be a tough act to follow for Pettitte. But he topped his 1996 effort in '97, posting his greatest season.

In 1997, Pettitte picked up where he left off the previous year, winning his first five decisions. He lost his first game on May 3 (Kansas City beat him 2-1 with an unearned run in the sixth), the start of a slump that kept him winless unless July 5. On that day he pitched the first shutout of his career, against Toronto. He then beat Detroit, Chicago, and Milwaukee—he allowed eight earned runs in his first four appearances in July—raising his record to 12-5.

Pettitte didn't lose a game after August 6. He shut out Minnesota 11-0 on August 11, allowing five hits and fanning nine in eight innings. On August 31, he carried a shutout into the eighth against Montreal. The Yankee bullpen nearly blew his lead but he ended up with a 3-2 victory. On September 5 he was hit in the face by a liner by

*Accomplished Yankee southpaw, Andy Pettite.*

# Game of Glory • April 2, 1997

In his first start of the season, on April 2, Pettitte stops the Mariners.

| NEW YORK | AB | R | H | RBI | | SEATTLE | AB | R | H | RBI |
|---|---|---|---|---|---|---|---|---|---|---|
| Jeter, ss | 5 | 1 | 1 | 1 | | Amaral, lf | 4 | 0 | 2 | 0 |
| Boggs, 3b | 3 | 3 | 0 | 0 | | Espinoza, ph | 1 | 0 | 0 | 0 |
| Williams, cf | 3 | 3 | 0 | 1 | | Rodriguez, ss | 5 | 0 | 1 | 0 |
| T. Martinez, 1b | 6 | 5 | 4 | 7 | | Griffey, cf | 4 | 2 | 2 | 0 |
| Fielder, dh | 5 | 1 | 1 | 2 | | Tinsley, ph | 1 | 0 | 0 | 0 |
| O'Neill, rf | 6 | 0 | 3 | 1 | | E. Martinez, dh | 3 | 0 | 0 | 0 |
| Strawberry, lf | 3 | 0 | 0 | 0 | | Buhner, rf | 3 | 0 | 1 | 1 |
| Whiten, ph, rf | 3 | 1 | 3 | 3 | | Blowers, 1b | 3 | 0 | 0 | 0 |
| Duncan, 2b | 2 | 0 | 0 | 0 | | Wilson, c | 3 | 0 | 1 | 1 |
| Kelly, 2b | 2 | 2 | 1 | 0 | | Davis, 3b | 4 | 0 | 1 | 0 |
| Posada, c | 6 | 0 | 1 | 1 | | Gates, 2b | 4 | 0 | 0 | 0 |
| **Totals** | **44** | **16** | **14** | **20** | | **Totals** | **35** | **2** | **8** | **2** |

| | | | | | | | | |
|---|---|---|---|---|---|---|---|---|
| New York | 3 0 2 | 0 1 1 | 0 2 7 | — | 16 | 14 | 0 |
| Seattle | 1 0 1 | 0 0 0 | 0 0 0 | — | 2 | 8 | 3 |

Doubles—Fielder, Kelly, Rodriguez, Griffey. Home runs—T. Martinez (3).
Errors—Blowers, Davis. Left on base—New York 15, Seattle 10.

| NEW YORK | IP | H | R | ER | BB | K |
|---|---|---|---|---|---|---|
| Pettitte (W, 1-0) | 6 | 7 | 2 | 2 | 4 | 4 |
| Weathers | 2 | 0 | 0 | 0 | 0 | 2 |
| Rivera | 1 | 1 | 0 | 0 | 0 | 1 |

| SEATTLE | IP | H | R | ER | BB | K |
|---|---|---|---|---|---|---|
| Sanders (L, 0-1) | 5 | 5 | 6 | 6 | 3 | 1 |
| Hurtado | .1 | 0 | 1 | 1 | 3 | 0 |
| McCarthy | 1.2 | 2 | 1 | 1 | 2 | 2 |
| Manzanillo | 1 | 2 | 1 | 1 | 2 | 1 |
| Torres | .1 | 3 | 1 | 1 | 2 | 0 |
| Wells | .2 | 2 | 0 | 0 | 1 | 1 |

Time—3:53. Attendance—30,961.

*1997*

> "I always had confidence that I would be a good big league ballplayer, but I never dreamed that I'd be able to win twenty games."
>
> —ANDY PETTITTE

Baltimore's Cal Ripken Jr. and had to leave the game with a bruised thumb, face, and lip and a cut on his nose. But he didn't miss a turn. He won again on September 11, allowing one run in seven innings in a 14-2 victory over Baltimore, and on the 16th, his last victory of the season.

There would be no World Series for the Yankees in 1997. They were eliminated by

Cleveland in the division playoffs, in which Pettitte lost two crucial games. On October 2, in the second game of the series, Pettitte gave up two runs in the fourth and two more in the fifth as the Indians posted a 7-5 victory. Four days later in the decisive Game 5, Pettitte surrendered three runs in the third and another run in the fourth as Cleveland eliminated the Yankees with a 4-3 victory. "I'm over it. I'm serious," he told reporters after the loss. "I'm ready to get out of here. I'm going to relax on the couch, watch TV and get ready for the deer season."

Although he finished with fewer victories (21 to 18), Pettitte's 1997 season rates an edge over his '96 campaign. He lowered his ERA by nearly a full run, and three of his seven losses were by one run; with a little luck he could have been 21-4. It didn't happen, but it's a good indication just how effective Pettitte was in 1997.

## Baseball News Of 1997

- The Phillies' Curt Schilling struck out 319 hitters.
- Interleague play was inaugurated, with the NL winning 117 of the 214 games.
- In the first franchise shift from one league to another, the Milwaukee Brewers moved from the AL to the NL.
- Mark McGwire became the first major-league home run champ to homer in both leagues (with Oakland and St. Louis) in the same season.
- On the fiftieth anniversary of Jackie Robinson's breaking the color barrier, every major-league team retired his number, 42.

## Around The World In 1997

- Britain handed over control of Hong Kong to China, ending a ninety-nine-year lease.
- Madeleine Albright became the first woman to serve as U.S. Secretary of State.
- The world's first surviving septuplets were born in Carlisle, Iowa.
- The U.S. spacecraft *Pathfinder* landed on Mars after a seven-month journey and began exploration of the Red Planet.

# Season of Glory

## Clete Boyer

### 1962

| AB | R | H | BA | OB% | SA | 2B | 3B | HR | RBI | BB/K | SB |
|----|---|---|----|----|----|----|----|----|-----|------|-----|
| 566 | 85 | 154 | .272 | .335 | .413 | 24 | 1 | 18 | 68 | 51/106 | 3 |

| | | | G | PO | A | DP | E | FA | FR | | |
|---|---|---|---|----|---|----|---|----|----|---|---|
| | | | 158 | 187 | 396 | 41 | 22 | .964 | 36 | | |

# 38

## Cletis LeRoy Boyer

**BORN**
February 9, 1937
Cassville, Missouri

**HEIGHT**
6-0

**WEIGHT**
182

**THREW**
right hand

**BATTED**
right hand

New York Yankees
1959–66

When considering the all-time top fifty seasons of individual Yankee players, there's a temptation to be distracted by flashy numbers—61 homers, a 56-game hitting streak, a .393 batting average, or a 41-victory season. But the complete player, one who can field his position as well as produce offensively, one who delivers clutch hits, one who, for lack of a better term, is a winner, cannot be overlooked.

That brings us to Clete Boyer. He didn't hit for power and he didn't have the highest batting average, but he deserves a spot in the top 50 just as much as Roger Maris, Joe DiMaggio, Babe Ruth, or Jack Chesbro. Why? Anyone who ever saw him play knows why. "Clete was the best third baseman I've ever seen, bar none," Tony Kubek wrote in his book *Sixty-One, The Team, The Record, The Men*. "Brooks Robinson was great. Graig Nettles was great. But Clete was a better defensive player." Another former teammate, pitcher Bill Stafford, agreed. "Clete was a much smoother fielder than Brooks," he told Kubek. "The play that Clete made that still amazes me was on the ball hit down the line. He'd dive for it, catch it across his body, and then throw from foul territory to first base, and the guy never got off his knees. It fascinated me that anyone could do it once a year, and he did it day after day."

But Boyer made amazing plays not only day after day, he kept it up years after year. Indeed, a strong case can be made that Boyer is the greatest defensive third baseman of all time. He was quick. He had good hands. He knew where to play opposing hitters. He had a great arm and tremendous range. Not bad for a guy who never won a Gold Glove in the American League.

Boyer was traded to the Yankee organization by Kansas City in 1957. He was promoted to the parent club during the '59 season, and by 1960 he had more or less become the Yankees' regular third baseman. In that magic Maris-Mantle world championship year of 1961, Boyer led AL third basemen in assists and chances per game and had—to that point—career highs in hits, runs, and RBIs. But it was Boyer's performance in 1962 that enabled him to crack the top fifty. In 1962 Boyer not only made invaluable contributions at third, as usual—he led American League third basemen in putouts, assists, double plays, and chances per game—but he also had career highs in runs scored, hits, doubles, batting average, and on-base percentage.

That year, the defending world champs opened their season with a 7-6 victory over Baltimore on April 10 at Yankee Stadium. It was a

*Clete Boyer, master craftsman at the hot-corner.*

# Game of Glory • June 24, 1962

It took seven hours and twenty-two innings, but the Yankees beat Detroit 9-7 on June 24, their version of *The Longest Day*. Boyer has three hits, including a homer, in nine at-bats and three RBIs.

| NEW YORK | AB | R | H | RBI | | DETROIT | AB | R | H | RBI |
|---|---|---|---|---|---|---|---|---|---|---|
| Tresh, ss | 9 | 0 | 2 | 0 | | Boros, 3b,1b | 10 | 1 | 1 | 0 |
| Richardson, 2b | 11 | 2 | 3 | 0 | | Bruton, cf | 9 | 2 | 2 | 0 |
| Maris, cf | 9 | 2 | 2 | 2 | | Goldy, rf | 10 | 1 | 1 | 3 |
| Mantle, rf | 3 | 1 | 1 | 0 | | Colavito, lf | 10 | 1 | 7 | 1 |
| Pepitone, rf | 1 | 0 | 0 | 0 | | Cash, 1b | 8 | 1 | 2 | 0 |
| Linz, ph | 0 | 0 | 0 | 0 | | McAuliffe, 2b | 5 | 0 | 1 | 0 |
| Reed, rf | 4 | 1 | 1 | 2 | | Morton, ph | 1 | 0 | 0 | 0 |
| Blanchard, lf | 10 | 1 | 1 | 0 | | Osborne, 1b | 1 | 0 | 0 | 0 |
| Berra, c | 10 | 0 | 3 | 1 | | Fernandez, ss | 10 | 1 | 1 | 1 |
| Skowron, 1b | 10 | 1 | 2 | 1 | | Roarke, c | 5 | 0 | 2 | 2 |
| Boyer, 3b | 9 | 1 | 3 | 3 | | Wood, ph | 0 | 0 | 0 | 0 |
| Turley, p | 1 | 0 | 0 | 0 | | Brown, c | 4 | 0 | 1 | 0 |
| Coates, p | 0 | 0 | 0 | 0 | | Lary, p | 0 | 0 | 0 | 0 |
| Lopez, ph | 1 | 0 | 1 | 0 | | Maxwell, ph | 1 | 0 | 1 | 0 |
| Stafford, p | 0 | 0 | 0 | 0 | | Casale, p | 1 | 0 | 0 | 0 |
| Bridges, p | 0 | 0 | 0 | 0 | | Wertz, ph | 1 | 0 | 0 | 0 |
| Howard, ph | 1 | 0 | 0 | 0 | | Nischwitz, p | 0 | 0 | 0 | 0 |
| Clevenger, p | 2 | 0 | 0 | 0 | | Kline, p | 1 | 0 | 0 | 0 |
| Cerv, ph | 1 | 0 | 0 | 0 | | Aguirre, p | 2 | 0 | 0 | 0 |
| Daley, p | 1 | 0 | 0 | 0 | | Fox, p | 2 | 0 | 0 | 0 |
| Bouton, p | 2 | 0 | 1 | 0 | | Mossi, ph | 1 | 0 | 0 | 0 |
| | | | | | | Regan, p | 0 | 0 | 0 | 0 |
| **Totals** | **85** | **9** | **20** | **9** | | **Totals** | **82** | **7** | **19** | **7** |

| | | | | | | | | | | | | | | | | | |
|---|---|---|---|---|---|---|---|---|---|---|---|---|---|---|---|---|---|
| New York | 6 1 0 | 0 0 0 | 0 0 0 | 0 0 0 | 0 0 0 | 0 0 0 | 0 0 0 2 — 9 20 4 |
| Detroit | 3 0 3 | 0 0 1 | 0 0 0 | 0 0 0 | 0 0 0 | 0 0 0 | 0 0 0 0 — 7 19 3 |

Doubles—Richardson, Roarke. Triple—Colavito. Home runs—Boyer, Reed, Goldy. Sacrifices—Tresh, Fox, Brown. Sacrifice fly—Berra. Double plays—New York, 4. Stolen bases—Tresh, Bruton. Left on base—New York 21, Detroit 22.

| NEW YORK | IP | H | R | ER | BB | K |
|---|---|---|---|---|---|---|
| Turley | .1 | 1 | 3 | 3 | 3 | 0 |
| Coates | 2.2 | 4 | 3 | 3 | 1 | 6 |
| Stafford | 2.2 | 4 | 1 | 1 | 1 | 3 |
| Bridges | .1 | 0 | 0 | 0 | 0 | 0 |
| Clevenger | 6.1 | 5 | 0 | 0 | 3 | 1 |
| Daley | 2.2 | 2 | 0 | 0 | 0 | 2 |
| Bouton (W, 2-1) | 7 | 3 | 0 | 0 | 2 | 6 |

| DETROIT | IP | H | R | ER | BB | K |
|---|---|---|---|---|---|---|
| Lary | 2 | 7 | 7 | 7 | 1 | 1 |
| Casale | 3 | 1 | 0 | 0 | 2 | 0 |
| Nischwitz | 1.2 | 2 | 0 | 0 | 2 | 0 |
| Kline | 1 | 0 | 0 | 0 | 2 | 0 |
| Aguirre | 5.1 | 2 | 0 | 0 | 1 | 8 |
| Fox | 8 | 7 | 0 | 0 | 0 | 1 |
| Regan (L, 4-7) | 1 | 1 | 2 | 2 | 1 | 2 |

Time—7:00. Attendance—35,638.

*1962*

# Something's Missing

In 1962 Clete Boyer ranked as the best third baseman in both leagues, but the AL award went to Baltimore's Brooks Robinson (San Francisco's Jim Davenport won the NL award). Here's a look at the game's top third basemen in 1962, ranked according to Fielding Runs.

| Player, Team | G | A | E | FA | FR |
|---|---|---|---|---|---|
| Clete Boyer, NY (AL) | 157 | 396 | 22 | .964 | 36 |
| Ron Santo, Chicago (NL) | 157 | 332 | 23 | .955 | 12 |
| Brooks Robinson, Baltimore | 162 | 339 | 11 | .979 | 7 |
| Frank Malzone, Boston | 156 | 313 | 16 | .967 | 5 |
| Ken Boyer, St. Louis | 160 | 318 | 22 | .956 | 4 |
| Ed Charles, Kansas City | 140 | 285 | 16 | .964 | 4 |
| Jim Davenport, San Francisco | 141 | 256 | 19 | .952 | 4 |
| Bob Aspromonte, Houston | 142 | 233 | 13 | .967 | 3 |
| Eddie Mathews, Milwaukee | 140 | 283 | 16 | .964 | 3 |
| Rich Rollins, Minnesota | 159 | 324 | 28 | .943 | -1 |

typical early-'60s Yankee victory: homers by Mickey Mantle, Roger Maris and Bill Skowron, and strong pitching from Whitey Ford, Ralph Terry and Luis Arroyo. Boyer was 2-for-4 and made two excellent defensive plays that day.

By Memorial Day the Yankees were locked in a tight race for first place with Cleveland and Minnesota. Off to his best start ever, Boyer provided plenty of punch at the bottom of manager Ralph Houk's batting order. He was hitting over .400 well into May, then began to slow down, ending the month at .317. By early June, the Yankees had taken the lead, but Boyer was struggling at the plate. An 0-for-5 day on June 9 dropped him below .300. He got hot over the last week of June—he was 12-for-26 between June 22 and 26—and ended the month at .284 with 10 homers and 31 RBIs.

The Yankees had a one-game lead at the first All-Star break—there were two All-Star Games that season—then pulled away during mid-July, winning nine in a row between July 14 and 21. The catalyst was Boyer, who was 13-for-29 during the first week after the All-Star Game. At the end of July, Boyer had another streak, hitting safely in eight straight games. New York had a six-game lead on

August 1, then kept its challengers at arm's length for the rest of the summer, ending the season five games ahead of second-place Minnesota.

"Brooks and Graig received more publicity because they were better hitters than Clete. Brooks and Nettles played deep, daring hitters to bunt on them. Clete played shallow and took away the bunt. He was quick enough to cover the ground in both directions, and no one could dive to the right, backhand the all and throw from his knees like Clete."

—TONY KUBEK

Boyer was a key player for the Yanks in the 1962 World Series. In Game 1, on October 4 in San Francisco, he hit a home run in the seventh inning that broke a 2-2 tie and helped the Yankees defeat the Giants. He hit .318 with four RBIs in the Series, which the Yankees won in seven games.

Boyer played for New York until 1966, when he was traded to Atlanta (he hit a career-best 26 homers in his first year with the

Braves). He finished his major-league playing career in '71 with a .242 career batting average—and the reputation as one of the best defensive third basemen ever to play the game.

"Even when we took infield practice," he once said, "I knew people were watching me. . . . I loved it. No distraction bothered me. A third baseman has got to be like that, loaded with confidence."

## Baseball News Of 1962

- The Houston Colt .45's and New York Mets were welcomed into the National League.
- The National League rejected Commissioner Ford Frick's proposal for interleague play.
- Jackie Robinson, Bob Feller, Edd Rousch, and Bill McKechnie were elected to the Hall of Fame.
- The Yankees' Joe Pepitone became the first rookie to hit two home runs in one inning.
- The Angels' Bo Belinsky no-hit the Orioles on May 5.
- The Giants beat the Dodgers in a three-game NL playoff.

## Around The World In 1962

- Tony Bennett won a Grammy for his rendition of "I Left My Heart in San Francisco."
- Reconnaisance flights detected fully equipped misile bases in Cuba, prompting the Cuban Missile Crisis.
- An earthquake in Iran killed more than 12,000 people.
- Johnny Carson replaced Jack Paar on "The Tonight Show."
- James Meredith became the first black student admitted to the University of Mississippi.
- Rachel Carson's *Silent Spring* helped launch the environmental movement.

# 39 Season of Glory

## Dave Winfield

### 1984

| AB | R | H | BA | OB% | 2B | 3B | HR | K/BB | RBI | BR | SB |
|----|---|---|-----|------|-----|-----|-----|-------|------|-----|-----|
| 567 | 106 | 193 | .340 | .397 | 34 | 4 | 19 | 71/53 | 100 | 43 | 6 |

| | | G | PO | A | DP | E | FA | FR | | | |
|--|--|----|-----|---|----|---|------|----|--|--|--|
| | | 141 | 306 | 3 | 1 | 2 | .994 | 2 | | | |

# 39 David Mark Winfield

**BORN**
October 3, 1951
St. Paul, Minnesota

**HEIGHT**
6-6

**WEIGHT**
220

**THREW**
right hand

**BATTED**
right hand

New York Yankees
1981–90

**HALL OF FAME**
2001

*1984*

Although Dave Winfield had a terrific career with the Yankees statistically—he hit 205 homers, had 818 runs batted in, had a .290 average, won five Gold Gloves, and appeared in eight All-Star Games in nine years—he always seemed to be playing under a cloud. Before Winfield ever even put on a Yankee uniform, he was at odds with the man who brought him to New York, George Steinbrenner. They sniped at each other in the press, they argued at private meetings, they fought in court. In the end, one cannot discuss Winfield's Yankee career without mentioning his disagreements with Steinbrenner.

Winfield was born on October 3, 1951 in St. Paul, Minn. He was a brilliant athlete, excelling in baseball (his first love), football and basketball. At the University of Minnesota, he played basketball, football and baseball and was the MVP in the College World Series in 1973. He was drafted by four pro teams—the NBA's Atlanta Hawks, the ABA's Utah Stars, the NFL's Minnesota Vikings and baseball's San Diego Padres. He signed with San Diego right out of school in June of '73 for $15,000. Going directly into the majors, Winfield hit .277 in 56 games—"the toughest three months of my life until then," he later called it—for the last-place Padres.

Winfield spent eight years in San Diego, averaging 19 homers and 78 runs batted in for some decidedly bland Padre teams (they finished over .500 only once during his time there). An All-Star his last four seasons as a Padre, but still largely ignored by the media, he became a free agent after the 1980 season.

The Yankees were one of ten teams that drafted Winfield under the free- agent rules that existed at the time. The field soon dwindled to four—the Yankees, Mets, Braves, and Astros—then the Mets offered Winfield the biggest contract in the history of baseball. Steinbrenner, refusing to be outdone by New York's other team, offered Winfield a $1 million signing bonus, $1.4 million a year for ten years, and salary increases (up to ten percent a year) that would match increases in the cost of living. Steinbrenner also agreed to give another $3 million to the David M. Winfield Foundation, an organization Winfield had started during his days as a Padre to help disadvantaged youth.

Winfield signed Steinbrenner's contract in December, and the conflict began when Steinbrenner realized he had miscalculated how much the deal was worth (originally, he thought the contract was worth $16 million; he later discovered it was worth as much as $23 million). The ink was hardly dry when he asked to renegotiate. After some prelimi-

"I pride myself on all elements of the game. Everything doesn't have to begin and end with the home run. To me, it's just as exhilarating to make a catch and a guy is tagging up and you throw him out."

—DAVE WINFIELD

# Game of Glory • May 9, 1984

Winfield leads a rout of Cleveland on May 9 with four hits.

| CLEVELAND | AB | R | H | RBI | | NEW YORK | AB | R | H | RBI |
|-----------|----|----|----|-----|---|----------|----|----|----|-----|
| Butler, cf | 2 | 0 | 0 | 0 | | Randolph, 2b | 4 | 2 | 2 | 0 |
| Nixon, cf | 2 | 0 | 0 | 0 | | Foli, 2b | 1 | 0 | 0 | 0 |
| Castillo, ph | 1 | 0 | 0 | 0 | | Harrah, 3b | 4 | 2 | 1 | 1 |
| Bernazard, 2b | 5 | 0 | 1 | 0 | | Griffey, rf | 3 | 1 | 1 | 0 |
| Franco, ss | 4 | 0 | 2 | 0 | | Gamble, rf | 2 | 0 | 0 | 0 |
| Thomson, dh | 2 | 1 | 0 | 0 | | Winfield, cf | 5 | 4 | 4 | 3 |
| Hargrove, lf | 4 | 1 | 0 | 0 | | Mattingly, 1b | 3 | 1 | 2 | 5 |
| Tabler, lf | 2 | 1 | 2 | 1 | | Kemp, lf | 3 | 0 | 1 | 1 |
| Hassey, c | 4 | 0 | 1 | 0 | | Smalley, dh | 4 | 1 | 1 | 1 |
| Jacoby, 3b | 4 | 1 | 2 | 2 | | Wynegar, c | 4 | 0 | 1 | 0 |
| Vukovich, rf | 4 | 0 | 1 | 1 | | Robertson, ss | 4 | 0 | 1 | 0 |
| **Totals** | **34** | **4** | **9** | **4** | | **Totals** | **37** | **11** | **14** | **11** |

```
Cleveland     0 1 0   0 0 3   0 0 0 — 4
New York      4 3 0   3 0 1   0 0 * — 11
```

Errors—Wynegar 2, Franco, Harrah, Winfield. Doubles—Franco, Winfield 2, Vukovich.
Triple—Harrah. Home runs—Mattingly, Winfield, Smalley.
Stolen bases—Bernazard, Franco. Sacrifice flies—Mattingly, Kemp, Tabler.
Double plays—New York 2. Left on base–Cleveland 7, New York 5.

| NEW YORK | IP | H | R | ER | BB | K |
|----------|----|----|----|----|----|----|
| P. Niekro (W, 5-1) | 7 | 8 | 4 | 1 | 3 | 4 |
| Shirley | 1 | 1 | 0 | 0 | 0 | 1 |
| Righetti | 1 | 0 | 0 | 0 | 0 | 0 |

| CLEVELAND | IP | H | R | ER | BB | K |
|-----------|----|----|----|----|----|----|
| Sutcliffe (L, 3-2) | 1.1 | 8 | 7 | 7 | 1 | 3 |
| Spillner | 6.2 | 6 | 4 | 4 | 0 | 0 |

Time—2:24. Attendance—20,453.

nary hesitancy, Winfield's lawyers agreed to work out a new deal. But the die was cast, and the Steinbrenner-Winfield relationship was off to a rocky start.

After the contract controversy cleared up, Winfield was able to focus on his new team. And he liked what he saw. "I knew the Yankees had an excellent chance of going all the way, and I knew I could help make it happen," he wrote in *Winfield: A Player's Life*. He also knew that because he was being paid so much, people expected a lot from him. "To prove anything to my teammates or to the New York fans, I knew I'd have to be pretty damn good," he wrote.

Overall, Winfield didn't disappoint during his first season in New York. He hit .294 and led the Yankees in hits (114), doubles (25), runs batted in (68), and slugging (.464), in a strike-shortened 107-game season. He played miserably in the 1981 World Series, however, hitting just .045.

Over the next two seasons, Winfield was one of the best players in the game. He hit 37 homers in 1982 and 32 the next season, drove in 222 runs over the two years, and was one of the best defensive outfielders in the game.

Meanwhile, Winfield and Steinbrenner had begun feuding because of Steinbrenner's refusal to fulfill his contractual obligations to the Winfield Foundation. Throughout Winfield's Yankee career, these disagreements with Steinbrenner overshadowed what was happening on the field. Winfield would complain about the late payments for the foundation; Steinbrenner would question the way it was being run; Winfield would say he just wanted to concentrate on baseball; Steinbrenner would point out his failure in the '81 World Series and a perceived poor performance down the stretch in September 1983, telling reporters "Winfield's not a winner," and referring to him as "Mr. May"; Winfield would respond by pointing out that without him, there would have been no September stretch run for the Yankees in '83 (32 homers, 116 RBIs, .283 batting average); Winfield would complain during spring training about the makeup of the 1984 ballclub; rumors would surface that the Yankees would try to trade him to Boston. That Winfield could put together his best season in 1984 was a tribute not only to his talent but to his ability to shut out the sideshows.

The '84 Yankees were a team in transition. Goose Gossage had left for and Graig Nettles was traded to San Diego, where they helped the Padres win the NL pennant. Shane Rawley was traded to Philadelphia for Marty Bystrom, who got hurt and pitched in just seven games. What's more, there were a number of new faces—Toby Harrah, Mike Pagliarulo, Bobby Meacham, and Steve Kemp, among them—and other returning players, like Omar Moreno and Ken Griffey, failed to produce as expected. Manager Yogi Berra, scrambling for the right combination, used eighteen different lineups over the first 21 games. The Yankees' opener, on April 3 in Kansas City, was a typical game for the 1984 campaign. The Royals' Onix Concepcion hit Ron Guidry's first pitch of the season for a home run—the first of Concepcion's career—while Winfield homered and drove in two runs in a losing cause.

Because the Yankees were struggling to pull it together and because the Detroit Tigers that year had a phenomenal start (they won 35 of their first 40 games), the Yankees soon found themselves in a deep hole. They were in last place, 10½ games out, by the end of April, and although they had climbed to sixth a month later, they were still 17½ games behind the Tigers by June 1. They improved dramatically after the All-Star break (51-30) and finished third, 17 games behind the runaway Tigers.

The season wasn't a total loss for Yankee fans, though, as Winfield and teammate Don Mattingly participated in one of the most memorable batting races in baseball history. Winfield had made a small adjustment in his batting style for 1984, shortening his stroke. The results were obvious by season's end: he hit 19 homers, 13 fewer than the year before, but raised his average by almost 60 points. Mattingly, in his first full season, would have the first of his 200-plus hit campaigns.

By the end of the first month of the season, Mattingly was at .315 and Winfield was on the disabled list with a hamstring injury and a .306 average. After missing 11 games, he returned on May 1. It took over a week for Winfield to regain his hitting eye—his average fell to .255—but then he began finding the groove. He went 4-for-5 with three RBIs in an 11-4 victory over Cleveland on May 9, contributed three hits to a victory over Seattle on May 13, had another four-hit game in a victory over Oakland on May 15, and beat the A's with a two-run, tenth-inning homer the next day. By the end of the month, his average was up to .295.

In June, Winfield shifted into high gear. He went 15 for 39 (.385) during the first ten days of the month. He ran his hitting streak to 17 games and improved his season average to .346, tops in the AL. The streak was snapped on June 11, and Mattingly briefly took the lead, but by the end of June, Winfield was leading the league at .368 (thanks in part to his three five-hit games that month, tying an AL record).

Winfield's average climbed to .377 in the days before the All-Star Game—he had a double in four at-bats in the game, which the AL lost—but he began slowing down as July wore on. (Steinbrenner took advantage of this slump to question his highly paid star's ability to win, setting off another round of quarreling.) By the end of August, Winfield's lead had dwindled to two points (.352 to .350). Mattingly became the frontrunner after his 8-for-15 streak from August 18 to 22, but Winfield regained the lead on September 28. He had a two-point edge (.341 to .339) going into the last game of the season, on September 30.

As Winfield saw it, he couldn't win. Impatient with Winfield's fights with Steinbrenner, the fans overwhelmingly supported Mattingly; in fact, when Winfield stepped to the plate on that last day, he was booed, when it was Mattingly's turn, the fans gave him a standing ovation. Mattingly got four hits in the game; when it was over, he was at .343, Winfield at .340. The two teammates put their arms around each other, doffed their caps to the cheering fans, and walked off the field together.

Winfield described his 1984 season as his most difficult and least rewarding. He did receive some praise after the season, however, when Berra told reporters that Winfield was his most valuable player.

Winfield's Yankee career lasted until May 1990, when he was traded to the California Angels. He had missed all of the 1989 season because of back surgery and was hitting just .213 when the deal was made. He hit .275 with 19 homers and 72 RBIs in 112 games for the Angels, and was named Comeback Player of the Year by *The Sporting News*.

## Baseball News Of 1984

- California's Reggie Jackson hit his 500th career home run on September 17 against Kansas City's Bud Black.

- Baseball personalities who died that year included Padres owner Ray Kroc (January 14); hitting coach extraordinaire Charlie Lau (March 18); Hall of Famer Stan Coveleski (March 20); baseball's clown prince Al Schacht (July 14); Hall of Famer Waite Hoyt (August 25); former AL president Joe Cronin (September 7); Hall of Famer Walter Alston; longtime utilityman Billy Goodman (October 1); and former NL batting champ Debs Garms (December 16).

- Marge Schott became the owner of the Cincinnati Reds.

- The Mets' Dwight Gooden fanned sixteen batters in two consecutive games.

## Around The World In 1984

- The U.S. embassy in Beirut was bombed, killing twenty-three, including two Americans.

- The top movie of the year was *Indiana Jones and the Temple of Doom*, which earned $42 million in its first six days of release.

- Michael Jackson's *Thriller* album topped the charts.

- The U.S. foreign trade deficit hit a record $107.6 billion.

- More than five million Americans kicked the habit in the Great American Smokeout in November.

- According to a Gallup poll, swimming, bicycling, and fishing were the most popular recreational activities among Americans.

- The Soviet Union boycotted the 1984 Olympics, which were held in Los Angeles, in retaliation for the United States' 1980 boycott of the Games in Moscow.

# 40

# Season of Glory

## Allie Reynolds

### 1952

| W | L | Pct. | IP | GS | CG | SH | SV | K/BB | Opp. BA | ERA |
|---|---|------|-----|----|----|----|----|------|---------|-----|
| 20 | 8 | .714 | 244.1 | 29 | 24 | 6 | 6 | 160/97 | .218 | 2.06 |

| | | GP | PO | A | DP | E | FA | ER/R | PR | DEF |
|---|---|----|----|---|----|----|----|------|----|-----|
| | | 35 | 13 | 35 | 1 | 2 | .960 | 70/56 | 34 | -1 |

# Allie Pierce Reynolds

**BORN**
February 10, 1915
Bethany, Oklahoma

**DIED**
December 26, 1994
Oklahoma City, Oklahoma

**HEIGHT**
6-0

**WEIGHT**
195

**THREW**
right hand

**BATTED**
right hand

New York Yankees
1947–54

*1952*

Allie Reynolds wasn't always a winner. In fact, during his first four years in the majors, with the Cleveland Indians, he developed a reputation as a pitcher who was unable to deliver in the clutch, a pitcher who was content to put in five or six good innings and then turn the game over to his bullpen. And he did nothing to improve his reputation after the Yankees traded for him following the 1946 season, on the advice of Joe DiMaggio. In his first season as a Yankee, Reynolds completed only 17 of 34 starts. In 1948 he went the distance only 11 times in 39 outings. And 1949 was an even worse year for Reynolds (in spite of his 17-6 record) as he completed only 4 of his 35 starts. "That season was my most miserable year," he later told sportswriter Tom Meany. "Complete games are as important to me as they are to any other starting pitcher, but people were acting as though I liked what was going on." The press didn't make matters any easier, referring to Reynolds, a Native American from Bethany, Olkahoma, as "The Vanishing American" or listing the winning pitcher as "Reynolds/Page," a reference to reliever Joe Page, who bailed Reynolds out on a regular basis in 1949.

But the bad rap disappeared on October 5, 1949, in the opening game of the World Series. Reynolds was pitching in front of 66,224 fans at Yankee Stadium, locked in a classic duel with Brooklyn's Don Newcombe. Neither allowed a run through eight innings, Reynolds holding the Dodgers to just two hits. In the bottom of the ninth, the Yankees' Tom Henrich homered to give Reynolds a 1-0 victory—and a new outlook. He later recalled, "Ever since I was a kid, I'd had the overpowering feeling that the breaks would never be mine. It was the first time I had come up with the right game in the right place." He returned in Game 4 with three perfect innings of relief—how's that for clutch?—in a 6-4 Yankee victory. They wrapped up the Series the next day.

So Reynolds had turned the corner. The next year he went 16-12, with 14 complete games. In 1951 he was 17-8, with two no-hitters and a league-best seven shutouts. But 1952 was the year Reynolds had an opportunity to really shine. That year the Yankees, who were three-time defending World Series champions, lost a number of key players, including DiMaggio, who had retired the previous December, Bobby Brown, Jerry Coleman, and Tom Morgan. Thus, the team's success would depend on the skills of the pitching staff, anchored by Vic Raschi, Ed Lopat, Johnny Sain, and, of course, Reynolds, whom manager Casey

*The Superchief, Allie Reynolds, overcame his early rap as a pitcher who couldn't deliver in the clutch.*

# Game of Glory • September 21, 1952

On September 21 Reynolds pitches his sixth shutout of the season to keep the Yankees a game-and-a-half ahead of Cleveland in the pennant race. His six strikeouts also move him into the AL lead in that department.

| PHILADELPHIA | AB | R | H | RBI | | NEW YORK | AB | R | H | RBI |
|---|---|---|---|---|---|---|---|---|---|---|
| Joost, ss | 4 | 0 | 0 | 0 | | Martin, 3b | 4 | 0 | 1 | 0 |
| Fain, 1b | 3 | 0 | 0 | 0 | | Rizzuto, ss | 0 | 0 | 0 | 0 |
| Philley, cf | 4 | 0 | 0 | 0 | | Collins, 1b | 3 | 1 | 0 | 0 |
| Valo, lf | 2 | 0 | 0 | 0 | | Mantle, cf | 3 | 0 | 1 | 0 |
| Robertson, lf | 3 | 0 | 1 | 0 | | Berra, c | 3 | 0 | 1 | 1 |
| Michaels, 2b | 2 | 0 | 1 | 0 | | Noren, lf | 4 | 0 | 0 | 0 |
| Hitchcock, 3b | 2 | 0 | 0 | 0 | | Bauer, rf | 3 | 0 | 1 | 0 |
| Thomas, ph | 0 | 0 | 0 | 0 | | McDougald, 3b | 2 | 0 | 1 | 0 |
| Murray, c | 2 | 0 | 0 | 0 | | Reynolds, p | 3 | 0 | 0 | 0 |
| Hamilton, ph | 1 | 0 | 0 | 0 | | | | | | |
| Astroth, c | 1 | 0 | 0 | 0 | | | | | | |
| Byrd, p | 3 | 0 | 1 | 0 | | | | | | |
| Clark, ph | 1 | 0 | 0 | 0 | | | | | | |
| **Totals** | **28** | **0** | **3** | **0** | | **Totals** | **25** | **1** | **5** | **1** |

| | | | | | | | | | |
|---|---|---|---|---|---|---|---|---|---|
| Philadelphia | 0 0 0 | 0 0 0 | 0 0 0 | — 0 |
| New York | 0 0 0 | 0 0 1 | 0 0 * | — 1 |

Errors—Joost, Hitchcock. Doubles—Mantle, Bauer. Triple—Michaels. Stolen base—Robertson. Sacrifices—Michaels, McDougald, Rizzuto. Double play—New York. Left on base—Philadelphia 9, New York 8.

| NEW YORK | IP | H | R | ER | BB | K |
|---|---|---|---|---|---|---|
| Reynolds (W, 19-8) | 9 | 3 | 0 | 0 | 3 | 6 |

| PHILADELPHIA | IP | H | R | ER | BB | K |
|---|---|---|---|---|---|---|
| Byrd (L, 15-14) | 8 | 5 | 1 | 1 | 0 | 5 |

*1952*

Stengel planned to use as a starter and reliever.

Reynolds made his 1952 debut on April 18 in the Yankees' third game of the season (their home opener). Before the game he was honored for his two 1951 no-hitters, and the team retired DiMaggio's jersey number (5). That was the high point for the Yankee faithful that day, as the Senators beat Reynolds 3-1. He allowed eight hits but was his own worst enemy, hitting one batter and walking another with the bases loaded.

Reynolds lost his next outing, 3-1 to Boston, then finally posted his first victory, a 4-1, eight-strikeout four-hitter against St. Louis on April 30. He was even sharper a week later versus Cleveland, scattering only five hits, but lost 1-0 to the Indians' Steve Gromek. He wouldn't be denied a victory in his next start, on May 11 against the Red Sox in New York. Reynolds allowed just two hits, a pair of singles in the first inning, then retired twenty-five men in a row, striking out eight and not walking a batter, as he beat Boston 1-0. It was the start of a six-game winning streak for Reynolds, after which he was 7-3 (all ten decisions were complete games). Highlights during this stretch included a two-hitter on May 27 against Washington and a three-hitter on June 7 against St. Louis.

The Yankees likewise started slowly, wallowing in fifth place in late May. But an early-June surge carried them to the top of the standings, and they took over first by percentage points when they beat Detroit on June 10. The Indians snapped Reynolds' winning streak at six with a 7-1 victory on June 13, dropping the Yankees into second, but New York regained first the next day with an 11-0 victory. The Yankees were 22-9 in June, which ended with them in first, 3½ games ahead of Boston and Chicago.

Reynolds won his last three decisions of the month and his first in July—a 5-4, 11-inning victory against the Browns, that brought his record to 11-4, all complete games. He failed to go the distance in his next start—the first time all season that had happened—as the Indians KO'd him in the second inning of an 11-6 loss.

The Yankees took their biggest lead of the season, 5½ games, on July 19 with a 4-2 victory over the White Sox. Try as they might, they couldn't shake the Indians or Red Sox in July. Cleveland moved back into first by .001 with a 6-4 victory over Reynolds on August 22—snapping his three-game winning streak—but the Yankees regained first the next day and remained there the rest of the season.

Stengel made Reynolds his go-to guy down the stretch. Not only did he win his last five starts—all complete games in which he allowed a total of just five earned runs—but he turned in several key relief appearances. On September 13 against Chicago, he came on in the ninth inning after Sain had given up hits to Jim Rivera and Sherm Lollar. He got the next two batters to hit into force plays at second, then got Chico Carrasquel to ground out to end the game. The next day he worked 3⅔ innings of shutout relief, allowing just one hit, in a 7-1 win over Cleveland. A week later he allowed only three hits against Philadelphia (his six strikeouts gave him the league lead over the

A's Bobby Shantz). The Yanks won 1-0, bringing Reynolds' record to 19–8.

He got his twentieth win on September 25 when the Yankees faced Boston at Fenway Park, going for the AL pennant-clincher. The Red Sox led 2-0 in the fourth, but the Yanks rallied to tie the score with single runs in the fifth and sixth. In the top of the ninth, a walk and two sacrifices put a man on third and brought Reynolds to the plate. "I didn't hesitate a second about letting Reynolds hit," Stengel later told reporters. "I expected him to come through." And Reynolds did, stroking Sid Hudson's third pitch over short for an RBI single that clinched a tie for the AL pennant and made Reynolds a twentieth-game winner for the first time in his career.

He wound up the regular season with six shutouts, 160 strikeouts, and a 2.06 ERA, all league-leading stats. This made him Stengel's obvious choice to start Game 1 of the World Series against Brooklyn. Reynolds'

> "I always had good stuff, only some days it didn't work as well as others."
>
> —ALLIE REYNOLDS

magic vanished, however, as Jackie Robinson, Duke Snider, and Pee Wee Reese homered to lead the Dodgers to a 4-2 victory in the opener. Reynolds lasted seven innings, allowing five hits and three earned runs.

The teams split the next two games, and Reynolds was back on the mound for Game 4 with only two days' rest. He responded with a masterful 2-0 four-hitter, striking out ten. "I never saw a fella pitch better with two days' rest," Stengel said.

Game 5 went to the Dodgers, however, and again Reynolds' heroics were needed to bail out the Yankees. Raschi was the starting pitcher for New York in Game 6. He had a 3-1 lead going into the bottom of the eighth, but then Snider homered and the Dodgers put another man on second with two out. That put Stengel on the spot. He needed to replace Raschi ("I could see he was getting tired") but was worried about depleting his pitching staff with a decisive Game 7 looming. His solution: bring on Reynolds. Reynolds got out of the immediate danger by fanning Roy Campanella to end the eighth. In the ninth he struck out pinch-hitter Rocky Nelson on three pitches, walked Carl Furillo and then got Andy Pafko to pop up and Billy Cox to ground out to save the victory and force Game 7.

Lopat started for the Yankees but left in the fourth after loading the bases with no one out. Reynolds was sent in to relieve him, and, despite having pitched just the day before, got out of the jam with minimal damage—the Dodgers scored only one run to take a 1-0 lead. By the time Reynolds left for a pinch-hitter in the seventh, he and the Yankees had a 4-2 lead. Southpaw Bob Kuzava shut the Dodgers down for 2⅔ hit-less innings to preserve the victory for Reynolds and give the Yankees their fourth straight world championship.

Reynolds had two more winning seasons with the Yankees, going 13-7 in 1953 and 13-4 in 1954. But a back injury, suffered when the team bus hit a railroad overpass in 1953, finally caught up with him, and he was forced to retire before the start of the 1955 season.

He left baseball with a 182-107 record and career 3.30 ERA. His .686 winning percentage (131-60) is the fourth highest in Yankee history for pitchers with 100 or more victories. He is fifth on the team's all-time shutout list (27), eighth on the strikeout list (967), and ninth on the victory list (131).

"You've got to distinguish between a pitcher and a thrower," Reynolds, who died in 1994, once reflected. "I was a thrower until that Series game in 1949."

## Baseball News Of 1952

- The A's Ferris Fain won his second consecutive AL batting crown.

- On April 23 New York Giants pitcher Hoyt Wilhelm homered in his first major-league at-bat. He didn't hit another homer in his twenty-one-year career.

- On May 20 Yankee manager Casey Stengel made Mickey Mantle his regular center-fielder.

- Pirates minor-league pitcher Ron Neccai struck out twenty-seven batters in a no-hitter on May 13. Eight days later he fanned twenty-four in another game.

- The Boston Braves purchased Henry Aaron's contract from the Indianapolis Clowns.

- Arky Vaughan, 40, drowned in a boating mishap on August 30 in California.

- Ted Williams went into the service and began flying combat missions in Korea.

## Around The World In 1952

- On November 4 Dwight Eisenhower was elected president, easily defeating Adlai Stevenson.

- Among the books published were *The Old Man and the Sea*, by Ernest Hemingway, *Invisible Man* , by Ralph Ellison, and *East of Eden*, by John Steinbeck.

- On April 8 the nation's steel mills were seized by presidential order to prevent a shutdown by strikers. The move was later declared unconstitutional, and a fifty-four-day steel strike followed.

- "Flying saucers" were spotted everywhere.

- A transatlantic speed record for ships was set on July 7 by the S.S. *United States* with a time of three days, ten hours, and forty minutes.

- The number of people employed in the United States reached a record 62.5 million.

# 41
## Season of Glory

## Mel Stottlemyre

### 1969

| W | L | Pct. | IP | GS | CG | SH | SV | K/BB | Opp. BA | ERA |
|---|---|------|------|----|----|----|----|------|---------|-----|
| 20 | 14 | .588 | 303.0 | 39 | 24 | 3 | 0 | 113/97 | .239 | 2.82 |

| | GP | PO | A | DP | E | FA | ER/R | PR | DEF |
|---|----|----|----|----|----|------|------|----|-----|
| | 39 | 24 | 88 | 3 | 5 | .957 | 105/95 | 22 | 8 |

BORN
November 13, 1941
Hazelton, Missouri

HEIGHT
6-2

WEIGHT
190

THREW
right hand

BATTED
right hand

New York Yankees
1964-74

# Melvin Leon Stottlemyre

**M**el Stottlemyre was a small-town guy who found success in the big city. Born in Hazelton, Missouri, on November 13, 1941, he was pitching for Yakima Valley College when he was discovered by a Yankee scout in 1960. Blessed with an effective sinker, decent fastball, and the kind of determination a pitcher needs to succeed, he moved through the Yankees' minor-league system and was named 1964 minor-league player of the year after a 13-3, 1.42 ERA season at Richmond.

In August 1964 the Yankees, in the midst of a three-way pennant race with Chicago and Baltimore, brought him to New York. While moving to New York was a big adjustment for Stottlemyre, he knew he couldn't afford to be distracted for very long. His concentration paid off: He went 9-3 to help the Yankees win the pennant and was 1-1 with a no-decision in the '64 World Series (he pitched against St. Louis' incomparable Bob Gibson all three games).

There would be no sophomore jinx for the young right-hander, who went 20-9 with a 2.63 ERA and 18 complete games in 1965. The Yankees, though, were slipping into mediocrity, and Stottlemyre became the ace for some lousy ball clubs. They didn't reach the .500 mark again until 1968, that thanks in large measure to Stottlemyre (21-12, 2.45), who was just warming up for his greatest season.

Before we examine Stottlemyre's top season, however, it is important to briefly review several events that made 1969—baseball's centennial—a year of change for the sport. First, expansion brought new teams to Kansas City, Seattle, San Diego, and Montreal, and the leagues were each split into two six-team divisions, giving baseball its first playoff setup. In addition, there was a new commissioner, Bowie Kuhn. What's more, eight teams started 1969 with new managers, and five others opened with managers who had taken over during the course of the 1968 season. Finally, team owners acted to solve what they deemed to be a problem with the game: the dominance of pitchers. In 1968 only six players hit over .300, and the American League had just one hitter over .290, Carl Yastrzemski at .301. Believing that fans wanted a faster- paced game with more action—apparently a low-scoring, well-pitched game didn't qualify as "exciting"—the owners approved two major changes. They lowered the mound from fifteen inches to ten and shrank the strike zone. The lowered pitching mound and smaller strike zone would help raise the AL's leaguewide batting average by sixteen points in 1969, but the

*Mel Stottlemyre, Yankee staff ace during the post-Mantle years, was a three-time, 20-game winner.*

# Game of Glory • April 12, 1969

In his second start of the season, Stottlemyre one-hits Detroit, allowing just a fifth-inning double by Jim Northrup. Only two other Tigers reached base, both on errors.

| NEW YORK | AB | R | H | RBI | | DETROIT | AB | R | H | RBI |
|---|---|---|---|---|---|---|---|---|---|---|
| Clarke, 2b | 5 | 2 | 3 | 1 | | McAuliffe, 2b | 4 | 0 | 0 | 0 |
| Kenney, cf | 5 | 0 | 2 | 1 | | Stanley, ss | 4 | 0 | 0 | 0 |
| Murcer, 3b | 5 | 0 | 1 | 1 | | Kaline, rf | 4 | 0 | 0 | 0 |
| White, lf | 4 | 0 | 1 | 1 | | Cash, 1b | 3 | 0 | 0 | 0 |
| Pepitone, 1b | 4 | 0 | 0 | 0 | | Horton, lf | 3 | 0 | 0 | 0 |
| Robinson, rf | 3 | 0 | 0 | 0 | | Northrup, cf | 3 | 0 | 1 | 0 |
| Gibbs, c | 4 | 0 | 2 | 0 | | Freehan, c | 3 | 0 | 0 | 0 |
| Michael, ss | 4 | 1 | 2 | 0 | | Wert, 3b | 3 | 0 | 0 | 0 |
| Stottlemyre, p | 4 | 1 | 1 | 0 | | McLain, p | 2 | 0 | 0 | 0 |
| | | | | | | Brown, ph | 1 | 0 | 0 | 0 |
| Totals | 38 | 4 | 12 | 4 | | Totals | 30 | 0 | 1 | 0 |

```
New York    0 0 2   0 1 0   0 0 1  — 4
Detroit     0 0 0   0 0 0   0 0 0  — 0
```

Errors—Clarke, Kaline, Murcer. Doubles—Michael, Murcer, Clarke, Northrup. Stolen bases—White, Murcer. Left on base—New York 9, Detroit 3.

| NEW YORK | IP | H | R | ER | BB | K |
|---|---|---|---|---|---|---|
| Stottlemyre (W, 2-0) | 9 | 1 | 0 | 0 | 0 | 3 |

| DETROIT | IP | H | R | ER | BB | K |
|---|---|---|---|---|---|---|
| McLain (L, 1-1) | 9 | 12 | 4 | 4 | 2 | 5 |

Time—2:00. Attendance—14,527.

changes did little to hinder Stottlemyre's effectiveness.

The 1969 season opened on April 7 in Washington, with the Yankees and Stottlemyre facing the Senators and their rookie manager, Ted Williams. Given an early 8-0 lead, Stottlemyre cruised to a complete-game, 8-4 victory in front of a Washington-record crowd of 45,113 that included President Richard Nixon. In his second start of the season, he thoroughly handcuffed Detroit, allowing just one hit—Jim Northrup's fifth-inning double—and only two other baserunners, both of whom reached on errors, in a 4-0 Yankee victory.

Stottlemyre was hot. He ran his record to 3-0 on April 17 with a ten-inning complete-game victory over Washington, and he beat Boston and Baltimore in his next two outings. Even in his first loss of the season, April 29 at Yankee Stadium, he was impressive, going the distance in a 2-1 loss to the Red Sox.

The Yankees weren't as fortunate, or as good, as Stottlemyre during the first month. Despite his pitching and Joe Pepitone's and Bobby Murcer's hitting (they each had seven homers in April), New York struggled to an 11-10 record and was in third place, four games behind first-place Baltimore. New York then lost ten of its first eleven games in May to effectively drop out of the AL East race. Stottlemyre lost two games during the slump—one loss was the result of five Yankee errors in one inning—but he rebounded to win his last three starts of the month. The highlight was a 5-3 win over the White Sox on May 27 in Chicago, in which he ripped a two-run homer off Wilbur Wood ("I guess it was a knuckler, but it didn't knuckle very much," Stottlemyre said) in the eighth to snap a 3-3 tie. The win left him with an 8-3 record and a 2.65 ERA.

The Yankees continued to fade during the rest of the first half of the season, through no fault of Stottlemyre. At the All-Star break, they were 46-52, in fifth place, 20 games out of first. Stottlemyre, though, was 14-7 with a 2.61 ERA, stats that earned him a spot on the AL All- Star squad.

Denny McLain, a 31-game winner in 1968, was scheduled to start the game. Less than an hour before gametime, he still hadn't arrived at Washington's RFK Stadium—McLain, who piloted his own jet, was circling the city, caught in heavy air traffic—and AL manager Mayo Smith turned to Stottlemyre. "I didn't find out I was going to start until forty-five minutes before the game, but that didn't have any effect on me," Stottlemyre told reporters afterward. "I knew I was going to pitch early anyway. I just threw a hanging curveball to Johnny Bench, that's all."

With a man on base, Johnny Bench put Stottlemyre's second-inning mistake well into the left-field mezzanine for a 3-0 NL lead (he had surrendered an unearned run in the first). Stottlemyre finished the inning, but wound up with the loss in the NL's 9-3 victory.

Stottlemyre continued to pitch well in the second half, but the spotlight was now on the Miracle Mets. "Being a Yankee and watching the Mets win was real tough," he once said. "They definitely owned the town that year. . . . I remember we suffered because they were winning."

Stottlemyre pitched some beauties over the last 2½ months of the season—a six-hit, 3-1 victory over California on July 27, a four-hit, 2-1 win over Oakland on August 9, and a 4-3 victory over Washington on September 18 for his twentieth win. And the Yankees were above .500 (34-29) in the second half. Still, they finished fifth, 28½ games behind Baltimore.

Stottlemyre finished with a 20-14 record, a 2.82 ERA and an AL-best 24 complete games, helping to give the Yankees the second-best pitching staff in the league. Stottlemyre remained a Yankee mainstay through four more full seasons, though he had a cumulative record of just 61-59 for some lackluster ball clubs. He suffered a shoulder injury during the '74 campaign and went 6-7. The next spring, as the five-time All-Star worked to come back from the injury, he was released, just as the Yankees were beginning a new era of success. Commenting once on what some saw as his unlucky timing, Stottlemyre was positive. "In gen-

> "(Stottlemyre) would stand on the mound, go into a miniature windup, snd take a small stride toward the plate. The ball would come in, nice and fast, but not _that_ fast, and then it would explode downward, dead flat down. He had great control and never seemed to throw a ball that was above the knees."
>
> —AUTHOR DAVID HALBERSTAM, ON MEL STOTTLEMYRE, IN OCTOBER 1964

eral," he said, "I was very fortunate to play for the Yankees and play alongside some of my boyhood idols, such as Whitey Ford, Mickey Mantle, Roger Maris, Thurman Munson, and Elston Howard. We had some super guys during that period; we just weren't able to put it together and win consistently."

# Baseball News Of 1969

- Both leagues expanded to twelve teams and were split into two six-team divisions.
- Bowie Kuhn became commissioner.
- Twins manager Billy Martin beat up one of his own pitchers, Dave Boswell, in a fight outside a Detroit restaurant on August 10.
- The save became an official statistic.
- On March 1 Mickey Mantle retired from baseball.
- Oakland's Reggie Jackson drove in ten runs in a 21-7 victory over the Red Sox on June 14.
- On August 11 Don Drysdale announced his retirement after a fourteen-year career.
- Willie Mays hit his 600th homer, off the Padres' Mike Corkins, on September 22.
- Heine Zimmerman, the 1912 Triple Crown winner who was banned from baseball for life for allegedly trying to fix games in 1919, died at age 82 on March 14.

# Around The World In 1969

- The worst rains in 100 years struck Southern California, causing floods and mudslides that left more than 100 dead and destroyed more than 10,000 homes.
- Among the obituaries were those of Senator Everett McKinley Dirksen (September 7, age 73), Joseph P. Kennedy (November 18, age 81), Judy Garland (June 22, age 47), Jack Kerouac (October 21, age 47), and Ludwig Mies van der Rohe (August 17, age 83).
- On February 8 the last issue of the *Saturday Evening Post* was published.
- James Earl Ray, admitted assassin of Rev. Martin Luther King, was sentenced to ninety-nine years in prison on March 10.
- On October 15 the first Vietnam Moratorium Day was observed by millions with prayer vigils, candlelight processions, and meetings.
- Obscenity laws prohibiting the private possession of obscene materials were declared unconstitutional by the U.S. Supreme Court.
- On July 20 Neil Armstrong became the first man to set foot on the moon.

# 42

## Season of Glory

## Catfish Hunter

### 1975

| W | L | Pct. | IP | GS | CG | SH | SV | K/BB | Opp. BA | ERA |
|---|---|------|-----|-----|-----|-----|-----|--------|---------|------|
| 23 | 14 | .622 | 328.0 | 39 | 30 | 7 | 0 | 177/83 | .208 | 2.58 |

| | GP | PO | A | DP | E | FA | ER/R | PR | DEF |
|---|-----|-----|-----|-----|-----|------|--------|-----|------|
| | 39 | 23 | 26 | 0 | 3 | .942 | 107/94 | 40 | -4 |

# James Augustus Hunter

**BORN**
April 8, 1946
Hertford, North Carolina

**DIED**
September 9, 1999
Hertford, North Carolina

**HEIGHT**
6-0

**WEIGHT**
195

**THREW**
right hand

**BATTED**
right hand

New York Yankees
1975–79

**HALL OF FAME**
1987

## 1975

December 31, 1974, had to be the most dismal New Year's Eve in Charlie Finley's life. Word was out that his prized pitcher, Jim "Catfish" Hunter, was about to sign a historic contract with the New York Yankees. Hunter, who had led the American League with twenty-five victories in 1974 and who had won 21 games in each of the three previous seasons, had been declared a free agent after he won a contract dispute with Finley.

Baseball had never seen anything quite like it. The best pitcher in the game, twenty-eight years old and in his prime, winner of the 1974 Cy Young Award and anchor of the pitching staff for three World Series championship teams in the '70s, was on the open market.

Twenty-three teams went Catfishing—only the San Francisco Giants stayed home—and the bidding soon reached uncharted territory with multimillion-dollar deals being tossed in James Augustus Hunter's direction. On New Year's Eve, Hunter made the Yankees the lucky winners, agreeing to a contract that was valued at nearly $3.5 million, a stunning amount for 1975, and that made him the richest player in the game. By adding Hunter and Bobby Bonds on the roster (not to mention Elliott Maddox, Sandy Alomar, Lou Piniella, Rudy May, and Larry Gura), the Yankees, who had finished second in the AL East by just two games the year before, hoped to become the team to beat in 1975.

But Hunter's first start as a Yankee, on April 11 in their home opener, wasn't exactly what George Steinbrenner was expecting from his $3.5 million investment. Hunter was touched for long home runs by Willie Horton and Nate Colbert, losing to Detroit 5-3. "I was a little bit nervous out there," Hunter admitted afterward. "I was pressing a little bit too much." His next three starts were no bargains either—he lost to Boston on April 15, was KO'd in the fourth inning in a loss to Detroit on April 19, and failed to get a decision on April 23, knocked out in the seventh of another loss to the Hunter was 0-3 with a 7.36 earned-run average.

Hunter didn't win a game until April 27, but it was a beauty. He held Milwaukee hitless for 7⅔ innings—Sexto Lezcano's single through the left side of the infield broke up the no-hitter—and settled for a three-hitter, with the Yankees winning 10-1. With the victory, Hunter found his groove, winning five of his next six outings. The wins included a two-hitter against his old Oakland teammates on May 10 and a four-hitter against the A's on May 18. He closed out the month with

*Catfish Hunter with the legendary Bob Feller.*

a one-hitter on May 31, beating Texas 6-0 with help from Bonds (3-for-5, two RBIs).

Like Hunter, the Yankees had started slowly. Bonds, who would have the first 30-homer, 30-stolen base season in Yankee history that year, struggled to get his average above .200 over the first six weeks of the season. The bullpen was shaky, and the starting rotation was slow to come around. As a result the Yankees were in fourth place with a 21-24 record when June started. They won their first six games of the month, moving to within two games of first. By June 23 they had won 19 of their last 24 games to come within .002 of first-place Boston. The Yankees finally took the lead on June 24, when Hunter beat Baltimore 3-1 on four hits.

New York was unable to hold onto the lead for more than a few days, however; from June 29 through July 5 they lost seven games in a row. With his team fading, in early August Steinbrenner replaced manager Bill Virdon with Billy Martin, who had been fired by Texas two weeks earlier. Martin's hiring may have been good theater, but it did little to change the fortunes of the Yankees, who would finish a distant third behind Boston and Baltimore.

Through the ups and downs, Hunter kept his poise, remaining the consummate professional that he continued to be

"My brothers taught me to throw strikes. Thanks to them, I gave up 379 home runs in the big leagues."

—CATFISH HUNTER AT HIS HALL OF FAME INDUCTION ON JULY 26, 1987

Hunter's winning four-hitter on June 24 against Baltimore and helps put the Yankees into first place.

| NEW YORK | AB | R | H | RBI | | BALTIMORE | AB | R | H | RBI |
|---|---|---|---|---|---|---|---|---|---|---|
| Coggins, cf | 2 | 0 | 1 | 0 | | Singleton, rf | 4 | 1 | 1 | 1 |
| White, lf | 4 | 0 | 0 | 0 | | Bumbry, lf | 4 | 0 | 1 | 0 |
| Blomberg, dh | 4 | 0 | 0 | 0 | | Davis, dh | 4 | 0 | 1 | 0 |
| Munson, c | 3 | 2 | 1 | 0 | | Blair, pr | 0 | 0 | 0 | 0 |
| Chambliss, 1b | 4 | 1 | 2 | 0 | | May, 1b | 4 | 0 | 0 | 0 |
| Nettles, 3b | 3 | 0 | 2 | 1 | | Northrup, cf | 4 | 0 | 1 | 0 |
| Whitfield, rf | 3 | 0 | 1 | 2 | | Shopay, pr | 0 | 0 | 0 | 0 |
| Mason, ss | 4 | 0 | 0 | 0 | | Grich, 2b | 3 | 0 | 0 | 0 |
| Alomar, 2b | 3 | 0 | 0 | 0 | | Robinson, 3b | 4 | 0 | 0 | 0 |
| | | | | | | Hendricks, c | 2 | 0 | 0 | 0 |
| | | | | | | Belanger, ss | 2 | 0 | 0 | 0 |
| Totals | 30 | 3 | 7 | 3 | | Totals | 31 | 1 | 4 | 1 |

```
New York     1 0 0   2 0 0   0 0 0 — 3
Baltimore    1 0 0   0 0 0   0 0 0 — 1
```

Double plays—Baltimore 2. Left on base—New York 6, Baltimore 6.
Home run—Singleton. Stolen base—Alomar. Sacrifice fly—Whitfield.

| NEW YORK | IP | H | R | ER | BB | K |
|---|---|---|---|---|---|---|
| Hunter (W, 11-6) | 9 | 4 | 1 | 1 | 1 | 5 |

| BALTIMORE | IP | H | R | ER | BB | K |
|---|---|---|---|---|---|---|
| Torrez (L,7-5) | 9 | 7 | 3 | 3 | 4 | 5 |

Hit by pitcher—by Torrez (Munson); by Hunter (Hendricks); by Hunter (Grich).

Time—2:12. Attendance—19,175.

*1975*

throughout his fifteen-year major-league career. He had some impressive wins: His fifth shutout of the season, on July 8 against Texas, left him at 12-8 with a 2.82 ERA at the All-Star break. But he also had some tough losses: He also wound up the loser in the Midsummer Classic when former A's teammate Claudell Washington misplayed two balls in the ninth inning in left field, breaking a 3-3 tie and helping the NL win 6-3. There were two 1-0 defeats and he dropped a 5-3 decision after two of his outfielders collided, turning a fly ball into a run-scoring triple.

He closed the season strong, winning seven of his last nine decisions. On September 7 he won his twentieth game, beating Baltimore 2-0—it was his twenty-sixth complete game and seventh shutout of the season—which made him a 20-game winner for the fifth consecutive season. Hunter was only the tenth major-league pitcher to accomplish the feat.

Hunter won the last game of his first season as a Yankee in impressive fashion, beating Baltimore 3-2 on September 27. He allowed six hits and struck out twelve as he ran his record to 23-14 and lowered his ERA to 2.58. Hunter's 23 victories, 30 complete

*1987 Hall of Fame inductee, the softspoken Hunter.*

games, 328 innings pitched, and .208 opponents' batting average were all league-leading figures.

Hunter played four more seasons in New York, with a combined 40-39 record. After a couple of years of arm trouble, he struggled through 1979 (2-9, 5.31) and then announced his retirement. Eight years later, he was inducted into baseball's Hall of Fame. And sitting in the audience, enjoying the show, was his old friend, Charlie Finley.

## Baseball News Of 1975

- Boston's Fred Lynn (.331, 21 HRs, 105 RBIs) became the only player in history to be named Rookie of the Year and MVP in the same year.

- In a historic decision on December 23, arbitrator Peter Seitz declared pitchers Dave McNally and Andy Messersmith free agents. Five days later Seitz was fired by the major-league owners.

- Harmon Killebrew retired after a twenty-two-year career that included 573 home runs and not one bunt hit.

- Houston's Bob Watson scored the one millionth run in major-league history on May 4 against San Francisco.

- Oakland's Billy Williams hit his 400th career homer on June 12.

- The Mets' Joe Torre hit into four consecutive double plays on July 21 against the Astros.

- Orioles manager Earl Weaver was ejected from both games of an August 15 double-header—both times by Ron Luciano.

- Thirty-year-old Tony Conigliaro was forced to retire from baseball because of injuries, not the least of which was a near-fatal beaning in 1967.

- On September 29 Casey Stengel, who won ten pennants in the twelve years he served as Yankees' manager, died at age 85.

- On December 1 former White Sox second baseman Nellie Fox died at age 47.

- Bill Veeck purchased the White Sox for the second time.

## Around The World In 1975

- The Vietnam War finally ended with the U.S. withdrawal on April 30.

- Literacy requirements for voting were abolished.

- President Ford survived two assassination attempts—the first on September 5 in Sacramento, California, and the second on September 22 in San Francisco.

- William O. Douglas, 77, announced his retirement after thirty-six years as a U.S. Supreme Court justice.

- Former Teamsters Union President Jimmy Hoffa disappeared.

- Heiress Patricia Hearst was captured after a nineteen-month odyssey that began with her kidnaping by the Symbionese Liberation Army.

- The creation of the first artificial animal gene was reported.

# 43

# Season of Glory

## Del Pratt

### 1919

| AB | R | H | BA | OB% | 2B | 3B | HR | K/BB | RBI | BR | SB |
|-----|-----|-----|------|------|-----|-----|-----|-------|-----|-----|-----|
| 527 | 69 | 154 | .292 | .342 | 27 | 7 | 4 | 24/36 | 56 | 3 | 22 |

| | | | | G | PO | A | DP | E | FA | FR | | |
|---|---|---|---|-----|-----|-----|-----|-----|------|-----|---|---|
| | | | | 140 | 315 | 491 | 64 | 26 | .969 | 28 | | |

# 43 Derril Burnham Pratt

**BORN**
January 10, 1888
Walhalla, South Carolina

**DIED**
September 30, 1977
Texas City, Texas

**HEIGHT**
5-11

**WEIGHT**
175

**THREW**
right hand

**BATTED**
right hand

New York Yankees
1918–20

*1919*

Del Pratt was the kind of ballplayer Miller Huggins was looking for—talented and tough minded—when he became manager of the Yankees before the start of the 1918 season. How talented was Pratt? Almost from the time he broke in with the St. Louis Browns in 1912, he was one of the premier second basemen in the American League, leading the league in chances per game from 1913 to 1917, in putouts from 1913 to 1916, and assists in 1916. And how tough was he? When Browns owner Phil Ball accused his men of not playing aggressively enough against certain teams, Pratt brought a lawsuit against Ball—and won an out-of-court settlement.

After that dispute Ball was anxious to get rid of Pratt. Huggins was glad to accommodate him. In January 1918 the Yankees sent Urban Shocker, Nick Cullop, Les Nunamaker, Fritz Maisel, and Elmer Gedeon to St. Louis for Pratt and pitcher Eddie Plank (who promptly retired).

Pratt was just the kind of player the new Yankee manager believed he needed to round out his veteran infield. He was smart, had a good arm, and covered a lot of territory. With Pratt at second, Roger Peckinpaugh at short, Home Run Baker at third, and Wally Pipp at first, Huggins had the best infielders in the league, men capable of playing the heads-up, air-tight defense he demanded. (Huggins was assembling the first team in a Yankee dynasty that lasted almost fifty years.) The new and improved infield helped the Yankees advance to fourth place in 1918 (they had been sixth the previous year).

The 1919 campaign would be another step in the right direction for Huggins and his team, as the Yankees moved up another notch. And a big factor in the team's success was Pratt. His defense was, as usual, superb. He led the league's second basemen in assists (491) and chances per game (5.9), and was second in double plays (64). (Pipp, Peckinpaugh, and Baker were likewise among the league leaders, each leading at least two defensive categories.) Pratt also had another solid year at bat—154 hits, 27 doubles, 56 RBIs and a .292 batting average.

In 1919 the main contenders in the pennant race were Chicago, Cleveland and New York. The White Sox grabbed control early in the season, but the Yankees stayed close behind and used an early-June streak during which they won 9 of 10 to move a half-game ahead of the White Sox. Pratt made valuable contributions, going 4-for-6 in two victories over Chicago on June 7 and 8, then going 4-for-10 in three games against the Tigers.

Pratt gets three hits in the Yankees' 4-3 victory over Detroit on September 21, helping the Yankees regain third place.

| DETROIT | AB | H | PO | A | E | NEW YORK | AB | H | PO | A | E |
|---|---|---|---|---|---|---|---|---|---|---|---|
| Bush, ss | 4 | 2 | 1 | 2 | 0 | Vick, rf | 4 | 1 | 3 | 1 | 1 |
| Young, 2b | 5 | 1 | 2 | 1 | 0 | Peckinpaugh, ss | 4 | 1 | 2 | 3 | 0 |
| Cobb, cf | 4 | 1 | 1 | 0 | 1 | Baker, 3b | 4 | 1 | 4 | 1 | 0 |
| Veach, lf | 4 | 2 | 2 | 0 | 0 | Pipp, 1b | 4 | 1 | 7 | 1 | 0 |
| Heilmann, 1b | 4 | 2 | 12 | 0 | 0 | Pratt, 2b | 4 | 3 | 2 | 2 | 0 |
| Flagstead, rf | 4 | 1 | 1 | 0 | 0 | Lewis, lf | 4 | 1 | 1 | 1 | 0 |
| Jones, 3b | 2 | 1 | 1 | 4 | 1 | Bodie, cf | 1 | 0 | 3 | 0 | 0 |
| Stanage, c | 4 | 0 | 2 | 1 | 0 | Fewster, cf | 2 | 0 | 1 | 0 | 0 |
| Dauss, p | 3 | 0 | 2 | 0 | 0 | Ruel, c | 3 | 0 | 4 | 1 | 0 |
| Shorten, ph | 1 | 0 | 0 | 0 | 0 | Mays, p | 3 | 1 | 0 | 4 | 0 |
| Myers, p | 0 | 0 | 0 | 0 | 0 | | | | | | |
| Totals | 35 | 10 | 24 | 8 | 2 | Totals | 33 | 9 | 27 | 14 | 1 |

```
Detroit      2 0 0   0 0 1   0 0 0 — 3 10 2
New York     0 1 0   0 2 0   1 0 * — 4  9 1
```

Doubles—Flagstead, Baker. Home runs—Pratt, Heilmann.
Stolen bases—Pratt, Bodie. Bases on balls—Mays 4, Dauss 1.
Strikeouts—Mays 3, Dauss 1, Ayers 1.
Hit by pitcher—Dauss (by Mays).
Wild pitch—Dauss.

*1919*

The Yanks held onto the lead for three weeks, until Washington's Walter Johnson beat them 1-0—Pratt, with a fourth-inning double, was the only Yankee to reach second base—and dropped them behind Chicago. Slowly, the team lost its momentum, fading to fourth. Finally, in late September, they climbed back to third after sweeping a three-game series against Detroit. In the third game, Pratt hit a homer in the second and had a two-run game-tying single in the sixth, raising his average to .299.

The Yankees finished in third, and Pratt ended the season with a respectable .292 average. But it was his defense that made his 1919 season his most productive. He was the best second baseman in the American League, and was rated seventh defensively among all players in the league, ranking behind only Babe Ruth, Walter Johnson, Ed Cicotte, Roger Peckinpaugh, George Sisler, and Bobby Veach.

Pratt's 1919 season was no fluke. He led the league in total chances per game five times during his career. During his Yankee years, he led second basemen in double plays and assists and once led them in putouts. It all adds up to a second baseman with better than average range and a good arm.

Pratt spent one more season in New York, hitting .314, then was traded in December 1920 to Boston in an eight-player swap. He spent two years with the Red Sox and two more in Detroit before retiring.

## Baseball News Of 1919

- Joe Wilhoit of Wichita (Western League) had a 69-game hitting streak, during which he hit .505.
- Cubs president and manager Fred Mitchell turned his front-office duties over to Bill Veeck Sr., a sportswriter.
- Philadelphia teams lost 194 of the 278 games they played.
- The White Sox became the Black Sox by throwing the World Series.
- Christy Mathewson returned from military service and accepted a position as pitching coach for the New York Giants.

## Around The World In 1919

- A New York Stock Exchange seat sold for $87,000.
- A theater fire in San Juan, Puerto Rico, killed 150 people.
- The National Easter Seal Society was formed in Chicago.
- Robert Goddard published an article on solid-fuel rockets.
- President Woodrow Wilson was awarded the Nobel Peace Prize.
- Sgt. Alvin York was welcomed home from France with a ticker-tape parade in New York.

# 44
# Season of Glory

## Thurmon Munson

### 1973

| AB | R | H | BA | OB% | 2B | 3B | HR | K/BB | RBI | BR | SB |
|---|---|---|---|---|---|---|---|---|---|---|---|
| 519 | 80 | 156 | .301 | .364 | 29 | 4 | 20 | 64/48 | 74 | 28 | 4 |

| | | G | PO | A | DP | E | FA | FR |
|---|---|---|---|---|---|---|---|---|
| | | 147 | 673 | 80 | 11 | 12 | .984 | 6 |

# Thurmon Lee Munson

**BORN**
June 7, 1947
Akron, Ohio

**DIED**
August 2, 1979
Canton, Ohio

**HEIGHT**
5-11

**WEIGHT**
191

**THREW**
right hand

**BATTED**
right hand

New York Yankees
1969-79

**1973**

*O*n his fifth birthday, Thurmon Munson got his first baseball glove. "It was a Hutch," he once recalled. "Don't remember what happened to it, but I remember it perfectly. I started playing every day. I was littler than all the rest of the kids, but I played longer than any of them." That competitive spirit would become his trademark two decades later when he was the captain and clubhouse leader of the New York Yankees, and enabled him to move quickly through the ranks and into the spotlight.

In high school Munson was all-state in football, basketball, and baseball. He received a baseball scholarship to Kent State University and was chosen by the Yankees in the June 1968 free-agent draft. He spent the rest of that season and the first half of 1969 in the minors and was called up by the Yankees in August of '69.

Munson made an immediate impact in his first full season, leading the 1970 ball club with a .302 average and, more important, proving himself one of the top catchers in the game. His performance earned him Rookie of the Year Award "His greatest asset is not his bat," *Newsday* reported after Munson was named Rookie of the Year. "It is his incredible ability to get rid of the ball. It sometimes seems that he throws it before he has caught it."

Munson's success as a catcher was due, in large part, not to his natural ability, but to his work ethic. After Yankee manager Ralph Houk told Munson that he'd "win more games catching than [he ever would] hitting," he began working even harder. And his work paid off: In 1971 he won his first Gold Glove Award. He made just one error that year, and his .998 fielding average was the tenth best among catchers in baseball history. His batting average, though, was a less-than-stellar .251, so Munson turned his attention to that part of his game, spending hours practicing his swing in front of a mirror at home. His hard work paid off again, as he added 30 points the next season.

Munson's reputation as a hard worker may have been exceeded only by his reputation as a sullen, uncommunicative person, at least as far as outsiders were concerned. In his words, he was a "grouch." He didn't like to deal with the press, especially in New York, the media center of the country.

Munson explained his uncongenial behavior in his autobiography *Thurmon Munson* which he coauthored with Marty Appel:

> There were times after a tough loss when I just hated to come in [to the clubhouse] and see that mass of humanity swarming around. Those were

*Thurmon Munson was the inspirational leader of the Yankees during the '70s.*

# Danger In the Air

Thurman Munson was one in a long line of athletes to die in air crashes:

- March 21, 1931: Notre Dame football coach Knute Rockne in Kansas.

- October 28, 1949: Former middleweight champion Marcel Cerdan in the Azores.

- September 20, 1956: Baltimore Orioles catcher Tom Gastall in Chesapeake Bay.

- February 6, 1958: Seven members of the Manchester United soccer team in Munich.

- October 29, 1960: Sixteen members of the California Polytechnic football team in Toledo.

- February 15, 1961: Eighteen members of the U.S. Olympic figure skating team in Belgium.

- February 13, 1964: Chicago Cubs second baseman Ken Hubbs in Provo, Utah.

- July 24, 1966: Golfer Tony Lema in Lansing, Illinois.

- June 4, 1969: Tennis star Rafael Osuna in Mexico.

- September 1, 1969: Former heavyweight champion Rocky Marciano in Newton, Iowa.

- October 2, 1970: Wichita State's football coach and thirteen players in Loveland, Colorado.

- November 12, 1970: Thirty-eight Marshall University football players, five coaches and a trainer in Huntington, West Virginia.

- December 31, 1972: Pittsburgh Pirates outfielder Roberto Clemente off the coast of Puerto Rico.

- June 24, 1975: New York Nets forward Wendell Lander in New York.

- November 29, 1975: Auto racing driver Graham Hill near London.

- December 13, 1977: The entire University of Evansville basketball team in Evansville.

- April 23, 1978: Eight USAC officials near Indianapolis.

- March 14, 1980: Fourteen members of the U.S. amateur boxing team in Poland.

- August 16, 1987: Phoenix Suns forward Nick Vanos in Romulus, Michigan.

- April 1, 1993: Defending Winston Cup driving champion Alan Kulwicki in Blountville, Tennessee.

- July 13, 1993: Winston Cup driver Davey Allison at Talladega, Alabama.

the days when I made good use of my reputation as a grouch.

Writers always said I was grumpy and surly. This image grew out of my sarcastic sense of humor, which goes over all right among players, but writers usually don't understand it. So when I'd give gruff and angry answers early in my career, they'd write stories about how grouchy I was. . . .

My teammates knew better, and my family knew better, and that's all I was concerned with. And if being a grouch meant people wouldn't bother me with silly questions and silly requests, then it worked to my benefit.

It also worked against him, though. His lack of cooperation with the media meant less publicity; as a result, the media instead anointed Boston's Carlton Fisk as the AL's top catcher. Munson chose to blame the snub not on his attitude toward the media, but on his appearance. "My build works against me," he rationalized. "I'm a short, chunky guy; I'm not the athletic hero type. Fisk is tall, lean, and more attractive."

At no time was this lack of recognition more obvious than in 1973, Munson's greatest season. He had a tremendous year and led Fisk in every offensive category except home runs. As much as he was liked by his

# Game of Glory • May 16, 1973

On May 16 Munson gets three hits, including a double and a home run, and drives in four runs to lead an 11-4 rout of Milwaukee.

| MILWAUKEE | AB | R | H | RBI | NEW YORK | AB | R | H | RBI |
|---|---|---|---|---|---|---|---|---|---|
| Johnson, ss | 5 | 1 | 1 | 1 | Clarke, 2b | 4 | 1 | 1 | 0 |
| Money, 3b | 5 | 0 | 1 | 0 | White, lf | 5 | 1 | 2 | 0 |
| May, cf | 3 | 0 | 1 | 0 | M. Alou, cf | 4 | 1 | 0 | 1 |
| Coluccio, cf | 1 | 0 | 1 | 2 | Murcer, cf | 5 | 1 | 2 | 2 |
| Scott, 1b | 3 | 0 | 0 | 0 | Nettles, 3b | 4 | 1 | 2 | 1 |
| Felske, 1b | 1 | 0 | 0 | 0 | Hart, dh | 5 | 0 | 2 | 1 |
| Briggs, lf | 3 | 0 | 0 | 0 | Callison, rf | 2 | 0 | 0 | 0 |
| Lahoud, lf | 1 | 0 | 0 | 0 | F. Alou, 1b | 3 | 2 | 1 | 1 |
| Rodriguez, c | 4 | 1 | 1 | 0 | Munson, c | 4 | 3 | 3 | 4 |
| Brown, dh | 4 | 0 | 3 | 0 | Michael, ss | 3 | 1 | 1 | 1 |
| Thomas, rf | 4 | 0 | 1 | 0 | Kline, p | 0 | 0 | 0 | 0 |
| Garcia, 2b | 3 | 2 | 2 | 1 | Lyle, p | 0 | 0 | 0 | 0 |
| Slaton, p | 0 | 0 | 0 | 0 | | | | | |
| Ryerson, p | 0 | 0 | 0 | 0 | | | | | |
| Parsons, p | 0 | 0 | 0 | 0 | | | | | |
| Newman, p | 0 | 0 | 0 | 0 | | | | | |
| Totals | 37 | 4 | 11 | 4 | Totals | 39 | 11 | 14 | 11 |

```
Milwaukee    0 0 0   0 0 1   0 2 1 — 4
New York     0 0 0   2 1 6   2 0 * — 11
```

Error—Nettles. Double play—New York 1. Left on base—Milwaukee 7, New York 8. Doubles—Brown, Michael, Hart, Munson, Coluccio. Triple—Brown. Home runs—Garcia, Munson.

| NEW YORK | IP | H | R | ER | BB | K |
|---|---|---|---|---|---|---|
| Kline (W, 3-4) | 5.1 | 5 | 1 | 1 | 1 | 1 |
| Lyle (S, 4) | 3.2 | 6 | 3 | 1 | 0 | 6 |

| MILWAUKEE | IP | H | R | ER | BB | K |
|---|---|---|---|---|---|---|
| Slaton (L, 2-3) | 4 | 6 | 3 | 3 | 0 | 0 |
| Ryerson | 1.1 | 2 | 2 | 2 | 0 | 0 |
| Parsons | .1 | 1 | 4 | 4 | 3 | 1 |
| Newman | 2.1 | 5 | 2 | 2 | 1 | 2 |

Time—2:29. Attendance—4,721.

*1973*

teammates and respected by other players around the league, he finished a half-million votes behind Fisk in the AL All-Star voting and was a distant twelfth in the MVP balloting.

But we're jumping ahead of ourselves here. Let's look at what went into Munson's greatest Yankee season. The Yankees stumbled out of the gate in 1973, losing their opener at Boston 15-5. Munson, hitting eighth for

Houk, went 0-for-3. Worse, perhaps in his eyes, was the fact that Fisk had two homers, one a grand slam, and six runs batted in. The Yankees dropped their next two in Boston, then lost their home opener April 9, and by the middle of the month, they were just percentage points out of last place.

Munson fared better. He had three hits in the Boston series, a double and three RBIs in the home opener, and two hits and an RBI on April 11, when the Yankees beat Cleveland for their first victory of the year. By the end of April, he was hitting .382.

In May the Yankees put it together and made a charge at first-place Detroit. On May 16, Munson, whose average had dropped to .311, had three hits, three runs scored, and

> "For those who never knew him and didn't like him, I feel sorry for them. He was a good man. . . . We not only lost a great competitor, but a leader and a husband and a devoted family man. He was a close friend. I loved him."
>
> —BILLY MARTIN ON MUNSON'S DEATH

four runs batted in against first-place Milwaukee. The Yankees climbed into second place the next day with a 4-2 victory over the Brewers. By the end of the month, they were finally over .500 and holding on to second place at 24-23. Munson was hitting .310 with 23 RBIs.

The Yankees briefly moved into first place with a win on June 9, but dropped to second the next day. On June 20, though, they took over the lead and would remain on top for most of the next month and a half. The hero in the charge was Munson. His double helped New York beat Baltimore 5-4 on June 19, and after the Yankees had moved into first on June 20 he helped keep them there, going 4-for-6 with two homers in the next two games, both Yankee wins. At the end of June, the Yankees had won eleven in a row at home and had a two-game lead over the

Orioles, and Munson's batting average was .288.

The Yankees lost eight of their first 13 games in July—including four of five to Boston between July 2 and 5—and fell into second. But they won seven of their next nine to move back into first and were 57-44 with a 1½-game lead at the July 23 All-Star break.

Munson, who was 0-for-2 as Fisk's backup in the All-Star Game, opened the second half in glorious fashion: In a twelve-inning game against Milwaukee, he went 4-for-5 and drove in the game's only run. He added three more hits the next afternoon—his average was up to .311—in another victory over the Brewers. The Yankees lost the next two games of the series (they had a one-game lead over Baltimore at this point) and then traveled to Boston for what would be a memorable four-game series.

The Red Sox won the opener, on July 30, pushing a run across in the bottom of the ninth. The Yankees came back to win the second game the next day, scoring three runs in the top of the ninth to win 5-4 and maintain a one-game lead over Baltimore.

The third game of the series, August 1, may have been the season's turning point. With the score tied 2-2, Munson opened the ninth with a double down the left-field line. He took third on an infield out by Graig Nettles. Felipe Alou was walked intentionally, bringing up Gene Michael. On John Curtis' second pitch, the Yankees tried a squeeze play. But the pitch was wide and Michael missed it. Fisk caught it, shoved Michael out of the way, and lunged at the approaching Munson. The two collided violently, with Fisk holding onto the ball for the out. Fisk tried to scramble to his feet and flipped Munson off of him. An angry Munson came up throwing punches. Fisk got in a few licks of his own before the two wrapped each other up. "There's no question I threw the first punch," Munson said. "But he started it."

Both were ejected, and the Red Sox won the game in the bottom of the ninth. The loss also cost the Yankees the AL East lead. The Orioles beat Cleveland that day to move

.004 ahead of New York. The Yankees wouldn't reach first place again that season.

As the Yankees slowly faded—they finished the season in fourth place at 80-82, 17 games back—Munson kept his average around the .300 mark. Some of his best games during this period included a victory over Oakland on August 10 in which he had a three-run homer and four RBIs, a five-game stretch a week later during which he was 12-for-17, and a game on August 29 against the Angels in which his pop single was the only hit off Nolan Ryan, who had already pitched two no- hitters that season. He finished with a .301 average, 156 runs, 156 hits, 29 doubles, 20 homers, and 74 RBIs, and led AL catchers in assists (80) and double plays (12) on his way to another Gold Glove.

Munson had five more full seasons behind the plate. Although his numbers had begun to drop by 1979, he was still an essential team member, still "The Captain." But on August 2 of that year, he was killed when the private plane he was piloting crashed at Akron-Canton Airport in Ohio. The *New York Daily News'* Mike Lupica delivered perhaps the best eulogy, one that even might have brought a smile from Munson:

He thought his job with the Yankees consisted of this one important thing: playing baseball hard, all the time. Walk up to the plate when the pain in the knees was like daggers. Make the throw to second base when the right arm was aching and useless. Run the bases like a fullback when one more collision might take him out for good.

That was his job. He did not feel he had to talk to the press; he did not have to be cordial to them; he could insult them in a mean way if his mood dictated. There was no reason for anyone to get to know Thurman Munson, as far as he was concerned.

Just watch me play, Munson seemed to say. That is all anyone needs to know.

---

## Baseball News Of 1973

- White Sox knuckleballer Wilbur Wood was the first pitcher in fifty-seven years to win and lose 20 games in the same season. He went 24-20.

- A group of investors, headed by George Steinbrenner, bought the Yankees from CBS for $10 million on January 3.

- Yankee pitchers Mike Kekich and Fritz Peterson swapped wives, families, houses and dogs. Kekich was traded to the Indians in June and released in 1974. Peterson was also sent to Cleveland in '74.

- The American League adopted the designated hitter rule. The first player to DH was Ron Blomberg of the Yankees; he hit .329 in 100 games as the Yankees' DH.

- On March 26 the Braves released Denny McLain, ending his career at age 28.

- On July 21 Hank Aaron homered off Philadelphia's Ken Brett for the 700th homer of his career.

- On September 20 Willie Mays announced he would retire at the end of the season.

- In Game 2 of the World Series, on October 14, A's second baseman Mike Andrews made two errors that helped the Mets win 10-7. The next day A's owner Charlie Finley tried to drop Andrews from the World Series roster, claiming he was injured. He was reinstated by commissioner Bowie Kuhn.

# *Around The World In 1973*

- The 110-story Sears Tower in Chicago was topped out at 1,450 feet, making it the world's tallest building.

- A peace agreement between Vietnam and the United States was signed in Paris on January 22.

- The following officials resigned after they were implicated in the Watergate scandal: acting FBI director L. Patrick Gray; Nixon White House officials H.R. Haldeman, John Ehrlichman, and John Dean; and Attorney General Richard Kleindienst. G. Gordon Liddy and James W. McCord, former Nixon re-election committee officials, were convicted of the Watergate break-in.

- On October 10 Vice President Spiro Agnew resigned after pleading no contest to a charge of income-tax evasion.

- Among the obituaries were those of Lyndon Johnson (January 22, age 64), W.H. Auden (September 28, age 66), Pearl S. Buck (March 6, age 80), Lon Chaney Jr. (July 12, age 67), John Ford (August 31, age 78), Betty Grable (July 2, age 56), Gene Krupa (October 16, age 64) and Edward G. Robinson (January 26, age 79).

- Skylab, the first U.S. space station, was launched into orbit on May 14.

- Eleven Mideast nations began an oil embargo on exports to the United States on October 17.

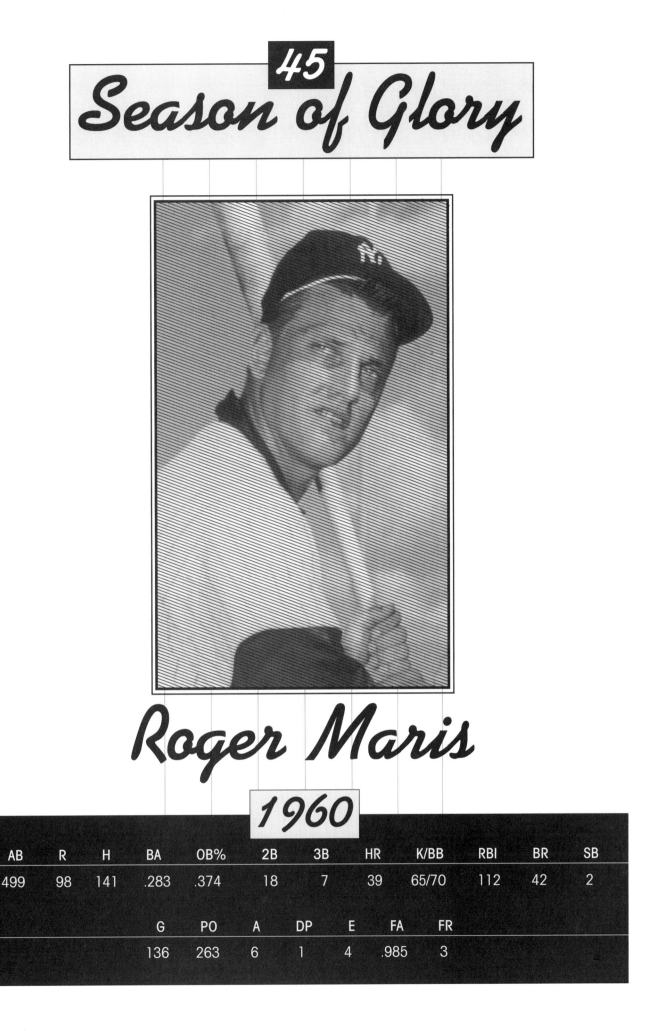

**45**

# Season of Glory

## Roger Maris

### 1960

| AB | R | H | BA | OB% | 2B | 3B | HR | K/BB | RBI | BR | SB |
|----|---|---|-----|------|----|----|----|-------|-----|----|----|
| 499 | 98 | 141 | .283 | .374 | 18 | 7 | 39 | 65/70 | 112 | 42 | 2 |

| | | G | PO | A | DP | E | FA | FR | |
|---|---|---|-----|---|----|---|------|----|---|
| | | 136 | 263 | 6 | 1 | 4 | .985 | 3 | |

# 45

## Roger Eugene Maris

**BORN**
September 10, 1934
Hibbing, Minnesota

**DIED**
December 14, 1985
Houston, Texas

**HEIGHT**
6-0

**WEIGHT**
204

**THREW**
right hand

**BATTED**
left hand

New York Yankees
1960–66

*1960*

*H*e broke baseball's most hallowed record—Babe Ruth's single-season mark of 60 homers—but all Roger Maris got was criticism and abuse. We won't even talk about the asterisk.

And at first glance, the fact that Maris' tremendous feat of 1961 isn't presented here as his greatest season might seem to be another slap. But as good as '61 was, Maris was even more valuable in 1960.

Maris was a twenty-five-year-old, three-year major-league veteran when he came to the Yankees after the 1959 season, "the best man I ever got in a deal," manager Casey Stengel later said.

He posted MVP numbers in 1960 and '61, but his pursuit of Ruth created a poisoned atmosphere—he warred with the media and even the fans turned against him—that would sour Maris on New York. And vice versa. The man who could have owned the city instead was unceremoniously traded after the 1966 season.

To understand what happened to Maris, it's useful to examine Maris, the man, as we discuss Maris, the player.

Maris—he was born Roger Maras, but he changed his name when he started playing professional ball—grew up in Grand Forks and Fargo, North Dakota. He was quiet and serious, traits that were later often misconstrued as sullenness and unfriendliness. He could also be stubborn; and when he thought he was right about something, he stuck to his guns.

"One of the things you heard about Roger through the years was that he was aloof," former teammate and lifelong friend Rocky Colavito told Maury Allen in his book *Roger Maris, A Man for All Seasons.*

"He may have been that way with guys he didn't know, but he certainly wasn't that way with guys he knew. He was easy to talk to, easy to get along with, a real straight shooter. See, Roger never changed through the years, he never put on airs.

"If he made up his mind to do something his way, that was just his way. He was not a wishy-washy guy, which was one of the things I liked about him. He gave loyalty as a friend and he expected loyalty in return. I think some of the things he said in New York put him in hot water with a lot of people, but Roger just couldn't be a politician."

Maris played football in high school and was offered several college football scholarships. But Maris wasn't very interested in continuing his studies, so he decided to concentrate on baseball. And there was plenty of interest. The Cubs brought him to Chicago for a tryout,

*The American League MVP in 1960 and 1961, Roger Maris.*

# Game of Glory • August 6, 1960

On August 6 Maris has three hits, including his 34th and 35th homers, to raise his average over .300 and spark the Yankees to a 16-4 rout of Kansas City.

| NEW YORK | AB | R | H | RBI | | KANSAS CITY | AB | R | H | RBI |
|----------|----|----|----|-----|---|-------------|----|----|----|-----|
| McDougald, 2b | 4 | 0 | 0 | 1 | | Tuttle, cf | 5 | 2 | 2 | 2 |
| Richardson, 2b | 1 | 0 | 0 | 0 | | Lumpe, 2b | 5 | 1 | 2 | 0 |
| Kubek, ss, cf | 6 | 4 | 3 | 2 | | Bauer, rf | 2 | 0 | 0 | 0 |
| Mantle, cf | 5 | 2 | 4 | 1 | | Snyder, rf | 1 | 0 | 1 | 1 |
| DeMaestri, ss | 1 | 0 | 0 | 0 | | Siebern, lf | 4 | 0 | 1 | 0 |
| Maris, rf | 4 | 2 | 3 | 6 | | Williams, 1b | 4 | 1 | 1 | 0 |
| Lopez, rf | 0 | 0 | 0 | 0 | | Jablonski, 3b | 4 | 0 | 1 | 0 |
| Skowron, 1b | 4 | 1 | 2 | 1 | | Daley, c | 4 | 0 | 2 | 1 |
| Hadley, 1b | 1 | 0 | 0 | 0 | | Johnson, ss | 4 | 0 | 0 | 0 |
| Blanchard, c | 5 | 1 | 1 | 0 | | Hall, p | 1 | 0 | 0 | 0 |
| Howard, c | 0 | 0 | 0 | 0 | | Kutyna, p | 0 | 0 | 0 | 0 |
| Cerv, lf | 5 | 3 | 3 | 1 | | Carey, ph | 1 | 0 | 0 | 0 |
| Boyer, 1b | 4 | 1 | 2 | 2 | | Briggs, p | 0 | 0 | 0 | 0 |
| Short, p | 4 | 2 | 1 | 2 | | Garver, p | 1 | 0 | 0 | 0 |
| Maas, p | 1 | 0 | 0 | 0 | | Herzog, ph | 1 | 0 | 0 | 0 |
| **Totals** | **45** | **16** | **19** | **16** | | **Totals** | **37** | **4** | **10** | **4** |

| | | | | | | | |
|--|--|--|--|--|--|--|--|
| New York | 1 0 1 | 4 7 0 | 1 1 0 | — 16 |
| Kansas City | 0 1 1 | 0 1 0 | 1 0 0 | — 4 |

Errors—Johnson (2). Doubles—Boyer, Short, Cerv (2).
Triple—Lumpe. Home runs—Maris (2), Tuttle (2).
Sacrifice—McDougald.
Sacrifice fly—Maris. Double play—Kansas City.
Left on base—New York 6, Kansas City 7.

| NEW YORK | IP | H | R | ER | BB | K |
|----------|----|----|----|----|----|----|
| Short (W, 3-4) | 5.2 | 8 | 3 | 3 | 1 | 2 |
| Maas | 3.1 | 2 | 1 | 1 | 0 | 3 |

| KANSAS CITY | IP | H | R | ER | BB | K |
|-------------|----|----|----|----|----|----|
| Hall (L, 6-8) | 3.1 | 7 | 6 | 4 | 0 | 0 |
| Kutyna | .2 | 2 | 1 | 0 | 0 | 0 |
| Briggs | 0 | 3 | 4 | 4 | 1 | 0 |
| Garve | 5 | 7 | 5 | 4 | 0 | 2 |

Passed balls—Blanchard, Daley.

Time—2:40. Attendance—24,039.

then the 6-foot, 175-pound teenager was told he was too small. No matter—the Indians were waiting.

After an impressive tryout in Cleveland, Maris was offered and signed a $15,000 contract with the Indians. He asked to be assigned to Cleveland's Fargo-Morehead minor-league team and played a season there, hitting .325 with 74 RBIs in 114 games. The following season (1954) he was assigned to the Indians' Keokuk, Iowa, farm team, where he hit .315 with 32 homers and 111 RBIs. He also led the Triple-I League in putouts.

In 1955 Maris was promoted to Tulsa, where his strong will precipitated a confrontation with his manager, Dutch Meyer. Early in the season, Maris made a bad throw from right field that sailed into the seats and cost Tulsa a game. Meyer berated his young outfielder, then ordered him to come out early the next day to work on his defense. Meyer hit ball after ball to Maris and had him make the throw to the cutoff man. Finally, Maris had enough. He caught a ball, tucked it in his glove, and walked off the field, followed by a screaming Meyer. "I'm not going to throw my arm out in practice for you," Maris said. "I don't want to play here any longer."

Maris wasn't bluffing: He left Tulsa and went home to Fargo. The next day the Indians assigned him to their Reading, Pennsylvania, farm club. Maris, who was hitting .233 at Tulsa, played 113 games for Reading, hitting .289 with 19 homers and 78 RBIs.

Maris split his 1956 season between Reading and Triple-A Indianapolis, hitting almost .300 and proving to the Indians that he was ready to jump to the majors. Soon after Maris was promoted to the parent team, however, he started having problems with Indians manager Bobby Bragan, who had misjudged the rookie's approach to the game and had told reporters that Maris wasn't giving it his all. Maris confronted his manager, and the two had an uneasy peace the rest of the 1957 season. Maris hit just .235 in his rookie year, and after he got off to another lackluster start in '58—he hit .225 during the first two months—he was traded to Kansas City.

A's manager Harry Craft was impressed by his new player's attitude. "He is intelligent, stubborn, opinionated," Craft said, "but he is a heck of a guy to have on the ballclub. He wants to win."

Maris got off to a brilliant start in 1959, his first full season with Kansas City. In late May he had a .328 average but then was stricken with a case of appendicitis that required surgery. He returned after a month off and experienced several long slumps be-

> "I give the man a point for speed. I do this because Maris can run fast. Then I can give him a point because he can slide fast. I give him another point because he can bunt. I also give him a point because he can field. He is very good around fences—sometimes on top of fences. Next, I give him a point because he can throw. A right-fielder has to be a thrower or he's not a right-fielder. So I add up my points and I've got five for him before I even come to his hitting. I would say this is a good man."
>
> —CASEY STENGEL'S ANALYSIS OF ROGER MARIS

fore he regained his batting eye. Maris finished the season with a .273 average, his best thus far in the majors.

During the off-season, the Yankees, who had finished third, 15 games behind the first-place White Sox, began negotiating with the A's for Maris. A left-handed pull hitter, he had a swing that was made for Yankee Stadium's short right-field porch. The Yanks had scouted him extensively during the '59 season, and on December 11 they put together a deal. The Yankees got Maris, Joe DeMaestri, and Kent Hadley from Kansas City in exchange for Hank Bauer, Don Larsen, Marv Throneberry, and Norm Siebern.

The trade received mixed reviews in both cities. Even Maris wasn't particularly thrilled. He preferred Kansas City, where he and his family had a comfortable home and where the fans had stuck with him during a couple of prolonged slumps in 1959. "That year I went 6-for-110 and never got booed once in Kansas City," he said. "People asked me why I liked playing in Kansas City. Well, they had good fans."

Maris adjusted slowly to life in New York (not wanting to uproot his family, he moved to New York alone and shared an apartment with Bob Cerv and, later, Cerv and Mantle). But he quickly got comfortable with his new teammates, who all liked and respected him. In Tony Kubek's book, *Sixty-One*, Cerv related a story that said a lot about Maris.

> Roger and Mickey loved country music. I couldn't stand it, and I used to take my Jewish records and play them. If you're not Jewish, those songs will drive you crazy. Even if country music stinks, you can at least understand the words. Mickey and Roger would humor me for a while before they would change the record. But one day, Roger really surprised me. I took him to a friend's bar mitzvah, and Roger stood up and sang "Hava Nagila." He had learned the whole thing from listening to my record when I wasn't around. It really meant a lot to me, Roger singing that song like he did. He didn't do it as a joke, but as something to please a friend.

Maris's teammates also fully appreciated his talent, unlike many members of the press, who wrote about his home runs but didn't report on the other facets of his game. Maris was a good fielder, he had a strong throwing arm, was speedy in the outfield and on the bases, and was willing to do the little things. "There were a lot of things he did that people didn't know about," teammate Clete Boyer pointed out.

"He was the best guy I saw in going from first to third, the best on breaking up a double play, the best at getting a run in from third with less than two out. I saw Roger many times, with a guy on third, hit the weakest grounder in the world to the right side. I mean weak. But the guy from third can score. That's a lot better than hitting a bullet that the first baseman catches.

"Roger could also bunt. There were quite a few times with the third baseman back, Roger bunted for a hit. He wasn't just a home run hitter."

That, though, was what fans and the press came to expect. And Maris reinforced those expectations in the Yankees' 1960 season opener, on April 19 in Boston. He had two home runs, a single, and a double, with four runs batted in, in an 8-4 victory. Maris didn't hit another homer until April 30, when he put one over the center-field fence at Yankee Stadium with two men on against Baltimore. He added two doubles, raising his average to .429, as the Yankees coasted to a 16-0 victory that moved them into first place, a half game ahead of the White Sox, the defending AL champions.

The Yankees fell out of first the next day. Maris, though, stayed hot: He had two hits, one a homer, on May 3; three hits, including two doubles, on May 4; three hits, three runs, and two RBIs on May 6; and a hit and an RBI the next day. One week into May, he was still at .429, with four homers and 17 RBIs.

In spite of Maris's wonderful start, the crowd began booing him. As Maris later explained to Mike Shannon, with whom he played in St. Louis, New York fans had booed Mickey Mantle when he first replaced Joe DiMaggio. "Mickey was still hearing a few boos when Roger showed up in New York," Shannon told Kubek for his book.

"But then they got off Mickey and made Roger their whipping boy. Roger couldn't figure out what was with the fans. He was having an MVP year in 1960, and a few people started to boo him. I mean, all of a sudden Mickey was the hero and Roger was the bad guy. Mickey never deserved to be booed. And Roger sure as hell never should have been booed."

Luckily, Maris was able to take the fans' fickleness in stride and continue with his season. At the end of May, Maris had a .319 average and the Yankees were in fourth place

*The M and M Boys—Maris and Mantle.*

at 19-17, four games out of first. On June 14 Maris went 3-for-5, hitting his 18th homer and driving in five runs as the Yankees beat Kansas City to move within percentage points of first. He had four hits the next day in a game suspended after thirteen innings. After Cleveland split a double-header the same day, the Yankees and Indians were tied for first.

Maris went hitless in his next two games, as New York lost its hold on first place, then had a 3-for-5 day on June 18, raising his average to .346 and helping the Yankees to a 12-5 victory that put them back on top. June ended with a 10-3 victory over Kansas City—the Yankees' twenty-first in their last 29 games—that gave New York a 1½-game lead. In that contest, Maris hit his major-league-leading 25th home run. He also got his 62nd and 63rd RBIs of the season, second best in baseball, and raised his average to .323.

Maris may not have been the darling of New York fans, but his accomplishments weren't going unnoticed among his peers. He received the most votes in the All-Star balloting, which was conducted among players. (He went 0-for-2 in the first All-Star Game, played on July 11 in Kansas City, and 0-for-4 two days later in the second contest, played in New York.)

Despite having a sore wrist, Maris stayed hot as the second half began. His 28th homer on July 16 helped New York beat Detroit; he hit his 29th on July 18, his 30th the next day, and his 31st on July 20. But then both Maris and the Yankees had a dry spell. New York lost three of four to the White Sox between July 21 and 24 to lose the lead. And Maris, who went 0-for-22 at one point and whose average fell below .300, did not hit No. 32 until August 2, when a victory put the Yankees back in first.

In early August Maris emerged from his slump. He hit a two-run homer on Agust 5, helping beat Kansas City, and hit Nos. 34 and 35 and had six RBIs the next day in another victory. On August 13 Maris tripled in the seventh inning against Washington then scored the game's only run on a Mantle sacrifice fly. But on August 14, during the course of an eight-hour double-header that

the Yankees lost to Washington, Maris reinjured his wrist. Not only were the Yankees in third after they lost the double-header, they were without Maris for two weeks.

By the beginning of September started, the Yankees had regained the lead. The pennant race was by no means over, however, as the Yankees promptly lost three straight games to the second-place Orioles, falling two games back. Once again, Maris came through. He hit an inside-the-park homer on September 8 against Chicago, his first homer in more than a month; a home run the next day that helped beat Detroit; and another on September 11 in a victory over Cleveland.

Maris was also a key player in a four-game series in the middle of the month that pitted the Yankees (whose lead over second-place Baltimore was .001) against the Orioles. In the opener Maris sent his 39th homer, which would be his last of the campaign, deep into the right-field seats, helping his team to a 4-2 victory. New York swept the series, giving the Yankees a solid four-game lead. They clinched on September 25 with a 4-3 victory in Boston—Maris was 6-for-13 in the series—and wound up winning the AL pennant by a comfortable eight games.

The 1960 World Series is still remembered as one of the most exciting ever. Maris hit a homer his first time up in Game 1 (he hit .267 in the Series) but the Pittsburgh Pirates got three runs in the bottom of the first and went on to a 6-4 victory. The Series lasted seven games, and while the Yankees outscored the Pirates 55-27, it was that 27th run—Bill Mazeroski's dramatic homer in the bottom of the ninth in Game 7—that gave the underdogs the world championship.

Although Maris hit just eight homers in his last 53 games, at the end of his greatest season he was only one behind league-leader Mantle. Maris led the AL in RBIs (112) and slugging percentage (.581) and was second in runs (98) and total bases (290). Defensively, he had a fielding percentage of .985, with just four errors.

To see why 1960 and not 1961 was chosen as Maris's best season, one needs to look at not only his offense —in 1961 Maris hit more homers (61), had more RBIs (142), runs (132), and walks (94 to 70), and had a higher slugging percentage (.620). The difference was his defense. In 1961 he made nine errors and had a fielding percentage of .968. Those miscues were just enough to give his 1960 season the edge.

Maris's 1960 accomplishments in 1960 earned him Most Valuable Player honors.

The election was the second closest in the award's history. Maris finished with 225 votes to the 222 of Mantle—giving New York fans yet another reason to boo Maris in 1961. And while Maris broke Ruth's home run record in 1961, he never got the recognition he deserved. Even Commissioner Ford Frick denigrated the accomplishment by saying that for Ruth's record to be broken, it had to be done in 154 games, the length of Ruth's

## Baseball News Of 1960

- Another first for White Sox owner Bill Veeck: He put players' names on the backs of their uniforms. Other owners were not amused.

- On June 17, Ted Williams hit home run No. 500. Other home run landmarks included Hank Aaron's 200th on July 3 and Mickey Mantle's 300th on July 4.

- Hall of Famer Fred Clarke, the stellar left-fielder and manager for the Pittsburgh Pirates during their glory years in the first decade of the century, died at age 87.

- Phillies manager Eddie Sawyer quit on April 14 after an Opening Day loss. "I'm 49 and I want to live to be 50," he said.

- Cleveland GM Frank "Trader" Lane was at it again: On August 3 he sent Indians manager Joe Gordon to Detroit for Tigers manager Jimmie Dykes.

- In his last at-bat in his final game, September 28 at Fenway Park, Ted Williams hit an eighth-inning home run off the Orioles' Jack Fisher to close out his nineteen-year career. He finished with 521 homers and a .344 lifetime average.

- The Negro American League, last of the black leagues, disbanded after the 1960 season.

## Around The World In 1960

- The Soviet Union shot down a U-2 U.S. spy plane on May 7 and captured the pilot, Francis Gary Powers, turning Cold War tensions up a notch.

- The fifty-star U.S. flag, reflecting the admission of Alaska and Hawaii in 1959, became official on July 4.

- The first Nixon-Kennedy debate was televised on September 26. Kennedy was elected on November 8.

- Among the books published was *To Kill a Mockingbird* by Harper Lee. It won the Pulitzer in 1961.

- *Lady Chatterley's Lover* by D.H. Lawrence was ruled not obscene by a court of appeals on March 25 and therefore mailable.

- Radio's payola scandal broke.

- *Tiros I*, the first weather satellite, was launched and orbited the Earth, sending back thousands of photos of cloud cover.

season. No matter that Maris hit his 61 homers in fewer at-bats. In effect, Frick was setting Ruth's numbers aside as the all-time standard. Anyone else would be listed in the record books separately. An imaginary asterisk, if you will.

The press and the fans didn't help the situation. As the pressure of 1961 increased, Maris became more withdrawn, tired of answering the same questions from a growing mob of reporters. "I remember one time when he didn't hit a homer," Boyer later recalled. "They asked him if he was choking. Can you imagine that? He wouldn't talk after that."

Relations between Maris and the public never improved. He had 33 homers and 100 RBIs in 1962, which were great numbers, but not Ruthian enough for the press or Yankee fans. He played hurt for much of the rest of his time in New York, but people didn't care. Everything came to a head in 1965. He had injured his wrist in a play at second base; the Yankees said it was not much more than a sprain. Maris said it was much more. It turned out he had chipped a bone. The Yankees wanted him to have surgery, but he refused, convinced the team had known the extent of the injury all along but had tried to pressure him into playing.

Despite eventual surgery, Maris' swing was never the same. He hit just .233 with 13 homers in 119 games in 1966. The Yankees finally decided they'd had enough of him, and traded Maris to St. Louis for journeyman infielder Charley Smith. In what amounted to a final, unintentional dig, the Yankees gave Smith Maris' uniform No. 9.

"The trade that sent Roger Maris from the Yankees to the Cardinals was an insult to him," wrote Arthur Daley in *The New York Times*. "He was disdainfully dealt off for the equivalent of a couple of broken bats and a scuffed baseball."

Maris had already decided he would retire rather than play another season in New York. (He later told one writer that his last six years in the American League had been "mental hell . . . years of anguish for me.") But he decided to give St. Louis a try. Lucky for the Cardinals, and Maris, that he did.

He enjoyed a rebirth in St. Louis, starting with his first game when he got three standing ovations—one before his first at-bat, one when he first took his spot in the outfield, and one after beating out a bunt single. Maris, still the team player who did the little things to win, hit .261 with nine homers that year to help the Cardinals win the NL pennant. Then he hit .385 to lead St. Louis past Boston in the World Series. In 1968, he hit .255 as the Cardinals won another pennant. After the season, he told the Cardinals he was done, and would rather be with his family.

Maris retired to Florida, where he ran a successful beer distributorship. His life—happily out of the spotlight, much of it spent on the golf course—took a tragic turn in 1983 when he was diagnosed with lymphatic cancer. After a two-year fight, he died on December 14, 1985 at the age of 51.

"There are lessons to be learned from the mistreatment of Roger Maris," wrote Bob Verdi in the *Chicago Tribune* after Maris's death, "but none more important than these: Treat an athlete for the person he is, not the person we think he ought to be; and judge what he accomplishes according to his era, not another irrelevant time-frame of reference. . . .

"Superior athletes, just as superior salesmen or superior airline pilots, encounter enough pressures each morning. They needn't be artificially compared with other people in other decades. If we so honor records that are made to be broken, we should respect whoever breaks them, whenever, however. Achievers are achievers, and that is the only equitable barometer. If only life had been so fair while it lasted for Roger Maris . . ."

## 46
## Season of Glory

## Herb Pennock

## 1924

| W | L | Pct. | IP | GS | CG | SH | SV | K/BB | Opp. BA | ERA |
|---|---|------|-----|-----|-----|-----|-----|--------|---------|------|
| 21 | 9 | .700 | 286.1 | 34 | 25 | 4 | 3 | 101/64 | .273 | 2.83 |

| GP | PO | A | DP | E | FA | ER/R | PR | DEF |
|----|-----|-----|-----|-----|-------|--------|-----|------|
| 40 | 10 | 61 | 5 | 0 | 1.000 | 90/104 | 42 | -1 |

BORN
**February 10, 1894**
**Kennett Square, Pennsylvania**

DIED
**January 30, 1948**
**New York, New York**

HEIGHT
**6-0**

WEIGHT
**160**

THREW
**left hand**

BATTED
**both**

**New York Yankees**
**1923–33**

HALL OF FAME
**1948**

**1924**

During the summer of 1911, a seventeen-year-old student from the prestigious Cedarcroft Academy, on the outskirts of Philadelphia, was picking up a little spending money—and indulging his passion for baseball—by pitching for a semipro team in Atlantic City. One afternoon the young left-hander threw a no-hitter against a black team from St. Louis. In the crowd was Earle Mack, son of Philadelphia A's owner Connie Mack, who related what he saw that day to his father. Less than a year later, Herb Pennock was pitching for Mack's defending American League champions. It was the start of Pennock's twenty-two-year major-league career, during which he won 240 games and had a 5-0 World Series record, and after which he was elected to the Hall of Fame.

Herbert Jefferis Pennock hardly fit the mold of an early-twentieth century ballplayer. He was born into a wealthy and refined Pennsylvania family and grew up on the family estate about forty miles from Philadelphia. At prep school, Pennock was introduced to baseball. It was love at first sight.

Pennock started out as a first baseman, but his natural ability to throw curves soon put him on the pitcher's mound. In May 1912, while Pennock was still in school, he got a wire from the elder Mack, offering him a job with the A's. On his third day with the team, Mack brought him in for mop-up duty in a game against the Chicago White Sox. Pennock, just eighteen years old, allowed only one hit over four innings in his debut.

The rookie pitcher appeared in 16 more games that season, going 1-2. He was 2-1 the following year, then had a tremendous year in 1914, when he was 11-4 with a 2.79 ERA. Herb Pennock was on his way. Mack, though, saw things differently.

Early in the 1915 season, the two had a disagreement. Mack told his young pitcher that he needed to take the game more seriously, and Pennock responded that if he didn't like the way he was playing, he should trade him. Mack, in the process of one of his periodic dismantlings of the A's, did just that, sending Pennock to Boston in June. (In his later years, Mack admitted that it was the worst mistake he ever made in baseball.)

Pennock appeared in only five games for the Red Sox in 1915, then was sent to the minors for part of the 1916 season. He had a 5-5 record for Boston in 1917, then spent a year in the service. Pennock was in top form in 1919, going 16-8. He played three more years in Boston,

*The Knight of Kennett Square, Herb Pennock.*

# Game of Glory • July 5, 1924

On July 5 Pennock outduels Walter Johnson to beat Washington 2-0.

| NEW YORK | AB | R | H | RBI | WASHINGTON | AB | R | H | RBI |
|---|---|---|---|---|---|---|---|---|---|
| Witt, cf | 5 | 1 | 3 | 0 | Rice, rf | 4 | 0 | 0 | 0 |
| Dugan, 3b | 5 | 0 | 1 | 0 | Mathews, cf | 3 | 0 | 2 | 0 |
| Ruth, rf | 3 | 1 | 3 | 0 | Harris, 2b | 3 | 0 | 0 | 0 |
| Meusel, lf | 3 | 0 | 0 | 0 | Goslin, lf | 4 | 0 | 1 | 0 |
| Pipp, 1b | 4 | 0 | 1 | 0 | Judge, 1b | 4 | 0 | 0 | 0 |
| Schang, c | 4 | 0 | 0 | 1 | Ruel, c | 3 | 0 | 1 | 0 |
| Ward, 2b | 4 | 0 | 1 | 0 | Peckinpaugh, ss | 3 | 0 | 0 | 0 |
| Scott, ss | 3 | 0 | 1 | 0 | Bluege, 3b | 3 | 0 | 1 | 0 |
| Pennock, p | 3 | 0 | 0 | 0 | Johnson, p | 3 | 0 | 2 | 0 |
| Totals | 34 | 2 | 10 | 1 | Totals | 30 | 0 | 7 | 0 |

New York     1 0 0    0 0 1    0 0 0 — 2
Washington   0 0 0    0 0 0    0 0 0 — 0

Doubles—Ruth (2).
Bases on balls—Johnson 2, Pennock 2.
Strikeouts—Johnson 1.

*1924*

going 38-44 and polishing the skills that would make him a big winner with the Yankees.

By this point in his career, Pennock had developed into a mature pitcher. He knew how to translate his intelligence into baseball smarts—he had to face a batter only once, it was said, and he had a book on him. He also had outstanding control (in 3,571 innings for his career, he walked only 916 men, an average of less than 1½ per nine innings). His best pitch was his curveball, which he delivered overhand as well as sidearm. He also had an excellent change and occasionally threw a screwball, a pitch he learned from Chief Bender during their days as teammates in Philadelphia.

In January 1923, the Red Sox and Yankees made a trade, and Pennock, following in the footsteps of Babe Ruth, Carl Mays, Waite Hoyt, and a dozen others, was sent from Boston to New York. He paid immediate dividends for the Yankees, going 19-6 and winning two World Series games for the 1923 world champions.

The Yankees were again the favorites in '24. Pennock got his first win in the Yankees' home opener, a 13-4 victory over the Red Sox. He couldn't maintain the momentum, however, and was a .500 pitcher (5-5) well into June.

Midway through the season, as the Senators were battling for first place (the competition was tougher than in 1923), Pennock shifted into high gear. He won 16 of his last 20 decisions, several in impressive fashion:

# Trading Partners

Herb Pennock was one of more than a dozen players who came to the Yankees on the Boston-to-New York shuttle. Some, like Babe Ruth, were huge stars. Others didn't pan out. But most made solid contributions to the Yankees.

| Player | Years with Yankees | Accomplishments as a Yankee | Number of World Series |
|--------|--------------------|-----------------------------|------------------------|
| Babe Ruth | 1919–32 | .342 batting average | 7 |
| Carl Mays | 1919–23 | 80–39 pitching record | 3 |
| Ernie Shore | 1919–20 | 7–10 pitching record | 0 |
| Duffy Lewis | 1919–20 | .272 batting average | 0 |
| Harry Harper | 1921 | 4–3 pitching record | 1 |
| Mike McNally | 1921–24 | .252 batting average | 3 |
| Waite Hoyt | 1921–30 | 157–98 pitching record | 6 |
| Wally Schang | 1921–25 | .297 batting average | 3 |
| Everett Scott | 1922–25 | .254 batting average | 2 |
| Sam Jones | 1922–26 | 47–36 pitching record | 3 |
| Joe Bush | 1922–24 | 62–38 pitching record | 2 |
| Joe Dugan | 1922–28 | .286 batting average | 5 |
| Elmer Smith | 1922–23 | .290 batting average | 2 |
| George Pipgras | 1923–33 | 93–64 pitching record | 6 |
| Harry Hendrik | 1923–24 | .268 batting average | 1 |
| Herb Pennock | 1923–33 | 162–90 pitching record | 5 |

- On June 28, he beat Boston 4-3 in twelve innings.
- On July 5, he outdueled Walter Johnson, allowing just seven hits in a 2-0 victory over Washington.
- Six days later, his complete-game eight-hitter beat Chicago 6-1 and moved New York into first place.
- On August 13, he blanked St. Louis 1-0 on a four-hitter.
- Four days later, he beat Chicago 2-1 in another masterful performance.

Over a stretch of 32 innings between August 13 and 23, he allowed just two earned runs. And during one twelve-game span, he had an ERA of 2.60. That was some accomplishment in light of what was going on around the rest of the majors, when 16-12, 11-9 and 17-10 games were common. Pennock finished the season with a 2.83 ERA, one of only nine pitchers in the majors below 3.00.

Pennock wound up the season with a 5-1

September. It wasn't enough, though. Other members of the Yankee pitching staff failed to pull their weight—although Hoyt was 18-13, Joe Bush was just 17-16 and Sam Jones was only 9-6. In addition, heralded rookie Earle Combs played in only 24 games (hitting .400) before a broken ankle ended his season. The Yankees were also wiithout Mays, who was traded to Cincinnati before the season (he won 20 games for the Reds that year). In the end, the Yankees were unable to fend off the Senators, losing the pennant race by two games.

"He was a left-handed Mathewson. He had one of the easiest, most graceful deliveries of any pitcher I have ever known. Certainly Rube Waddell and Lefty Grove had more smoke, but they didn't have Pennock's class."

—BABE RUTH

Pennock struggled to a hard-luck 17-19 record in 1925—he lost 10 games by one run—then had three more strong seasons (23-11, 19-8, 17-6). Over the next five seasons, he went 47-33 for New York. He was released after the 1933 season, then spent a year in Boston, going 2-0 in 30 games for the Red Sox, before retiring.

Pennock, a classy gentleman who made hundreds if not thousands of friends during his playing career, remained in baseball as an executive and coach for the Red Sox. In 1943 he accepted an offer to become general manager of the Philadelphia Phillies. He spent four years there putting together the 1nucleus of the team that would become the 1950 pennant-winning "Whiz Kids."

In January of 1948, Pennock suffered a stroke and died. Later that year, he was voted into the Hall of Fame.

## Baseball News Of 1924

- The Cubs began broadcasting their games, with Hal Totten at the WMAQ microphone.
- Yankee third baseman Joe Dugan had four unassisted double plays in one game, a major-league record.
- Walter Johnson won 13 games in a row and threw six shutouts, leading the Senators to their first pennant.
- Yankee pitchers struck out only 420 batters, a record low for a season.
- Cardinals pitcher Jesse Haines no-hit Boston on July 17.

## Around The World In 1924

- Wyoming and Texas elected America's first female governors.
- Frozen Foods, later to become Birdseye, was founded.
- Thirty-five-year-old Clarence DeMar won the Boston Marathon in the record time of 2:29.40.
- George Gershwin's *Rhapsody in Blue* was debuted in New York's Aeolian Hall.
- The Pulitzer Prize for letters was awarded to Robert Frost for his *Poem With Notes* and *Grace Notes*.

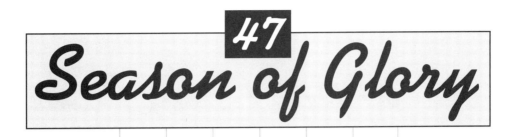

# 47
# Season of Glory

## Willie Randolph

1980

| AB | R | H | BA | OB% | 2B | 3B | HR | K/BB | RBI | BR | SB |
|----|----|----|----|----|----|----|----|----|----|----|----|
| 513 | 99 | 151 | .294 | .429 | 23 | 7 | 7 | 46/119 | 46 | 31 | 30 |

| | G | PO | A | DP | E | FA | FR | | | |
|----|----|----|----|----|----|----|----|----|----|----|
| | 138 | 361 | 401 | 97 | 19 | .976 | -7 | | | |

# Willie Larry Randolph

**BORN**
July 6, 1954
Holly Hill, South Carolina

**HEIGHT**
5-11

**WEIGHT**
166

**THREW**
right hand

**BATTED**
right hand

New York Yankees
1976–88

On December 11, 1975, Yankee president Gabe Paul made two of the most important trades in franchise history. In the first, he sent slugger Bobby Bonds, who had played for New York for just a year, to California in exchange for Mickey Rivers and Ed Figueroa. In the second deal, he sent 16-game winner Doc Medich to Pittsburgh in exchange for Dock Ellis, Ken Brett, and a young infield prospect, Willie Randolph.

Paul was reshaping the Yankees for 1976; they'd played the two previous seasons at Shea Stadium while Yankee Stadium underwent renovations. Back home in a ballpark that gave outfielders much room to roam, Paul put the emphasis on pitching (Figueroa and Ellis) and speed (Rivers and Randolph). The speedy Rivers would be a key player for the Yankees in the late '70s, Figueroa would win 19 games in 1976 and 20 two years later, Ellis would go 17-8 in '76, and Randolph—perhaps, in the end, the most valuable player obtained during Paul's busy day at the 1975 Winter Meetings—would go on to an illustrious thirteen-year career with New York.

Randolph grew up in Brooklyn and was drafted by the Pirates out of high school. During the 3½ years he played in the Pirates' farm system, he twice led his league in walks, once led in runs scored, and stole 105 bases. In the spring of 1975, he attracted attention when he played well in several exhibition games against New York. With the Yankees keeping an eye on him, he went on to hit .339 for Charleston that season. In December the Pirates traded him to the Yankees.

Randolph not only made the team in 1976, he won the starting second base job, beating out incumbent Sandy Alomar, who had led the AL in fielding the year before. That year Randolph hit .267, stole 37 bases and, with 58 walks, had an on-base percentage of .358. He was the first rookie in baseball history to be listed on the All-Star ballot (he made the team) and he helped the Yankees win the 1976 pennant, their first in twelve years.

The quiet, dependable Randolph quickly entrenched himself as the Yankees' second baseman. He steadily went about is work in a businesslike manner—hitting in the .270s, fielding his position well, making the big plays—making real contributions to the team's success. Randolph was also a presence in the usually chaotic Yankee clubhouse, but not in the way of a Reggie Jackson, a Thurman Munson or a Graig Nettles.

In 1980, Randolph's finest year as a Yankee, the team didn't hit its

*Willie Randolph, as classy a Yank as has ever donned pinstripes.*

# Game of Glory • April 27, 1980

On April 27 Randolph has a big day in a losing cause against Chicago.

| CHICAGO | AB | R | H | RBI | | NEW YORK | AB | R | H | RBI |
|---|---|---|---|---|---|---|---|---|---|---|
| Kuntz, rf | 2 | 0 | 0 | 0 | | Randolph, 2b | 6 | 2 | 2 | 1 |
| Bosley, rf | 2 | 1 | 1 | 0 | | Jones, cf | 6 | 0 | 2 | 2 |
| Bannister, lf | 5 | 3 | 2 | 0 | | Watson, 1b | 6 | 0 | 0 | 0 |
| Nordhagen, dh | 3 | 1 | 1 | 1 | | Jackson, rf | 5 | 0 | 0 | 0 |
| Molinaro, dh | 3 | 1 | 2 | 2 | | Piniella, lf | 4 | 1 | 1 | 0 |
| Johnson, 1b | 3 | 1 | 2 | 0 | | Brown ,lf | 0 | 0 | 0 | 0 |
| Squires, 1b | 1 | 0 | 1 | 2 | | Murcer, lf | 2 | 0 | 0 | 0 |
| Lemon, cf | 4 | 1 | 1 | 1 | | Soderholm, dh | 2 | 1 | 1 | 0 |
| Morrison, 2b | 5 | 0 | 0 | 0 | | Spencer, dh | 2 | 0 | 0 | 0 |
| Kimm, c | 3 | 0 | 1 | 0 | | Nettles, 3b | 4 | 2 | 2 | 1 |
| Foley, c | 2 | 0 | 0 | 0 | | Cerone, c | 2 | 1 | 1 | 0 |
| Pryor, ss | 5 | 0 | 1 | 2 | | Gamble, ph | 0 | 0 | 0 | 1 |
| Bell, 3b | 5 | 0 | 0 | 0 | | Oates, c | 2 | 0 | 0 | 0 |
| | | | | | | Stanley, ss | 5 | 0 | 2 | 2 |
| **Totals** | **43** | **8** | **12** | **8** | | **Totals** | **46** | **7** | **11** | **7** |

```
Chicago      0 0 0   0 2 2   0 2 0   1 0 1 — 8
New York     0 0 3   0 0 1   1 1 0   1 0 0 — 7
```

Doubles—Stanley, Lemon, Piniella. Triples—Randolph (2), Nordhagen.
Home runs—Molinaro, Nettles. Stolen bases—Jones, Bosley. Sacrifice—Squires.
Sacrifice fly—Gamble. Double plays—Chicago 1, New York 2.
Left on base—Chicago 6, New York 9.

| CHICAGO | IP | H | R | ER | BB | K |
|---|---|---|---|---|---|---|
| Kravec | 5.1 | 6 | 4 | 4 | 2 | 0 |
| Proly | 1.2 | 2 | 1 | 1 | 0 | 0 |
| Wortham | .1 | 1 | 1 | 1 | 2 | 0 |
| Farmer (W, 3-0) | 3.2 | 2 | 1 | 1 | 1 | 3 |
| Scarberry (S,1) | 1 | 0 | 0 | 0 | 0 | 1 |

| NEW YORK | IP | H | R | ER | BB | K |
|---|---|---|---|---|---|---|
| Guidry | 7 | 7 | 4 | 4 | 2 | 6 |
| Gossage | 2 | 2 | 2 | 2 | 2 | 1 |
| Underwood (L, 1-2) | 3 | 3 | 2 | 2 | 2 | 1 |

Wild pitch—Guidry.

Time—3:42. Attendance—18,020.

stride until the season was well under way. At the end of April, the team was 9-9 and Randolph was hitting .266. Randolph had a couple of memorable games, however. He had three hits and scored the winning run in an April 20 victory over Milwaukee; on April 27 he laced an 0-2 inside slider from Britt Burns to right ("On paper there's no way he can hit that ball," Burns later said) for a single that drove in the only run in a 1-0 victory over Chicago; and he had a pair of hits and two RBIs in a 4-3 win in Baltimore.

In May the Yankees and Randolph began to turn things around. The team won 19 of 26 games, moving into first place. Randolph hit .330 that month—he was 24-for-53 (.453) over a two-week period from May 14 to 28—finishing May at .305. Randolph also demonstrated that the game is not just about getting hits. On June 11 against California, for example, he had four walks and stole second three times. The last walk was in the 11th, and he later scored the winning run on a Munson pinch single.

The Yankees reached the All-Star break at 51-27, leading the AL East by 7½ games. Randolph, with a .283 average, was the AL's starting second baseman. This wasn't one of his most memorable All-Star performancess (he selected for the team six times). He made two errors—the second of which enabled the NL to score the go-ahead run—and was picked off first. The American League lost 4-2.

A week after the All-Star Game, the Yankees were in the lead by 9½ games. Between July 18 and August 27, however, they were 18-21 and their lead shrank to as little as a half-game on August 22. Randolph, too, was having problems. He strained his left hip on August 15 and was out of the lineup for 11 of the next 12 games. He returned on August 29, contributing three hits and a pair of RBIs in a victory over Seattle.

"We're not the same team without Randolph leading off," manager Dick Howser said after the win over the Mariners. "And now that he's back, things happen." Indeed, Randolph's return coincided with the Yankees' regaining control of the AL East race. They won 16 of 18 games after he returned to the lineup—including was a four-game sweep at Fenway—and by September 15 they were in first place by five games ahead and pulling away. They finished at 103-59—the best record in baseball that year—three games ahead of Baltimore.

Randolph ended the year at .294—it was his best season to date. He also led the American League in walks with 119 (he walked in each of his last 15 games) and was second only to Kansas City's George Brett in on-base percentage (.429).

Surprisingly, the Yankees lost the ALCS to the Royals that year in just three games. Randolph played a pivotal role in the series. He led off Game 1 with a double but never got past third. Had he scored, the complexion of the series certainly would have been different. As it turned out, the Royals romped 7-2 in the opener. In the eighth inning of Game 2, Randolph was involved in a play that, through no fault of his own, probably marked the turning point in the series. Kansas City had a 3-2 lead, the Yankees had two outs, and Randolph was on first. Bob Watson ripped a double to left field; Kansas City's Willie Wil-

> "Willie was respected, low-key, a family man, no-nonsense on the field, a true professional all the way. If there were 'wrong' people and 'right' people to hang around with, Willie would definitely be one of the 'rightest.' "
>
> —FORMER TEAMMATE DAVE WINFIELD

son fielded it cleanly, but Yankee third-base coach Mike Ferraro waved Randolph, who had stumbled briefly leaving first, home. It looked like a great decision when Wilson overthrew the cutoff man. But Brett, backing up the play, fielded the errant throw, turned, and fired a strike to catcher Darrell Porter, who tagged Randolph out to end the inning. "I think that changed the momentum," Brett said of the play. "If they've had scored the run, we might have been intimidated. We went into the dugout fired up, and I saw the look of disbelief in their eyes." The Yankees didn't roll over and die in Game 3, taking a 2-1 lead into the seventh inning, but then a bloop double and infield chopper put two men on base, and Brett crushed a three-run homer off Goose Gossage to put Kansas City ahead to stay.

Over the next eight seasons, Randolph continued to be a valuable, contributing member of the Yankees. After the 1988 season, owner George Steinbrenner signed free-agent second baseman Steve Sax. Randolph, realizing he didn't fit in the Yankees' plans, took the free-agent route to the Los Angeles Dodgers, for whom he hit .282 in 1989. He played for Oakland, Milwaukee, and the Mets and then retired after the 1992 season. He returned to the Yankees as a coach in 1994.

## Baseball News Of 1980

- On October 4, fifty-seven-year-old Minnie Minoso pinch-hit for the White Sox against the Angels. He thus became the second major-eaguer—Nick Altrock was the first—to appear in games in five decades.

- Elston Howard, who in 1955 became the first black player for the Yankees, died at 51 on December 14.

- Bob Shawkey, who pitched the first game at Yankee Stadium, died at age 90 on December 31.

- Montreal's Ron LeFlore led the NL with 97 stolen bases, becoming the first player to have led both leagues in steals (he had 68 for the Tigers in 1978).

- Cubs reliever Bruce Sutter was awarded the then-incredible salary of $700,000 in arbitration. After the season he was traded to St. Louis.

- The Phillies won their first World Series.

## Around The World In 1980

- The United States broke diplomatic relations with Iran as the hostage crisis continued.

- Regulations prohibiting sexual harassment of women in the workplace by their superiors were issued by the Equal Opportunity Commission.

- Mount St. Helens erupted in Washington, triggering fires, mudslides, and floods and leaving more than fifty people dead or missing.

- Draft registration for men ages nineteen and twenty was reinstated.

- *Voyager I*, launched in 1977, flew within 77,000 miles of Saturn and discovered previously unknown rings.

- Among the obituaries were those of Jimmy Durante (January 29, age 86), Henry Miller (June 7, age 88), Mae West (November 22, age 87), George Meany (January 10, age 85), and Colonel Harland Sanders (December 16, age 90).

# 48
# Season of Glory

## Tommy John

### 1979

| W | L | Pct. | IP | GS | CG | SH | SV | K/BB | Opp. BA | ERA |
|---|---|------|----|----|----|----|----|------|---------|-----|
| 21 | 9 | .700 | 276 | 36 | 17 | 3 | 0 | 111/65 | .268 | 2.96 |

| | GP | PO | A | DP | E | FA | ER/R | PR | DEF |
|---|----|----|---|----|---|----|------|----|----|
| | 37 | 15 | 51 | 5 | 3 | .957 | 109/91 | 34 | 2 |

# 48

# *Thomas Edward John*

**BORN**
May 22, 1943
Terre Haute, Indiana

**HEIGHT**
6-3

**WEIGHT**
185

**THREW**
left hand

**BATTED**
right hand

New York Yankees
1979–82
1986–1989

*S*ometimes, talent isn't enough. Sometimes, it takes luck, or a medical miracle, or maybe even help from a higher power to succeed. Take Tommy John. He had loads of potential when he made his major-league debut in 1963 with the Cleveland Indians. But the twenty-year-old left- hander was slow in living up to that potential. It wasn't until he was traded to the White Sox and was taken under the wing of Chicago pitching coach Ray Berres that his talent emerged.

"I asked Ray Berres, the White Sox pitching coach, why Chicago wanted me," John wrote in *The Tommy John Story*. "My big-league record to that point was a pathetic 2-11. Berres said he had marked down in his scorebook a game I lost 2-1 to Chicago, where Al Weis beat me with a home run.

"Berres said I had made a half-dozen outstanding pitches, and after that game he told White Sox manager Al Lopez that 'When that kid out there had his arm in the proper position, he was unhittable. Keep an eye on him.'" Lopez, in turn, instructed general manager Ed Short to pursue John, and he made a deal that brought John and Tommie Agee to Chicago.

Blessed with a good curve and sinker and excellent control—he was an expert at working the edges of the plate—and coached by Berres, John became a winner. He was 14-7 in 1965 and 14-11 the following year. That he was able to accomplish this while playing for one of baseball's most punchless teams was impressive (the Sox hit .246 in '65, .231 in '66, and a feeble .225 in '67, when John still managed to go 10-13).

John's fortunes, and those of the White Sox, soon changed. The team became a second-division ball club in 1968 and hit bottom in 1970, going 56-106. A new manager, Chuck Tanner, came aboard for 1971 and turned things around—the Sox, with John going 13-16, placed third in the AL West that year. After the season, Tanner, who needed to add some power to his lineup, sent John to the Los Angeles Dodgers for Dick Allen. In the long run, it may have been the luckiest thing ever to happen to John.

In his first season in the National League, he went 11-5. He was 16-7, with the best winning percentage in the league, in 1973. The turning point in John's career—in his life—occurred on July 17, 1974. In the fourth inning of a game against Montreal, he was facing Hal Breeden. "As I came forward and released the ball, I felt a kind of nothingness, as if my arm weren't there, then I heard a 'pop' from

*When "T.J." had a tendon transplanted from his right forearm to his left elbow,
he became, in a manner of speaking, baseball's first right-handed southpaw.*

# Game of Glory • May 20, 1979

John shuts out Boston on May 20, allowing only two hits, to improve his record to 9-0.

| NEW YORK | AB | R | H | RBI | | BOSTON | AB | R | H | RBI |
|---|---|---|---|---|---|---|---|---|---|---|
| Rivers, cf | 4 | 0 | 2 | 0 | | Remy, 2b | 3 | 0 | 1 | 0 |
| Randolph, 2b | 2 | 0 | 0 | 0 | | Wolfe, ph | 1 | 0 | 0 | 0 |
| Munson, c | 4 | 0 | 0 | 0 | | Burleson, ss | 3 | 0 | 0 | 0 |
| Nettles, 3b | 4 | 1 | 1 | 1 | | Lynn, cf | 3 | 0 | 1 | 0 |
| Jackson, rf | 4 | 1 | 1 | 1 | | Rice, dh | 3 | 0 | 0 | 0 |
| Chambliss, 1b | 4 | 0 | 2 | 0 | | Yastrzemski, lf | 3 | 0 | 0 | 0 |
| White, lf | 4 | 0 | 0 | 0 | | Hobson, 3b | 3 | 0 | 0 | 0 |
| Spence, dh | 4 | 0 | 0 | 0 | | Scott, 1b | 3 | 0 | 0 | 0 |
| Dent, ss | 3 | 0 | 0 | 0 | | Evans, rf | 3 | 0 | 0 | 0 |
| | | | | | | Allenson, c | 2 | 0 | 0 | 0 |
| Totals | 33 | 2 | 6 | 2 | | Totals | 28 | 0 | 2 | 0 |

```
New York     0 0 0   1 0 0   0 0 1 — 2  6  1
Boston       0 0 0   0 0 0   0 0 0 — 0  2  1
```

Doubles—Chambliss, Lynn. Home runs—Jackson, Nettles.
Errors—Scott, Nettles. Double plays—New York 1, Boston 1.
Left on base—New York 6, Boston 1.

| NEW YORK | IP | H | R | ER | BB | K |
|---|---|---|---|---|---|---|
| John (W, 9-0) | 9 | 2 | 0 | 0 | 0 | 5 |

| BOSTON | IP | H | R | ER | BB | K |
|---|---|---|---|---|---|---|
| Eckersley (L, 6-3) | 9 | 6 | 2 | 2 | 2 | 8 |

Time—1:58. Attendance—33,932.

*1979*

inside my arm, and the ball just blooped to the plate," he recalled in *T.J.: My 26 Years in Baseball*. "I didn't feel soreness or pain at this point, but just a strange sensation that my arm wasn't there."

He had ruptured a tendon in his left elbow. What's more, he had nerve damage, and no pitcher had ever come back from such an injury. John's career appeared to be over.

Enter Dr. Frank Jobe. The famed orthopedist suggested that John undergo an experimental operation, in which Jobe would take a six-inch tendon from John's right forearm and use it to rebuild his left elbow. With his left arm virtually useless, and after several days of prayer and discussions with his wife, Sally, and the Dodgers, John agreed to the surgery. "Baseball is my life," John wrote of what went into his decision. "God gave me the gift of throwing a baseball better than most other people. My gift to God is to play baseball the best I can—so I (had) to pitch again."

The operation was performed in September 1974, and John embarked on a long, painful, and sometimes frustrating rehabilitation process. "One piece of Scripture sustained me, and became like a mantra to me," he later recalled, "and that was Phil. 4:13. 'For with God, nothing shall be impossible.'" He missed the entire 1975 season, and it wasn't until the spring of the following year that he regained strength, velocity, and control in his injured arm. He returned to the Dodgers and had a 10-10 record that season—it earned him the NL Comeback Player of the Year Award. In 1977 he demonstrated just how far he had come back by going 20-7 with a 2.78 ERA and a second-place finish in the NL Cy Young Award voting. In 1978 John was 17-10 and helped the Dodgers reach the World Series, which they lost to the Yankees.

John's disappointment at losing the Series was short-lived. A month later he signed a five-year, $1 million-plus free-agent contract with the Yankees. And as the 1979 season unfolded, it looked like the Yankees had made a great investment, with John winning his first nine decisions.

In his first American League start in seven years, on April 8, John held Milwaukee to six hits in seven innings, helping the Yankees to their first victory of the season. It was a typical John victory. He made only two mistakes—fat pitches to Robin Yount and Gorman Thomas—and both the resulting long drives were chased down in Yankee Stadium's spacious outfield. "When I signed, I said this was a very forgiving ballpark," John pointed out to reporters. "And you can make some mistakes." The rest of the Brewers struggled with John's awesome sinker—14 of the 21 outs he recorded were ground balls as the Milwaukee hitters pounded the ball into the dirt. "Sinker, sinker, sinker," muttered Milwaukee's Don Money, shaking his head.

In John's next outing, on April 12 in Baltimore, he got his thirty-fourth career shutout. With 18 of his hitters going out on grounders, Orioles manager Earl Weaver repeatedly asked umpires to check the balls for scuffs. It didn't help; John allowed only three hits and the Yankees won 5-0. (Six days later John hammered home the point when he beat the Orioles 3-1, allowing eight hits in 7⅔ innings and lowering his ERA to 0.76.)

On April 19 relief ace Rich Gossage got into a clubhouse fight with teammate Cliff Johnson and tore a ligament in his thumb. Gossage was sidelined until July, and while he was recovering, the Yankee bullpen faltered. Nevertheless, Tommy John won five games in a row in early May, ending a five-game Yankee losing streak, helping New York advance to third place, and bringing his record to 9-0 and dropping his ERA to 1.72.

John lost his next outing, on May 26 in Cleveland, giving up six runs, three of them earned, on seven hits in 4⅓ innings, then rebounded, allowing only one unearned run in 7⅔ innings against Milwaukee four days later (he didn't get the decision). He ended May at 9-1 with a 1.69 ERA.

Between July 30 and August 31, John had another five-game winning streak, which brought his record to 18-6. But by then, the Yankees were out of the race. The bullpen's early season problems had been costly, and the tragic death of Munson on August 2 had seriously dampened the team's spirit. From that point on, the stunned Yankees were just going through the motions. They finished fourth in the AL East.

John won three of his last six decisions and finished at 21-9. He had a 2.96 ERA (second best in the AL), 17 complete games (tied for second), and three shutouts—remarkable

> "I pitched my first big league game when John F. Kennedy was still in the White House, and my last with the presidency occupied by another baseball fan, George Bush. I was the last active pitcher to give up a home run to Mickey Mantle. In my twenty-six years in the major leagues, more than 49,000 ballgames were played; about one third of all the games in history. No one plays that long without developing an ability to overcome obstacles and bounce back from defeat. To make comebacks. I've been coming back, it seems, most of my professional life."
>
> —TOMMY JOHN

numbers for a thirty-six-year-old pitcher whose career was supposedly over five years earlier.

But John had fooled them all. And he kept fooling them. He was 22-9 in 1980 and 19-18 over the next season and a half. He was then traded to California. He spent parts of four seasons with the Angels and half season with Oakland, going 26-38. When he was let go by the A's after the 1985 season, it seemed that the end had arrived.

John wasn't ready to hang it up just yet. Invited to the Yankees' camp in the spring of 1986 as a nonroster player, he made the team. His playing time was limited to 13 games because of a variety of injuries, but he still had a 5-3 record and a 2.93 ERA. He bounced back in '87—at the age of 44—with a 13-6 record. In 1988 John was 9-8—he would have had an even better record had not Yankee relievers blown six leads he had turned over to them. He finally reached the end of the road on May 30, 1989, at the age of forty-six (he was the Yankees' Opening Day pitcher that season, beating Minnesota for his 287th career victory) when he was given his release, ending his stellar twenty-six-year pitching career.

"There's a sense of relief when I look back on my career, knowing that it's over," he once reflected. "The only thing I would have done differently is learn the changeup much earlier, because it's such a devastating pitch. Other than that, I wouldn't change a thing. I feel things happened the way God intended."

## Baseball News Of 1979

- After a forty-five-day strike, umpires returned to major-league diamonds $7,000 richer, with improved vacation and pension benefits.

- Disco Demolition Night at Chicago's Comiskey Park turned into a riot and caused the Sox to forfeit the second game of a double-header against Detroit.

- Boston's Bob Watson became the first player to hit for the cycle in both leagues.

- Phil and Joe Niekro became the second pair of brothers (Jim and Gaylord Perry were the first) to win twenty games in the same season.

- Keith Hernandez and Willie Stargell shared the NL MVP Award.

## Around The World In 1979

- The Shah of Iran was overthrown, and the Ayatollah Ruhollah Khomeini was installed as the nation's leader.

- Margaret Thatcher became Britain's first female prime minister.

- The nuclear plant at Three Mile Island in Pennsylvania malfunctioned, nearly causing a major disaster.

- An American Airlines DC-10 crashed as it was taking off from Chicago's O'Hare International Airport, killing 275 persons. It was the worst air disaster in U.S. history.

- Rick Mears won the Indy 500.

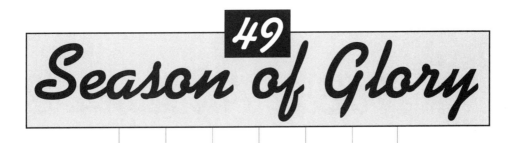

**49**

# Season of Glory

# Wade Boggs

## 1994

| AB | R | H | BA | OB% | 2B | 3B | HR | K/BB | RBI | BR | SB |
|----|----|----|------|------|----|----|----|-------|-----|----|----|
| 366 | 61 | 125 | .342 | .437 | 19 | 1 | 11 | 29/61 | 55 | 27 | 2 |

| | | G | PO | A | DP | E | FA | FR | | | |
|---|---|----|----|-----|----|----|------|----|---|---|---|
| | | 97 | 40 | 214 | 19 | 10 | .962 | 13 | | | |

# 49 Wade Anthony Boggs

**BORN**
June 15, 1958
Omaha, Nebraska

**HEIGHT**
6-2

**WEIGHT**
197

**THROWS**
right hand

**BATS**
left hand

New York Yankees
1992-97

*1994*

In late 1992, Wade Boggs reached a crossroads in his career. The eleven-year Boston veteran had been unable to agree on a new contract with the Red Sox. Consequently, he had filed for free agency. Several teams had expressed interest in the thirty-three-year-old third baseman—players with lifetime .338 batting averages don't come on the market every day—but in the end Boggs had to choose between the New York Yankees and Los Angeles Dodgers. The Dodgers were offering a two-year deal with an option for a third; the Yankees were offering three years. An easy choice, right? Not for Boggs.

Boggs had never liked Yankee Stadium, and it had nothing to do with baseball. In 1986, Boggs happened to be in Yankee Stadium when he received a phone call informing him that his mother had been killed in an auto accident. The memory had haunted him since. "[Yankee Stadium] always made me sad," he recalled several years later. "I never thought I would play here. But when I did sign with the Yankees, I sat down with my dad and had a long talk. I decided it was time to block that out. It helped." Boggs signed the three-year deal, worth $11 million, on December 15, 1992.

In his first season in New York, he managed to put his problems from 1992 behind him—he had a career-low .259 average and trouble with Red Sox management and teammate Roger Clemens—and reach the .300 level again. Wade Boggs was back.

From his major-league debut in 1982 with the Red Sox, Boggs had always been the picture of consistency. He always hit above .300. He always had an on-base percentage over .400. He always made the big play in the field. He always wanted to be the best.

There's a story that illustrates Boggs' discipline and determination to succeed. As a high school junior in Tampa, he batted .522, the best average in the state. Halfway through his senior season, though, he was struggling badly, his average was more than 200 points lower than the previous year. His father got a copy of Ted Williams's *The Science of Hitting* from the public library, and Boggs spent a weekend studying it. Applying Williams's words on the field, Boggs hit .788 in his last 11 games to finish the season at .485.

Boggs had demonstrated he could hit, but his weaknesses as a player—he wasn't great defensively, he was a slow runner, and he was basically a singles hitter—turned off major-league scouts. The Red Sox chose him in the June 1976 draft, but not until the seventh round. Boggs spent the next 4½ years in the minors, batting .263, .332, .311, .325, and .306.

*After the Yanks' World Series victory in 1996, Boggs toured the Stadium on horseback with one of New York's finest.*

# Game of Glory • May 15, 1994

Boggs contributes a double and homer to a 12-1 rout of Milwaukee on May 15.

| NEW YORK | AB | R | H | RBI | | MILWAUKEE | AB | R | H | RBI |
|---|---|---|---|---|---|---|---|---|---|---|
| Polonia, lf | 6 | 2 | 2 | 2 | | Diaz, cf | 4 | 0 | 0 | 0 |
| Boggs, 3b | 4 | 2 | 2 | 3 | | Spiers, 3b | 4 | 0 | 1 | 0 |
| Eenhoorn, ss | 0 | 0 | 0 | 0 | | Cirillo, 3b | 0 | 0 | 0 | 0 |
| Mattingly, 1b | 5 | 1 | 4 | 2 | | Ward, lf | 3 | 0 | 0 | 0 |
| Melvin, pr-1b | 0 | 0 | 0 | 0 | | Brunansky, rf | 1 | 0 | 0 | 0 |
| Tartabull, dh | 5 | 0 | 1 | 0 | | Vaughn, dh | 4 | 0 | 0 | 0 |
| O'Neill, rf | 3 | 2 | 2 | 0 | | Nilsson, 1b | 4 | 1 | 2 | 0 |
| G. Williams, ph-rf | 1 | 0 | 0 | 0 | | Harper, c | 4 | 0 | 2 | 1 |
| Leyritz, c | 4 | 2 | 1 | 1 | | Matheny, c | 0 | 0 | 0 | 0 |
| B. Williams, cf | 5 | 1 | 1 | 2 | | Reed, 2b | 3 | 0 | 0 | 0 |
| Velarde, ss-3b | 5 | 1 | 2 | 1 | | Valentin, ss | 4 | 0 | 0 | 0 |
| Gallego, 2b | 5 | 1 | 2 | 1 | | Miske, rf-lf | 1 | 0 | 0 | 0 |
| Totals | 43 | 12 | 17 | 12 | | Totals | 32 | 1 | 5 | 1 |

| | | | | | | | | | |
|---|---|---|---|---|---|---|---|---|---|
| New York | 0 0 2 | 5 0 0 | 4 1 0 — 12 |
| Milwaukee | 0 0 0 | 0 0 1 | 0 0 0 — 1 |

Errors—Velarde (2). Doubles—Polonia, Boggs, Tartabull, O'Neill, Leyritz, Gallego, Harper (2). Triple—Polonia. Home runs—Boggs, Mattingly, B. Williams. Sacrifice fly—Boggs. Left on base—New York 7, Milwaukee 8.

| NEW YORK | IP | H | R | ER | BB | K |
|---|---|---|---|---|---|---|
| Kamieniecki (W, 3-0) | 85 | 1 | 1 | 4 | 1 | |
| Hutton | 1 | 0 | 0 | 0 | 0 | 0 |

| MILWAUKEE | IP | H | R | ER | BB | K |
|---|---|---|---|---|---|---|
| Navarro (L, 2-3) | 3.1 | 7 | 6 | 6 | 1 | 5 |
| Kiefer | 3 | 5 | 5 | 5 | 1 | 2 |
| Henry | 1.2 | 2 | 1 | 1 | 0 | 1 |
| Fetters | 1 | 2 | 0 | 0 | 0 | 1 |

Time—2:48. Attendance—32,293.

1994

Despite his solid hitting, Boggs wasn't part of the Red Sox plans. It was the same old story: Major-league teams can't afford singles-hitting third basemen who are below average defensively. So Boggs went to work, practicing to improve his defensive skills and trying to hit for power. The hard work paid off: In 1981 at Pawtucket, he hit a league-leading .335. He had 41 doubles, an increase of twenty over the year before, and

five homers, one more than he had hit in the four previous seasons combined.

The Red Sox could no longer ignore him. He made the team in 1982 and became the regular third baseman in June, when Carney Lansford was injured. Boggs made a big splash, hitting over .400 during his first month as a regular. In all he played 44 games at third and 49 at first that year, finishing his rookie season at .349 (he was third in Rookie of the Year voting behind Cal Ripken, Jr., and Kent Hrbek). It was the start of a remarkably productive eleven-year career in Boston: five batting titles, seven consecutive seasons of 200 or more hits, and six years leading the league in on-base percentage. But then came 1992. Not only did his average tumble, he had problems with management—trouble started after they haggled over a contract extension in spring training—and Clemens, who became angry with Boggs after a late-season incident. During a game that Clemens was pitching, Boggs had been charged with an error. The next day he persuaded the official scorer to change his call, ruling the error a hit. That nudged Clemens' ERA slightly higher. Clemens, with an eye on the Cy Young Award and a $125,000 bonus that went with it, expressed his anger to reporters. That turned out to close the book on Boggs' Boston career. It was time for a change, and the Yankees were only happy to sign him.

Boggs came out swinging in the Yankees' 1994 opener on April 4 against Texas, going 4-for-5 and scoring twice in the 5-3 Yankee victory. He got four more hits in New York's next game, and by the middle of April, he was at .419. A month into the season, Boggs was at .309 and the Yankees were challenging the Red Sox for first in the AL East. The Yankees swept a three-game series against Boston in early May, moving within a half game of the lead. On May 9 the Yankees defeated Cleveland, taking over first, then won their next six games, solidifying their hold on first.

Boggs went 14-for-25 (.560) over the last week of May, raising his average to .342. He continued his hitting spree in June, which included a three-run homer on May 7 against Texas; another three-run homer on May 12 versus Toronto; a game-winning RBI single in the ninth against Baltimore's ace reliever Lee Smith on May 15; and a 12-for-24 stretch from May 18 through the May 24.

It was beginning to look like the Yankees'—and Boggs'—year. By July 1 they had the best record in the American League (47-28) and a 4½-game lead in their division. And Boggs was at .332 and climbing.

The Yankees stumbled slightly heading around the time of the All-Star break, losing five of seven games and having their lead cut to a half game. After the second half of the season—or, what was scheduled to be the second half—began, however, New York was unstoppable, winning 10 of 11 and increasing their lead to 5½ games. Boggs, who had contributed a hit in three at-bats in the All-Star Game, was a big factor in the Yankees' success, going 16-for-33 (which raised his average to .343).

"I try to hit the ball as far as I can without making an out. Home-run hitters pop out and strike out more often than line-drive hitters, but everybody wants to see a guy hit thirty home runs even if he bats .240. . . . Why try to hit thirty home runs when you could try to get 250 hits and contribute more to the team?"

—WADE BOGGS IN THE MARCH 1987 EDITION OF *INSIDE SPORTS*

There was no letup. Less than two weeks later, the Yankees were leading by ten games and Boggs was hitting .360. And then it was over.

All season, the owners and the players' union had been at odds over free agency, revenue sharing, a salary cap, arbitration, minimum salaries, pensions, and just about everything this side of the price of hot dogs. The players walked off the job after their games on August 12 . . . and that was it. Negotiations broke down, and after weeks of talking, the rest of the season was canceled. Boggs' pursuit of a sixth batting title ended. The Yankees' pennant express was derailed.

For the record, Boggs finished seventh in the American League at .342, his best average in six years. He hit .352 with runners in scoring position, .353 against right-handers, .359 at Yankee Stadium, and .333 when he had two strikes on him. He also won his first Gold Glove, made *The Sporting News*' All-

Star team, and placed thirteenth in the AL MVP voting.

Boggs' Yankee career ended after the 1997 season. At thirty-nine, he had been relegated to part-time duties that year, replaced at third by Charlie Hayes. While he hit .292 with four homers that season, he clearly didn't fit into the Yankees' plans, and on December 9 he signed as a free agent with the expansion Tampa Bay Devil Rays.

## Baseball News Of 1994

- Baseball personalities who died that year included former Pittsburgh pitcher Harvey Haddix (January 9), former NL president Chub Feeney (January 10), Negro Leagues star Ray Dandridge (February 12), longtime umpire and beer pitchman Jim Honochick (March 10), ex-Padres pitcher Eric Show (March 16), former Met and beer pitchman Marv Throneberry (June 23), ex-Twin Cesar Tovar (July 14), former pitcher Hank Aguirre (September 5), ex-Yankee pitcher Allie Reynolds (December 27).

- Milwaukee's Robin Yount retired after a stellar twenty-one-year career.

- Cubs rookie Karl "Tuffy" Rhodes homered in his first three at-bats on Opening Day. He was the first man ever to hit three in an opener.

## Around The World In 1994

- Sergei Krikalev became the first Russian to fly aboard a U.S. space shuttle.

- Fragments of the Shoemaker-Levy 9 comet struck Jupiter in mid-July, producing a spectacular light show.

- Colorado's antigay law was overturned by that state's Supreme Court.

- The United States ended its trade embargo against Vietnam on February 3.

- The Church of England ordained its first women priests on March 12 in London.

- Richard Nixon died on April 22.

- Jacqueline Kennedy Onassis died on May 19.

# Season of Glory

**50**

## Joe Page

### 1949

| W | L | Pct. | IP | GS | CG | SH | SV | K/BB | Opp. BA | ERA |
|---|---|------|-----|-----|-----|-----|-----|------|---------|------|
| 13 | 8 | .619 | 135.1 | 0 | 0 | 0 | 27 | 99/75 | .215 | 2.59 |

| | GP | PO | A | DP | E | FA | ER/R | PR | DEF |
|---|-----|-----|-----|-----|-----|------|------|-----|-----|
| | 60 | 4 | 15 | 1 | 1 | .950 | 44/39 | 22 | -2 |

# 50

BORN
October 28, 1917
Cherry Valley, Pennsylvania

DIED
April 21, 1980
Latrobe, Pennsylvania

HEIGHT
6-2

WEIGHT
205

THREW
left hand

BATTED
left hand

New York Yankees
1944–50

## 1949

# Joseph Francis Page

*I*t was the beginning of the 1947 season, and Joe Page was in the doghouse so deep, he later recalled, that "it would have taken a bloodhound to find me." Page, 29, had three unimpressive years of work under his belt for the Yankees, and had a reputation as a free spirit, someone who was more interested in having fun than concentrating on the task at hand. For that reason, he hadn't been a particular favorite of manager Joe McCarthy, and, aside from Joe DiMaggio, he wasn't close to any of his teammates.

New Yankee manager Bucky Harris, though, refused to give up on the big, hard-throwing left-hander, who relied on a fastball, forkball, and occasional spitter. He did what he could to boost Page's confidence, using him in key situations. Unfortunately, Page didn't always live up to his manager's expectations. But on May 26, 1947, Page pitched a game that showed Harris' faith in him was justified and that marked a turning point in his career.

In the third inning of a game against the Red Sox, the defending American League champions, Harris brought in Page. New York was trailing 3-1, and Boston had two men on and no outs. Then, an error loaded the bases and Rudy York came up to bat. Page went 3-0 on York, then struck him out on the next three pitches. Bobby Doerr, one of the game's best clutch hitters, was next. It was the same story: Page went 3-0 on him, then struck him out. The next batter, Eddie Pellagrini hit a harmless fly, and the inning was over.

The Yankees went on to win 9-3, and the Joe Page legend was born. He nourished it that season by going 14-8 with 17 saves and a 2.48 ERA in 56 appearances (all but two in relief). He also won Game 7 of the World Series. It appeared that Page's reputation was improving—he was now becoming known as one of the game's first great relievers. "He was the beginning of relief pitchers being stars rather than just guys who couldn't start," Yankee announcer Mel Allen said in *Pen Men*, by Bob Cairns. "The lasting memory, the one I'll never forget, is seeing him come in out of that bullpen in Yankee Stadium. He'd sling his jacket over his shoulder and jump over the right-field fence."

Joseph Francis Page was born on October 28, 1917, in Cherry Valley, Pennsylvania. After high school, he went to work in the coal mines, but at nineteen, with his father's blessing, began to play semipro ball. In 1940 he caught on with the Yankees' Class D farm team in Butler, Pennsylvania, moved to Class B Augusta, Georgia, in 1941, and spent 1942 and '43 with Newark, the Yankees' top minor-league team (Page was exempted from the service because of a severe leg injury he suffered in 1938).

The handsome, curly-haired Page came up for the 1944 season and made an immediate impression, winning five of his first six decisions and earning a spot on the AL All-Star team. His second half was another story. Bothered by a sore shoulder suffered when he fell rounding second base in June (an injury he was reluctant to report), he lost his next six decisions and was shipped back to Newark by McCarthy in August. He got another opportunity in 1945. His numbers were impressive—6-3 with a 2.82 ERA—but his love of good times infuriated McCarthy. "I had won little more than a reputation as a playboy," Page told the *Saturday Evening Post* in 1948.

McCarthy stepped down early in the 1946 season, but Page, still splitting his time between starting and relieving, didn't fare much better under Bill Dickey and Johnny Neun, going 9-8 with a 3.57 ERA. And after his big 1947, Page suffered through a 7-8, 4.26 season in '48.

The question, then, as 1949 arrived, was whether Page's performance in 1947 was an aberration. Page gave an early indication of what kind of season 1949 would be. On April 22, in the Yankees' fourth game of the season, he relieved Allie Reynolds in the seventh and pitched three hitless innings to save a 5-3 victory in Boston.

Page had some lousy outings during the first couple of weeks—he gave up the winning run in the tenth on April 27 against Washington; he surrendered a two-run, game-tying single to the first batter he faced three days later against Boston; and he struggled (three hits and three walks in three innings) in a May 5 victory in Chicago. But snapped out of it on May 28, pitching six shutout innings, allowing just four hits, and getting the win when the Yankees pushed a

*Joe Page, first winner of the Babe Ruth Memorial Award (the World Series MVP) in 1949.*

run across in the fourteenth inning. And he was equally impressive his next time out, on June 2. The Yankees led Chicago 9-6 when he came on with the bases loaded in the fourth. He immediately walked in a run, then allowed just one hit, fanning five, over the next 4⅔ innings to run his record to 4-1.

The greatest beneficiary of Page's heroics in '49 was Allie Reynolds. All season long Page came to his rescue, giving Reynolds an undeserved—and unwelcome—reputation as a pitcher who couldn't finish. But there were too many instances to ignore: Page ended a threat by Washington on May 30, he saved a victory over Cleveland on June 11, four days later he saved yet another Reynolds victory, he bailed Reynolds out on June 24 and got the victory himself, and on

# Game of Glory • July 16, 1949

Page, making his fifty-fourth relief appearance of the season, allows two hits over three innings as the Yankees hold off the Indians, the defending AL champions. It was the thirty-ninth time that the Yankees won a game in which Page appeared.

| NEW YORK | AB | R | H | RBI | | CLEVELAND | AB | R | H | RBI |
|---|---|---|---|---|---|---|---|---|---|---|
| Rizzuto, ss | 5 | 1 | 2 | 1 | | Mitchell, lf | 5 | 0 | 1 | 0 |
| Mapes, cf | 5 | 0 | 2 | 1 | | Boudreau, ss | 4 | 1 | 2 | 0 |
| Brown, 3b | 5 | 2 | 2 | 0 | | Vernon, 1b | 4 | 1 | 1 | 1 |
| Berra, c | 4 | 1 | 1 | 0 | | Doby, rf-cf | 2 | 1 | 0 | 0 |
| Silvera, c | 0 | 0 | 0 | 0 | | Gordon, 2b | 4 | 0 | 0 | 0 |
| Keller, lf | 2 | 1 | 1 | 0 | | Kennedy, 3b | 4 | 0 | 1 | 0 |
| Bauer, rf | 4 | 1 | 3 | 3 | | Tucker, cf | 3 | 0 | 0 | 0 |
| Collins, 1b | 3 | 1 | 1 | 1 | | Peck, rf | 0 | 0 | 0 | 0 |
| Coleman, 2b | 0 | 0 | 0 | 0 | | Hegan, c | 3 | 0 | 1 | 0 |
| Buxton, p | 0 | 0 | 0 | 0 | | Benton, p | 1 | 0 | 0 | 0 |
| Casey, p | 0 | 0 | 0 | 0 | | Wynn, p | 2 | 0 | 0 | 0 |
| Page, p | 1 | 0 | 0 | 0 | | Boone, ph | 1 | 0 | 1 | 0 |
| Woodling, ph | 1 | 0 | 0 | 1 | | Berardino, ph | 1 | 0 | 0 | 0 |
| Delsing, ph | 1 | 0 | 0 | 0 | | | | | | |
| Mize, ph | 1 | 0 | 0 | 0 | | | | | | |
| Raschi, p | 0 | 0 | 0 | 0 | | | | | | |
| Henrich, ph | 0 | 0 | 0 | 0 | | | | | | |
| Stirnweiss, 2b | 2 | 0 | 0 | 0 | | | | | | |
| **Totals** | **34** | **3** | **7** | **1** | | **Totals** | **34** | **7** | **12** | **7** |

```
New York    0 3 1   0 0 0   2 1 * — 7
Cleveland   3 0 0   0 0 0   0 0 0 — 3
```

Doubles—Vernon, Rizzuto, Bauer. Triples—Hegan, Mitchell, Bauer.
Stolen bases—Doby (2), Tucker, Rizzuto. Left on base— Cleveland 8, New York 8.

| NEW YORK | IP | H | BB | K |
|---|---|---|---|---|
| Buxton | 1 | 0 | 0 | 0 |
| Casey (W, 1-0) | 3 | 2 | 2 | 2 |
| Page | 3 | 2 | 1 | 3 |
| Raschi | 2 | 3 | 1 | 3 |

| CLEVELAND | IP | H | BB | K |
|---|---|---|---|---|
| Benton (L, 8-6) | 2.2 | 0 | 2 | 2 |
| Wynn | 5.1 | 7 | 2 | 4 |

Balk—Raschi. Hit by pitch—by Benton (Henrich). Wild pitch—Raschi.

Time—2:41. Attendance—64,549.

June 28 he came on in the ninth and preserved Reynolds' eighth win in nine decisions.

With Reynolds winning 11 of his first 12 decisions (Page [8-4] relieved in ten of those victories), the Yankees, under first-year manager Casey Stengel, were able to jump into first place on Opening Day and remain there until the last week of the season. By September 1 it was a three-way race, with New York leading Boston by two games and Cleveland by 4½. Down the stretch Page was the man Stengel relied on. Here's what he did during the first three weeks of September:

- On September 1 against St. Louis, he came on in the ninth with the bases loaded and one out. He walked in a run, then saved the 4-3 victory when the next two batters hit harmless fly balls.
- Six days later, in the opener of a crucial three-game series with Boston, he struck out four of the five men he faced—in relief of Reynolds—to preserve a 5-2 win that left New York 2½ games ahead of the Red Sox.
- On September 11, after the Senators had cut the Yankees' lead to 2-1, Page came on with a man on second to end the threat and save another victory.
- On September 17, making his 53rd relief appearance of the season, he allowed two hits in 2⅔ innings to save a 5-4 victory over Detroit.
- A day later he pitched three shutout innings in a 7-3 win over Cleveland.
- On September 20 he saved Reynolds' 17th victory with two mediocre (1 hit, 3 walks) innings of work against Chicago.

The Red Sox, who had been twelve games back on July 4, finally caught the Yankees on September 25 with a 4-1 victory. Boston also won the next afternoon—Page, thanks to an error and a walk, was the loser—to take a one-game lead. At the end of the month, Boston still led by one game and was scheduled to play a season-ending two-game series at Yankee Stadium.

In the first game, on October 1, the Red Sox quickly took advantage of a shaky Reynolds, scoring a run in the first and three more in the third. Page came on in the third (the bases were loaded and there was one out) and walked in two runs—both charged to Reynolds—to put Boston up 4-0. But Page allowed just one hit the rest of the way. The Yankees, meanwhile, chipped away at Boston's lead, finally tying the score in the fifth and scoring the winner in the bottom of the eighth.

The season came down to one game. Behind Vic Raschi's five-hit pitching and Jerry Coleman's three-run double in the eighth, the Yankees won 5-3 to capture their sixteenth American League pennant and earn a World Series berth against Brooklyn.

In the Series opener, Reynolds didn't need help from Page or anyone else. He held the Dodgers to two hits, striking out nine, as the Yankees won 1-0. Brooklyn came back to win

> "(Joe Page) was probably the biggest dissipater in the history of baseball—drinker, women . . . They'd send detectives out to follow him and he'd end up getting the detectives drunk. Well the Yankees were on a road trip, and in those days we used to be on the road three, three and a half weeks. So Page gets off the train at Grand Central Station and he's with a writer, Bill Roeder, a friend of mine who wrote for the *(New York) Telegram*. He's with Bill and now here comes Page's wife. Joe isn't expecting to see her there so when he goes to introduce Roeder he says, 'Bill, I want you to meet my wife . . . uh, Mrs. Page.' He forgot her first name! That's a true story, that was Joe Page."
>
> —FORMER PITCHER REX BARNEY IN *PEN MEN*

Game 2, 1-0—Page pitched one shutout inning—but the Yankees won the next three games for the world championship.

Page was the World Series hero that year (for Yankee fans, anyway). He got the win in Game 3, allowing three hits in 5⅔ innings, then worked 2⅓ shutout innings to get the save in the decisive Game 5. In the nine innings that Page pitched in the World Series, he allowed six hits, two earned runs, and three walks and had eight strikeouts. For the regular season, he was 13-8 with a 2.59 earned-run average and a league-leading 27 saves in 60 appearances (also most in the league). For the second time in three years, Page had proven himself to be the best reliever in baseball.

He was rewarded by being named winner of the first Babe Ruth Memorial Award, given to the World Series MVP, and with a reported $35,000 salary for 1950 (the highest salary ever for a Yankee pitcher to that time). "It even surprised me," he told reporters.

Not surprisingly, Page expected a lot out of himself in 1950. "I guess I can work as many as 90 games if I have to," he said. But the 1950 season was another disappointment. He suffered a hip injury in May (which he refused to tell management about) and went 3-7 record with 5.04 ERA. The following spring he tore a muscle in his throwing arm and was released by Stengel. He kicked around the minors for a couple of seasons and tried to make a comeback with Pittsburgh in 1954, but with his arm gone, and with years of the high life catching up to him, Page's career was over.

A heart ailment slowed him down in the '70s and eventually ended his life. He died of heart failure on April 21, 1980. He was only sixty-two years old.

## Baseball News Of 1949

- Joe DiMaggio, who underwent surgery for bone spurs in his heel after the 1948 season, became the first ballplayer to receive a $100,000 salary. But recurring foot problems kept him out of 65 games that season.

- Phillies first baseman Eddie Waitkus was shot by an obsessed fan in his Chicago hotel room on June 14.

- The Yankees signed seventeen-year-old prospect Mickey Mantle on June 24.

- Boston's Dom DiMaggio hit in 34 consecutive games. His streak was broken on August 9 against the Yankees.

- Pirates pitcher Ernie Bonham, 36, died while undergoing an emergency appendectomy on September 15.

- The White Sox acquired Nellie Fox from the Philadelphia A's in exchange for catcher Joe Tipton.

- Ted Williams went 0-for-2 on the last day of the season and lost the AL batting race to Detroit's George Kell, .3429 to .34275.

## Around The World In 1949

- NATO was formed on April 4.

- The first nonstop around-the-world flight was completed on March 2 when the U.S. superfortress *Lucky Lady II* landed at Carswell Air Force Base in Texas.

- The discovery of cortisone was announced.

- Among the books published that year were *The Man With the Golden Arm*, by Nelson Algren, *The Brave Bulls*, by Tom Lea, *The Greatest Story Ever Told*, by Fulton Oursler, and *Peace of Soul*, by Fulton J. Sheen.

- UN headquarters was dedicated in New York on October 24.

- The bikini bathing suit became the rage.

- Arthur Miller's *Death of a Salesman* won the Pulitzer Prize for Drama.

# More Than an Afterthought

Beyond Joe Page at the number fifty spot, there was another group of superb players who deserve recognition. From among those strong challengers, headed by Hall of Famers Earle Combs and Waite Hoyt, we present fifteen for honorable mention, listed alphabetically.

## Bobby Bonds, Rightfielder, 1975

**BORN: MARCH 15, 1946          YANKEES: 1975**

| AB | R | H | Avg. | HR | RBI | BR | FR |
|----|----|----|----|----|----|----|----|
| 529 | 93 | 143 | .270 | 32 | 85 | 37 | 7 |

Bobby Bonds made a one-year stop at Yankee Stadium, then moved on to six other teams before retiring. His New York stint was short but eventful, as he helped manager Billy Martin, Catfish Hunter, Thurman Munson, Sparky Lyle, et al., to a third-place finish in the AL East. Bonds was third in the league in runs scored and fifth in slugging and, despite a knee injury that slowed him down from June on, was more than adequate in Yankee Stadium's sun field.

## Joe Bush, Right-handed Pitcher, 1922

**BORN: NOVEMBER 27, 1892          DIED: NOVEMBER 1, 1974          YANKEES: 1922–1924**

| W | L | Pct. | Starts | CG | K | BB | Saves | PR | Def | ERA |
|----|----|----|----|----|----|----|----|----|----|----|
| 26 | 7 | .788 | 30 | 20 | 92 | 85 | 3 | 21 | 1 | 3.31 |

The man with the aristocratic name of Leslie Ambrose Bush was called "Bullet Joe" by those who faced him. Possessing a bedeviling forkball and potent fastball, he helped his team win the pennant in 1922. Opponents batted just .252 against him, and he allowed just 8.46 hits per nine innings. Always a good hitting pitcher, Bush batted .326 that year.

# Ben Chapman, Rightfielder, 1931

**BORN: DECEMBER 25, 1908**     **DIED: JULY 7, 1993**     **YANKEES: 1930–1936**

| AB | R | H | Avg. | HR | RBI | BR | FR |
|----|---|---|------|----|-----|----|----|
| 600 | 120 | 189 | .315 | 17 | 122 | 33 | 8 |

Mercurial Ben Chapman zipped through his second year in pinstripes stealing a league-high 61 bases in 149 games. Hitting behind leadoff man Earle Combs, he set the table for Gehrig, Lazzeri, Ruth, and Dickey. Despite the heroics of Chapman and his teammates, the Yankees finished behind the Philadelphia A's in 1931. He also possessed a strong arm and was strong defensively, as evidenced in his eight Fielding Runs.

# Earle Combs, Centerfielder, 1927

**BORN: MAY 14, 1899**     **DIED: JULY 2, 1976**     **YANKEES: 1924–1935**

| AB | R | H | Avg. | HR | RBI | BR | FR |
|----|---|---|------|----|-----|----|----|
| 648 | 137 | 231 | .356 | 6 | 64 | 40 | 2 |

When Earle Combs was in his prime, it seemed he was on base just about every time the Yankees came to bat. The best leadoff hitter in Yankee history, he had a .414 on-base percentage and a .511 slugging average to go with his league-high 231 hits in 1927. He also had 23 triples. A class act, the Kentucky Colonel was a determined and intelligent outfielder who also ran the bases with speed and smarts. The '27 Yankees, often called the greatest ballclub ever, were a notch or two higher because of Combs, who was elected to the Hall of Fame in 1970.

# Tommy Henrich, Rightfielder, 1948

**BORN: FEBRUARY 20, 1913**     **YANKEES: 1937–1942, 1946–1950**

| AB | R | H | Avg. | HR | RBI | BR | FR |
|----|---|---|------|----|-----|----|----|
| 588 | 138 | 181 | .308 | 25 | 100 | 40 | 0 |

Tommy Henrich's greatest year ended in disappointment when the Yankees finished third in a three-way pennant race with Boston and Cleveland that went down to the final series of the season. Still, "Old Reliable" had a lot to be proud of that year: He led the AL in runs (138) and triples (14), was second in total bases (326), and third in slugging (.554). And he played Yankee Stadium's tricky right field about as well as anyone before or since.

# Waite Hoyt, Right-handed pitcher, 1927

**BORN: SEPTEMBER 9, 1899**      **DIED: AUGUST 25, 1984**      **YANKEES: 1921–1930**

| W | L | Pct. | Starts | CG | K | BB | Saves | PR | Def | ERA |
|---|---|------|--------|----|----|----|-------|----|-----|-----|
| 22 | 7 | .759 | 32 | 23 | 86 | 54 | — | 35 | 0 | 2.63 |

Largely on the strength of his Yankee career, Waite Hoyt was elected to the Hall of Fame in 1969. Another Yankee who put it all together in that 1927 season, Hoyt led the league in wins and winning percentage, then won the first game of the World Series in Pittsburgh. A money pitcher of the first order, Hoyt put the Yankees in first place to stay on April 12, 1927, with an 8–3 victory over Philadelphia. He closed out the season October 1, relieving Wilcy Moore in a 4–3 victory over Washington. In between were winning streaks of five and seven games and that steady composure that helped keep the Yankees on top from wire to wire.

# Jimmy Key, Left-handed pitcher, 1994

**BORN: APRIL 22, 1961**      **YANKEES: 1993–1996**

| W | L | Pct. | Starts | CG | K | BB | Saves | PR | Def | ERA |
|---|---|------|--------|----|----|----|-------|----|-----|-----|
| 17 | 4 | .810 | 25 | 1 | 97 | 52 | — | 24 | 3 | 3.27 |

The best left-handed pitcher in the history of the Toronto Blue Jays moved on to the Yankees in 1993 and promptly went 18–6. For an encore Jimmy Key went 17–4 in the strike-shortened season of 1994. He was the American League's pitching success story that season—he won his tenth game by June 16 and was the majors' first 17-game winner by the end of July. Key finished second to Kansas City's David Cone in the Cy Young Award voting.

# Lyn Lary, Shortstop, 1931

**BORN: JANUARY 28, 1906**      **DIED: JANUARY 9, 1973**      **YANKEES: 1929–1934**

| AB | R | H | Avg. | HR | RBI | BR | FR |
|----|---|---|------|----|-----|----|----|
| 610 | 100 | 171 | .280 | 10 | 107 | 14 | 9 |

They called him "Broadway," and that's where he started—New York—in 1929. He soon wrested the shortstop job away from Mark Koenig and Leo Durocher, and by 1931 he was ready for what turned out to be his greatest season as a Yankee. Scoring 100 times and adding 107 RBIs to the Yankee attack, he also teamed with second baseman Tony Lazzeri to form the smartest shortstop-second base combination in the AL. Playing every game in 1931, he had 484 assists and participated in 85 double plays. Offensively, he also had 35 doubles and 13 stolen bases.

# Eddie Lopat, Left-handed pitcher, 1951

**BORN: JUNE 21, 1918**    **DIED: JUNE 15, 1992**    **YANKEES: 1948–1955**

| W | L | Pct. | Starts | CG | K | BB | Saves | PR | Def | ERA |
|---|---|------|--------|----|----|----|-------|----|-----|-----|
| 21 | 9 | .700 | 31 | 20 | 71 | 12 | — | 31 | 2 | 2.91 |

Eddie Lopat—born Edmund Walter Lopatynski—was the kind of pitcher who could be touched for a lot of hits but would surrender few runs. He knew his strengths and weaknesses and rarely got them confused. That made life easier for Yogi Berra, who loved to catch him. In 1951, he teamed with Vic Raschi to form the Yankees' 1–2 punch, a combination that rivaled the neighboring Giants' Larry Jansen and Sal Maglie. But in the World Series, it was Lopat who starred, throttling the Giants on one earned run in eighteen innings of work.

# Lindy McDaniel, Right-handed pitcher, 1970

**BORN: DECEMBER 13, 1935**    **YANKEES: 1968–1973**

| W | L | Pct. | Starts | CG | K | BB | Saves | PR | Def | ERA |
|---|---|------|--------|----|----|----|-------|----|-----|-----|
| 9 | 5 | .643 | 62 | 29 | 81 | 23 | — | 19 | 1 | 2.01 |

A seasoned pitcher at thirty-four, Lindy McDaniel came up with a gem of a season in 1970. One of baseball's all-time great relievers, McDaniel issued only 23 walks, five of them intentional, that season. A master of control, the quiet right-hander figured in 38 decisions, winning nine and saving 29 others. His 2.01 ERA was a career best.

# Al Orth, Right-handed pitcher, 1906

**BORN: SEPTEMBER 5, 1872**    **DIED: OCTOBER 8, 1948**    **YANKEES: 1904–1909**

| W | L | Pct. | Starts | CG | K | BB | Saves | PR | Def | ERA |
|---|---|------|--------|----|----|----|-------|----|-----|-----|
| 27 | 17 | .614 | 39 | 36 | 133 | 66 | — | 13 | -1 | 2.34 |

Smilin' Al, also known as the Curveless Wonder, got by on changing speeds, meticulous control, and the occasional spitter. It all worked in 1906, when he was the go-to guy for manager Clark Griffith's Highlanders. He kept the ballclub in the pennant race while leading the league in ERA, complete games, and innings pitched (338⅔). He also had a .274 batting average and 17 RBIs. One highlight of the 1906 season was an eleven-day stretch during which the Highlanders won fifteen games, including five consecutive double-headers. Orth contributed three victories to the streak.

# Fritz Peterson, Left-handed pitcher, 1969

**BORN: FEBRUARY 8, 1942**     **YANKEES: 1966–1974**

| W | L | Pct. | Starts | CG | K | BB | Saves | PR | Def | ERA |
|---|---|------|--------|----|----|----|-------|----|-----|-----|
| 17 | 16 | .515 | 37 | 16 | 150 | 43 | — | 28 | 2 | 2.55 |

Many of baseball's most bizarre stories seem to involve left-handers. Fritz Peterson is no exception. His story has become part of baseball lore: Peterson and teammate Mike Kekich, another lefty, traded families—wives, kids, dogs, and all. Still, Peterson could pitch. Between 1968 and 1972 he went 81–66 for some mighty weak post-Mantle teams. His 2.55 ERA in '69 was in the AL's top five, and he led the league with only 1.42 walks per nine innings. Opposing batters got on base only 26 percent of the time when Peterson was pitching. He had a better record in 1970, but overall, his 1969 season was his best.

# Bobby Shantz, Left-handed pitcher, 1957

**BORN: SEPTEMBER 26, 1925**     **YANKEES: 1957–1960**

| W | L | Pct. | Starts | CG | K | BB | Saves | PR | Def | ERA |
|---|---|------|--------|----|----|----|-------|----|-----|-----|
| 11 | 5 | .688 | 21 | 9 | 5 | 72 | 40 | 22 | 6 | 2.45 |

The mighty mite (5-foot-6, 142 pounds) who almost single-handedly kept Jimmie Dykes' A's over .500 with an MVP season in 1952, came to New York for a distinguished four-year stint, helping the Yankees to three pennants. The Gold Glove, first awarded in 1957, went to Shantz that year—and the next three. By 1957 the little lefty with the baffling curve—Ted Williams claimed it was the best in the league — was used more sparingly, usually in tough spots. Manager Casey Stengel, adept at finding the right player for the right situation, used Shantz as a starter and reliever. Shantz responded with the best ERA in the league.

# Danny Tartabull, Rightfielder, 1992

**BORN: OCTOBER 30, 1962**     **YANKEES: 1992–1995**

| AB | R | H | Avg. | HR | RBI | BR | FR |
|----|---|---|------|----|----|----|----|
| 421 | 72 | 112 | .266 | 25 | 85 | 31 | 1 |

Powerfully built Danny Tartabull had baseball in his blood. His father, Jose, an outfielder for Kansas City, Boston, and Oakland in the 1960s, had just completed his first major-league season when Danny was born in Puerto Rico. Danny came to the Yankees from Kansas City in 1991, which was also an excellent season for him (.316, 100 RBIs, 31 HRs). He had a .410 on-base percentage in 1992, second in the league, as well as 85 RBIs and 25 homers in just 112 games (he spent more than a month on the disabled list).

# Bernie Williams, Centerfielder, 1995

BORN: SEPTEMBER 13, 1968     YANKEES: 1991–PRESENT

| AB | R | H | Avg. | HR | RBI | BR | FR |
|----|----|----|------|----|-----|----|----|
| 563 | 93 | 173 | .307 | 18 | 82 | 25 | 16 |

Playing in New York is tough enough without having George Steinbrenner as a boss. And 1995, a post-strike season, was an especially tough year. How did Williams handle the situation? Masterfully, playing super ball and quietly enjoying the most productive part of his career. With Paul O'Neill and Wade Boggs, he led the Yankees to a wild-card spot in the AL playoffs, where he hit .469. Unfortunately, the season ended in Seattle, not at the World Series. Through a torrid September stretch, he hit .370 (61-for-165) and scored 33 runs to keep the Yankees in the race. Without him, they wouldn't have made the playoffs.

# Total Player Ratings (TPR)

This listing presents the top fifty individual Yankee seasons regardless of the number of times a player's name might appear (Babe Ruth had so many outstanding seasons, for example, that his name appears no less then ten times). TPR below designates the Total Player Rating for an individual season, representing both pitchers and position players. Ties are listed chronologically.

| NAME | YEAR | TPR |
|------|------|-----|
| Ruth | 1923 | 10.6 |
| Ruth | 1921 | 9.4 |
| Ruth | 1927 | 9.2 |
| Mantle | 1956 | 8.7 |
| Ruth | 1920 | 8.6 |
| Mantle | 1957 | 8.6 |
| Ruth | 1924 | 8.5 |
| Ruth, | 1926 | 8.4 |
| Gehrig, | 1927 | 8.1 |
| Mantle | 1961 | 8.0 |
| Gehrig | 1934 | 7.8 |
| Henderson | 1985 | 7.4 |
| Ruth | 1930 | 7.3 |
| Ruth, | 1931 | 7.3 |
| Stirnweiss, | 1945 | 7.2 |
| Stirnweiss, | 1944 | 7.1 |
| Ruth | 1928 | 7.0 |
| Gehrig | 1930 | 6.9 |
| Gomez | 1937 | 6.5 |
| Mantle | 1958 | 6.5 |
| Gehrig | 1936 | 6.4 |
| DiMaggio | 1941 | 6.4 |
| Mantle | 1955 | 6.3 |

| NAME | YEAR | TPR | |
|---|---|---|---|
| Guidry | 1978 | | 6.2 |
| DiMaggio | 1937 | | 6.0 |
| C. Mays | 1921 | | 5.8 |
| Gehrig | 1931 | | 5.8 |
| Ruth | 1932 | | 5.8 |
| DiMaggio | 1939 | | 5.7 |
| Chandler | 1943 | | 5.7 |
| Murcer | 1971 | | 5.5 |
| Murcer | 1972 | | 5.5 |
| Gordon | 1942 | | 5.4 |
| Gordon | 1943 | | 5.4 |
| Williams | 1999 | | 5.2 |
| Peckinpaugh | 1919 | | 5.1 |
| Gehrig | 1928 | | 5.1 |
| Dickey | 1937 | | 5.1 |
| Mantle | 1962 | | 5.0 |
| Gehrig | 1932 | | 4.9 |
| Mattingly | 1984 | | 4.9 |
| W. Moore | 1927 | | 4.8 |
| Lazzeri | 1929 | | 4.8 |
| Gehrig | 1935 | | 4.8 |
| Gomez | 1938 | | 4.8 |
| Rivera | 1997 | | 4.8 |
| Ruffing | 1939 | | 4.7 |
| Gossage | 1978 | | 4.7 |
| Henderson | 1988 | | 4.7 |
| Mantle | 1952 | | 4.6 |
| DiMaggio | 1940 | | 4.5 |
| E. Ford | 1956 | | 4.5 |
| R. White | 1971 | | 4.5 |
| Rivera | 1999 | | 4.5 |

# About the Authors

**WILLIAM HAGEMAN**, author of a biography of Honus Wagner and coauthor of *Chicago Cubs: Seasons at the Summit*, is an editor in the Features Department of the *Chicago Tribune*. He previously worked as a sportswriter, editor, and columnist for newspapers in Michigan and Delaware. Bill resides in Aurora, Illinois, with his wife and three daughters.

· · ·

**WARREN WILBERT**, dean *emeritus* of Lifelong Learning Services at Concordia University, Ann Arbor, Michigan, has served as a Lutheran educator and as a football, basketball, and baseball coach. Coauthor with Bill Hageman of *Chicago Cubs: Seasons at the Summit*, he has also written for athletic and sports journals. His article "20-Year Men" appears in the 1996 edition of the *Baseball Research Journal*, a publication of the Society for American Baseball Research. Warren and his wife, Ginny, reside in Fort Wayne, Indiana, where Warren maintains a lively interest in adult education, baseball (especially the White Sox), and his grandchildren.